Modern Library College Editions

The Later Plays of Eugene O'Neill

Ah, Wilderness!

A Touch of the Poet

Hughie

A Moon for the Misbegotten

EDITED BY *Travis Bogard*
UNIVERSITY OF CALIFORNIA, BERKELEY

The Modern Library NEW YORK

Frontispiece photograph by Louis Sheaffer.

THE MODERN LIBRARY

is published by RANDOM HOUSE, INC.

Manufactured in the United States of America

CONTENTS

Introduction

BY TRAVIS BOGARD

In 1913 at the age of 25, Eugene O'Neill wrote his first work for the stage — an inconsequential sketch such as an established actor might have used for a personal appearance tour in vaudeville. It was not a promising debut, yet the play marked a turning point in O'Neill's life. Behind its writing lay a long adolescence, a waste of years marked by hardship and dereliction, a life that had been formless, self-destructive and governed by no clear purpose. Ahead lay forty years of a life in art, of a dedication to a single purpose that was so complete as to cause the sacrifice of almost all the ordinary diversions and sustaining relationships that most men need to provide a sense of fulfillment in their lives.

When he died in 1953, O'Neill had written nearly 70 dramatic works. Some were unfinished and some destroyed; some exist only in manuscript. They range in length from one-act plays to such massive works as *Strange Interlude;* the trilogy, *Mourning Becomes Electra;* and the incomplete cycle of nine plays, *A Tale of Possessors, Self-Dispossessed*. Many are experiments, attempting somewhat uncertainly to employ new theatrical modes; others must rank among the finest plays of the first half of the twentieth century, fully worthy to stand beside the best of Chekhov, Shaw, Pirandello, Giraudoux, Brecht — and even those of O'Neill's two principal masters, Ibsen and Strindberg.

It is with Strindberg's work that O'Neill's bears the closest kinship. Like the Swedish dramatist, O'Neill wrote plays that were directly autobiographical, depicting on stage with little disguising fiction the facts of his own personal life. Perhaps the stage provided opportunity to achieve a better self-understanding, for both dramatists attempted not only to depict the facts of their experiences, but, in O'Neill's phrase, to go "behind life," in order to explore the hidden forces, the obscure motives, that had led to their bewilderment and pain. In pursuing their self-investigations, both playwrights worked in the two major styles of twentieth-century theatre: the realistic and the expressionistic; and their works are thus similar in many points both of theme and theatrical technique.

O'Neill's imitation of Strindberg arose out of a sense of shared concerns. However, Strindberg's autobiographical dramas are at once bitter and guilt-ridden, filled with hatred that, as a dramatist, he was sometimes able to turn into a gesture of forgiveness toward what afflicted him. O'Neill's work is not like this. He is less concerned with the hostile external world than with that private world in which every man is isolated, as if in a cell. It is a little room, but O'Neill explored it thoroughly and with obsessive intensity.

The manuscript of *The Emperor Jones,* for example, is written on three sheets — six pages of paper, each measuring 8½ by 11 inches — in a handwriting that is nearly microscopic. It is as if O'Neill's entire intellectual and emotional power had been concentrated in his hand and forced through the fine point of his pencil, not so much to write the words as to carve them onto the page. In his later plays, his extraordinary concentration was to be directed to the projection of the substance of his own inner life fully and directly into his dramas. What he sought was self-knowledge and forgiveness, an attempt that brought him, in the end, to the creation of major works of dramatic art, conceived in a highly individual mode that was marked by an essential lyricism.

The search for understanding informed even his earliest writing. When in 1912, he entered a tuberculosis sanitarium, he had drifted to the limits of endurance. Behind him lay a forced marriage and a degrading divorce. He was the father of a son he had not seen. He had knocked around the waterfronts of New York and Buenos Aires, and had become one of the pieces of human flotsam who inhabited the saloons and flophouses. He had attempted suicide, and finally, as if his body were attempting to complete a process of self-destruction, his lungs failed him. O'Neill's youth was a plunge toward death, but in the sanitarium, he checked this downward course. When he emerged from it, he devoted his life to exploring the forces that had led him to so perilous an edge.

His efforts were in the end to produce the plays for which he received four Pulitzer Prizes and the Nobel Prize for Literature. Studied in sequence, the large body of completed works tells the story of a remarkable progress. O'Neill grew steadily as an artist, and as he did so, his insight into his characters deepened; his awareness of the philosophical and theological significance of the actions he depicted became clearer; and his mastery of technique provided him with theatrical resources no other American dramatist possessed. In the later plays, his work fulfilled and transcended his initial personal motivation for writing, and his work, finally, stood before the world as a clear indication of the coming-of-age of the American theatre.

I

Among the characters that O'Neill required in order to enable him to make his explorations was a self-portrait. The character who was ultimately to become Edmund

Tyrone first appears as the Poet in *Fog,* a one-act fantasy written in 1914.[1] The work is a dialogue between a Businessman and a Poet, adrift in a lifeboat on a fog-bound sea. The atmosphere of the play is derived from that of *The Rime of the Ancient Mariner;* and its argument — that the greatest human evil is poverty — is borrowed from Shaw's *Major Barbara.* All that is worthy of notice in the play is the face of the Poet. O'Neill describes it as oval, with "big, dark eyes and a black mustache and black hair pushed back from a high forehead."

A face with the same characteristics will appear often in the plays that follow. In an unpublished play, *Bread and Butter* (1914), it is the face of the hero, John Brown, a young painter at odds with small-town Connecticut society:

His naturally dark complexion has been burnt to a gold bronze by the sun. His hair, worn long and brushed straight back from his forehead, is black, as are his abnormally large dreamer's eyes, deep-set and far apart, in the oval of his face. His mouth is full-lipped and small, almost weak in its general character; his nose straight and thin with the nostrils of the enthusiast.

It is also the face Robert Mayo, the protagonist of *Beyond the Horizon* (1918):

There is a touch of the poet about him expressed in his high forehead and wide dark eyes. His features are delicate and refined, leaning to weakness in the mouth and chin.

The mask of Dion Anthony in *The Great God Brown* (1925) is a refinement of the face: "dark, spiritual, poetic,

[1] All dates assigned to O'Neill's plays are those of composition. Plays not contained in this volume are contained in *The Plays of Eugene O'Neill,* or *Ten Lost Plays,* with the exception of *Long Day's Journey into Night* and *More Stately Mansions.*

passionately supersensitive, helplessly unprotected. . . ."
Finally, in *Long Day's Journey into Night* (1940), Edmund
Tyrone is described in these terms:

> Edmund looks like both his parents, but is more like his
> mother. Her big, dark eyes are the dominant feature in
> his long, narrow Irish face. His mouth has the same qual-
> ity of hypersensitiveness hers possesses. His high forehead
> is hers accentuated, with dark brown hair, sunbleached
> to red at the ends, brushed straight back from it.

The face appears to be O'Neill's own — drawn at first, perhaps, in juvenile narcissism, but emerging in its final devel-
opment as a necessary part of O'Neill's means of achieving
clear self-knowledge.

As the self-portrait evolves, O'Neill learns more about his
own image. The immature railer against social evils in *Fog*
develops, through the character of Robert Mayo, into a
study of a man who is seeking his home in nature. Although he dreams of sailing "beyond the horizon" and of
giving himself to the sea, Mayo has elected instead to remain
on the land and to work his father's farm. In making his
choice between the natural polarities of sea and land, however, Mayo has forgotten that he is the sea's creature, not
the land's. In denying the sea, he has denied some mysterious element in his own heritage, and his choice, therefore,
condemns him to misery and death. In describing his hero,
O'Neill first uses the phrase "a touch of the poet" in order
to suggest the quality that has set him apart from other
men and that has caused him to yearn after half-understood
necessities—a destination, a home, where he can fully belong.

In the tradition of the naturalistic writers of Europe and
America, the young O'Neill saw men as controlled by a
"life force" that determined their destinies. From this, however, he did not derive the pessimistic overview of a

Hardy, a Zola, or a Frank Norris. Instead, he argued that
when man commits himself without thought of alternatives
to the element that is his proper earth, he achieves thereby
a contentment that, while it may not be happiness, is nevertheless the best destiny man can find. The sailors on the
S. S. Glencairn, for instance, are children of the sea. So long
as they follow where the sea leads them, they remain un-
tortured by any destructive sensibilities. Cradled by the
element to which they belong, they achieve a coarse contentment that passes for happiness.

Most men, O'Neill suggested, do not recognize their
relationship to the life force, but live as if under a spell,
passing their lives as do the sailors in *The Moon of the
Caribbees* (1917), in an animal-like existence, freed both
from the torture of thought and from the perspective on self
that thought brings. Self-awareness is man's demon; thought
makes men orphans. Smitty, the alien on the *Glencairn,*
sees the other sailors for what they are, but his perspective
causes him to be more critical of himself than he is of his
fellows. He longs for, yet cannot achieve, their unaware
identification with the sea. Similarly, when the Hairy Ape
sees himself as an animal, he runs from the source of his
life in the engine room where he belongs and comes to his
death. In the same way, the end comes to Robert Mayo,
whose life, once he has denied the sea, is consumed by a
sense of alienation.

Robert Mayo, however, reveals another aspect of O'Neill's
characteristic *dramatis personae.* The "touch of the poet"
gives him an awareness such as most men do not possess of
man's *need* to belong. The true poet is fully aware of the
kinship between man and nature, and understands and re-
joices in the identification that he feels with all of creation.
O'Neill drew this figure of the true poet only once, in the
resurrected Lazarus of *Lazarus Laughed* (1926–7), who
preaches:

Once as squirming specks we crept from the tides of the sea. Now we return to the sea! Once as quivering flecks of rhythm we beat down from the sun. Now we re-enter the sun! . . . Laughing we lived with our gift, now with laughter give we back that gift to become again the Essence of the Giver!

Edmund Tyrone describes the transitory mystical experience when "the veil of things as they seem" is drawn back by an unseen hand, and when "For a second you see — and seeing the secret are the secret." For Lazarus, the philosopher-poet, there is no veil; there is instead the secure knowledge that is like a saint's "vision of beatitude."

For those who are only touched with poetry, however, the sense of the secret brings only transitory identification with the life force. In O'Neill's most explicit analysis of this yearning toward identification — the monologue of Edmund Tyrone in the fourth act of *Long Day's Journey into Night* — he makes clear that, for men who are not gods, the vision of Lazarus is impossible. Although unexpectedly, when the veil is removed, a man may receive a sense of his mysterious, ultimate unity with all nature, when the veil drops again into place, man forgets the reality of his vision and is condemned to wander disconsolately in the fog, waiting for another of those rare moments when the veil is removed.

As a foil to the self-portrait, O'Neill developed the figure of a man who has no touch of the poet in him and therefore cannot see. Unlike the *Glencairn* sailors, however, he cannot belong simply, without thought. Something moves in him — an awareness of the possibility of vision in others, perhaps — that disturbs him because it causes him to doubt his own self-identification. Moved by fear, he becomes a denier of dreams and in his blindness seeks to possess, rather than to belong to, the earth. The first full portrait of this character is that of Andrew Mayo, Robert's brother. Andrew has none of Robert's vision, yet he belongs to the land. Had he stayed, working close to the earth on the family farm, his life would have been fulfilled. He, however, goes to sea, travelling beyond the horizon, yet sees nothing of the mysteries of which Robert dreamed. Instead, he returns disgusted with the stench of the places he has visited, and he reveals himself as a materialist without a soul, denying his heritage by speculating in wheat, and thus betraying the source of his identity for gain. The satirical picture of Marco Polo in *Marco Millions* (1925) is a full-length portrait of this figure. O'Neill's most savage depiction of him, however, is in the characterization of William Brown in *The Great God Brown*. There, in a kind of satyr play that follows the tragedy of the poet, O'Neill causes the betrayer of the poet's dream to caper to his death in the poet's mask in a frenetic attempt to possess the poet's dreams and to assume both his vision and his power.

Like the poet himself, the antagonist of the poet emerges from O'Neill's own experiences. Some aspects are perhaps derived from O'Neill's father, but he is essentially drawn after O'Neill's brother Jamie, who was to become the Jamie Tyrone of *Long Day's Journey into Night* and of *A Moon for the Misbegotten* (1941-3).[2]

Jamie O'Neill had a minor talent as an actor, a talent that he failed to foster. Less adventurous and less capable of self-discipline than his brother, he drifted through a similar pattern of self-destruction, and died at last in a sanitarium. The relationship between Eugene and his brother, as presented in *Long Day's Journey into Night,* is that of hostility mingled with love. In a way, O'Neill seems to have felt that Jamie was his own hostile *alter ego:* "Hell," Jamie Tyrone says to Edmund, "You're more than my brother. I made you! You're my Frankenstein!" The waste of spir-

---

[2] Something of Jamie may appear as well in the character of Erie Smith in *Hughie* and Simon Harford in the unfinished *More Stately Mansions.*

itual substance that O'Neill fought in himself was Jamie's disease, and Jamie remained in the plays as the omnipresent shadow of the poet. Where the poet goes, the *doppelgänger* follows, and since his presence threatens the poet's vision, the essential conflict between the poet and his opposite takes shape.

The relationship that is first sketched in the characters of Andrew and Robert Mayo is to be found in many of the plays of O'Neill's maturity. From this conflict, for instance, he developed the unsuccessful experiment of *Days Without End* (1932), in which the two figures, here seen as projections of the dual nature of the same individual, are played by two actors. This same opposition forms the basis of the conflict between Hickey and the bums of Harry Hope's saloon in *The Iceman Cometh* (1939), and it underlies the schizoid fragmentations in the character of Major Cornelius Melody in *A Touch of the Poet* (1939–42).

Into this pattern, O'Neill introduced the figure of the woman as both destroyer and preserver. Early in his career, while he was still strongly imitative of Strindberg, O'Neill tended to portray woman as by nature incapable of understanding, and, therefore, as inevitably draining the creative life of the poet. Ruth Mayo, Robert's wife, might well be the female in a rural *Dance of Death*. Later, however, O'Neill combines the woman's predatory nature with another quality that makes her supremely desirable: she becomes the object, in part, of the poet's quest. She is not only the destroying wife, but also the mother, in whose love the poet seeks to find forgetfulness, and the sense of home and unity with nature.

The first appearance of the mother figure in O'Neill's plays is in *Bound East for Cardiff* (1914), where the dying Yank sees a vision of a "pretty lady dressed in black" — an image that is intended to suggest the sea mourning like a mother for its children in pain. After *Welded* in 1922, the dual wife-mother character becomes the dominant female personality, appearing, for example, as Abbie in *Desire Under the Elms* (1924); as Cybel, the earth-mother of *The Great God Brown;* as Nina Leeds in *Strange Interlude* (1926); and as Mrs. Light in *Dynamo* (1928). Elements of the character enter into the portrait of Mrs. Miller in *Ah, Wilderness!* (1932), and of Nora Melody in *A Touch of the Poet.* In O'Neill's last play, *A Moon for the Misbegotten,* he draws her portrait fully as Josie Hogan, the virgin mother who cradles Jamie Tyrone through the long and peaceful night.

The source of the characters of these women, like those of the men, lay in O'Neill's family. They were drawn chiefly after O'Neill's own mother, who, placed on stage as Mary Tyrone, reveals both the negative qualities of the women of the early plays and the more fulfilling maternal nature that dominates those of the later. O'Neill used his mother's name, Ella, for that of the heroine of *All God's Chillun Got Wings* (1923), and it is remarkable, too, how closely the description of the young Nina Leeds parallels the initial description of Mary Tyrone. In each appearance, when the woman gives herself fully to the man, he finds a peace that is like "belonging," like arriving at the end of a quest. When she denies him, however, he is lost in agony. As with the characters of the men, so in the depiction of the women, more than simple portraiture is involved; O'Neill's sense of the dual nature of woman reflects much of his own fear and his needs — rooted deeply in the facts of his own experience.

II

From this central structure of relationships, evolved in patterns of positive and negative, of quest and frustration, O'Neill formed his tragedies. He was never greatly concerned, as were many of his contemporaries in Europe and

America, with social conditions. *The Hairy Ape* (1921), his most explicit work of social criticism, becomes in the end a drama of a private quest for "belonging." The world through which Yank moves is, like the forest in *The Emperor Jones,* a projection of the hero's being; it is not explored for any general critical or corrective purpose. O'Neill's customary area of investigation was the private life of the inner man, and he tended to set his plays in a world that was sealed off from an extensively detailed social milieu. Only in those plays that were set in a historical context — *Desire Under the Elms, Marco Millions, Mourning Becomes Electra, A Touch of the Poet,* and *Ah, Wilderness!* — was he concerned with creating a complete social context in which his characters might move as men do in the world. In these plays, his ability to project a historical *milieu* is superb. It is difficult to conceive of Con Melody and his family as living in any other period than that in which O'Neill placed them. Similarly, despite the intensely psychoanalytic interpretation of the interrelationships in the Mannon family, the characters in *Mourning Becomes Electra* seem to be truly of their period, even though that period is not recreated with any extensive elaboration on stage.

Elsewhere, however, O'Neill was less concerned with narrating events in time, and more with projecting states of being, set to some extent out of time. The technical equipment he developed for this purpose was formidable. Several characteristics which he developed in the writing of his earlier plays were to serve him well in the later. Among them note should be taken of his use of light and sound and of his characteristic handling of dialogue.

In *All God's Chillun Got Wings,* O'Neill dramatizes the psychological trap in which his characters are caught by diminishing, as the play progresses, the physical dimensions of the room in which they live. This is the most elaborate manifestation of a characteristic element of his style: the decrease of the physical setting of the play, in order that he and his audience may concentrate on its inner action. Normally, he does this by contracting the area of light in which his characters are permitted to move. *Long Day's Journey into Night,* for instance, begins in morning sunlight, but gradually, as the night comes and fog surrounds the house, the stage is reduced to a dim circle of light surrounded by outer darkness. The broad full stage of *Moon for the Misbegotten* is reduced in the third act to the moonlit steps on which Josie Hogan sits holding Jamie Tyrone in her arms. The action of *Hughie* (1940), is set entirely in the dimly lighted lobby that serves the two characters as a refuge from the dark and hostile city outside. The light-pattern, closely keyed to the play's theme and action, stresses in visual terms O'Neill's sense that isolation is the natural condition of man, who, lacking vision, is condemned to wander through the surrounding blackness in search of something he cannot name.

The pattern of sound complements the pattern of light. In his first fully characteristic play, *Bound East for Cardiff,* O'Neill called for a rich and expressive use of sound. There, the foghorn, the cry of "All's well," the laughter of the crew, serve as ironic counterpoint to the despair of Yank and Driscoll, who are isolated in the close forecastle. In *The Moon of the Caribbees,* the native chant that drifts from shore to ship is "like the mood of the moonlight made audible." The pulse-beat of the drums in *The Emperor Jones* (1920), the hum of electrical power in *Dynamo,* the laughter in *Lazarus Laughed* — all these result from what might be called O'Neill's "ear" for drama. In the late plays, especially in *Hughie* and *Long Day's Journey into Night,* the use of sound, like that of light, skilfully emphasizes the hostile environment that condemns man to loneliness.

A third technical element, the dialogue, also stresses man's isolation. O'Neill's language is perhaps the most severely criticized single aspect of his dramas, and he himself repeatedly lamented that he was not a poet capable of writing a subtle and fully-expressive language. Although his language is rarely beautiful, and although on the printed page it often reads awkwardly, his self-criticism was unwarranted. On the stage, when it is heard as one part of the total complex of sound, light and action, his language becomes the authentic dialect of the special kingdom of feeling that he created for his characters. It is a poetic creation, essentially lyric in its final effect.

It should be noted that O'Neill sometimes asked of his language something that very few playwrights have dared to ask, something that language alone perhaps cannot do. At times, he attempted to make his characters speak thoughts that, in reality, lie below the level of conscious thought and are, therefore, subverbal. Normally, theatrical language, even the Shakespearean soliloquy, emerges from the conscious levels of a character's mind. O'Neill taxed language heavily in his attempt to make it express the welling up of the character's deepest inner motives and desires for which no words can entirely suffice.

His concentration on the "poets" who are isolated questers, caught in a structure of alienated relationships, led O'Neill to write dialogue that was not in any normal sense fully communicative. His characters often tend to make private, not public utterances. They are presented less through the external communication normal to most men moving through the world in time, than through the solitary outpourings that they voice when they are alone. For this reason, O'Neill turns to the use of monologues, soliloquies and asides — the voices of the questers, who can only imperfectly communicate the nature of their search. Speech in O'Neill's dramas is often not so much heard as over-heard; if it becomes communication, it does so almost in spite of itself. In the usual sense of the term it is not "dramatic"; rather, it formulates itself in a series of lyrics, whose source in the play's action, however, is fully dramatic.

O'Neill's lyric mode has many memorable peaks. There is, for instance, Ephraim Cabot's monologue in *Desire Under the Elms* (II:ii), and there is Tiberius' narrative in *Lazarus Laughed* (IV:i). The Hairy Ape's hymn to the essence of steel in himself is of this order, as are the monologues in the forest scenes of *The Emperor Jones*. In the late plays, the monologue, almost uninterrupted, comes to comprise major sections of the drama, as in Hickey's confession in *The Iceman Cometh*, the scenes between Edmund and James Tyrone in Act Four of *Long Day's Journey into Night*, those between Jamie and Josie in *Moon for the Misbegotten*, Deborah Harford's appearance in *A Touch of the Poet*, and the entire *Hughie*. Given emphasis by a pattern of sound and centered in an intense concentration of light, these monologues stand forth as essentially lyric expressions, a kind of song expressive of human need.

Their effect in the late plays is strange, for they serve to reinforce the sense that the action is somehow outside of time, suspended in a void of consciousness between dreaming and waking where loneliness becomes a fluid process of pain and man cannot quite attain his only anodyne — being heard and touching another human being in the dark. It is perhaps not fanciful to suggest that these lyric expressions stand in the same relation to the characters in the plays as the plays themselves did to their author.

O'Neill's special use of sound, light, and dialogue remains a constant part of his technical equipment through all the experimental dramas of his middle years. His experiments with scenery and masks, like his turn toward the expressionistic theatre, following the lead of Strindberg and influenced, perhaps, by friends who were seeking to promote the idea of "Art Theatre" in America, led him to increasingly unsuccessful dramaturgy and farther from the style characteristic of his peculiar genius, which had manifested itself early, in the poetic realism of *The Moon of the Caribbees*. After writing *The Great God Brown,* O'Neill undertook to write plays that appeared to seek after a strangeness of manner, an experimental difference of mode. Uncharitably viewed, these works might be called instances of "experiment for the sake of experiment." They were not this. O'Neill's high seriousness can never rightly be called into question. He appears to have adopted some of the techniques of expressionism in an effort to set forth on his stage what his early realistic style did not permit him to deal with: the nature of the force that lay at the end of the quest.

That this force, which was associated with either land or sea, was also associated with an idea of a god was already clear in O'Neill's early plays. In *"Anna Christie"* (1920), for instance, at the precise moment when Old Chris cries out, "Dat ole davil, sea, she ain't God!," both he and his daughter Anna hear the cry that signals the arrival of Mat Burke, who has been, in effect, tossed by the sea at Anna's feet, and through whose love Anna will complete the restoration to health and happiness that has been begun by her return to the sea. Similarly, in *The Emperor Jones,* the forces of the jungle appear to have something of a god's power to reclaim those apostates who would deny or scoff at his supremacy.

As O'Neill matured, the simple idea of a "life force" that was oriented in nature, in the land or the sea, grew more complex, and he became increasingly concerned with "the death of the old God and failure of science and materialism to give any satisfying new one for the surviving primitive religious instinct to find a meaning for life in, and to comfort its fears of death with." [3] Such concerns led him almost inevitably to attempt to explicate the nature of the god of modern man. The experimental plays of the 1920's and early 1930's, including *Strange Interlude,* are all religious dramas. Their purpose is to determine something of the aspect of that god, as well as to demonstrate man's need to unite with his power. O'Neill's work in this period is to some extent an effort to find his own salvation, less through understanding himself as a quester than by way of exploring the nature of what lay at the end of the quest. For the most part, as the bleak symbolism of *Dynamo* and *Days Without End* attest, the endeavor caused him to move far from the central sources of his genius.

Finally, however, O'Neill renounced the attempt to know the nature of the modern god and to explicate it directly on stage. A change comes over his work, signaled by the writing of *Mourning Becomes Electra* during the years 1929–31. In this play, he stopped his experimentation, and turned back to Aeschylus and the primary source of modern tragedy. As if he were attempting to rediscover the taproots of his own creative life, he rewrote the *Oresteia* as a modern, realistic tragedy. Two experimental plays about the nature of god remained as evidence of commitments to the old concerns, but neither is a major achievement. While he was writing *Days Without End,* fighting his way through its tangled expressionistic commitments, he conceived the autobiographical comedy *Ah, Wilderness!,* and wrote it quickly, almost as if the play had thrust itself upon his imagination. *Ah, Wilderness!* is the first of his directly autobiographical works, and serves as a prelude to the final tragedies, in which O'Neill put to one side his attempt to develop a modern theology. From that work forth, he

[3] From a letter to George Jean Nathan printed in *The American Mercury,* XVI (January 1929), p. 119.

sought only to know himself and those who were closest to him.

III

Read without reference to the O'Neill canon, *Ah, Wilderness!* [4] is a pleasant comedy of turn-of-the-century American life, comparable to Thornton Wilder's *Our Town* in its recreation of a simple life that has long vanished. It is rich in detail, satisfying in its comedic action, and it skirts sentimentality without ever finally yielding to it. Biographical studies of O'Neill have shown the extent to which he drew on the materials of his own life in creating the story of Richard Miller and his family. O'Neill himself said that the play was his life as he would have liked it to be. Read in the perspective that *Long Day's Journey into Night* provides, it appears as the bright counterpart to the dramatist's final self-assessment.

The central setting of the comedy, the Millers' living room, is in most details identical with that of the tragedy. The chief differences are that, in the comedy, the wallpaper is cheerful and that the characters at the end are suffused by moonlight, rather than by fog. More important, however, is the fact that the comedy is rooted in the same life experience as the tragedy, contains the same basic materials, and tells the same essential story. Like the tragedy, it centers in the lives of four people, a father, a mother and two brothers — the O'Neill family circle. In the comedy, however, O'Neill separates each of the complex source-figures of his own life and of the tragedy into simpler components, each one of which becomes a character. By such division, he takes from the figures of his family the burden of responsibility and guilt.

[4] *Ah, Wilderness!* was written in 1932 and produced by The Theatre Guild in October, 1933. It was filmed in 1935, and again in 1948, as a musical entitled *Summer Holiday*. In 1960, it served as the basis of a musical play entitled *Take Me Along*.

Thus, James O'Neill, rendered in the tragedy as a man who is both a success and a failure, as one who is capable of love yet incapable of fulfilling its obligations, becomes in the comedy both the father, Nat Miller, and Uncle Sid. Nat's actions are wise, his manner gentle; Sid is a drunkard and a roisterer, who bears no responsibility in the world, and therefore cannot be charged with guilt. Ella O'Neill, who, when freed of her morphine addiction, could become the mother that Eugene and Jamie needed, but who when the morphine claimed her, retired into a lonely drifting spinsterhood, is projected in the comedy both as Mrs. Miller and as Lily, her spinster sister-in-law. Jamie is present, in part at least, as Richard Miller's older brother, but it is not he who introduces Richard to the woman from New York. Rather, it is the brother's college friend who serves as the agent of Richard's partial corruption. It is perhaps worth noting, finally, that O'Neill's own brief adolescent romance with a girl named Maybelle Scott is recreated and brought to shy fulfillment in the play's last act, when Richard and his girl are reunited under the beneficent influence of the moonlight, to which all the characters respond with a sense of belonging and a dim awareness of their participation in a cycle of nature.

Such participation lies at the root of most great comedy. The characters in Shakespearean comedy, for instance, begin by making a series of withdrawals from life — into walled gardens, into the artifices of lover's melancholy, into what amounts to a denial of sexual possibility by transvestitism. Yet, for all their wilful denial of its positive power, nature has its way with the would-be spinsters; in the end it restores them securely into the mainstream of common experience. In O'Neill's earlier tragedies, withdrawal from and denial of the life force had formed the basis of the action. The consequences of such denial had been demonstrated by the consumptive wasting away of

Robert Mayo and by the violent reclaiming of such apostates as Brutus Jones or the Hairy Ape by the god to whom each "belonged."

Richard Miller, for all his difference of quality, stands alongside the earlier protagonists as one whom the god-force also reclaims. Now, however, the consequences are not absolute, and the theological implications are altogether absent. In the moonlight, Richard comes to harmony with himself and his girl, held by the moon and sea, much as the sailors on the *Glencairn* were held, in painless bondage. Although he has embarked on a self-destructive action, drawing away from the normal, "right" course set for him, at the end of the play, he returns to the natural cycle of life suggested by Nat Miller's final words:

Well, Spring isn't everything, is it, Essie? There's a lot to be said for Autumn. That's got beauty, too. And Winter — if you're together.

The action and meaning of *Ah, Wilderness!* are at no great remove from those of *A Moon for the Misbegotten*.[5] If the former can be taken as a sort of curtain-raiser to *Long Day's Journey into Night*, then the latter, which is O'Neill's most lyric statement, is a gentle epilogue to the tragedy. It begins in comedy — some of O'Neill's best — reminiscent of, and entirely comparable to, Synge's work in genre realism. Yet, as night comes, as the light narrows, the tone modulates slowly. Laughter disappears, narrative is suspended, and the play hangs in time, as Jamie and Josie speak of what they are. The shift from the realistic to the lyric mode is skilfully made, and although the lyri-

---

[5] *A Moon for the Misbegotten* was O'Neill's last completed play, written between 1941 and 1943. It opened, in a production by the Theatre Guild, in Columbus, Ohio, in February, 1947. Trouble with the censors plagued its out-of-town tryout, and it closed at its second stop, Detroit. It was revived in May, 1957 for its first New York production.

cism of the latter part of the play moves the characters and action toward the symbolic, O'Neill does not lose his essentially realistic perspective on his people as he sometimes did in the expressionistic experiments of the 1930's.

Although Josie Hogan becomes a symbol, she does not thereby lose her human characteristics. She has in her the essence of most of O'Neill's later heroines: she is Nina Leeds, she is Cybel — whore, mother, and wife in one. Her grotesque size has forced her into a life-lie, and thus led her to mask herself with coarseness. Only once does she set the mask aside, when she speaks of herself to the child and lover who is lying asleep in her arms. At that moment, O'Neill creates a moving symbol of the *Pietà;* Josie, at peace with herself and nature, and blessed by "the silly mug of the moon," becomes an image of nature itself. Yet here, as contrasted with the expressionistic plays, the symbolism is kept firmly within the realistic frame, and the lyricism that gave rise to the symbols remains a true idiom of the characters. Josie and Jamie, who are touched with poetry, nevertheless are not poets except when loneliness presses in upon them.

The story that Jamie tells Josie is a true one. Ella O'Neill died in Los Angeles, and Jamie brought her body to New York under the circumstances described in the play. The train arrived in New York City the night *The Hairy Ape* opened, and O'Neill was forced to care not only for his mother's body but for his drunken brother as well. Cancelled passages in the typescript of the play reveal Jamie's concern for his brother's animosity, but O'Neill eliminated these vestiges of his own presence, perhaps in an effort to allow his brother to find peace of soul in the end.

Like *Ah, Wilderness!, A Moon for the Misbegotten* is an experience that should have, but probably did not, happen. Jamie's need to find love, to discover somewhere the woman who could provide him surcease from the self-destructive course on which he had set himself was never satisfied in life. Yet, in devising the fiction of this play, O'Neill remained true to what his brother was and performed a gesture of forgiveness and of love. For Jamie needed once to touch deeply another human being, and it is to this that O'Neill brings him, in the night, in the circle of moonlight, as he confesses and then sleeps against the breast of the giant woman whose need is like his own.

To touch another person in momentary contact is the only good that can come to the gropers in darkness who stumble through O'Neill's final tragedies. In *Hughie*,[6] both Erie and Hughes move through black isolation in the echoing spaces of a dead city. Hughes, who is incapable of speaking out the nihilism with which he reacts to his loneliness, is caught up in an unspoken interior monologue.[7] Erie reaches like a blind man through the dark void of his life and arrives at only an awareness of his sense of loss. As in Sartre's play, there is, in *Hughie,* no exit. The reality of life for these men denies life. For this reason, life must be created where it does not exist; man must take refuge in the life-lie, the pipe-dream. Here perhaps is an essential difference between *Hughie* and *A Moon for the Misbegotten*: what Josie and Jamie speak is truth, and it is in the speaking of that truth that they find communion and a transitory salvation. For Hughes and Erie, the truth itself is so ter-

---

[6] *Hughie* was the only completed work of a projected six-play cycle of one-act dramas, to be called *By Way of Obit*. It was written in 1940 and first produced in Stockholm in 1958. Its New York premiere took place in 1964.

[7] That many of Hughes' thoughts remain unheard presents no significant difficulty on stage. It is an error to attempt to voice them. Hughes' silence should be remarkable, fully a part of the pattern of sound that creates the sense of night and the dead city. The interior monologue should be played by an actor exactly as if his words were being heard. The result will be eloquent silence.

rifying that no salvation can come of it. For them, therefore, the only point of human contact is in relation to a
lie. Yet, whether it be truth or lie, what matters is the
contact, and the warmth that is generated by their hud-
dled human souls.

The salvation of the life-lie is explored further in the
first and only completed play of the projected historical
cycle, *A Tale of Possessors, Self-Dispossessed. A Touch
of the Poet,*[8] although it is not autobiographical, spins
its material from the same impulses as the other late plays
were woven from. The events, however, are clothed in
historical and narrative fact, which gives them an altogether different quality on stage. Con Melody is an actor.
He plays his role with bravado, but with his red coat and
cavalier manner he masks an emptiness of soul and a sense
of failure that is comparable to that displayed by James
Tyrone. Nora and Sara, the subjects of his tyranny, support him, love him, and in the end mourn for him. For
them, and for Con, the difference between truth and lie
matters. Con, like the inhabitants of Harry Hope's saloon
in *The Iceman Cometh,* is caught in the waste-land between the life-lie and the truth. Role-playing for him
amounts to a violent splitting of his identity, which leads
to an almost schizoid madness as he sacrifices the symbol
of his lie, the mare. Disappearing into the bar at the play's
end, he enters, perhaps, the actionless world of Harry

---

[8] *A Touch of the Poet* was begun in 1939 and finished in 1942. It was first
produced in Stockholm in 1957 and its first New York production was in
1958. Its title was once given to the cycle as a whole, and it was originally
conceived as the first play of the work. In the final plan, it was put third,
to be preceded by *Greed of the Meek* and *And Give Me Death*. It was to
be followed by *More Stately Mansions,* which carries on the story of the
marriage of Sara and Simon, and by *The Calms of Capricorn, The Earth
Is the Limit!, Nothing Lost Save Honor, Man on Iron Horseback,* and
Hair of the Dog. All the unfinished plays except *More Stately Mansions*
were destroyed by O'Neill shortly before his death.

Hope's saloon, no longer attempting to carry the dream into reality, and instead relapsing into drunkenness, which for a time may cause him to forget his dreams.

Deborah Harford, in describing her family to Sara, says of them, "The Harfords never give up their dreams, even though they deny them." So it is with Con, and so it will prove to be for Sara Melody in *More Stately Mansions*. To attempt to live in the dream clearly leads the dreamer toward madness, as Con's murder of the mare reveals. Deborah's deliberate choice of madness at the end of *More Stately Mansions* is of the same order. Yet the alternative to the insanity of dreams is no better; for in a dreamless life, man moves far from his gods in a wilderness without vision or hope, haunted as was the jungle of *The Emperor Jones* by nightmare projections of another life, only dimly comprehended.

The implications of *A Touch of the Poet,* as extended incompletely in *More Stately Mansions,* are altogether dark: those who once were possessed by a vision that was more than a dream — the poets who shaped America, men whose names were Emerson and Thoreau — proved to be incapable of sustaining that vision. Instead, they sought to possess and draw profit from the land in which at first they had moved so harmoniously. Simon Harford, who had sought the wilderness cabin in order to write his idealistic book, will never write it. He will turn instead into an outrageously corrupt capitalist. Sara, in whom lies the gentle spirit of her mother, will become a woman tarnished by passion and wealth, renouncing dreams of love for the sake of power over all she touches. And Con and Deborah retreat from the world, seeking salvation in vain flight.

In his early plays, O'Neill had suggested that "Life's all right, if you let it alone," [9] for in that case, the god-

---

[9] Cybel's words in *The Great God Brown,* I, iii.

force would lead men to their necessary end without pain. In the cycle plays, there is no suggestion that god exists. Man is alone, and is bent on self-dispossession. He has proved incapable of creating a life consonant with the golden forms of promise he has seen in his vision, and he sets it aside and attempts to forget it. Yet the memory will not die. It lives in him, mocking him, and in the end destroying him.

The view of America that is projected by O'Neill's last historical plays is unredeemed by any saving possibilities. The dramas form a bitter, uncompromising indictment of the failure of vision in a land of hope. Set in a carefully drawn social matrix, they provide a counterpoint to the lyrical autobiographies that form O'Neill's final statement, in that they show the world beyond the fog, the unlighted cities, the source of the terror that finally causes men to seek their reason for being, if not their salvation, by withdrawing into darkness, journeying into night.

Selected Bibliography

ALEXANDER, DORIS. *The Tempering of Eugene O'Neill*. New York, Harcourt, Brace and World, 1962.

BOULTON, AGNES. *Part of a Long Story*. Garden City, N.Y., Doubleday, 1958.

BOWEN, CROSWELL. *The Curse of the Misbegotten*. New York, McGraw-Hill, 1959.

CARGILL, OSCAR, N. B. FAGIN, W. J. FISHER (eds.). *O'Neill and His Plays*. New York, New York University Press, 1961.

CARPENTER, FREDERIC I. *Eugene O'Neill*. New York, Twayne Publishers, 1964.

CLARK, BARRETT. *Eugene O'Neill*. New York, Dover Press, 1947.

ENGLE, EDWIN A. *The Haunted Heroes of Eugene O'Neill*. Cambridge, Mass., Harvard University Press, 1953.

FALK, DORIS. *Eugene O'Neill and the Tragic Tension*. Rutgers, N.J., Rutgers University Press, 1958.

GASSNER, JOHN (ed.). *O'Neill: A Collection of Critical Essays*. Englewood Cliffs, N.J., Prentice-Hall, 1964.

GELB, ARTHUR and BARBARA. *O'Neill*. New York, Harper, 1962.

LEECH, CLIFFORD. *O'Neill*. Edinburgh, Oliver and Boyd, 1963.

MILLER, JORDAN Y. *Playwright's Progress: O'Neill and the Critics*. Chicago, Scott, Foresman and Company, 1965.

O'NEILL, EUGENE G. *Hughie*. New Haven, Conn., Yale University Press, 1959.

O'NEILL, EUGENE G. *Inscriptions: Eugene O'Neill to Carlotta Monterey O'Neill*. New Haven, Conn., Yale University Press, 1960.

O'NEILL, EUGENE G. *A Long Day's Journey into Night*. New

Haven, Conn., Yale University Press, 1955.

O'NEILL, EUGENE G. *A Moon for the Misbegotten.* New York, Random House, 1952.

O'NEILL, EUGENE G. *More Stately Mansions.* New Haven, Conn., Yale University Press, 1964.

O'NEILL, EUGENE G. *The Plays of Eugene O'Neill.* 3 volumes. New York, Random House, 1955.

O'NEILL, EUGENE G. *Ten "Lost" Plays.* New York, Random House, 1964. (Includes *"Thirst"* and other one-act plays.)

O'NEILL, EUGENE G. *A Touch of the Poet.* New Haven, Conn., Yale University Press, 1967.

RALEIGH, JOHN HENRY. *Eugene O'Neill.* Carbondale, Ill., Southern Illinois University Press, 1965.

SKINNER, RICHARD. *Eugene O'Neill: A Poet's Quest.* New York, Russell and Russell, 1964.

WINTHER, SOPHUS KEITH. *Eugene O'Neill: A Critical Study.* New York, Russell and Russell, 1961.

WYLIE, MAX. *Trouble in the Flesh.* Garden City, N.Y., Doubleday, 1959.

,

Ah, Wilderness!

A PLAY IN FOUR ACTS

Characters

NAT MILLER, *owner of the* Evening Globe

ESSIE, *his wife*

ARTHUR

RICHARD

MILDRED

TOMMY

their children

SID DAVIS, *Essie's brother*

LILY MILLER, *Nat's sister*

DAVID MCCOMBER

MURIEL MCCOMBER, *his daughter*

WINT SELBY, *a classmate of Arthur's at Yale*

BELLE

NORAH

BARTENDER

SALESMAN

Scenes

ACT ONE

Sitting-room of the Miller home in a large small-town in Connecticut—early morning, July 4th, 1906.

ACT TWO

Dining-room of the Miller home—evening of the same day.

ACT THREE

SCENE I: Back room of a bar in a small hotel—10 o'clock the same night.

SCENE II: Same as Act One—the sitting-room of the Miller home—a little after 11 o'clock the same night.

ACT FOUR

SCENE I: The Miller sitting-room again—about 1 o'clock the following afternoon.

SCENE II: A strip of beach along the harbor—about 9 o'clock that night.

SCENE III: Same as Scene I—the sitting-room—about 10 o'clock the same night.

Act One

—*Sitting-room of the Miller home in a large small-town in Connecticut—about 7:30 in the morning of July 4th, 1906.*

The room is fairly large, homely looking and cheerful in the morning sunlight, furnished with scrupulous medium-priced tastelessness of the period. Beneath the two windows at left, front, a sofa with silk and satin cushions stands against the wall. At rear of sofa, a bookcase with glass doors, filled with cheap sets, extends along the remaining length of wall. In the rear wall, left, is a double doorway with sliding doors and portières, leading into a dark, windowless, back parlor. At right of this doorway, another bookcase, this time a small open one, crammed with boys' and girls' books and the best-selling novels of many past years—books the family really have read. To the right of this bookcase is the mate of the double doorway at its left, with sliding doors and portières, this one leading to a well-lighted front parlor. In the right wall, rear, a screen door opens on a porch. Farther forward in this wall are two windows, with a writing desk and a chair between them. At center is a big, round table with a green-shaded reading lamp, the cord of the lamp running up to one of five sockets in the chandelier above. Five chairs are grouped about the table—three rockers at left, right, and right rear of it, two armchairs at rear and left rear. A medium-priced, inoffensive

*rug covers most of the floor. The walls are papered white
with a cheerful, ugly blue design.*

*Voices are heard in a conversational tone from the dining-
room beyond the back parlor, where the family are just
finishing breakfast. Then* MRS. MILLER's *voice, raised commandingly,* "Tommy! Come back here and finish your
milk!" *At the same moment* TOMMY *appears in the doorway from the back parlor—a chubby, sun-burnt boy of
eleven with dark eyes, blond hair wetted and plastered
down in a part, and a shiny, good-natured face, a rim of
milk visible about his lips. Bursting with bottled-up energy
and a longing to get started on the Fourth, he nevertheless
has hesitated obediently at his mother's call.*

TOMMY (*calls back pleadingly*): Aw, I'm full, Ma. And I
said excuse me and you said all right. (*His* FATHER's
voice is heard speaking to his mother. Then she calls:
"All right, Tommy," *and* TOMMY *asks eagerly*) Can I go
out now?

MOTHER'S VOICE (*correctingly*): May I!

TOMMY (*fidgeting, but obediently*): May I, Ma?

MOTHER'S VOICE: Yes. (TOMMY *jumps for the screen door to
the porch at right like a sprinter released by the starting
shot.*)

FATHER'S VOICE (*shouts after him*): But you set off your
crackers away from the house, remember! (*But* TOMMY
*is already through the screen door, which he leaves open
behind him.*)

(*A moment later the family appear from the back parlor, coming from the dining-room. First are* MILDRED
and ARTHUR. MILDRED *is fifteen, tall and slender, with
big, irregular features, resembling her father to the
complete effacing of any pretense at prettiness. But her
big, gray eyes are beautiful; she has vivacity and a*

fetching smile, and everyone thinks of her as an attractive girl. She is dressed in shirtwaist and skirt in the fashion of the period.)

(ARTHUR, *the eldest of the Miller children who are still living home, is nineteen. He is tall, heavy, barrelchested and muscular, the type of football linesman of that period, with a square, stolid face, small blue eyes and thick sandy hair. His manner is solemnly collegiate. He is dressed in the latest college fashion of that day, which has receded a bit from the extreme of preceding years, but still runs to padded shoulders and pants half-pegged at the top, and so small at their widecuffed bottoms that they cannot be taken off with shoes on.)*

MILDRED (*as they appear—inquisitively*): Where are you going today, Art?

ARTHUR (*with superior dignity*): That's my business. (*He ostentatiously takes from his pocket a tobacco pouch with a big Y and class numerals stamped on it, and a heavy bulldog briar pipe with silver Y and numerals, and starts filling the pipe.*)

MILDRED (*teasingly*): Bet I know, just the same! Want me to tell you her initials? E.R.! (*She laughs.* ARTHUR, *pleased by this insinuation at his lady-killing activities, yet finds it beneath his dignity to reply. He goes to the table, lights his pipe and picks up the local morning paper, and slouches back into the armchair at left rear of table, beginning to whistle "Oh, Waltz Me Around Again, Willie" as he scans the headlines.* MILDRED *sits on the sofa at left, front.*)

(*Meanwhile, their mother and their* AUNT LILY, *their father's sister, have appeared, following them from the back parlor.* MRS. MILLER *is around fifty, a short, stout woman with fading light-brown hair sprinkled with gray, who must have been decidedly pretty as a girl in a round-faced, cute, small-featured, wide-eyed fashion. She has big brown eyes, soft and maternal—a bustling, mother-of-a-family manner. She is dressed in shirtwaist and skirt.)*

(LILY MILLER, her sister-in-law, is forty-two, tall, dark and thin. She conforms outwardly to the conventional type of old-maid school teacher, even to wearing glasses. But behind the glasses her gray eyes are gentle and tired, and her whole atmosphere is one of shy kindliness. Her voice presents the greatest contrast to her appearance—soft and full of sweetness. She, also, is dressed in a shirtwaist and skirt.)

MRS. MILLER *(as they appear)*: Getting milk down him is like— *(Suddenly she is aware of the screen door standing half open)* Goodness, look at that door he's left open! The house will be alive with flies! *(Rushing out to shut it)* I've told him again and again—and that's all the good it does! It's just a waste of breath! *(She slams the door shut.)*

LILY *(smiling)*: Well, you can't expect a boy to remember to shut doors—on the Fourth of July. *(She goes diffidently to the straight-backed chair before the desk at right, front, leaving the comfortable chairs to the others.)*

MRS. MILLER: That's you all over, Lily—always making excuses for him. You'll have him spoiled to death in spite of me. *(She sinks in rocker at right of table)* Phew, I'm hot, aren't you? This is going to be a scorcher. *(She picks up a magazine from the table and begins to rock, fanning herself.)*

(Meanwhile, her husband and her brother have appeared from the back parlor, both smoking cigars. NAT MILLER is in his late fifties, a tall, dark, spare man, a little stoop-shouldered, more than a little bald, dressed

with an awkward attempt at sober respectability imposed upon an innate heedlessness of clothes. His long face has large, irregular, undistinguished features, but he has fine, shrewd, humorous gray eyes.)

(SID DAVIS, *his brother-in-law, is forty-five, short and fat, bald-headed, with the puckish face of a Peck's Bad Boy who has never grown up. He is dressed in what had once been a very natty loud light suit but is now a shapeless and faded nondescript in cut and color.)*

SID (*as they appear*): Oh, I like the job first rate, Nat. Waterbury's a nifty old town with the lid off, when you get to know the ropes. I rang in a joke in one of my stories that tickled the folks there pink. Waterwagon—Waterbury—Waterloo!

MILLER (*grinning*): Darn good!

SID (*pleased*): I thought it was pretty fair myself. (*Goes on a bit ruefully, as if oppressed by a secret sorrow*) Yes, you can see life in Waterbury, all right—that is, if you're looking for life in Waterbury!

MRS. MILLER: What's that about Waterbury, Sid?

SID: I was saying it's all right in its way—but there's no place like home. (*As if to punctuate this remark, there begins a series of bangs from just beyond the porch outside, as* TOMMY *inaugurates his celebration by setting off a package of firecrackers. The assembled family jump in their chairs.*)

MRS. MILLER: That boy! (*She rushes to the screen door and out on the porch, calling*) Tommy! You mind what your Pa told you! You take your crackers out in the back yard, you hear me!

ARTHUR (*frowning scornfully*): Fresh kid! He did it on purpose to scare us.

MILLER (*grinning through his annoyance*): Darned youngster! He'll have the house afire before the day's out.

SID (*grins and sings*):

> "*Dunno what ter call 'im*
> *But he's mighty like a Rose—velt.*"

(*They all laugh.*)

LILY: Sid, you Crazy! (SID *beams at her.* MRS. MILLER *comes back from the porch, still fuming.*)

MRS. MILLER: Well, I've made him go out back at last. Now we'll have a little peace. (*As if to contradict this, the bang of firecrackers and torpedoes begins from the rear of the house, left, and continues at intervals throughout the scene, not nearly so loud as the first explosion, but sufficiently emphatic to form a disturbing punctuation to the conversation.*)

MILLER: Well, what's on the tappee for all of you today? Sid, you're coming to the Sachem Club picnic with me, of course.

SID (*a bit embarrassedly*): You bet. I mean I'd like to, Nat —that is, if—

MRS. MILLER (*regarding her brother with smiling suspicion*): Hmm! I know what that Sachem Club picnic's always meant!

LILY (*breaks in in a forced joking tone that conceals a deep earnestness*): No, not this time, Essie. Sid's a reformed character since he's been on the paper in Waterbury. At least, that's what he swore to me last night.

SID (*avoiding her eyes, humiliated—joking it off*): Pure as the driven snow, that's me. They're running me for president of the W.C.T.U. (*They all laugh.*)

MRS. MILLER: Sid, you're a caution. You turn everything into a joke. But you be careful, you hear? We're going to have dinner in the evening tonight, you know—the best shore dinner you ever tasted and I don't want you coming home—well, not able to appreciate it.

LILY: Oh, I know he'll be careful today. Won't you, Sid?

SID (*more embarrassed than ever—joking it off melodramatically*): Lily, I swear to you if any man offers me a drink, I'll kill him—that is, if he changes his mind! (*They all laugh except* LILY, *who bites her lip and stiffens.*)

MRS. MILLER: No use talking to him, Lily. You ought to know better by this time. We can only hope for the best.

MILLER: Now, you women stop picking on Sid. It's the Fourth of July and even a downtrodden newspaperman has a right to enjoy himself when he's on his holiday.

MRS. MILLER: I wasn't thinking only of Sid.

MILLER (*with a wink at the others*): What, are you insinuating I ever—?

MRS. MILLER: Well, to do you justice, no, not what you'd really call— But I've known you to come back from this darned Sachem Club picnic— Well, I didn't need any little bird to whisper that you'd been some place besides to the well! (*She smiles good-naturedly.* MILLER *chuckles.*)

SID (*after a furtive glance at the stiff and silent* LILY— *changes the subject abruptly by turning to* ARTHUR): How are you spending the festive Fourth, Boola-Boola? (ARTHUR *stiffens dignifiedly.*)

MILDRED (*teasingly*): I can tell you, if he won't.

MRS. MILLER (*smiling*): Off to the Rands', I suppose.

ARTHUR (*with dignity*): I and Bert Turner are taking Elsie and Ethel Rand canoeing. We're going to have a picnic lunch on Strawberry Island. And this evening I'm staying at the Rands' for dinner.

MILLER: You're accounted for, then. How about you, Mid?

MILDRED: I'm going to the beach to Anne Culver's.

ARTHUR (*sarcastically*): Of course, there won't be any boys present! Johnny Dodd, for example?

MILDRED (*giggles—then with a coquettish toss of her head*):
Pooh! What do I care for him? He's not the only pebble
on the beach.

MILLER: Stop your everlasting teasing, you two. How about
you and Lily, Essie?

MRS. MILLER: I don't know. I haven't made any plans.
Have you, Lily?

LILY (*quietly*): No. Anything you want to do.

MRS. MILLER: Well, I thought we'd just sit around and rest
and talk.

MILLER: You can gossip any day. This is the Fourth. Now,
I've got a better suggestion than that. What do you say
to an automobile ride? I'll get out the Buick and we'll
drive around town and out to the lighthouse and back.
Then Sid and I will let you off here, or anywhere you
say, and we'll go on to the picnic.

MRS. MILLER: I'd love it. Wouldn't you, Lily?

LILY: It would be nice.

MILLER: Then, that's all settled.

SID (*embarrassedly*): Lily, want to come with me to the
fireworks display at the beach tonight?

MRS. MILLER: That's right, Sid. You take her out. Poor Lily
never has any fun, always sitting home with me.

LILY (*flustered and grateful*): I—I'd like to, Sid, thank
you. (*Then an apprehensive look comes over her face*)
Only not if you come home—you know.

SID (*again embarrassed and humiliated—again joking it
off, solemnly*): Evil-minded, I'm afraid, Nat. I hate to
say it of your sister. (*They all laugh. Even LILY cannot
suppress a smile.*)

ARTHUR (*with heavy jocularity*): Listen, Uncle Sid. Don't
let me catch you and Aunt Lily spooning on a bench
tonight—or it'll be my duty to call a cop! (SID *and* LILY
both look painfully embarrassed at this, and the joke

falls flat, except for MILDRED *who can't restrain a giggle at the thought of these two ancients spooning.*)

MRS. MILLER (*rebukingly*): Arthur!

MILLER (*dryly*): That'll do you. Your education in kicking a football around Yale seems to have blunted your sense of humor.

MRS. MILLER (*suddenly—startledly*): But where's Richard? We're forgetting all about him. Why, where is that boy? I thought he came in with us from breakfast.

MILDRED: I'll bet he's off somewhere writing a poem to Muriel McComber, the silly! Or pretending to write one. I think he just copies—

ARTHUR (*looking back toward the dining-room*): He's still in the dining-room, reading a book. (*Turning back—scornfully*) Gosh, he's always reading now. It's not my idea of having a good time in vacation.

MILLER (*caustically*): He read his school books, too, strange as that may seem to you. That's why he came out top of his class. I'm hoping before you leave New Haven they'll find time to teach you reading is a good habit.

MRS. MILLER (*sharply*): That reminds me, Nat. I've been meaning to speak to you about those awful books Richard is reading. You've got to give him a good talking to— (*She gets up from her chair*) I'll go up and get them right now. I found them where he'd hid them on the shelf in his wardrobe. You just wait till you see what— (*She bustles off, rear right, through the front parlor.*)

MILLER (*plainly not relishing whatever is coming—to* SID, *grumblingly*): Seems to me she might wait until the Fourth is over before bringing up— (*Then with a grin*) I know there's nothing to it, anyway. When I think of the books I used to sneak off and read when I was a kid.

SID: Me, too. I suppose Dick is deep in Nick Carter or Old Cap Collier.

MILLER: No, he passed that period long ago. Poetry's his

red meat nowadays, I think—love poetry—and socialism, too, I suspect, from some dire declarations he's made. (*Then briskly*) Well, might as well get him on the carpet. (*He calls*) Richard. (*No answer—louder*) Richard. (*No answer—then in a bellow*) Richard!

ARTHUR (*shouting*): Hey, Dick, wake up! Pa's calling you.

RICHARD'S VOICE (*from the dining-room*): All right. I'm coming.

MILLER: Darn him! When he gets his nose in a book, the house could fall down and he'd never—

(RICHARD *appears in the doorway from the back parlor, the book he has been reading in one hand, a finger marking his place. He looks a bit startled still, reluctantly called back to earth from another world.*)

(*He is going on seventeen, just out of high school. In appearance he is a perfect blend of father and mother, so much so that each is convinced he is the image of the other. He has his mother's light-brown hair, his father's gray eyes; his features are neither large nor small; he is of medium height, neither fat nor thin. One would not call him a handsome boy; neither is he homely. But he is definitely different from both of his parents, too. There is something of extreme sensitiveness added—a restless, apprehensive, defiant, shy, dreamy, self-conscious intelligence about him. In manner he is alternately plain simple boy and a posey actor solemnly playing a role. He is dressed in prep school reflection of the college style of ARTHUR.*)

RICHARD: Did you want me, Pa?

MILLER: I'd hoped I'd made that plain. Come and sit down a while. (*He points to the rocking chair at the right of table near his.*)

RICHARD (*coming forward—seizing on the opportunity to play up his preoccupation—with apologetic superiority*):

I didn't hear you, Pa. I was off in another world. (MILDRED *slyly shoves her foot out so that he trips over it, almost falling. She laughs gleefully. So does* ARTHUR.)

ARTHUR: Good for you, Mid! That'll wake him up!

RICHARD (*grins sheepishly—all boy now*): Darn you, Mid! I'll show you! (*He pushes her back on the sofa and tickles her with his free hand, still holding the book in the other. She shrieks.*)

ARTHUR: Give it to her, Dick!

MILLER: That's enough, now. No more roughhouse. You sit down here, Richard. (RICHARD *obediently takes the chair at right of table, opposite his father*) What were you planning to do with yourself today? Going out to the beach with Mildred?

RICHARD (*scornfully superior*): That silly skirt party! I should say not!

MILDRED: He's not coming because Muriel isn't. I'll bet he's got a date with her somewheres.

RICHARD (*flushing bashfully*): You shut up! (*Then to his father*) I thought I'd just stay home, Pa—this morning, anyway.

MILLER: Help Tommy set off firecrackers, eh?

RICHARD (*drawing himself up—with dignity*): I should say not. (*Then frowning portentously*) I don't believe in this silly celebrating the Fourth of July—all this lying talk about liberty—when there is no liberty!

MILLER (*a twinkle in his eye*): Hmm.

RICHARD (*getting warmed up*): The land of the free and the home of the brave! Home of the slave is what they ought to call it—the wage slave ground under the heel of the capitalist class, starving, crying for bread for his children, and all he gets is a stone! The Fourth of July is a stupid farce!

MILLER (*putting a hand to his mouth to conceal a grin*):

Hmm. Them are mighty strong words. You'd better not repeat such sentiments outside the bosom of the family or they'll have you in jail.

SID: And throw away the key.

RICHARD (*darkly*): Let them put me in jail. But how about the freedom of speech in the Constitution, then? That must be a farce, too. (*Then he adds grimly*) No, you can celebrate your Fourth of July. I'll celebrate the day the people bring out the guillotine again and I see Pierpont Morgan being driven by in a tumbril! (*His father and* SID *are greatly amused;* LILY *is shocked but, taking her cue from them, smiles.* MILDRED *stares at him in puzzled wonderment, never having heard this particular line before. Only* ARTHUR *betrays the outraged reaction of a patriot.*)

ARTHUR: Aw say, you fresh kid, tie that bull outside! You ought to get a punch in the nose for talking that way on the Fourth!

MILLER (*solemnly*): Son, if I didn't know it was you talking, I'd think we had Emma Goldman with us.

ARTHUR: Never mind, Pa. Wait till we get him down to Yale. We'll take that out of him!

RICHARD (*with high scorn*): Oh, Yale! You think there's nothing in the world besides Yale. After all, what is Yale?

ARTHUR: You'll find out what!

SID (*provocatively*): Don't let them scare you, Dick. Give 'em hell!

LILY (*shocked*): Sid! You shouldn't swear before—

RICHARD: What do you think I am, Aunt Lily—a baby? I've heard worse than anything Uncle Sid says.

MILDRED: And said worse himself, I bet!

MILLER (*with a comic air of resignation*): Well, Richard, I've always found I've had to listen to at least one stump speech every Fourth. I only hope getting your extra strong one right after breakfast will let me off for the rest of the day. (*They all laugh now, taking this as a cue.*)

RICHARD (*somberly*): That's right, laugh! After you, the deluge, you think! But look out! Supposing it comes before? Why shouldn't the workers of the world unite and rise? They have nothing to lose but their chains! (*He recites threateningly*) "The days grow hot, O Babylon! 'Tis cool beneath thy willow trees!"

MILLER: Hmm. That's good. But where's the connection, exactly? Something from that book you're reading?

RICHARD (*superior*): No. That's poetry. This is prose.

MILLER: I've heard there was a difference between 'em. What is the book?

RICHARD (*importantly*): Carlyle's "French Revolution."

MILLER: Hmm. So that's where you drove the tumbril from and piled poor old Pierpont in it. (*Then seriously*) Glad you're reading it, Richard. It's a darn fine book.

RICHARD (*with unflattering astonishment*): What, have you read it?

MILLER: Well you see, even a newspaper owner can't get out of reading a book every now and again.

RICHARD (*abashed*): I—I didn't mean—I know you— (*Then enthusiastically*) Say, isn't it a great book, though—that part about Mirabeau—and about Marat and Robespierre—

MRS. MILLER (*appears from the front parlor in a great state of flushed annoyance*): Never you mind Robespierre, young man! You tell me this minute where you've hidden those books! They were on the shelf in your wardrobe and now you've gone and hid them somewheres else. You go right up and bring them to your father! (*RICHARD, for a second, looks suddenly guilty and crushed. Then he bristles defensively.*)

MILLER (*after a quick understanding glance at him*): Never mind his getting them now. We'll waste the whole morn-

ing over those darned books. And anyway, he has a right
to keep his library to himself—that is, if they're not too—
What books are they, Richard?

RICHARD (*self-consciously*): Well—there's—

MRS. MILLER: I'll tell you, if he won't—and you give him
a good talking to. (*Then, after a glance at* RICHARD,
mollifiedly) Not that I blame Richard. There must be
some boy he knows who's trying to show off as advanced
and wicked, and he told him about—

RICHARD: No! I read about them myself, in the papers and
in other books.

MRS. MILLER: Well, no matter how, there they were on his
shelf. Two by that awful Oscar Wilde they put in jail
for heaven knows what wickedness.

ARTHUR (*suddenly—solemnly authoritative*): He committed
bigamy. (*Then as* SID *smothers a burst of ribald laughter*)
What are you laughing at? I guess I ought to know. A
fellow at college told me. His father was in England
when this Wilde was pinched—and he said he remembered once his mother asked his father about it and he
told her he'd committed bigamy.

MILLER (*hiding a smile behind his hand*): Well then, that
must be right, Arthur.

MRS. MILLER: I wouldn't put it past him, nor anything
else. One book was called the Picture of something or
other.

RICHARD: "The Picture of Dorian Gray." It's one of the
greatest novels ever written!

MRS. MILLER: Looked to me like cheap trash. And the
second book was poetry. The Ballad of I forget what.

RICHARD: "The Ballad of Reading Gaol," one of the greatest poems ever written. (*He pronounces it Reading
Goal* [*as in goalpost*].)

MRS. MILLER: All about someone who murdered his wife
and got hung, as he richly deserved, as far as I could

make out. And then there were two books by that Bernard Shaw—

RICHARD: The greatest playwright alive today!

MRS. MILLER: To hear him tell it, maybe! You know, Nat, the one who wrote a play about—well, never mind— that was so vile they wouldn't even let it play in New York!

MILLER: Hmm. I remember.

MRS. MILLER: One was a book of his plays and the other had a long title I couldn't make head or tail of, only it wasn't a play.

RICHARD (*proudly*): "The Quintessence of Ibsenism."

MILDRED: Phew! Good gracious, what a name! What does it mean, Dick? I'll bet he doesn't know.

RICHARD (*outraged*): I do, too, know! It's about Ibsen, the greatest playwright since Shakespeare!

MRS. MILLER: Yes, there was a book of plays by that Ibsen there, too! And poems by Swin something—

RICHARD: "Poems and Ballads" by Swinburne, Ma. The greatest poet since Shelley! He tells the truth about real love!

MRS. MILLER: Love! Well, all I can say is, from reading here and there, that if he wasn't flung in jail along with Wilde, he should have been. Some of the things I simply couldn't read, they were so indecent— All about— well, I can't tell you before Lily and Mildred.

SID (*with a wink at* RICHARD—*jokingly*): Remember, I'm next on that one, Dick. I feel the need of a little poetical education.

LILY (*scandalized, but laughing*): Sid! Aren't you ashamed?

MRS. MILLER: This is no laughing matter. And then there was Kipling—but I suppose he's not so bad. And last there was a poem—a long one—the Rubay— What is it, Richard?

RICHARD: "The Rubaiyat of Omar Khayyam." That's the best of all!

MILLER: Oh, I've read that, Essie—got a copy down at the office.

SID (*enthusiastically*): So have I. It's a pippin!

LILY (*with shy excitement*): I—I've read it, too—at the library. I like—some parts of it.

MRS. MILLER (*scandalized*): Why, Lily!

MILLER: Everybody's reading that now, Essie—and it don't seem to do them any harm. There's fine things in it, seems to me—true things.

MRS. MILLER (*a bit bewildered and uncertain now*): Why, Nat, I don't see how you— It looked terrible blasphemous—parts I read.

SID: Remember this one: (*He quotes rhetorically*) "Oh Thou, who didst with pitfall and gin beset the path I was to wander in—" Now, I've always noticed how beset my path was with gin—in the past, you understand! (*He casts a joking side glance at* LILY. *The others laugh. But* LILY *is in a melancholy dream and hasn't heard him.*)

MRS. MILLER (*tartly, but evidently suppressing her usual smile where he is concerned*): You would pick out the ones with liquor in them!

LILY (*suddenly—with a sad pathos, quotes awkwardly and shyly*): I like—because it's true

> "The Moving Finger writes, and having writ,
> Moves on: nor all your Piety nor Wit
> Shall lure it back to cancel half a Line,
> Nor all your Tears wash out a Word of it."

MRS. MILLER (*astonished, as are all the others*): Why, Lily, I never knew you to recite poetry before!

LILY (*immediately guilty and apologetic*): I—it just stuck in my memory somehow.

RICHARD (*looking at her as if he had never seen her be-*

fore): Good for you, Aunt Lily! (*Then enthusiastically*) But that isn't the best. The best is

"*A Book of Verses underneath the Bough,
A Jug of Wine, A Loaf of Bread—and Thou
Beside me singing in the Wilderness—*"

ARTHUR (*who, bored to death by all this poetry quoting, has wandered over to the window at rear of desk, right*): Hey! Look who's coming up the walk— Old Man Mc-Comber!

MILLER (*irritably*): Dave? Now what in thunder does that damned old— Sid, I can see where we never are going to get to that picnic.

MRS. MILLER (*vexatiously*): He'll know we're in this early, too. No use lying. (*Then appalled by another thought*) That Norah—she's that thick, she never can answer the front door right unless I tell her each time. Nat, you've got to talk to Dave. I'll have her show him in here. Lily, you run up the back stairs and get your things on. I'll be up in a second. Nat, you get rid of him the first second you can! Whatever can the old fool want— (*She and* LILY *hurry out through the back parlor.*)

ARTHUR: I'm going to beat it—just time to catch the eight-twenty trolley.

MILDRED: I've got to catch that, too. Wait till I get my hat, Art! (*She rushes into the back parlor.*)

ARTHUR (*shouts after her*): I can't wait. You can catch up with me if you hurry. (*He turns at the back-parlor door —with a grin*) McComber may be coming to see if your intentions toward his daughter are dishonorable, Dick! You'd better beat it while your shoes are good! (*He disappears through the back-parlor door, laughing.*)

RICHARD (*a bit shaken, but putting on a brave front*): Think I'm scared of him?

MILLER (*gazing at him—frowning*): Can't imagine what—

But it's to complain about something, I know that. I only wish I didn't have to be pleasant with the old buzzard—but he's about the most valuable advertiser I've got.

SID (*sympathetically*): I know. But tell him to go to hell, anyway. He needs that ad more than you.

(*The sound of the bell comes from the rear of the house, off left from back parlor.*)

MILLER: There he is. You clear out, Dick—but come right back as soon as he's gone, you hear? I'm not through with you, yet.

RICHARD: Yes, Pa.

MILLER: You better clear out, too, Sid. You know Dave doesn't approve jokes.

SID: And loves me like poison! Come on, Dick, we'll go out and help Tommy celebrate. (*He takes* RICHARD's *arm and they also disappear through the back-parlor door.* MILLER *glances through the front parlor toward the front door, then calls in a tone of strained heartiness.*)

MILLER: Hello, Dave. Come right in here. What good wind blows you around on this glorious Fourth?

(*A flat, brittle voice answers him: "Good morning," and a moment later* DAVID MC COMBER *appears in the doorway from the front parlor. He is a thin, dried-up little man with a head too large for his body perched on a scrawny neck, and a long solemn horse face with deep-set little black eyes, a blunt formless nose and a tiny slit of a mouth. He is about the same age as* MILLER *but is entirely bald, and looks ten years older. He is dressed with a prim neatness in shiny old black clothes.*)

MILLER: Here, sit down and make yourself comfortable. (*Holding out the cigar box*) Have a cigar?

MC COMBER (*sitting down in the chair at the right of table—acidly*): You're forgetting. I never smoke.

MILLER (*forcing a laugh at himself*): That's so. So I was. Well, I'll smoke alone then. (*He bites off the end of the cigar viciously, as if he wished it were* MC COMBER's *head, and sits down opposite him.*)

MC COMBER: You asked me what brings me here, so I'll come to the point at once. I regret to say it's something disagreeable—disgraceful would be nearer the truth—and it concerns your son, Richard!

MILLER (*beginning to bristle—but calmly*): Oh, come now, Dave, I'm sure Richard hasn't—

MC COMBER (*sharply*): And I'm positive he has. You're not accusing me of being a liar, I hope.

MILLER: No one said anything about liar. I only meant you're surely mistaken if you think—

MC COMBER: I'm not mistaken. I have proof of everything in his own handwriting!

MILLER (*sharply*): Let's get down to brass tacks. Just what is it you're charging him with?

MC COMBER: With being dissolute and blasphemous—with deliberately attempting to corrupt the morals of my young daughter, Muriel.

MILLER: Then I'm afraid I will have to call you a liar, Dave!

MC COMBER (*without taking offense—in the same flat, brittle voice*): I thought you'd get around to that, so I brought some of the proofs with me. I've a lot more of 'em at home. (*He takes a wallet from his inside coat pocket, selects five or six slips of paper, and holds them out to* MILLER) These are good samples of the rest. My wife discovered them in one of Muriel's bureau drawers hidden under the underwear. They're all in his handwriting, you can't deny it. Anyway, Muriel's confessed to me he wrote them. You read them and then say I'm a liar. (*MILLER has taken the slips and is reading them frowningly.* MC COMBER *talks on*) Evidently you've been too busy to take the right care about Richard's bringing up or what's he's allowed to read—though I can't see why his mother failed in her duty. But that's your misfortune, and none of my business. But Muriel is my business and I can't and I won't have her innocence exposed to the contamination of a young man whose mind, judging from his choice of reading matter, is as foul—

MILLER (*making a tremendous effort to control his temper*): Why, you damned old fool! Can't you see Richard's only a fool kid who's just at the stage when he's out to rebel against all authority, and so he grabs at everything radical to read and wants to pass it on to his elders and his girl and boy friends to show off what a young hellion he is! Why, at heart you'd find Richard is just as innocent and as big a kid as Muriel is! (*He pushes the slips of paper across the table contemptuously*) This stuff doesn't mean anything to me—that is, nothing of what you think it means. If you believe this would corrupt Muriel, then you must believe she's easily corrupted! But I'll bet you'd find she knows a lot more about life than you give her credit for—and can guess a stork didn't bring her down your chimney!

MC COMBER: Now you're insulting my daughter. I won't forget that.

MILLER: I'm not insulting her. I think Muriel is a darn nice girl. That's why I'm giving her credit for ordinary good sense. I'd say the same about my own Mildred, who's the same age.

MC COMBER: I know nothing about your Mildred except that she's known all over as a flirt. (*Then more sharply*) Well, I knew you'd prove obstinate, but I certainly never dreamed you'd have the impudence, after reading those papers, to claim your son was innocent of all wrongdoing!

MILLER: And what did you dream I'd do?

MC COMBER: Do what it's your plain duty to do as a citizen to protect other people's children! Take and give him a hiding he'd remember to the last day of his life! You'd ought to do it for his sake, if you had any sense—unless you want him to end up in jail!

MILLER (*his fists clenched, leans across the table*): Dave, I've stood all I can stand from you! You get out! And get out quick, if you don't want a kick in the rear to help you!

MC COMBER (*again in his flat, brittle voice, slowly getting to his feet*): You needn't lose your temper. I'm only demanding you do your duty by your own as I've already done by mine. I'm punishing Muriel. She's not to be allowed out of the house for a month and she's to be in bed every night by eight sharp. And yet she's blameless, compared to that—

MILLER: I said I'd had enough out of you, Dave! (*He makes a threatening movement.*)

MC COMBER: You needn't lay hands on me. I'm going. But there's one thing more. (*He takes a letter from his wallet*) Here's a letter from Muriel for your son. (*Puts it on the table*) It makes clear, I think, how she's come to think about him, now that her eyes have been opened. I hope he heeds what's inside—for his own good and yours—because if I ever catch him hanging about my place again I'll have him arrested! And don't think I'm not going to make you regret the insults you've heaped on me. I'm taking the advertisement for my store out of your paper—and it won't go in again, I tell you, not unless you apologize in writing and promise to punish—

MILLER: I'll see you in hell first! As for your damned old ad, take it out and go to hell!

MC COMBER: That's plain bluff. You know how badly you need it. So do I. (*He starts stiffly for the door.*)

MILLER: Here! Listen a minute! I'm just going to call *your* bluff and tell you that, whether you want to reconsider your decision or not, I'm going to refuse to print your damned ad after tomorrow! Put that in your pipe and smoke it! Furthermore, I'll start a campaign to encourage outside capital to open a dry-goods store in opposition to you that won't be the public swindle I can prove yours is!

MC COMBER (*a bit shaken by this threat—but in the same flat tone*): I'll sue you for libel.

MILLER: When I get through, there won't be a person in town will buy a dishrag in your place!

MC COMBER (*more shaken, his eyes shifting about furtively*): That's all bluff. You wouldn't dare— (*Then finally he says uncertainly*) Well, good day. (*And turns and goes out.* NAT *stands looking after him. Slowly the anger drains from his face and leaves him looking a bit sick and disgusted.* SID *appears from the back parlor. He is nursing a burn on his right hand, but his face is one broad grin of satisfaction.*)

SID: I burned my hand with one of Tommy's damned firecrackers and came in to get some vaseline. I was listening to the last of your scrap. Good for you, Nat! You sure gave him hell!

MILLER (*dully*): Much good it'll do. He knows it was all talk.

SID: That's just what he don't know, Nat. The old skinflint has a guilty conscience.

MILLER: Well, anyone who knows me knows I wouldn't use my paper for a dirty, spiteful trick like that—no matter what he did to me.

SID: Yes, everyone knows you're an old sucker, Nat, too decent for your own good. But McComber never saw you like this before. I tell you you scared the pants off him. (*He chuckles.*)

MILLER (*still dejectedly*): I don't know what made me let go like that. The hell of skunks like McComber is that after being with them ten minutes you become as big skunks as they are.

SID (*notices the slips of paper on the table*): What's this? Something he brought? (*He picks them up and starts to read.*)

MILLER (*grimly*): Samples of the new freedom—from those books Essie found—that Richard's been passing on to Muriel to educate her. They're what started the rumpus. (*Then frowning*) I've got to do something about that young anarchist or he'll be getting me, and himself, in a peck of trouble. (*Then pathetically helpless*) But what can I do? Putting the curb bit on would make him worse. Then he'd have a harsh tyrant to defy. He'd love that, darn him!

SID (*has been reading the slips, a broad grin on his face—suddenly he whistles*): Phew! This is a warm lulu for fair! (*He recites with a joking intensity*)

> *"My life is bitter with thy love; thine eyes*
> *Blind me, thy tresses burn me, thy sharp sighs*
> *Divide my flesh and spirit with soft sound—"*

MILLER (*with a grim smile*): Hmm. I missed that one. That must be Mr. Swinburne's copy. I've never read him, but I've heard something like that was the matter with him.

SID: Yes, it's labelled Swinburne—"Anactoria." Whatever that is. But wait, watch and listen! The worst is yet to come! (*He recites with added comic intensity*)

> *"That I could drink thy veins as wine, and eat*
> *Thy breasts like honey, that from face to feet*
> *Thy body were abolished and consumed,*
> *And in my flesh thy very flesh entombed!"*

MILLER (*an irrepressible boyish grin coming to his face*):
Hell and hallelujah! Just picture old Dave digesting
that for the first time! Gosh, I'd give a lot to have seen
his face! (*Then a trace of shocked reproof showing in
his voice*). But it's no joking matter. That stuff *is* warm
—too damned warm, if you ask me! I don't like this a
damned bit, Sid. That's no kind of thing to be sending
a decent girl. (*More worriedly*) I thought he was really
stuck on her—as one gets stuck on a decent girl at his
age—all moonshine and holding hands and a kiss now
and again. But this looks—I wonder if he is hanging
around her to see what he can get? (*Angrily*) By God,
if that's true, he deserves that licking McComber says
it's my duty to give him! I've got to draw the line somewhere!

SID: Yes, it won't do to have him getting any decent girl in
trouble.

MILLER: The only thing I can do is put it up to him straight.
(*With pride*) Richard'll stand up to his guns, no matter
what. I've never known him to lie to me.

SID (*at a noise from the back parlor, looks that way—
in a whisper*): Then now's your chance. I'll beat it
and leave you alone—see if the women folks are ready
upstairs. We ought to get started soon—if we're ever
going to make that picnic. (*He is halfway to the entrance to the front parlor as* RICHARD *enters from the
back parlor, very evidently nervous about* MC COMBER'S
call.)

RICHARD (*adopting a forced, innocent tone*): How's your
hand, Uncle Sid?

SID: All right, Dick, thanks—only hurts a little. (*He disappears.* MILLER *watches his son frowningly.* RICHARD
*gives him a quick side glance and grows more guiltily
self-conscious.*)

RICHARD (*forcing a snicker*): Gee, Pa, Uncle Sid's a bigger kid than Tommy is. He was throwing firecrackers in the air and catching them on the back of his hand and throwing 'em off again just before they went off—and one came and he wasn't quick enough, and it went off almost on top of—

MILLER: Never mind that. I've got something else to talk to you about besides firecrackers.

RICHARD (*apprehensively*): What, Pa?

MILLER (*suddenly puts both hands on his shoulders— quietly*): Look here, Son. I'm going to ask you a question, and I want an honest answer. I warn you beforehand if the answer is "yes" I'm going to punish you and punish you hard because you'll have done something no boy of mine ought to do. But you've never lied to me before, I know, and I don't believe, even to save yourself punishment, you'd lie to me now, would you?

RICHARD (*impressed—with dignity*): I won't lie, Pa.

MILLER: Have you been trying to have something to do with Muriel—something you shouldn't—you know what I mean.

RICHARD (*stares at him for a moment, as if he couldn't comprehend—then, as he does, a look of shocked indignation comes over his face*): No! What do you think I am, Pa? I never would! She's not that kind! Why, I—I love her! I'm going to marry her—after I get out of college! She's said she would! We're engaged!

MILLER (*with great relief*): All right. That's all I wanted to know. We won't talk any more about it. (*He gives him an approving pat on the back.*)

RICHARD: I don't see how you could think— Did that old idiot McComber say that about me?

MILLER (*joking now*): Shouldn't call your future father-in-law names, should you? 'Tain't respectful. (*Then after a glance at* RICHARD's *indignant face—points to the slips of paper on the table*) Well, you can't exactly blame

old Dave, can you, when you read through that literature
you wished on his innocent daughter?

RICHARD (*sees the slips for the first time and is overcome by
embarrassment, which he immediately tries to cover up
with a superior carelessness*): Oh, so that's why. He
found those, did he? I told her to be careful— Well, it'll
do him good to read the truth about life for once and
get rid of his old-fogy ideas.

MILLER: I'm afraid I've got to agree with him, though, that
they're hardly fit reading for a young girl. (*Then with
subtle flattery*) They're all well enough, in their way, for
you who're a man, but— Think it over, and see if you
don't agree with me.

RICHARD (*embarrassedly*): Aw, I only did it because I liked
them—and I wanted her to face life as it is. She's so
darned afraid of life—afraid of her Old Man—afraid of
people saying this or that about her—afraid of being in
love—afraid of everything. She's even afraid to let me
kiss her. I thought, maybe, reading those things—they're
beautiful, aren't they, Pa?—I thought they would give
her the spunk to lead her own life, and not be—always
thinking of being afraid.

MILLER: I see. Well, I'm afraid she's still afraid. (*He takes
the letter from the table*) Here's a letter from her he
said to give you. (RICHARD *takes the letter from him uncertainly, his expression changing to one of apprehension.*
MILLER *adds with a kindly smile*) You better be prepared for a bit of a blow. But never mind. There's lots
of other fish in the sea. (RICHARD *is not listening to him,
but staring at the letter with a sort of fascinated dread.*
MILLER *looks into his son's face a second, then turns away,
troubled and embarrassed*) Darn it! I better go upstairs
and get rigged out or I never will get to that picnic. (*He
moves awkwardly and self-consciously off through the
front parlor.* RICHARD *continues to stare at the letter for a*

moment—then girds up his courage and tears it open and begins to read swiftly. As he reads his face grows more and more wounded and tragic, until at the end his mouth draws down at the corners, as if he were about to break into tears. With an effort he forces them back and his face grows flushed with humiliation and wronged anger.)

RICHARD (*blurts out to himself*): The little coward! I hate her! She can't treat me like that! I'll show her! (*At the sound of voices from the front parlor, he quickly shoves the letter into the inside pocket of his coat and does his best to appear calm and indifferent, even attempting to whistle "Waiting at the Church." But the whistle peters out miserably as his mother,* LILY *and* SID *enter from the front parlor. They are dressed in all the elaborate paraphernalia of motoring at that period—linen dusters, veils, goggles,* SID *in a snappy cap.*)

MRS. MILLER: Well, we're about ready to start at last, thank goodness! Let's hope no more callers are on the way. What did that McComber want, Richard, do you know? Sid couldn't tell us.

RICHARD: You can search me. Ask Pa.

MRS. MILLER (*immediately sensing something "down" in his manner—going to him worriedly*): Why, whatever's the matter with you, Richard? You sound as if you'd lost your last friend! What is it?

RICHARD (*desperately*): I— I don't feel so well—my stomach's sick.

MRS. MILLER (*immediately all sympathy—smoothing his hair back from his forehead*): You poor boy! What a shame— on the Fourth, too, of all days! (*Turning to the others*) Maybe I better stay home with him, if he's sick.

LILY: Yes, I'll stay, too.

RICHARD (*more desperately*): No! You go, Ma! I'm not really sick. I'll be all right. You go. I want to be alone!

(*Then, as a louder bang comes from in back as* TOMMY *sets off a cannon cracker, he jumps to his feet*) Darn Tommy and his darned firecrackers! You can't get any peace in this house with that darned kid around! Darn the Fourth of July, anyway! I wish we still belonged to England! (*He strides off in an indignant fury of misery through the front parlor.*)

MRS. MILLER (*stares after him worriedly—then sighs philosophically*): Well, I guess he can't be so very sick— after that. (*She shakes her head*) He's a queer boy. Sometimes I can't make head or tail of him.

MILLER (*calls from the front door beyond the back parlor*): Come along folks. Let's get started.

SID: We're coming, Nat. (*He and the two women move off through the front parlor.*)

Curtain

Act Two

SCENE—*Dining-room of the* MILLER *home—a little after 6 o'clock in the evening of the same day.*

The room is much too small for the medium-priced, formidable dining-room set, especially now when all the leaves of the table are in. At left, toward rear, is a double doorway with sliding doors and portières leading into the back parlor. In the rear wall, left, is the door to the pantry. At the right of door is the china closet with its display of the family cut glass and fancy china. In the right wall are two windows looking out on a side lawn. In front of the windows is a heavy, ugly sideboard with three pieces of old silver on its top. In the left wall, extreme front, is a screen door opening on a side porch. A dark rug covers most of the floor. The table, with a chair at each end, left and right, three chairs on the far side, facing front, and two on the near side, their backs to front, takes up most of the available space. The walls are papered in a somber brown and dark-red design.

MRS. MILLER *is supervising and helping the Second Girl,* NORAH, *in the setting of the table.* NORAH *is a clumsy, heavy-handed, heavy-footed, long-jawed, beamingly good-natured young Irish girl—a "greenhorn."*

MRS. MILLER: I really think you better put on the lights, Norah. It's getting so cloudy out, and this pesky room is so dark, anyway.

NORAH: Yes, Mum. (*She stretches awkwardly over the*

table to reach the chandelier that is suspended from the middle of the ceiling and manages to turn one light on —scornfully) Arrah, the contraption!

MRS. MILLER *(worriedly)*: Careful!

NORAH: Careful as can be, Mum. *(But in moving around to reach the next bulb she jars heavily against the table.)*

MRS. MILLER: There! I knew it! I do wish you'd watch—!

NORAH *(a flustered appeal in her voice)*: Arrah, what have I done wrong now?

MRS. MILLER *(draws a deep breath—then sighs helplessly)*: Oh, nothing. Never mind the rest of the lights. You might as well go out in the kitchen and wait until I ring.

NORAH *(relieved and cheerful again)*: Yes, Mum. *(She starts for the pantry.)*

MRS. MILLER: But there's one thing— *(NORAH turns apprehensively)* No, two things—things I've told you over and over, but you always forget. Don't pass the plates on the wrong side at dinner tonight, and do be careful not to let that pantry door slam behind you. Now you will try to remember, won't you?

NORAH: Yes, Mum. *(She goes into the pantry and shuts the door behind her with exaggerated care as MRS. MILLER watches her apprehensively. MRS. MILLER sighs and reaches up with difficulty and turns on another of the four lights in the chandelier. As she is doing so, LILY enters from the back parlor.)*

LILY: Here, let me do that, Essie. I'm taller. You'll only strain yourself. *(She quickly lights the other two bulbs.)*

MRS. MILLER *(gratefully)*: Thank you, Lily. It's a stretch for me, I'm getting so fat.

LILY: But where's Norah? Why didn't she—?

MRS. MILLER *(exasperatedly)*: Oh, that girl! Don't talk about her! She'll be the death of me! She's that thick, you honestly wouldn't believe it possible.

LILY *(smiling)*: Why, what did she do now?

MRS. MILLER: Oh, nothing. She means all right.

LILY: Anything else I can do, Essie?

MRS. MILLER: Well, she's got the table all wrong. We'll have to reset it. But you're always helping me. It isn't fair to ask you—in your vacation. You need your rest after teaching a pack of wild Indians of kids all year.

LILY (*beginning to help with the table*): You know I love to help. It makes me feel I'm some use in this house. instead of just sponging—

MRS. MILLER (*indignantly*): Sponging! You pay, don't you?

LILY: Almost nothing. And you and Nat only take that little to make me feel better about living with you. (*Forcing a smile*) I don't see how you stand me—having a cranky old maid around all the time.

MRS. MILLER: What nonsense you talk! As if Nat and I weren't only too tickled to death to have you! Lily Miller, I've no patience with you when you go on like that. We've been over this a thousand times before, and still you go on! Crazy, that's what it is! (*She changes the subject abruptly*) What time's it getting to be?

LILY (*looking at her watch*): Quarter past six.

MRS. MILLER: I do hope those men folks aren't going to be late for dinner. (*She sighs*) But I suppose with that darned Sachem Club picnic it's more likely than not. (LILY *looks worried, and sighs*. MRS. MILLER *gives her a quick side glance*) I see you've got your new dress on.

LILY (*embarrassedly*): Yes, I thought—if Sid's taking me to the fireworks—I ought to spruce up a little.

MRS. MILLER (*looking away*): Hmm. (*A pause—then she says with an effort to be casual*) You mustn't mind if Sid comes home feeling a bit—gay. I expect Nat to— and we'll have to listen to all those old stories of his about when he was a boy. You know what those picnics are, and Sid'd be running into all his old friends.

LILY (*agitatedly*): I don't think he will—this time—not after his promise.

MRS. MILLER (*avoiding looking at her*): I know. But men are weak. (*Then quickly*) That was a good notion of Nat's, getting Sid the job on the Waterbury *Standard*. All he ever needed was to get away from the rut he was in here. He's the kind that's the victim of his friends. He's easily led—but there's no real harm in him, you know that. (LILY *keeps silent, her eyes downcast.* MRS. MILLER *goes on meaningly*) He's making good money in Waterbury, too—thirty-five a week. He's in a better position to get married than he ever was.

LILY (*stiffly*): Well, I hope he finds a woman who's willing—though after he's through with his betting on horse races, and dice, and playing Kelly pool, there won't be much left for a wife—even if there was nothing else he spent his money on.

MRS. MILLER: Oh, he'd give up all that—for the right woman. (*Suddenly she comes directly to the point*) Lily, why don't you change your mind and marry Sid and reform him? You love him and always have—

LILY (*stiffly*): I can't love a man who drinks.

MRS. MILLER: You can't fool me. I know darned well you love him. And he loves you and always has.

LILY: Never enough to stop drinking for. (*Cutting off* MRS. MILLER'S *reply*) No, it's no good in your talking, Essie. We've been over this a thousand times before and I'll always feel the same as long as Sid's the same. If he gave me proof he'd—but even then I don't believe I could. It's sixteen years since I broke off our engagement, but what made me break it off is as clear to me today as it was then. It was what he'd be liable to do now to anyone who married him—his taking up with bad women.

MRS. MILLER (*protests half-heartedly*): But he's always

sworn he got raked into that party and never had anything to do with those harlots.

LILY: Well, I don't believe him—didn't then and don't now. I do believe he didn't deliberately plan to, but—Oh, it's no good talking, Essie. What's done is done. But you know how much I like Sid—in spite of everything. I know he was just born to be what he is—irresponsible, never meaning to harm but harming in spite of himself. But don't talk to me about marrying him—because I never could.

MRS. MILLER (*angrily*): He's a dumb fool—a stupid dumb fool, that's what he is!

LILY (*quietly*): No. He's just Sid.

MRS. MILLER: It's a shame for you—a measly shame—you that would have made such a wonderful wife for any man—that ought to have your own home and children!

LILY (*winces but puts her arm around her affectionately—gently*): Now don't you go feeling sorry for me. I won't have that. Here I am, thanks to your and Nat's kindness, with the best home in the world; and as for the children, I feel the same love for yours as if they were mine, and I didn't have the pain of bearing them. And then there are all the boys and girls I teach every year. I like to feel I'm a sort of second mother to them and helping them to grow up to be good men and women. So I don't feel such a useless old maid, after all.

MRS. MILLER (*kisses her impulsively—her voice husky*): You're a good woman, Lily—too good for the rest of us. (*She turns away, wiping a tear furtively—then abruptly changing the subject*) Good gracious, if I'm not forgetting one of the most important things! I've got to warn that Tommy against giving me away to Nat about the fish. He knows, because I had to send him to market for it, and he's liable to burst out laughing—

LILY: Laughing about what?

MRS. MILLER (*guiltily*): Well, I've never told you, because it seemed sort of a sneaking trick, but you know how Nat carries on about not being able to eat bluefish.

LILY: I know he says there's a certain oil in it that poisons him.

MRS. MILLER (*chuckling*): Poisons him, nothing! He's been eating bluefish for years—only I tell him each time it's weakfish. We're having it tonight—and I've got to warn that young imp to keep his face straight.

LILY (*laughing*): Aren't you ashamed, Essie!

MRS. MILLER: Not much, I'm not! I like bluefish! (*She laughs*) Where is Tommy? In the sitting-room?

LILY: No, Richard's there alone. I think Tommy's out on the piazza with Mildred. (MRS. MILLER *bustles out through the back parlor. As soon as she is gone, the smile fades from* LILY's *lips. Her face grows sad and she again glances nervously at her watch.* RICHARD *appears from the back parlor, moving in an aimless way. His face wears a set expression of bitter gloom; he exudes tragedy. For* RICHARD, *after his first outburst of grief and humiliation, has begun to take a masochistic satisfaction in his great sorrow, especially in the concern which it arouses in the family circle. On seeing his aunt, he gives her a dark look and turns and is about to stalk back toward the sitting-room when she speaks to him pityingly*) Feel any better, Richard?

RICHARD (*somberly*): I'm all right, Aunt Lily. You mustn't worry about me.

LILY (*going to him*): But I do worry about you. I hate to see you so upset.

RICHARD: It doesn't matter. Nothing matters.

LILY (*puts her arm around him sympathetically*): You really mustn't let yourself take it so seriously. You know,

something happens and things like that come up, and we
think there's no hope—

RICHARD: Things like what come up?

LILY: What's happened between you and Muriel.

RICHARD (*with disdain*): Oh, her! I wasn't even thinking
about her. I was thinking about life.

LILY: But then—if we really, *really* love—why, then something else is bound to happen soon that changes everything again, and it's all as it was before the misunderstanding, and everything works out all right in the end.
That's the way it is with life.

RICHARD (*with a tragic sneer*): Life! Life is a joke! And
everything comes out all wrong in the end!

LILY (*a little shocked*): You mustn't talk that way. But I
know you don't mean it.

RICHARD: I do too mean it! You can have your silly op-
timism, if you like, Aunt Lily. But don't ask me to be
so blind. I'm a pessimist! (*Then with an air of cruel
cynicism*) As for Muriel, that's all dead and past. I was
only kidding her, anyway, just to have a little fun, and
she took it seriously, like a fool. (*He forces a cruel smile
to his lips*) You know what they say about women and
trolley cars, Aunt Lily: there's always another one along
in a minute.

LILY (*really shocked this time*): I don't like you when
you say such horrible, cynical things. It isn't nice.

RICHARD: Nice! That's all you women think of! I'm proud
to be a cynic. It's the only thing you can be when you
really face life. I suppose you think I ought to be heartbroken about Muriel—a little coward that's afraid to say
her soul's her own, and keeps tied to her father's apron
strings! Well, not for mine! There's plenty of other fish
in the sea! (*As he is finishing, his mother comes back
through the back parlor.*)

MRS. MILLER: Why, hello. You here, Richard? Getting hungry, I suppose?

RICHARD (*indignantly*): I'm not hungry a bit! That's all you think of, Ma—food!

MRS. MILLER: Well, I must say I've never noticed you to hang back at meal times. (*To* LILY) What's that he was saying about fish in the sea?

LILY (*smiling*): He says he's through with Muriel now.

MRS. MILLER (*tartly—giving her son a rebuking look*): She's through with him, he means! The idea of your sending a nice girl like her things out of those indecent books! (*Deeply offended,* RICHARD *disdains to reply but stalks woundedly to the screen door at left, front, and puts a hand on the knob*) Where are you going?

RICHARD (*quotes from "Candida" in a hollow voice*): "Out, then, into the night with me!" (*He stalks out, slamming the door behind him.*)

MRS. MILLER (*calls*): Well, don't you go far, 'cause dinner'll be ready in a minute, and I'm not coming running after you! (*She turns to* LILY *with a chuckle*) Goodness, that boy! He ought to be on the stage! (*She mimics*) "Out—into the night"—and it isn't even dark yet! He got that out of one of those books, I suppose. Do you know, I'm actually grateful to old Dave McComber for putting an end to his nonsense with Muriel. I never did approve of Richard getting so interested in girls. He's not old enough for such silliness. Why, seems to me it was only yesterday he was still a baby. (*She sighs—then matter-of-factly*) Well, nothing to do now till those men turn up. No use standing here like gawks. We might as well go in the sitting-room and be comfortable.

LILY (*the nervous, worried note in her voice again*): Yes, we might as well. (*They go out through the back parlor. They have no sooner disappeared than the screen door is opened cautiously and* RICHARD *comes back in the room.*)

RICHARD (*stands inside the door, looking after them—quotes bitterly*): "They do not know the secret in the poet's heart." (*He comes nearer the table and surveys it, especially the cut-glass dish containing olives, with contempt and mutters disdainfully*) Food! (*But the dish of olives seems to fascinate him and presently he has approached nearer, and stealthily lifts a couple and crams them into his mouth. He is just reaching out for more when the pantry door is opened slightly and* NORAH *peers in.*)

NORAH: Mister Dick, you thief, lave them olives alone, or the missus'll be swearing it was me at them!

RICHARD (*draws back his hand as if he had been stung—too flustered to be anything but guilty boy for a second*): I—I wasn't eating—

NORAH: Oho, no, of course not, divil fear you, you was only feeling their pulse! (*Then warningly*) Mind what I'm saying now, or I'll have to tell on you to protect me good name! (*She draws back into the pantry, closing the door.* RICHARD *stands, a prey to feelings of bitterest humiliation and seething revolt against everyone and everything. A low whistle comes from just outside the porch door. He starts. Then a masculine voice calls:* "Hey, Dick." *He goes over to the screen door grumpily—then as he recognizes the owner of the voice, his own as he answers becomes respectful and admiring.*)

RICHARD: Oh, hello, Wint. Come on in. (*He opens the door and* WINT SELBY *enters and stands just inside the door.* SELBY *is nineteen, a classmate of* ARTHUR's *at Yale. He's a typical, good-looking college boy of the period, not the athletic but the hell-raising sport type. He is tall, blond, dressed in extreme collegiate cut.*)

WINT (*as he enters—warningly, in a low tone*): Keep it quiet, Kid. I don't want the folks to know I'm here. Tell Art I want to see him a second—on the Q.T.

RICHARD: Can't. He's up at the Rands'—won't be home before ten, anyway.

WINT (*irritably*): Damn, I thought he'd be here for dinner. (*More irritably*) Hell, that gums the works for fair!

RICHARD (*ingratiatingly*): What is it, Wint? Can't I help?

WINT (*gives him an appraising glance*): I might tell you, if you can keep your face shut.

RICHARD: I can.

WINT: Well, I ran into a couple of swift babies from New Haven this after, and I dated them up for tonight, thinking I could catch Art. But now it's too late to get anyone else and I'll have to pass it up. I'm nearly broke and I can't afford to blow them both to drinks.

RICHARD (*with shy eagerness*): I've got eleven dollars saved up. I could loan you some.

WINT (*surveys him appreciatively*): Say, you're a good sport. (*Then shaking his head*) Nix, Kid, I don't want to borrow your money. (*Then getting an idea*) But say, have you got anything on for tonight?

RICHARD: No.

WINT: Want to come along with me? (*Then quickly*) I'm not trying to lead you astray, understand. But it'll be a help if you would just sit around with Belle and feed her a few drinks while I'm off with Edith. (*He winks*) See what I mean? You don't have to do anything, not even take a glass of beer—unless you want to.

RICHARD (*boastfully*): Aw, what do you think I am—a rube?

WINT: You mean you're game for anything that's doing?

RICHARD: Sure I am!

WINT: Ever been out with any girls—I mean, real swift ones that there's something doing with, not these dead Janes around here?

RICHARD (*lies boldly*): Aw, what do you think? Sure I have!

WINT: Ever drink anything besides sodas?

RICHARD: Sure. Lots of times. Beer and sloe-gin fizz and—Manhattans.

WINT (*impressed*): Hell, you know more than I thought. (*Then considering*) Can you fix it so your folks won't get wise? I don't want your old man coming after me. You can get back by half-past ten or eleven, though, all right. Think you can cook up some lie to cover that? (*As* RICHARD *hesitates—encouraging him*) Ought to be easy—on the Fourth.

RICHARD: Sure. Don't worry about that.

WINT: But you've got to keep your face closed about this, you hear?—to Art and everybody else. I tell you straight, I wouldn't ask you to come if I wasn't in a hole—and if I didn't know you were coming down to Yale next year, and didn't think you're giving me the straight goods about having been around before. I don't want to lead you astray.

RICHARD (*scornfully*): Aw, I told you that was silly.

WINT: Well, you be at the Pleasant Beach House at half-past nine then. Come in the back room. And don't forget to grab some cloves to take the booze off your breath.

RICHARD: Aw, I know what to do.

WINT: See you later, then. (*He starts out and is just about to close the door when he thinks of something*) And say, I'll say you're a Harvard freshman, and you back me up. They don't know a damn thing about Harvard. I don't want them thinking I'm traveling around with any high-school kid.

RICHARD: Sure. That's easy.

WINT: So long, then. You better beat it right after your dinner while you've got a chance, and hang around until it's time. Watch your step, Kid.

RICHARD: So long. (*The door closes behind* WINT. RICHARD *stands for a moment, a look of bitter, defiant rebellion coming over his face, and mutters to himself*) I'll show her she can't treat me the way she's done! I'll show them all! (*Then the front door is heard slamming, and a moment later* TOMMY *rushes in from the back parlor.*)

TOMMY: Where's Ma?

RICHARD (*surlily*): In the sitting-room. Where did you think, Bonehead?

TOMMY: Pa and Uncle Sid are coming. Mid and I saw them from the front piazza. Gee, I'm glad. I'm awful hungry, ain't you? (*He rushes out through the back parlor, calling*) Ma! They're coming! Let's have dinner quick! (*A moment later* MRS. MILLER *appears from the back parlor accompanied by* TOMMY, *who keeps insisting urgently*) Gee, but I'm awful hungry, Ma!

MRS. MILLER: I know. You always are. You've got a tapeworm, that's what I think.

TOMMY: Have we got lobsters, Ma? Gee, I love lobsters.

MRS. MILLER: Yes, we've got lobsters. And fish. You remember what I told you about that fish. (*He snickers*) Now, do be quiet, Tommy! (*Then with a teasing smile at* RICHARD) Well, I'm glad to see you've got back out of the night, Richard. (*He scowls and turns his back on her.* LILY *appears through the back parlor, nervous and apprehensive. As she does so, from the front yard* SID's *voice is heard singing "Poor John!"* MRS. MILLER *shakes her head forebodingly—but, so great is the comic spell for her even in her brother's voice, a humorous smile hovers at the corners of her lips*) Mmm! Mmm! Lily, I'm afraid—

LILY (*bitterly*): Yes, I might have known. (MILDRED *runs in through the back parlor. She is laughing to herself a bit shamefacedly. She rushes to her mother.*)

MILDRED: Ma, Uncle Sid's— (*She whispers in her ear.*)

MRS. MILLER: Never mind! You shouldn't notice such things —at your age! And don't you encourage him by laughing at his foolishness, you hear!

TOMMY: You needn't whisper, Mid. Think I don't know? Uncle Sid's soused again.

MRS. MILLER (*shakes him by the arm indignantly*): You be quiet! Did I ever! You're getting too smart! (*Gives him a push*) Go to your place and sit right down and not another word out of you!

TOMMY (*aggrieved—rubbing his arm as he goes to his place*): Aw, Ma!

MRS. MILLER: And you sit down, Richard and Mildred. You better, too, Lily. We'll get him right in here and get some food in him. He'll be all right then. (RICHARD, *preserving the pose of the bitter, disillusioned pessimist, sits down in his place in the chair at right of the two whose backs face front.* MILDRED *takes the other chair facing back, at his left.* TOMMY *has already slid into the end chair at right of those at the rear of table facing front.* LILY *sits in the one of those at left, by the head of the table, leaving the middle one* [SID's] *vacant. While they are doing this, the front screen door is heard slamming and* NAT's *and* SID's *laughing voices, raised as they come in and for a moment after, then suddenly cautiously lowered.* MRS. MILLER *goes to the entrance to the back parlor and calls peremptorily*) You come right in here! Don't stop to wash up or anything. Dinner's coming right on the table.

MILLER'S VOICE (*jovially*): All right, Essie. Here we are! Here we are!

MRS. MILLER (*goes to pantry door, opens it and calls*): All right, Norah. You can bring in the soup. (*She comes back to the back-parlor entrance just as* MILLER *enters. He isn't drunk by any means. He is just mellow and benignly ripened. His face is one large, smiling, happy beam of utter appreciation of life. All's right with the world, so satisfyingly right that he becomes sentimentally moved even to think of it.*)

MILLER: Here we are, Essie! Right on the dot! Here we are! (*He pulls her to him and gives her a smacking kiss on the ear as she jerks her head away.* MILDRED *and* TOMMY *giggle.* RICHARD *holds rigidly aloof and disdainful, his brooding gaze fixed on his plate.* LILY *forces a smile.*)

MRS. MILLER (*pulling away—embarrassedly, almost blushing*): Don't, you Crazy! (*Then recovering herself—tartly*) So I see, you're here! And if I didn't, you've told me four times already!

MILLER (*beamingly*): Now, Essie, don't be critical. Don't be carpingly critical. Good news can stand repeating, can't it? 'Course it can! (*He slaps her jovially on her fat buttocks.* TOMMY *and* MILDRED *roar with glee. And* NORAH, *who has just entered from the pantry with a huge tureen of soup in her hands, almost drops it as she explodes in a merry guffaw.*)

MRS. MILLER (*scandalized*): Nat! Aren't you ashamed!

MILLER: Couldn't resist it! Just simply couldn't resist it! (NORAH, *still standing with the soup tureen held out stiffly in front of her, again guffaws.*)

MRS. MILLER (*turns on her with outraged indignation*): Norah! Bring that soup here this minute! (*She stalks with stiff dignity toward her place at the foot of the table, right.*)

NORAH (*guiltily*): Yes, Mum. (*She brings the soup around the head of the table, passing* MILLER.)

MILLER (*jovially*): Why, hello, Norah!

MRS. MILLER: Nat! (*She sits down stiffly at the foot of the table.*)

NORAH (*rebuking him familiarly*): Arrah now, don't be making me laugh and getting me into trouble!

MRS. MILLER: Norah!

NORAH (*a bit resentfully*): Yes, Mum. Here I am. (*She sets *the soup tureen down with a thud in front of* MRS. MILLER *and passes around the other side, squeezing with difficulty between the china closet and the backs of chairs at the rear of the table.*)

MRS. MILLER: Tommy! Stop spinning your napkin ring! How often have I got to tell you? Mildred! Sit up straight in your chair! Do you want to grow up a humpback? Richard! Take your elbows off the table!

MILLER (*coming to his place at the head of the table, rubbing his hands together genially*): Well, well, well. Well, well, well. It's good to be home again. (NORAH *exits into the pantry and lets the door slam with a bang behind her.*)

MRS. MILLER (*jumps*): Oh! (*Then exasperatedly*) Nat, I do wish you wouldn't encourage that stupid girl by talking to her, when I'm doing my best to train—

MILLER (*beamingly*): All right, Essie. Your word is law! (*Then laughingly*) We did have the darndest fun today! And Sid was the life of that picnic! You ought to have heard him! Honestly, he had that crowd just rolling on the ground and splitting their sides! He ought to be on the stage.

MRS. MILLER (*as* NORAH *comes back with a dish of saltines —begins ladling soup into the stack of plates before her*): He ought to be at this table eating something to sober him up, that's what he ought to be! (*She calls*) Sid! You come right in here! (*Then to* NORAH, *handing her a soup plate*) Here, Norah. (NORAH *begins passing soup*) Sit down, Nat, for goodness sakes. Start eating, everybody. Don't wait for me. You know I've given up soup.

MILLER (*sits down but bends forward to call to his wife in a confidential tone*): Essie—Sid's sort of embarrassed about coming—I mean I'm afraid he's a little bit—not too much, you understand—but he met such a lot of friends and—well, you know, don't be hard on him. Fourth of July is like Christmas—comes but once a year. Don't pretend to notice, eh? And don't you kids, you hear! And don't you, Lily. He's scared of you.

LILY (*with stiff meekness*): Very well, Nat.

MILLER (*beaming again—calls*): All right, Sid. The coast's clear. (*He begins to absorb his soup ravenously*) Good soup, Essie! Good soup! (*A moment later* SID *makes his entrance from the back parlor. He is in a condition that can best be described as blurry. His movements have a hazy uncertainty about them. His shiny fat face is one broad, blurred, Puckish, naughty-boy grin; his eyes have a blurred, wondering vagueness. As he enters he makes a solemnly intense effort to appear casual and dead, cold sober. He waves his hand aimlessly and speaks with a silly gravity.*)

SID: Good evening. (*They all answer* "Good evening," *their eyes on their plates. He makes his way vaguely toward his place, continuing his grave effort at conversation*) Beautiful evening. I never remember seeing—more beautiful sunset. (*He bumps vaguely into* LILY's *chair as he attempts to pass behind her—immediately he is all grave politeness*) Sorry—sorry, Lily—deeply sorry.

LILY (*her eyes on her plate—stiffly*): It's all right.

SID (*manages to get into his chair at last—mutters to himself*): Wha' was I sayin'? Oh, sunsets. But why butt in? Hasn't sun—perfect right to set? Mind y'r own business. (*He pauses thoughtfully, considering this—then looks around from face to face, fixing each with a vague, blurred, wondering look, as if some deep puzzle were confronting him. Then suddenly he grins mistily and nods with satisfaction*) And there you are! Am I right?

MILLER (*humoring him*): Right.

SID: Right! (*He is silent, studying his soup plate, as if it*

were some strange enigma. Finally he looks up and regards his sister and asks with wondering amazement)
Soup?

MRS. MILLER: Of course, it's soup. What did you think it was? And you hurry up and eat it.

SID (*again regards his soup with astonishment*): Well! (*Then suddenly*) Well, all right then! Soup be it! (*He picks up his spoon and begins to eat, but after two tries in which he finds it difficult to locate his mouth, he addresses the spoon plaintively*) Spoon, is this any way to treat a pal? (*Then suddenly comically angry, putting the spoon down with a bang*) Down with spoons! (*He raises his soup plate and declaims*) "We'll drink to the dead already, and hurrah for the next who dies." (*Bowing solemnly to right and left*) Your good health, ladies and gents. (*He starts drinking the soup.* MILLER *guffaws and* MILDRED *and* TOMMY *giggle. Even* RICHARD *forgets his melancholy and snickers, and* MRS. MILLER *conceals a smile. Only* LILY *remains stiff and silent.*)

MRS. MILLER (*with forced severity*): Sid!

SID (*peers at her muzzily, lowering the soup plate a little from his lips*): Eh?

MRS. MILLER: Oh, nothing. Never mind.

SID (*solemnly offended*): Are you—publicly rebuking me before assembled—? Isn't soup liquid? Aren't liquids drunk? (*Then considering this to himself*) What if they are drunk? It's a good man's failing. (*He again peers mistily about at the company*) Am I right or wrong?

MRS. MILLER: Hurry up and finish your soup, and stop talking nonsense!

SID (*turning to her—again offendedly*): Oh, no, Essie, if I ever so far forget myself as to drink a leg of lamb, then you might have some—excuse for— Just think of waste effort eating soup with spoons—fifty gruelling lifts per plate—billions of soup-eaters on globe—why, it's

simply staggering! (*Then darkly to himself*) No more
spoons for me! If I want to develop my biceps, I'll buy
a Sandow Exerciser! (*He drinks the rest of his soup in a
gulp and beams around at the company, suddenly all
happiness again*) Am I right, folks?

MILLER (*who has been choking with laughter*): Haw, haw!
You're right, Sid.

SID (*peers at him blurredly and shakes his head sadly*):
Poor old Nat! Always wrong—but heart of gold, heart
of purest gold. And drunk again, I regret to note. Sister, my heart bleeds for you and your poor fatherless
chicks!

MRS. MILLER (*restraining a giggle—severely*): Sid! Do shut
up for a minute! Pass me your soup plates, everybody.
If we wait for that girl to take them, we'll be here all
night. (*They all pass their plates, which* MRS. MILLER
*stacks up and then puts on the sideboard. As she is do-
ing this,* NORAH *appears from the pantry with a platter
of broiled fish. She is just about to place these before*
MILLER *when* SID *catches her eye mistily and rises to his
feet, making her a deep, uncertain bow.*)

SID (*raptly*): Ah, Sight for Sore Eyes, my beautiful Ma-
cushla, my star-eyed Mavourneen—

MRS. MILLER: Sid!

NORAH (*immensely pleased—gives him an arch, flirtatious
glance*): Ah sure, Mister Sid, it's you that have kissed
the Blarney Stone, when you've a drop taken!

MRS. MILLER (*outraged*): Norah! Put down that fish!

NORAH (*flusteredly*): Yes, Mum. (*She attempts to put
the fish down hastily before* MILLER, *but her eyes are fixed
nervously on* MRS. MILLER *and she gives* MILLER *a nasty
swipe on the side of the head with the edge of the dish.*)

MILLER: Ouch! (*The children, even* RICHARD, *explode into
laughter.*)

NORAH (*almost lets the dish fall*): Oh, glory be to God! Is it hurted you are?

MILLER (*rubbing his head—good-naturedly*): No, no harm done. Only careful, Norah, careful.

NORAH (*gratefully*): Yes, sorr. (*She thumps down the dish in front of him with a sigh of relief.*)

SID (*who is still standing—with drunken gravity*): Careful, Mavourneen, careful! You might have hit him some place besides the head. Always aim at his head, remember—so as not to worry us. (*Again the children explode. Also* NORAH. *Even* LILY *suddenly lets out an hysterical giggle and is furious with herself for doing so.*)

LILY: I'm so sorry, Nat. I didn't mean to laugh. (*Turning on* SID *furiously*) Will you please sit down and stop making a fool of yourself? (SID *gives her a hurt, mournful look and then sinks meekly down on his chair.*)

NORAH (*grinning cheerfully, gives* LILY *a reassuring pat on the back*): Ah, Miss Lily, don't mind him. He's only under the influence. Sure, there's no harm in him at all.

MRS. MILLER: Norah! (NORAH *exits hastily into the pantry, letting the door slam with a crash behind her. There is silence for a moment as* MILLER *serves the fish and it is passed around.* NORAH *comes back with the vegetables and disappears again, and these are dished out.*)

MILLER (*is about to take his first bite—stops suddenly and asks his wife*): This isn't, by any chance, bluefish, is it, my dear?

MRS. MILLER (*with a warning glance at* TOMMY): Of course not. You know we never have bluefish, on account of you.

MILLER (*addressing the table now with the gravity of a man confessing his strange peculiarities*): Yes, I regret to say, there's a certain peculiar oil in bluefish that invariably poisons me. (*At this,* TOMMY *cannot stand it any more but explodes into laughter.* MRS. MILLER, *after a helpless glance at him, follows suit; then* LILY *goes off into uncontrollable, hysterical laughter, and* RICHARD *and* MILDRED *are caught in the contagion.* MILLER *looks around at them with a weak smile, his dignity now ruffled a bit*) Well, I must say I don't see what's so darned funny about my being poisoned.

SID (*peers around him—then with drunken cunning*): Aha! Nat, I suspect—plot! This fish looks blue to me—very blue—in fact despondent, desperate, and— (*He points his fork dramatically at* MRS. MILLER) See how guilty she looks a ver—veritable Lucretia Georgia! Can it be this woman has been slowly poisoning you all these years? And how well—you've stood it! What an iron constitution! Even now, when you are invariably at death's door, I can't believe— (*Everyone goes off into uncontrollable laughter.*)

MILLER (*grumpily*): Oh, give us a rest, you darned fool! A joke's a joke, but— (*He addresses his wife in a wounded tone*) Is this true, Essie?

MRS. MILLER (*wiping the tears from her eyes—defiantly*): Yes, it is true, if you must know, and you'd never have suspected it, if it weren't for that darned Tommy, and Sid poking his nose in. You've eaten bluefish for years and thrived on it and it's all nonsense about that peculiar oil.

MILLER (*deeply offended*): Kindly allow me to know my own constitution! Now I think of it, I've felt upset afterwards every damned time we've had fish! (*He pushes his plate away from him with proud renunciation*) I can't eat this.

MRS. MILLER (*insultingly matter-of-fact*): Well, don't then. There's lots of lobster coming and you can fill up on that. (RICHARD *suddenly bursts out laughing again.*)

MILLER (*turns to him caustically*): You seem in a merry

mood, Richard. I though you were the original of the Heart Bowed Down today.

SID (*with mock condolence*): Never mind, Dick. Let them —scoff! What can they understand about girls whose hair sizzchels, whose lips are fireworks, whose eyes are red-hot sparks—

MILDRED (*laughing*): Is that what he wrote to Muriel? (*Turning to her brother*) You silly goat, you!

RICHARD (*surlily*): Aw, shut up, Mid. What do I care about her? I'll show all of you how much I care!

MRS. MILLER: Pass your plates as soon as you're through, everybody. I've rung for the lobster. And that's all. You don't get any dessert or tea after lobster, you know. (*NORAH appears bearing a platter of cold boiled lobsters which she sets before MILLER, and disappears.*)

TOMMY: Gee, I love lobster! (*MILLER puts one on each plate, and they are passed around and everyone starts in pulling the cracked shells apart.*)

MILLER (*feeling more cheerful after a couple of mouthfuls —determining to give the conversation another turn, says to his daughter*): Have a good time at the beach, Mildred?

MILDRED: Oh, fine, Pa, thanks. The water was wonderful and warm.

MILLER: Swim far?

MILDRED: Yes, for me. But that isn't so awful far.

MILLER: Well, you ought to be a good swimmer, if you take after me. I used to be a regular water rat when I was a boy. I'll have to go down to the beach with you one of these days—though I'd be rusty, not having been in in all these years. (*The reminiscent look comes into his eyes of one about to embark on an oft-told tale of childhood adventure*) You know, speaking of swimming, I never go down to that beach but what it calls to mind the day I and Red Sisk went in swimming there and I saved his life. (*By this time the family are beginning to exchange amused, guilty glances. They all know what is coming.*)

SID (*with a sly, blurry wink around*): Ha! Now we—have it again!

MILLER (*turning on him*): Have what?

SID: Nothing—go on with your swimming—don't mind me.

MILLER (*glares at him—but immediately is overcome by the reminiscent mood again*): Red Sisk—his father kept a blacksmith shop where the Union Market is now—we kids called him Red because he had the darndest reddest crop of hair—

SID (*as if he were talking to his plate*): Remarkable!— the curious imagination—of little children.

MRS. MILLER (*as she sees* MILLER *about to explode—interposes tactfully*): Sid! Eat your lobster and shut up! Go on, Nat.

MILLER (*gives* SID *a withering look—then is off again*): Well, as I was saying, Red and I went swimming that day. Must have been—let me see—Red was fourteen, bigger and older than me, I was only twelve—forty-five years ago—wasn't a single house down there then— but there was a stake out where the whistling buoy is now, about a mile out. (TOMMY, *who has been having difficulty restraining himself, lets out a stifled giggle.* MILLER *bends a frowning gaze on him*) One more sound out of you, young man, and you'll leave the table!

MRS. MILLER (*quickly interposing, trying to stave off the story*): Do eat your lobster, Nat. You didn't have any fish, you know.

MILLER (*not liking the reminder—pettishly*): Well, if I'm going to be interrupted every second anyway— (*He turns to his lobster and chews in silence for a moment.*)

MRS. MILLER (*trying to switch the subject*): How's Anne's mother's rheumatism, Mildred?

MILDRED: Oh, she's much better, Ma. She was in wading today. She says salt water's the only thing that really helps her bunion.

MRS. MILLER: Mildred! Where are your manners? At the table's no place to speak of—

MILLER (*fallen into the reminiscent obsession again*): Well, as I was saying, there was I and Red, and he dared me to race him out to the stake and back. Well, I didn't let anyone dare me in those days. I was a spunky kid. So I said all right and we started out. We swam and swam and were pretty evenly matched; though, as I've said, he was bigger and older than me, but finally I drew ahead. I was going along easy, with lots in reserve, not a bit tired, when suddenly I heard a sort of gasp from behind me—like this— "Help." (*He imitates. Everyone's eyes are firmly fixed on his plate, except* SID's) And I turned and there was Red, his face all pinched and white, and he says weakly: "Help, Nat! I got a cramp in my leg!" Well, I don't mind telling you I got mighty scared. I didn't know what to do. Then suddenly I thought of the pile. If I could pull him to that, I could hang on to him till someone'd notice us. But the pile was still—well, I calculate it must have been two hundred feet away.

SID: Two hundred and fifty!

MILLER (*in confusion*): What's that?

SID: Two hundred *and* fifty! I've taken down the distance every time you've saved Red's life for thirty years and the mean average to that pile is two hundred and fifty feet! (*There is a burst of laughter from around the table.* SID *continues complainingly*) Why didn't you let that Red drown, anyway, Nat? I never knew him but I know I'd never have liked him.

MILLER (*really hurt, forces a feeble smile to his lips and pretends to be a good sport about it*): Well, guess you're right, Sid. Guess I have told that one too many times and bored everyone. But it's a good true story for kids because it illustrates the danger of being foolhardy in the water—

MRS. MILLER (*sensing the hurt in his tone, comes to his rescue*): Of course it's a good story—and you tell it whenever you've a mind to. And you, Sid, if you were in any responsible state, I'd give you a good piece of my mind for teasing Nat like that.

MILLER (*with a sad, self-pitying smile at his wife*): Getting old, I guess, Mother—getting to repeat myself. Someone ought to stop me.

MRS. MILLER: No such thing! You're as young as you ever were. (*She turns on* SID *again angrily*) You eat your lobster and maybe it'll keep your mouth shut!

SID (*after a few chews—irrepressibly*): Lobster! Did you know, Tommy, your Uncle Sid is the man invented lobster? Fact! One day—when I was building the Pyramids—took a day off and just dashed off lobster. He was bigger'n' older than me and he had the darndest reddest crop of hair but I dashed him off just the same! Am I right, Nat? (*Then suddenly in the tones of a side-show barker*) Ladies *and* Gents—

MRS. MILLER: Mercy sakes! Can't you shut up?

SID: In this cage you see the lobster. You will not believe me, ladies *and* gents, but it's a fact that this interesting bivalve only makes love to his mate once in every thousand years—but, dearie me, how he does enjoy it! (*The children roar.* LILY *and* MRS. MILLER *laugh in spite of themselves—then look embarrassed.* MILLER *guffaws —then suddenly grows shocked.*)

MILLER: Careful, Sid, careful. Remember you're at home.

TOMMY (*suddenly in a hoarse whisper to his mother, with*

an awed glance of admiration at his uncle): Ma! Look at him! He's eating that claw, shells and all!

MRS. MILLER (*horrified*): Sid, do you want to kill yourself? Take it away from him, Lily!

SID (*with great dignity*): But I prefer the shells. All famous epicures prefer the shells—to the less delicate, coarser meat. It's the same with clams. Unless I eat the shells there is a certain, peculiar oil that invariably poisons— Am I right, Nat?

MILLER (*good-naturedly*): You seem to be getting a lot of fun kidding me. Go ahead, then. I don't mind.

MRS. MILLER: He better go right up to bed for a while, that's what he better do.

SID (*considering this owlishly*): Bed? Yes, maybe you're right. (*He gets to his feet*) I am not at all well—in very delicate condition—we are praying for a boy. Am I right, Nat? Nat, I kept telling you all day I was in delicate condition and yet you kept forcing demon chowder on me, although you knew full well—even if you were full—that there is a certain, peculiar oil in chowder that invariably— (*They are again all laughing—LILY, hysterically.*)

MRS. MILLER: *Will* you get to bed, you idiot!

SID (*mutters graciously*): Immediately—if not sooner. (*He turns to pass behind LILY, then stops, staring down at her*) But wait. There is still a duty I must perform. No day is complete without it. Lily, answer once and for all, will you marry me?

LILY (*with an hysterical giggle*): No, I won't—never!

SID (*nodding his head*): Right! And perhaps it's all for the best. For how could I forget the pre-precepts taught me at mother's dying knee. "Sidney," she said, "never marry a woman who drinks! Lips that touch liquor shall never touch yours!" (*Gazing at her mournfully*) Too bad! So fine a woman once—and now such a slave to rum! (*Turning to* NAT) What can we do to save her, Nat? (*In a hoarse, confidential whisper*) Better put her in institution where she'll be removed from temptation! The mere smell of it seems to drive her frantic!

MRS. MILLER (*struggling with her laughter*): You leave Lily alone, and go to bed!

SID: Right! (*He comes around behind* LILY's *chair and moves toward the entrance to the back parlor—then suddenly turns and says with a bow*) Good night, ladies —and gents. We will meet—bye and bye! (*He gives an imitation of a Salvation Army drum*) Boom! Boom! Boom! Come and be saved, Brothers! (*He starts to sing the old Army hymn*)

> "In the sweet
>   Bye and bye
>   We will meet on that beautiful shore."

(*He turns and marches solemnly out through the back parlor, singing*)

> "Work and pray
>   While you may.
>   We will meet in the sky bye and bye."

(MILLER *and his wife and the children are all roaring with laughter.* LILY *giggles hysterically.*)

MILLER (*subsiding at last*): Haw, haw. He's a case, if ever there was one! Darned if you can help laughing at him —even when he's poking fun at you!

MRS. MILLER: Goodness, but he's a caution! Oh, my sides ache, I declare! I was trying so hard not to—but you can't help it, he's so silly! But I suppose we really shouldn't. It only encourages him. But, my lands—!

LILY (*suddenly gets up from her chair and stands rigidly, her face working—jerkily*): That's just it—you shouldn't —even I laughed—it does encourage—that's been his downfall—everyone always laughing, everyone always saying what a card he is, what a case, what a caution, so funny—and he's gone on—and we're all responsible—making it easy for him—we're all to blame—and all we do is laugh!

MILLER (*worriedly*): Now, Lily, now, you mustn't take on so. It isn't as serious as all that.

LILY (*bitterly*): Maybe—it is—to me. Or was—once. (*Then contritely*) I'm sorry, Nat. I'm sorry, Essie. I didn't mean to—I'm not feeling myself tonight. If you'll excuse me, I'll go in the front parlor and lie down on the sofa awhile.

MRS. MILLER: Of course, Lily. You do whatever you've a mind to. (LILY *goes out.*)

MILLER (*frowning—a little shamefaced*): Hmm. I suppose she's right. Never knew Lily to come out with things that way before. Anything special happened, Essie?

MRS. MILLER: Nothing I know—except he'd promised to take her to the fireworks.

MILLER: That's so. Well, supposing I take her? I don't want her to feel disappointed.

MRS. MILLER (*shaking her head*): Wild horses couldn't drag her there now.

MILLER: Hmm. I thought she'd got completely over her foolishness about him long ago.

MRS. MILLER: She never will.

MILLER: She'd better. He's got fired out of that Waterbury job—told me at the picnic after he'd got enough Dutch courage in him.

MRS. MILLER: Oh, dear! Isn't he the fool!

MILLER: I knew something was wrong when he came home. Well, I'll find a place for him on my paper again, of course. He always was the best news-getter this town ever had. But I'll tell him he's got to stop his damn nonsense.

MRS. MILLER (*doubtfully*): Yes.

MILLER: Well, no use sitting here mourning over spilt milk.

(*He gets up, and* RICHARD, MILDRED, TOMMY *and* MRS.
MILLER *follow his example, the children quiet and a bit
awed*) You kids go out in the yard and try to keep
quiet for a while, so's your Uncle Sid'll get to sleep and
your Aunt Lily can rest.

TOMMY (*mournfully*): Ain't we going to set off the sky-
rockets and Roman candles, Pa?

MILLER: Later, Son, later. It isn't dark enough for them
yet anyway.

MILDRED: Come on, Tommy. I'll see he keeps quiet, Pa.

MILLER: That's a good girl. (MILDRED *and* TOMMY *go out
through the screen door.* RICHARD *remains standing, sunk
in bitter, gloomy thoughts.* MILLER *glances at him—then
irritably*) Well, Melancholy Dane, what are you doing?

RICHARD (*darkly*): I'm going out—for a while. (*Then
suddenly*) Do you know what I think? It's Aunt Lily's
fault, Uncle Sid's going to ruin. It's all because he loves
her, and she keeps him dangling after her, and eggs
him on and ruins his life—like all women love to ruin
men's lives! I don't blame him for drinking himself to
death! What does he care if he dies, after the way she's
treated him! I'd do the same thing myself if I were in
his boots!

MRS. MILLER (*indignantly*): Richard! You stop that talk!

RICHARD (*quotes bitterly*):

*"Drink! for you know not whence you come nor why.
Drink! for you know not why you go nor where!"*

MILLER (*losing his temper—harshly*): Listen here, young
man! I've had about all I can stand of your nonsense for
one day! You're growing a lot too big for your size,
seems to me! You keep that damn fool talk to yourself,
you hear me—or you're going to regret it! Mind now!
(*He strides angrily away through the back parlor.*)

MRS. MILLER (*still indignant*): Richard, I'm ashamed of

you, that's what I am. (*She follows her husband.* RICHARD *stands for a second, bitter, humiliated, wronged, even his father turned enemy, his face growing more and more rebellious. Then he forces a scornful smile to his lips.*)

RICHARD: Aw, what the hell do I care? I'll show them! (*He turns and goes out the screen door.*)

Curtain

Act Three

SCENE—*The back room of a bar in a small hotel—a small, dingy room, dimly lighted by two fly-specked globes in a fly-specked gilt chandelier suspended from the middle of the ceiling. At left, front, is the swinging door leading to the bar. At rear of door, against the wall, is a nickel-in-the-slot player-piano. In the rear wall, right, is a door leading to the "Family Entrance" and the stairway to the upstairs rooms. In the middle of the right wall is a window with closed shutters. Three tables with stained tops, four chairs around each table, are placed at center, front, at right, toward rear, and at rear, center. A brass cuspidor is on the floor by each table. The floor is unswept, littered with cigarette and cigar butts. The hideous saffron-colored wall-paper is blotched and spotted.*

It is about 10 o'clock the same night. RICHARD *and* BELLE *are discovered sitting at the table at center,* BELLE *at left of it,* RICHARD *in the next chair at the middle of table, rear, facing front.*

BELLE *is twenty, a rather pretty peroxide blonde, a typical college "tart" of the period, and of the cheaper variety, dressed with tawdry flashiness. But she is a fairly recent recruit to the ranks, and is still a bit remorseful behind her make-up and defiantly careless manner.*

BELLE *has an empty gin-rickey glass before her,* RICHARD *a half-empty glass of beer. He looks horribly timid, em-*

barrassed and guilty, but at the same time thrilled and proud of at last mingling with the pace that kills.

The player-piano is grinding out "Bedelia." The BAR-TENDER, *a stocky young Irishman with a foxily cunning, stupid face and a cynically wise grin, stands just inside the bar entrance, watching them over the swinging door.*

BELLE (*with an impatient glance at her escort—rattling the ice in her empty glass*): Drink up your beer, why don't you? It's getting flat.

RICHARD (*embarrassedly*): I let it get that way on purpose. I like it better when it's flat. (*But he hastily gulps down the rest of his glass, as if it were some nasty-tasting medicine. The* BARTENDER *chuckles audibly.* BELLE *glances at him.*)

BELLE (*nodding at the player-piano scornfully*): Say, George, is "Bedelia" the latest to hit this hick burg? Well, it's only a couple of years old! You'll catch up in time! Why don't you get a new roll for that old box?

BARTENDER (*with a grin*): Complain to the boss, not me. We're not used to having Candy Kiddoes like you around —or maybe we'd get up to date.

BELLE (*with a professionally arch grin at him*): Don't kid me, please. I can't bear it. (*Then she sings to the music from the piano, her eyes now on* RICHARD) "Bedelia, I'd like to feel yer." (*The* BARTENDER *laughs. She smirks at* RICHARD) Ever hear those words to it, Kid?

RICHARD (*who has heard them but is shocked at hearing a girl say them—putting on a blasé air*): Sure, lots of times. That's old.

BELLE (*edging her chair closer and putting a hand over one of his*): Then why don't you act as if you knew what they were all about?

RICHARD (*terribly flustered*): Sure, I've heard that old parody lots of times. What do you think I am?

BELLE: I don't know, Kid. Honest to God, you've got me
guessing.

BARTENDER (*with a mocking chuckle*): He's a hot sport,
can't you tell it? I never seen such a spender. My head's
dizzy bringing you in drinks!

BELLE (*laughs irritably—to* RICHARD): Don't let him kid
you. You show him. Loosen up and buy another drink,
what say?

RICHARD (*humiliated—manfully*): Sure. Excuse me. I was
thinking of something else. Have anything you like.
(*He turns to the* BARTENDER *who has entered from the
bar*) See what the lady will have—and have one on me
yourself.

BARTENDER (*coming to the table—with a wink at* BELLE):
That's talking! Didn't I say you were a sport? I'll take
a cigar on you. (*To* BELLE) What's yours, Kiddo—the
same?

BELLE: Yes. And forget the house rules this time and remember a rickey is supposed to have gin in it.

BARTENDER (*grinning*): I'll try to—seeing it's you. (*Then
to* RICHARD) What's yours—another beer?

RICHARD (*shyly*): A small one, please. I'm not thirsty.

BELLE (*calculatedly taunting*): Say, honest, are things that
slow up at Harvard? If they had you down at New
Haven, they'd put you in a kindergarten! Don't be such
a dead one! Filling up on beer will only make you
sleepy. Have a man's drink!

RICHARD (*shamefacedly*): All right. I was going to. Bring
me a sloe-gin fizz.

BELLE (*to* BARTENDER): And make it a real one.

BARTENDER (*with a wink*): I get you. Something that'll
warm him up, eh? (*He goes into the bar, chuckling.*)

BELLE (*looks around the room—irritably*): Christ, what a
dump! (RICHARD *is startled and shocked by this curse
and looks down at the table*) If this isn't the deadest

burg I ever struck! Bet they take the sidewalks in after nine o'clock! (*Then turning on him*) Say, honestly, Kid, does your mother know you're out?

RICHARD (*defensively*): Aw, cut it out, why don't you— trying to kid me!

BELLE (*glances at him—then resolves on a new tack—patting his hand*) All right. I didn't mean to, Dearie. Please don't get sore at me.

RICHARD: I'm not sore.

BELLE (*seductively*): You see, it's this way with me. I think you're one of the sweetest kids I've ever met—and I could like you such a lot if you'd give me half a chance —instead of acting so cold and indifferent.

RICHARD: I'm not cold and indifferent. (*Then solemnly tragic*) It's only that I've got—a weight on my mind.

BELLE (*impatiently*): Well, get it off your mind and give something else a chance to work. (*The* BARTENDER *comes in, bringing the drinks.*)

BARTENDER (*setting them down—with a wink at* BELLE): This'll warm him for you. Forty cents, that is—with the cigar.

RICHARD (*pulls out his roll and hands a dollar bill over— with exaggerated carelessness*): Keep the change. (BELLE *emits a gasp and seems about to protest, then thinks better of it. The* BARTENDER *cannot believe his luck for a moment—then pockets the bill hastily, as if afraid* RICHARD *will change his mind.*)

BARTENDER (*respect in his voice*): Thank you, sir.

RICHARD (*grandly*): Don't mention it.

BARTENDER: I hope you like the drink. I took special pains with it. (*The voice of the* SALESMAN, *who has just come in the bar, calls* "Hey! Anybody here?" *and a coin is rapped on the bar*) I'm coming. (*The* BARTENDER *goes out.*)

BELLE (*remonstrating gently, a new appreciation for her*

escort's possibilities in her voice): You shouldn't be so
generous, Dearie. Gets him in bad habits. A dime would
have been plenty.

RICHARD: Ah, that's all right. I'm no tightwad.

BELLE: That's the talk I like to hear. (*With a quick look
toward the bar, she stealthily pulls up her dress—to*
RICHARD'S *shocked fascination—and takes a package of
cheap cigarettes from her stocking*) Keep an eye out for
that bartender, Kid, and tell me if you see him coming.
Girls are only allowed to smoke upstairs in the rooms,
he said.

RICHARD (*embarrassedly*): All right. I'll watch.

BELLE (*having lighted her cigarette and inhaled deeply,
holds the package out to him*): Have a Sweet? You
smoke, don't you?

RICHARD (*taking one*): Sure! I've been smoking for the
last two years—on the sly. But next year I'll be allowed
—that is, pipes and cigars. (*He lights his cigarette with
elaborate nonchalance, puffs, but does not inhale—then,
watching her, with shocked concern*) Say, you oughtn't
to inhale like that! Smoking's awful bad for girls, anyway, even if they don't—

BELLE (*cynically amused*): Afraid it will stunt my growth?
Gee, Kid, you are a scream! You'll grow up to be a
minister yet! (RICHARD *looks shamefaced. She scans him
impatiently—then holds up her drink*) Well, here's how!
Bottoms up, now! Show me you really know how to
drink. It'll take that load off your mind. (RICHARD *follows
her example and they both drink the whole contents of
their glasses before setting them down*) There! That's
something like! Feel better?

RICHARD (*proud of himself—with a shy smile*): You bet.

BELLE: Well, you'll feel still better in a minute—and then
maybe you won't be so distant and unfriendly, eh?

RICHARD: I'm not.

BELLE: Yes, you are. I think you just don't like me.

RICHARD (*more manfully*): I do too like you.

BELLE: How much? A lot?

RICHARD: Yes, a lot.

BELLE: Show me how much! (*Then as he fidgets embarrassedly*) Want me to come sit on your lap?

RICHARD: Yes—I—(*She comes and sits on his lap. He looks desperately uncomfortable, but the gin is rising to his head and he feels proud of himself and devilish, too.*)

BELLE: Why don't you put your arm around me? (*He does so awkwardly*) No, not that dead way. Hold me tight. You needn't be afraid of hurting me. I like to be held tight, don't you?

RICHARD: Sure I do.

BELLE: 'Specially when it's by a nice handsome kid like you. (*Ruffling his hair*) Gee, you've got pretty hair, do you know it? Honest, I'm awfully strong for you! Why can't you be about me? I'm not so awfully ugly, am I?

RICHARD: No, you're—you're pretty.

BELLE: You don't say it as if you meant it.

RICHARD: I do mean it—honest.

BELLE: Then why don't you kiss me? (*She bends down her lips toward his. He hesitates, then kisses her and at once shrinks back*) Call that kissing? Here. (*She holds his head and fastens her lips on his and holds them there. He starts and struggles. She laughs*) What's the matter, Honey Boy? Haven't you ever kissed like that before?

RICHARD: Sure. Lot of times.

BELLE: Then why did you jump as if I'd bitten you? (*Squirming around on his lap*) Gee, I'm getting just crazy about you! What shall we do about it, eh? Tell me.

RICHARD: I—don't know. (*Then boldly*) I—I'm crazy about you, too.

BELLE (*kissing him again*): Just think of the wonderful time Edith and your friend, Wint, are having upstairs —while we sit down here like two dead ones. A room only costs two dollars. And, seeing I like you so much, I'd only take five dollars—from you. I'd do it for nothing—for you—only I've got to live and I owe my room rent in New Haven—and you know how it is. I get ten dollars from everyone else. Honest! (*She kisses him again, then gets up from his lap—briskly*) Come on. Go out and tell the bartender you want a room. And hurry. Honest, I'm so strong for you I can hardly wait to get you upstairs!

RICHARD (*starts automatically for the door to the bar—then hesitates, a great struggle going on in his mind—timidity, disgust at the money element, shocked modesty, and the guilty thought of* MURIEL, *fighting it out with the growing tipsiness that makes him want to be a hell of a fellow and go in for all forbidden fruit, and makes this tart a romantic, evil vampire in his eyes. Finally, he stops and mutters in confusion*) I can't.

BELLE: What, are you too bashful to ask for a room? Let me do it, then. (*She starts for the door.*)

RICHARD (*desperately*): No—I don't want you to—I don't want to.

BELLE (*surveying him, anger coming into her eyes*): Well, if you aren't the lousiest cheap skate!

RICHARD: I'm not a cheap skate!

BELLE: Keep me around here all night fooling with you when I might be out with some real live one—if there is such a thing in this burg!—and now you quit on me! Don't be such a piker! You've got five dollars! I seen it when you paid for the drinks, so don't hand me any lies!

RICHARD: I— Who said I hadn't? And I'm not a piker. If you need the five dollars so bad—for your room rent— you can have it without—I mean, I'll be glad to give—

(*He has been fumbling in his pocket and pulls out his nine-dollar roll and holds out the five to her.*)

BELLE (*hardly able to believe her eyes, almost snatches it from his hand—then laughs and immediately becomes sentimentally grateful*): Thanks, Kid. Gee—oh, thanks — Gee, forgive me for losing my temper and bawling you out, will you? Gee, you're a regular peach! You're the nicest kid I've ever met! (*She kisses him and he grins proudly, a hero to himself now on many counts*) Gee, you're a peach! Thanks, again!

RICHARD (*grandly—and quite tipsily*): It's—nothing—only too glad. (*Then boldly*) Here—give me another kiss, and that'll pay me back.

BELLE (*kissing him*): I'll give you a thousand, if you want 'em. Come on, let's sit down, and we'll have another drink—and this time I'll blow you just to show my appreciation. (*She calls*) Hey, George! bring us another round—the same!

RICHARD (*a remnant of caution coming to him*): I don't know as I ought to—

BELLE: Oh, another won't hurt you. And I want to blow you, see. (*They sit down in their former places.*)

RICHARD (*boldly draws his chair closer and puts an arm around her—tipsily*): I like you a lot—now I'm getting to know you. You're a darned nice girl.

BELLE: Nice is good! Tell me another! Well, if I'm so nice, why didn't you want to take me upstairs? That's what I don't get.

RICHARD (*lying boldly*): I did want to—only I— (*Then he adds solemnly*) I've sworn off. (*The* BARTENDER *enters with the drinks.*)

BARTENDER (*setting them on the table*): Here's your pleasure. (*Then regarding* RICHARD's *arm about her waist*) Ho-ho, we're coming on, I see. (RICHARD *grins at him muzzily.*)

BELLE (*digs into her stocking and gives him a dollar*):

Here. This is mine. (*He gives her change and she tips him a dime, and he goes out. She puts the five* RICHARD *had given her in her stocking and picks up her glass*) Here's how—and thanks again. (*She sips.*)

RICHARD (*boisterously*): Bottoms up! Bottoms up! (*He drinks all of his down and sighs with exaggerated satisfaction*) Gee, that's good stuff, all right. (*Hugging her*) Give me another kiss, Belle.

BELLE (*kisses him*): What did you mean a minute ago when you said you'd sworn off?

RICHARD (*solemnly*): I took an oath I'd be faithful.

BELLE (*bristling*): I'm not good enough to talk about her, I suppose?

RICHARD: I didn't—mean that. You're all right. (*Then with tipsy gravity*) Only you oughtn't to lead this kind of life. It isn't right—for a nice girl like you. Why don't you reform?

BELLE (*sharply*): Nix on that line of talk! Can it, you hear! You can do a lot with me for five dollars—but you can't reform me, see. Mind your own business, Kid, and don't butt in where you're not wanted!

RICHARD: I—I didn't mean to hurt your feelings.

BELLE: I know you didn't mean. You're only like a lot of people who mean well, to hear them tell it. (*Changing the subject*) So you're faithful to your one love, eh? (*With an ugly sneer*) And how about her? Bet you she's out with a guy under some bush this minute, giving him all he wants. Don't be a sucker, Kid! Even the little flies do it!

RICHARD (*starting up his chair again—angrily*): Don't you say that! Don't you dare!

BELLE (*unimpressed—with a cynical shrug of her shoulders*): All right. Have it your own way and be a sucker! It cuts no ice with me.

RICHARD: You don't know her or—

BELLE: And don't want to. Shut up about her, can't you? (*She stares before her bitterly.* RICHARD *subsides into scowling gloom. He is becoming perceptibly more intoxicated with each moment now. The* BARTENDER *and the* SALESMAN *appear just inside the swinging door. The* BARTENDER *nods toward* BELLE, *giving the* SALESMAN *a wink. The* SALESMAN *grins and comes into the room, carrying his highball in his hand. He is a stout, jowly-faced man in his late thirties, dressed with cheap nattiness, with the professional breeziness and jocular, kid-'em-along manner of his kind.* BELLE *looks up as he enters and he and she exchange a glance of complete recognition. She knows his type by heart and he knows hers.*)

SALESMAN (*passes by her to the table at right—grinning genially*): Good evening.

BELLE: Good evening.

SALESMAN (*sitting down*): Hope I'm not butting in on your party—but my dogs were giving out standing at that bar.

BELLE: All right with me. (*Giving* RICHARD *a rather contemptuous look*) I've got no party on.

SALESMAN: That sounds hopeful.

RICHARD (*suddenly recites sentimentally*):

"But I wouldn't do such, 'cause I loved her too much,
But I learned about women from her."

(*Turns to scowl at the* SALESMAN—*then to* BELLE) Let's have 'nother drink!

BELLE: You've had enough. (RICHARD *subsides, muttering to himself.*)

SALESMAN: What is it—a child poet or a child actor?

BELLE: Don't know. Got me guessing.

SALESMAN: Well, if you could shake the cradle-robbing act, maybe we could do a little business.

BELLE: That's easy. I just pull my freight. (*She shakes* RICHARD *by the arm*) Listen, Kid. Here's an old friend of mine, Mr. Smith of New Haven, just come in. I'm going over and sit at his table for a while, see. And you better go home.

RICHARD (*blinking at her and scowling*): I'm never going home! I'll show them!

BELLE: Have it your own way—only let me up. (*She takes his arm from around her and goes to sit by the* SALESMAN. RICHARD *stares after her offendedly.*)

RICHARD: Go on. What do I care what you do? (*He recites scornfully*) "For a woman's only a woman, but a good cigar's a smoke."

SALESMAN (*as* BELLE *sits beside him*): Well, what kind of beer will you have, Sister?

BELLE: Mine's a gin rickey.

SALESMAN: You've got extravagant tastes, I'm sorry to see.

RICHARD (*begins to recite sepulchrally*):

> "Yet each man kills the thing he loves,
> By each let this be heard."

SALESMAN (*grinning*): Say, this is rich! (*He calls encouragement*) That's swell dope, young feller. Give us some more.

RICHARD (*ignoring him—goes on more rhetorically*):

> "Some do it with a bitter look,
> Some with a flattering word,
> The coward does it with a kiss,
> The brave man with a sword!"

(*He stares at* BELLE *gloomily and mutters tragically*) I did it with a kiss! I'm a coward.

SALESMAN: That's the old stuff, Kid. You've got something on the ball, all right, all right! Give us another—right over the old pan, now!

BELLE (*with a laugh*): Get the hook!

RICHARD (*glowering at her—tragically*):

> " 'Oho,' they cried, 'the world is wide,
> But fettered limbs go lame!
> And once, or twice, to throw the dice
> Is a gentlemanly game,
> But he does not win who plays with Sin
> In the secret House of Shame!' "

BELLE (*angrily*): Aw, can it! Give us a rest from that bunk!

SALESMAN (*mockingly*): This gal of yours don't appreciate poetry. She's a lowbrow. But I'm the kid that eats it up. My middle name is Kelly and Sheets! Give us some more of the same! Do you know "The Lobster and the Wise Guy"? (*Turns to* BELLE *seriously*) No kidding, that's a peacherino. I heard a guy recite it at Poli's. Maybe this nut knows it. Do you, Kid? (*But* RICHARD *only glowers at him gloomily without answering.*)

BELLE (*surveying* RICHARD *contemptuously*): He's copped a fine skinful—and gee, he's hardly had anything.

RICHARD (*suddenly—with a dire emphasis*): "And then—at ten o'clock—Eilert Lovborg will come—with vine leaves in his hair!"

BELLE: And bats in his belfry, if he's you!

RICHARD (*regards her bitterly—then starts to his feet bellicosely—to the* SALESMAN): I don't believe you ever knew her in New Haven at all! You just picked her up now! You leave her alone, you hear! You won't do anything to her—not while I'm here to protect her!

BELLE (*laughing*): Oh, my God! Listen to it!

SALESMAN: Ssshh! This is a scream! Wait! (*He addresses* RICHARD *in tones of exaggerated melodrama*) Curse you, Jack Dalton, if I won't unhand her, what then?

RICHARD (*threateningly*): I'll give you a good punch in the snoot, that's what! (*He moves toward their table.*)

SALESMAN (*with mock terror—screams in falsetto*): Help! Help! (*The* BARTENDER *comes in irritably.*)

BARTENDER: Hey. Cut out the noise. What the hell's up with you?

RICHARD (*tipsily*): He's too—damn fresh!

SALESMAN (*with a wink*): He's going to murder me. (*Then gets a bright idea for eliminating* RICHARD— *seriously to the* BARTENDER) It's none of my business, Brother, but if I were in your boots I'd give this young souse the gate. He's under age; any fool can see that.

BARTENDER (*guiltily*): He told me he was over eighteen.

SALESMAN: Yes, and I tell you I'm the Pope—but you don't have to believe me. If you're not looking for trouble, I'd advise you to get him started for some other gin mill and let them do the lying, if anything comes up.

BARTENDER: Hmm. (*He turns to* RICHARD *angrily and gives him a push*) Come on, now. On your way! You'll start no trouble in here! Beat it now!

RICHARD: I will not beat it!

BARTENDER: Oho, won't you? (*He gives him another push that almost sends him sprawling.*)

BELLE (*callously*): Give him the bum's rush! I'm sick of his bull! (RICHARD *turns furiously and tries to punch the* BARTENDER.)

BARTENDER (*avoids the punch*): Oho, you would, would you! (*He grabs* RICHARD *by the back of the neck and the seat of the pants and marches him ignominiously toward the swinging door.*)

RICHARD: Leggo of me, you dirty coward!

BARTENDER: Quiet now—or I'll pin a Mary Ann on your jaw that'll quiet you! (*He rushes him through the screen door and a moment later the outer doors are heard swinging back and forth.*)

SALESMAN (*with a chuckle*): Hand it to me, Kid. How was that for a slick way of getting rid of him?

BELLE (*suddenly sentimental*): Poor kid. I hope he makes home all right. I liked him—before he got soused.

SALESMAN: Who is he?

BELLE: The boy who's upstairs with my friend told me, but I didn't pay much attention. Name's Miller. His old man runs a paper in this one-horse burg, I think he said.

SALESMAN (*with a whistle*): Phew! He must be Nat Miller's kid, then.

BARTENDER (*coming back from the bar*): Well, he's on his way—with a good boot in the tail to help him!

SALESMAN (*with a malicious chuckle*): Yes? Well, maybe that boot will cost you a job, Brother. Know Nat Miller who runs the *Globe*? That's his kid.

BARTENDER (*his face falling*): The hell he is! Who said so?

SALESMAN: This baby doll. (*Getting up*) Say, I'll go keep cases on him—see he gets on the trolley all right, anyway. Nat Miller's a good scout. (*He hurries out.*)

BARTENDER (*viciously*): God damn the luck! If he ever finds out I served his kid, he'll run me out of town. (*He turns on* BELLE *furiously*) Why didn't you put me wise, you lousy tramp, you!

BELLE: Hey! I don't stand for that kind of talk—not from no hick beer-squirter like you, see!

BARTENDER (*furiously*): You don't, don't you? Who was it but you told me to hand him dynamite in that fizz? (*He gives her chair a push that almost throws her to the floor*) Beat it, you—and beat it quick—or I'll call Sullivan from the corner and have you run in for street-walking! (*He gives her a push that lands her against the family-entrance door*) Get the hell out of here—and no long waits!

BELLE (*opens the door and goes out—turns and calls back viciously*): I'll fix you for this, you thick Mick, if I have to go to jail for it. (*She goes out and slams the door.*)

BARTENDER (*looks after her worriedly for a second—then*

shrugs his shoulders): That's only her bull. (*Then with a sigh as he returns to the bar*) Them lousy tramps is always getting this dump in Dutch!

Curtain

ACT THREE

SCENE II

SCENE—*Same as Act one—Sitting-room of the Miller home —about 11 o'clock the same night.*

MILLER *is sitting in his favorite rocking-chair at left of table, front. He has discarded collar and tie, coat and shoes, and wears an old, worn, brown dressing-gown and disreputable-looking carpet slippers. He has his reading specs on and is running over items in a newspaper. But his mind is plainly preoccupied and worried, and he is not paying much attention to what he reads.*

MRS. MILLER *sits by the table at right, front. She also has on her specs. A sewing basket is on her lap and she is trying hard to keep her attention fixed on the doily she is doing. But, as in the case of her husband, but much more apparently, her mind is preoccupied, and she is obviously on tenterhooks of nervous uneasiness.*

LILY *is sitting in the armchair by the table at rear, facing right. She is pretending to read a novel, but her attention wanders, too, and her expression is sad, although now it has lost all its bitterness and become submissive and resigned again.*

MILDRED *sits at the desk at right, front, writing two words*

*over and over again, stopping each time to survey the re-
sult critically, biting her tongue, intensely concentrated on
her work.*

TOMMY *sits on the sofa at left, front. He has had a hard
day and is terribly sleepy but will not acknowledge it. His
eyes blink shut on him, his head begins to nod, but he isn't
giving up, and every time he senses any of the family
glancing in his direction, he goads himself into a bright-
eyed wakefulness.*

MILDRED (*finally surveys the two words she has been writing and is satisfied with them*): There. (*She takes the
paper over to her mother*) Look, Ma. I've been practising a new way of writing my name. Don't look at the
others, only the last one. Don't you think it's the real
goods?

MRS. MILLER (*pulled out of her preoccupation*): Don't talk
that horrible slang. It's bad enough for boys, but for a
young girl supposed to have manners—my goodness,
when I was your age, if my mother'd ever heard me—

MILDRED: Well, don't you think it's nice, then?

MRS. MILLER (*sinks back into preoccupation—scanning the
paper—vaguely*): Yes, very nice, Mildred—very nice, indeed. (*Hands the paper back mechanically.*)

MILDRED (*is a little piqued, but smiles*): Absent-minded!
I don't believe you even saw it. (*She passes around the
table to show her* AUNT LILY. MILLER *gives an uneasy
glance at his wife and then, as if afraid of meeting her
eye, looks quickly back at his paper again.*)

MRS. MILLER (*staring before her—sighs worriedly*): Oh, I
do wish Richard would come home!

MILLER: There now, Essie. He'll be in any minute now.
Don't you worry about him.

MRS. MILLER: But I do worry about him!

LILY (*surveying* MILDRED's *handiwork—smiling*): This is
fine, Mildred. Your penmanship is improving wonder-
fully. But don't you think that maybe you've got a little
too many flourishes?

MILDRED (*disappointedly*): But, Aunt Lily, that's just what
I was practising hardest on.

MRS. MILLER (*with another sigh*): What time is it now,
Nat?

MILLER (*adopting a joking tone*): I'm going to buy a
clock for in here. You have me reaching for my watch
every couple of minutes. (*He has pulled his watch out
of his vest pocket—with forced carelessness*) Only a
little past ten.

MRS. MILLER: Why, you said it was that an hour ago! Nat
Miller, you're telling me a fib, so's not to worry me. You
let me see that watch!

MILLER (*guiltily*): Well, it's quarter to eleven—but that's
not so late—when you remember it's Fourth of July.

MRS. MILLER: If you don't stop talking Fourth of July—!
To hear you go on, you'd think that was an excuse for
anything from murder to picking pockets!

MILDRED (*has brought her paper around to her father and
now shoves it under his nose*): Look, Pa.

MILLER (*seizes on this interruption with relief*): Let's see.
Hmm. Seems to me you've been inventing a new signa-
ture every week lately. What are you in training for—
writing checks? You must be planning to catch a rich
husband.

MILDRED (*with an arch toss of her head*): No wedding bells
for me! But how do you like it, Pa?

MILLER: It's overpowering—no other word for it, overpowering! You could put it on the Declaration of Independence and not feel ashamed.

MRS. MILLER (*desolately, almost on the verge of tears*):
It's all right for you to laugh and joke with Mildred! I'm

the only one in this house seems to care—(*Her lips tremble.*)

MILDRED (*a bit disgustedly*): Ah, Ma, Dick only sneaked off to the fireworks at the beach, you wait and see.

MRS. MILLER: Those fireworks were over long ago. If he had, he'd be home.

LILY (*soothingly*): He probably couldn't get a seat, the trolleys are so jammed, and he had to walk home.

MILLER (*seizing on this with relief*): Yes, I never thought of that, but I'll bet that's it.

MILDRED: Ah, don't let him worry you, Ma. He just wants to show off he's heartbroken about that silly Muriel— and get everyone fussing over him and wondering if he hasn't drowned himself or something.

MRS. MILLER (*snappily*): You be quiet! The way you talk at times, I really believe you're that hard-hearted you haven't got a heart in you! (*With an accusing glance at her husband*) One thing I know, you don't get that from me!(*He meets her eye and avoids it guiltily. She sniffs and looks away from him around the room. TOMMY, who is nodding and blinking is afraid her eye is on him. He straightens alertly and speaks in a voice that, in spite of his effort, is dripping with drowsiness.*)

TOMMY: Let me see what you wrote, Mid.

MILDRED (*cruelly mocking*): You? You're so sleepy you couldn't see it.

TOMMY (*valiantly*): I am not sleepy!

MRS. MILLER (*has fixed her eye on him*): My gracious, I was forgetting you were still up! You run up to bed this minute! It's hours past your bedtime!

TOMMY: But it's the Fourth of July. Ain't it, Pa?

MRS. MILLER (*gives her husband an accusing stare*): There! You see what you've done? You might know he'd copy your excuses! (*Then sharply to TOMMY*) You heard what I said, Young Man!

TOMMY: Aw, Ma, can't I stay up a *little* longer?

MRS. MILLER: I said, no! You obey me and no more arguing about it!

TOMMY (*drags himself to his feet*): Aw! I should think I could stay up till Dick—

MILLER (*kindly but firmly*): You heard your ma say no more arguing. When she says git, you better git. (TOMMY *accepts his fate resignedly and starts around kissing them all good night.*)

TOMMY (*kissing her*): Good night, Aunt Lily.

LILY: Good night, dear. Sleep well.

TOMMY (*pecking at* MILDRED): Good night, you.

MILDRED: Good night, you.

TOMMY (*kissing him*): Good night, Pa.

MILLER: Good night, Son. Sleep tight.

TOMMY (*kissing her*): Good night, Ma.

MRS. MILLER: Good night. Here! You look feverish. Let me feel of your head. No, you're all right. Hurry up, now. And don't forget your prayers.

(TOMMY *goes slowly to the doorway—then turns suddenly, the discovery of another excuse lighting up his face.*)

TOMMY: Here's another thing, Ma. When I was up to the water closet last—

MRS. MILLER (*sharply*): When you were *where?*

TOMMY: The bathroom.

MRS. MILLER: That's better.

TOMMY: Uncle Sid was snoring like a fog horn—and he's right next to my room. How can I ever get to sleep while he's—(*He is overcome by a jaw-cracking yawn.*)

MRS. MILLER: I guess you'd get to sleep all right if you were inside a fog horn. You run along now. (TOMMY *gives up, grins sleepily, and moves off to bed. As soon as he is off her mind, all her former uneasiness comes back on* MRS.

MILLER *tenfold. She sighs, moves restlessly, then finally asks*) What time is it now, Nat?

MILLER: Now, Essie, I just told you a minute ago.

MRS. MILLER (*resentfully*): I don't see how you can take it so calm! Here it's midnight, you might say, and our Richard still out, and we don't even know where he is.

MILDRED: I hear someone on the piazza. Bet that's him now, Ma.

MRS. MILLER (*her anxiety immediately turning to relieved anger*): You give him a good piece of your mind, Nat, you hear me! You're too easy with him, that's the whole trouble! The idea of him daring to stay out like this! (*The front door is heard being opened and shut, and someone whistling "Waltz Me Around Again, Willie."*)

MILDRED: No, that isn't Dick. It's Art.

MRS. MILLER (*her face falling*): Oh. (*A moment later* ARTHUR *enters through the front parlor, whistling softly, half under his breath, looking complacently pleased with himself.*)

MILLER (*surveys him over his glasses, not with enthusiasm —shortly*): So you're back, eh? We thought it was Richard.

ARTHUR: Is he still out? Where'd he go to?

MILLER: That's just what we'd like to know. You didn't run into him anywhere, did you?

ARTHUR: No. I've been at the Rands' ever since dinner. (*He sits down in the armchair at left of table, rear*) I suppose he sneaked off to the beach to watch the fireworks.

MILLER (*pretending an assurance he is far from feeling*): Of course. That's what we've been trying to tell your mother, but she insists on worrying her head off.

MRS. MILLER: But if he was going to the fireworks, why wouldn't he say so? He knew we'd let him.

ARTHUR (*with calm wisdom*): That's easy, Ma. (*He grins*

superiorly) Didn't you hear him this morning showing off bawling out the Fourth like an anarchist? He wouldn't want to reneg on that to you—but he'd want to see the old fireworks just the same. (*He adds complacently*) I know. He's at the foolish age.

MILLER (*stares at* ARTHUR *with ill-concealed astonishment, then grins*): Well, Arthur, by gosh, you make me feel as if I owed you an apology when you talk horse sense like that. (*He turns to his wife, greatly relieved*) Arthur's hit the nail right on the head, I think, Essie. That was what I couldn't figure out—why he—but now it's clear as day.

MRS. MILLER (*with a sigh*): Well, I hope you're right. But I wish he was home.

ARTHUR (*takes out his pipe and fills and lights it with solemn gravity*): He oughtn't to be allowed out this late at his age. I wasn't, Fourth or no Fourth—if I remember.

MILLER (*a twinkle in his eyes*): Don't tax your memory trying to recall those ancient days of your youth. (MILDRED *laughs and* ARTHUR *looks sheepish. But he soon regains his aplomb.*)

ARTHUR (*importantly*): We had a corking dinner at the Rands'. We had sweetbreads on toast.

MRS. MILLER (*arising momentarily from her depression*): Just like the Rands to put on airs before you! I never could see anything to sweetbreads. Always taste like soap to me. And no real nourishment to them. I wouldn't have the pesky things on my table! (ARTHUR *again feels sat upon.*)

MILDRED (*teasingly*): Did you kiss Elsie good night?

ARTHUR: Stop trying to be so darn funny all the time! You give me a pain in the ear!

MILDRED: And that's where she gives me a pain, the stuck-up thing!—thinks she's the whole cheese!

MILLER (*irritably*): And that's where your everlasting wrangling gives me a pain, you two! Give us a rest! (*There is silence for a moment.*)

MRS. MILLER (*sighs worriedly again*): I do wish that boy would get home!

MILLER (*glances at her uneasily, peeks surreptitiously at his watch—then has an inspiration and turns to* ARTHUR): Arthur, what's this I hear about your having such a good singing voice? Rand was telling me he liked nothing better than to hear you sing—said you did every night you were up there. Why don't you ever give us folks at home here a treat?

ARTHUR (*pleased, but still nursing wounded dignity*): I thought you'd only sit on me.

MRS. MILLER (*perking up—proudly*): Arthur has a real nice voice. He practises when you're not at home. I didn't know you cared for singing, Nat.

MILLER: Well, I do—nothing better—and when I was a boy I had a fine voice myself and folks used to say I'd ought—(*Then abruptly, mindful of his painful experience with reminiscence at dinner, looking about him guiltily*) Hmm. But don't hide your light under a bushel, Arthur. Why not give us a song or two now? You can play for him, can't you, Mildred?

MILDRED (*with a toss of her head*): I can play as well as Elsie Rand, at least!

ARTHUR (*ignoring her—clearing his throat importantly*): I've been singing a lot tonight. I don't know if my voice—

MILDRED (*forgetting her grudge, grabs her brother's hand and tugs at it*): Come on. Don't play modest. You know you're just dying to show off. (*This puts* ARTHUR *off it at once. He snatches his hand away from her angrily.*)

ARTHUR: Let go of me, you! (*Then with surly dignity*) I don't feel like singing tonight, Pa. I will some other time.

MILLER: You let him alone, Mildred! (*He winks at* ARTHUR, *indicating with his eyes and a nod of his head* MRS. MILLER, *who has again sunk into worried brooding. He makes it plain by this pantomime that he wants him to sing to distract his mother's mind.*)

ARTHUR (*puts aside his pipe and gets up promptly*): Oh— sure, I'll do the best I can. (*He follows* MILDRED *into the front parlor, where he switches on the lights.*)

MILLER (*to his wife*): It won't keep Tommy awake. Nothing could. And Sid, he'd sleep through an earthquake. (*Then suddenly, looking through the front parlor—grumpily*) Darn it, speak of the devil, here he comes. Well, he's had a good sleep and he'd ought to be sobered up. (LILY *gets up from her chair and looks around her huntedly, as if for a place to hide.* MILLER *says soothingly*) Lily, you just sit down and read your book and don't pay any attention to him. (*She sits down again and bends over her book tensely. From the front parlor comes the tinkling of a piano as* MILDRED *runs over the scales. In the midst of this,* SID *enters through the front parlor. All the effervescence of his jag has worn off and he is now suffering from a bad case of hangover— nervous, sick, a prey to gloomy remorse and bitter feelings of self-loathing and self-pity. His eyes are bloodshot and puffed, his face bloated, the fringe of hair around his baldness tousled and tufty. He sidles into the room guiltily, his eyes shifting about, avoiding looking at anyone.*)

SID (*forcing a sickly, twitching smile*): Hello.

MILLER (*considerately casual*): Hello, Sid. Had a good nap? (*Then, as* SID *swallows hard and is about to break into further speech,* MILDRED'S *voice comes from the front parlor,* "I haven't played that in ever so long, but I'll try," *and she starts an accompaniment.* MILLER *motions* SID *to be quiet*) Ssshh! Arthur's going to sing for us. (SID *flattens himself against the edge of the bookcase at center, rear, miserably self-conscious and ill-at-ease there but nervously afraid to move anywhere else.* AR-THUR *begins to sing. He has a fairly decent voice but his method is untrained sentimentality to a dripping degree. He sings that old sentimental favorite, "Then You'll Remember Me." The effect on his audience is instant.* MILLER *gazes before him with a ruminating melancholy, his face seeming to become gently sorrowful and old.* MRS. MILLER *stares before her, her expression becoming more and more doleful.* LILY *forgets to pretend to read her book but looks over it, her face growing tragically sad. As for* SID, *he is moved to his remorseful, guilt-stricken depths. His mouth pulls down at the corners and he seems about to cry. The song comes to an end.* MILLER *starts, then claps his hands enthusiastically and calls*) Well done, Arthur—well done! Why, you've got a splendid voice! Give us some more! You liked that, didn't you, Essie?

MRS. MILLER (*dolefully*): Yes—but it's sad—terrible sad.

SID (*after swallowing hard, suddenly blurts out*): Nat and Essie—and Lily—I—I want to apologize—for coming home—the way I did—there's no excuse—but I didn't mean—

MILLER (*sympathetically*): Of course, Sid. It's all forgotten.

MRS. MILLER (*rousing herself—affectionately pitying*): Don't be a goose, Sid. We know how it is with picnics. You forget it. (*His face lights up a bit but his gaze shifts to* LILY *with a mute appeal, hoping for a word from her which is not forthcoming. Her eyes are fixed on her book, her body tense and rigid.*)

SID (*finally blurts out desperately*): Lily—I'm sorry—about the fireworks. Can you—forgive me? (*But* LILY *remains implacably silent. A stricken look comes over* SID's *face. In the front parlor* MILDRED *is heard saying "But I only* know the chorus"—*and she starts another accompaniment.*)

MILLER (*comes to* SID's *rescue*): Ssshh! We're going to have another song. Sit down, Sid. (SID, *hanging his head, flees to the farthest corner, left, front, and sits at the end of the sofa, facing front, hunched up, elbows on knees, face in hands, his round eyes childishly wounded and woe-begone.* ARTHUR *sings the popular "Dearie," playing up its sentimental values for all he is worth. The effect on his audience is that of the previous song, intensified—especially upon* SID. *As he finishes,* MILLER *again starts and applauds*) Mighty fine, Arthur! You sang that darned well! Didn't he, Essie?

MRS. MILLER (*dolefully*): Yes—But I wish he wouldn't sing such sad songs. (*Then, her lips trembling*) Richard's always whistling that.

MILLER (*hastily—calls*): Give us something cheery, next one, Arthur. You know, just for variety's sake.

SID (*suddenly turns toward* LILY—*his voice choked with tears—in a passion of self-denunciation*): You're right, Lily!—right not to forgive me!—I'm no good and never will be!—I'm a no-good drunken bum!—you shouldn't even wipe your feet on me!—I'm a dirty, rotten drunk! —no good to myself or anybody else!—if I had any guts I'd kill myself, and good riddance!—but I haven't!—I'm yellow, too!—a yellow, drunken bum! (*He hides his face in his hands and begins to sob like a sick little boy. This is too much for* LILY. *All her bitter hurt and steely resolve to ignore and punish him vanish in a flash, swamped by a pitying love for him. She runs and puts her arm around him—even kisses him tenderly and impulsively on his bald head, and soothes him as if he were a little boy.* MRS. MILLER, *almost equally moved, has half risen to go to her brother, too, but* MILLER *winks and shakes his head vigorously and motions her to sit down.*)

LILY: There! Don't cry, Sid! I can't bear it! Of course, I forgive you! Haven't I always forgiven you? I know you're not to blame—So don't, Sid!

SID (*lifts a tearful, humbly grateful, pathetic face to her— but a face that the dawn of a cleansed conscience is already beginning to restore to its natural Puckish expression*): Do you really forgive me—I know I don't deserve it—can you really—?

LILY (*gently*): I told you I did, Sid—and I do.

SID (*kisses her hand humbly, like a big puppy licking it*): Thanks, Lily. I can't tell you— (*In the front parlor,* ARTHUR *begins to sing rollickingly "Waiting at the Church," and after the first line or two* MILDRED *joins in.* SID's *face lights up with appreciation and, automatically, he begins to tap one foot in time, still holding fast to* LILY's *hand. When they come to "sent around a note, this is what she wrote," he can no longer resist, but joins in a shaky bawl*): "Can't get away to marry you today, My wife won't let me!" (*As the song finishes, the two in the other room laugh.* MILLER *and* SID *laugh.* LILY *smiles at* SID's *laughter. Only* MRS. MILLER *remains dolefully preoccupied, as if she hadn't heard.*)

MILLER: That's fine, Arthur and Mildred. That's darned good.

SID (*turning to* LILY *enthusiastically*): You ought to hear Vesta Victoria sing that! Gosh, she's great! I heard her at Hammerstein's Victoria—you remember, that trip I made to New York.

LILY (*her face suddenly tired and sad again—for her memory of certain aspects of that trip is the opposite from what he would like her to recall at this moment— gently disengaging her hand from his—with a hopeless sigh*): Yes, I remember, Sid. (*He is overcome momentarily by guilty confusion. She goes quietly and sits down in her chair again. In the front parlor, from now on, MILDRED keeps starting to run over popular tunes but always gets stuck and turns to another.)*

MRS. MILLER (*suddenly*): What time is it now, Nat? (*Then without giving him a chance to answer*) Oh, I'm getting worried something dreadful, Nat! You don't know what might have happened to Richard! You read in the papers every day about boys getting run over by automobiles.

LILY: Oh, don't say that, Essie!

MILLER (*sharply, to conceal his own reawakened apprehension*): Don't get to imagining things, now!

MRS. MILLER: Well, why couldn't it happen, with everyone that owns one out tonight, and lots of those driving, drunk? Or he might have gone down to the beach dock, and fallen overboard! (*On the verge of hysteria*) Oh, I know something dreadful's happened! And you can sit there listening to songs and laughing as if— Why don't you do something? Why don't you go out and find him? (*She bursts into tears.*)

LILY (*comes to her quickly and puts her arm around her*): Essie, you mustn't worry so! You'll make yourself sick! Richard's all right. I've got a feeling in my bones he's all right.

MILDRED (*comes hurrying in from the front parlor*): What's the trouble? (*ARTHUR appears in the doorway beside her. She goes to her mother and also puts an arm around her*) Ah, don't cry, Ma! Dick'll turn up in a minute or two, wait and see!

ARTHUR: Sure, he will!

MILLER (*has gotten to his feet, frowning—soberly*): I was going out to look—if he wasn't back by twelve sharp. That'd be the time it'd take him to walk from the beach if he left after the last car. But I'll go now, if it'll ease your mind. I'll take the auto and drive out the beach road—and likely pick him up on the way. (*He has taken his collar and tie from where they hang from one* corner of the bookcase at rear, center, and is starting to put them on) You better come with me, Arthur.

ARTHUR: Sure thing, Pa. (*Suddenly he listens and says*) Ssshh! There's someone on the piazza now—coming around to this door, too. That must be him. No one else would—

MRS. MILLER: Oh, thank God, thank God!

MILLER (*with a sheepish smile*): Darn him! I've a notion to give him hell for worrying us all like this. (*The screen door is pushed violently open and* RICHARD *lurches in and stands swaying a little, blinking his eyes in the light. His face is a pasty pallor, shining with perspiration, and his eyes are glassy. The knees of his trousers are dirty, one of them torn from the sprawl on the sidewalk he had taken, following the* BARTENDER'S *kick. They all gape at him, too paralyzed for a moment to say anything.*)

MRS. MILLER: Oh, God, what's happened to him! He's gone crazy! Richard!

SID (*the first to regain presence of mind—with a grin*): Crazy, nothing. He's only soused!

ARTHUR: He's drunk, that's what! (*Then shocked and condemning*) You've got your nerve! You fresh kid! We'll take that out of you when we get you down to Yale!

RICHARD (*with a wild gesture of defiance—maudlinly dramatic*):

> "Yesterday this Day's Madness did prepare
> Tomorrow's Silence, Triumph, or Despair.
> Drink! for—"

MILLER (*his face grown stern and angry, takes a threatening step toward him*): Richard! How dare—!

MRS. MILLER (*hysterically*): Don't you strike him, Nat! Don't you—!

SID (*grabbing his arm*): Steady, Nat! Keep your temper!

No good bawling him out now! He don't know what he's doing!

MILLER (*controlling himself and looking a bit ashamed*): All right—you're right, Sid.

RICHARD (*drunkenly glorying in the sensation he is creating —recites with dramatic emphasis*): "And then—I will come—with vine leaves in my hair!" (*He laughs with a double-dyed sardonicism.*)

MRS. MILLER (*staring at him as if she couldn't believe her eyes*): Richard! You're intoxicated!—you bad, wicked boy, you!

RICHARD (*forces a wicked leer to his lips and quotes with ponderous mockery*): "Fancy that, Hedda!" (*Then suddenly his whole expression changes, his pallor takes on a greenish, sea-sick tinge, his eyes seem to be turned inward uneasily—and, all pose gone, he calls to his mother appealingly, like a sick little boy*) Ma! I feel—rotten! (MRS. MILLER *gives a cry and starts to go to him, but* SID *steps in her way.*)

SID: You let me take care of him, Essie. I know this game backwards.

MILLER (*putting his arm around his wife*): Yes, you leave him to Sid.

SID (*his arm around* RICHARD—*leading him off through the front parlor*): Come on, Old Sport! Upstairs we go! Your old Uncle Sid'll fix you up. He's the kid that wrote the book!

MRS. MILLER (*staring after them—still aghast*): Oh, it's too terrible! Imagine our Richard! And did you hear him talking about some Hedda? Oh, I know he's been with one of those bad women, I know he has—my Richard! (*She hides her face on* MILLER's *shoulder and sobs heartbrokenly.*)

MILLER (*a tired, harassed, deeply worried look on his face*

—*soothing her*) : Now, now, you mustn't get to imagining such things! You mustn't, Essie! (LILY *and* MILDRED *and* ARTHUR *are standing about awkwardly with awed, shocked faces.*)

Curtain

Act Four

SCENE—*The same—Sitting-room of the Miller house— about one o'clock in the afternoon of the following day.*

As the curtain rises, the family, with the exception of RICHARD, *are discovered coming in through the back parlor from dinner in the dining-room.* MILLER *and his wife come first. His face is set in an expression of frowning severity.* MRS. MILLER'S *face is drawn and worried. She has evidently had no rest yet from a sleepless, tearful night.* SID *is himself again, his expression as innocent as if nothing had occurred the previous day that remotely concerned him. And, outside of eyes that are bloodshot and nerves that are shaky, he shows no aftereffects except that he is terribly sleepy.* LILY *is gently sad and depressed.* ARTHUR *is self-consciously a virtuous young man against whom nothing can be said.* MILDRED *and* TOMMY *are subdued, covertly watching their father.*

They file into the sitting-room in silence and then stand around uncertainly, as if each were afraid to be the first to sit down. The atmosphere is as stiltedly grave as if they were attending a funeral service. Their eyes keep fixed on the head of the house, who has gone to the window at right and is staring out frowningly, savagely chewing a toothpick.

MILLER (*finally—irritably*): Damn it, I'd ought to be back at the office putting in some good licks! I've a whole pile of things that have got to be done today!

MRS. MILLER (*accusingly*): You don't mean to tell me you're going back without seeing him? It's your *duty—*!

MILLER (*exasperatedly*): 'Course I'm not! I wish you'd stop jumping to conclusions! What else did I come home for, I'd like to know? Do I usually come way back here for dinner on a busy day? I was only wishing this hadn't come up—just at this particular time. (*He ends up very lamely and is irritably conscious of the fact.*)

TOMMY (*who has been fidgeting restlessly—unable to bear the suspense a moment longer*): What is it Dick done? Why is everyone scared to tell me?

MILLER (*seizes this as an escape valve—turns and fixes his youngest son with a stern forbidding eye*): Young man, I've never spanked you yet, but that don't mean I never will! Seems to me that you've been just itching for it lately! You keep your mouth shut till you're spoken to—or I warn you something's going to happen!

MRS. MILLER: Yes, Tommy, you keep still and don't bother your pa. (*Then warningly to her husband*) Careful what you say, Nat. Little pitchers have big ears.

MILLER (*peremptorily*): You kids skedaddle—all of you. Why are you always hanging around the house? Go out and play in the yard, or take a walk, and get some fresh air. (*MILDRED takes TOMMY's hand and leads him out through the front parlor. ARTHUR hangs back, as if the designation "kids" couldn't possibly apply to him. His father notices this—impatiently*) You, too, Arthur. (*AR-THUR goes out with a stiff, wounded dignity.*)

LILY (*tactfully*): I think I'll go for a walk, too. (*She goes out through the front parlor. SID makes a movement as if to follow her.*)

MILLER: I'd like you to stay, Sid—for a while, anyway.

SID: Sure. (*He sits down in the rocking-chair at right, rear, of table and immediately yawns*) Gosh, I'm dead. Don't know what's the matter with me today. Can't seem to keep awake.

MILLER (*with caustic sarcasm*): Maybe that demon chowder you drank at the picnic poisoned you! (SID *looks sheepish and forces a grin. Then* MILLER *turns to his wife with the air of one who determinedly faces the unpleasant*) Where is Richard?

MRS. MILLER (*flusteredly*): He's still in bed. I made him stay in bed to punish him—and I thought he ought to, anyway, after being so sick. But he says he feels all right.

SID (*with another yawn*): 'Course he does. When you're young you can stand anything without it fazing you. Why, I remember when I could come down on the morning after, fresh as a daisy, and eat a breakfast of pork chops and fried onions and— (*He stops guiltily.*)

MILLER (*bitingly*): I suppose that was before eating lobster shells had ruined your iron constitution!

MRS. MILLER (*regards her brother severely*): If I was in your shoes, I'd keep still! (*Then turning to her husband*) Richard must be feeling better. He ate all the dinner I sent up, Norah says.

MILLER: I thought you weren't going to give him any dinner—to punish him.

MRS. MILLER (*guiltily*): Well—in his weakened condition— I thought it best— (*Then defensively*) But you needn't think I haven't punished him. I've given him pieces of my mind he won't forget in a hurry. And I've kept reminding him his real punishment was still to come— that you were coming home to dinner on purpose—and then he'd learn that you could be terrible stern when he did such awful things.

MILLER (*stirs uncomfortably*): Hmm!

MRS. MILLER: And that's just what it's your duty to do—punish him good and hard! The idea of him daring—(*Then hastily*) But you be careful how you go about it, Nat. Remember he's like you inside—too sensitive for his own good. And he never would have done it, I know, if it hadn't been for that darned little dunce, Muriel, and her numbskull father—and then all of us teasing him and hurting his feelings all day—and then you lost your temper and were so sharp with him right after dinner before he went out.

MILLER (*resentfully*): I see this is going to work round to where it's all my fault!

MRS. MILLER: Now, I didn't say that, did I? Don't go losing your temper again. And here's another thing. You know as well as I, Richard would never have done such a thing alone. Why, he wouldn't know how! He must have been influenced and led by someone.

MILLER: Yes, I believe that. Did you worm out of him who is was? (*Then angrily*) By God, I'll make whoever it was regret it!

MRS. MILLER: No, he wouldn't admit there was anyone. (*Then triumphantly*) But there is one thing I did worm out of him—and I can tell you it relieved my mind more'n anything. You know, I was afraid he'd been with one of those bad women. Well, turns out there wasn't any Hedda. She was just out of those books he's been reading. He swears he's never known a Hedda in his life. And I believe him. Why, he seemed disgusted with me for having such a notion. (*Then lamely*) So somehow—I can't kind of feel it's all as bad as I thought it was. (*Then quickly and indignantly*) But it's bad enough, goodness knows—and you punish him good just the same. The idea of a boy his age—! Shall I go up now and tell him to get dressed, you want to see him?

MILLER (*helplessly—and irritably*): Yes! I can't waste all day listening to you!

MRS. MILLER (*worriedly*): Now you keep your temper, Nat, remember! (*She goes out through the front parlor.*)

MILLER: Darn women, anyway! They always get you mixed up. Their minds simply don't know what logic is! (*Then he notices that* SID *is dozing—sharply*) Sid!

SID (*blinking—mechanically*): I'll take the same. (*Then hurriedly*) What'd you say, Nat?

MILLER (*caustically*): What I didn't say was what'll you have. (*Irritably*) Do you want to be of some help, or don't you? Then keep awake and try and use your brains! This is a damned sight more serious than Essie has any idea! She thinks there weren't any girls mixed up with Richard's spree last night—but I happen to know there were! (*He takes a letter from his pocket*) Here's a note a woman left with one of the boys downstairs at the office this morning—didn't ask to see me, just said give me this. He'd never seen her before—said she looked like a tart. (*He has opened the letter and reads*) "Your son got the booze he drank last night at the Pleasant Beach House. The bartender there knew he was under age but served him just the same. He thought it was a good joke to get him soused. If you have any guts you will run that bastard out of town." Well, what do you think of that? It's a woman's handwriting—not signed, of course.

SID: She's one of the babies, all right—judging from her elegant language.

MILLER: See if you recognize the handwriting.

SID (*with a reproachful look*): Nat, I resent the implication that I correspond with all the tramps around this town. (*Looking at the letter*) No, I don't know who this one could be. (*Handing the letter back*) But I de-

duce that the lady had a run-in with the barkeep and
wants revenge.

MILLER (*grimly*): And I deduce that before that she must
have picked up Richard—or how would she know who
he was?—and took him to this dive.

SID: Maybe. The Pleasant Beach House is nothing but a
bed house—(*Quickly*) At least, so I've been told.

MILLER: That's just the sort of damned fool thing he might
do to spite Muriel, in the state of mind he was in—pick
up some tart. And she'd try to get him drunk so—

SID: Yes, it might have happened like that—and it might
not. How're we ever going to prove it? Everyone at the
Pleasant Beach will lie their heads off.

MILLER (*simply and proudly*): Richard won't lie.

SID: Well, don't blame him if he don't remember everything that happened last night. (*Then sincerely concerned*) I hope you're wrong, Nat. That kind of baby is
dangerous for a kid like Dick—in more ways than one.
You know what I mean.

MILLER (*frowningly*): Yep—and that's just what's got me
worried. Damn it, I've got to have a straight talk with
him—about women and all those things. I ought to have
long ago.

SID: Yes. You ought.

MILLER: I've tried to a couple of times. I did it all right
with Wilbur and Lawrence and Arthur, when it came
time—but, hell, with Richard I always get sort of
ashamed of myself and can't get started right. You feel,
in spite of all his bold talk out of books, that he's so
darned innocent inside.

SID: I know. I wouldn't like the job. (*Then after a pause
—curiously*) How were you figuring to punish him for
his sins?

MILLER (*frowning*): To be honest with you, Sid, I'm
damned if I know. All depends on what I feel about

what he feels when I first size him up—and then it'll be like shooting in the dark.

SID: If I didn't know you so well, I'd say don't be too hard on him. (*He smiles a little bitterly*) If you remember, I was always getting punished—and see what a lot of good it did me!

MILLER (*kindly*): Oh, there's lots worse than you around, so don't take to boasting. (*Then, at a sound from the front parlor—with a sigh*) Well, here comes the Bad Man, I guess.

SID (*getting up*): I'll beat it. (*But it is* MRS. MILLER *who appears in the doorway, looking guilty and defensive.* SID *sits down again.*)

MRS. MILLER: I'm sorry, Nat—but he was sound asleep and I didn't have the heart to wake him. I waited for him to wake up but he didn't.

MILLER (*concealing a relief of which he is ashamed—exasperatedly*): Well, I'll be double damned! If you're not the—

MRS. MILLER (*defensively aggressive*): Now don't lose your temper at me, Nat Miller! You know as well as I do he needs all the sleep he can get today—after last night's ructions! Do you want him to be taken down sick? And what difference does it make to you anyway? You can see him when you come home for supper, can't you? My goodness, I never saw you so savage-tempered! You'd think you couldn't bear waiting to punish him!

MILLER (*outraged*): Well, I'll be eternally—(*Then suddenly he laughs*) No use talking, you certainly take the cake! but you know darned well I told you I'm not coming home to supper tonight. I've got a date with Jack Lawson that may mean a lot of new advertising and it's important.

MRS. MILLER: Then you can see him when you do come home.

MILLER (*covering his evident relief at this respite with a fuming manner*): All right! All right! I give up! I'm going back to the office. (*He starts for the front parlor*) Bring a man all the way back here on a busy day and then you— No consideration— (*He disappears, and a moment later the front door is heard shutting behind him.*)

MRS. MILLER: Well! I never saw Nat so bad-tempered.

SID (*with a chuckle*): Bad temper, nothing. He's so tickled to get out of it for a while he can't see straight!

MRS. MILLER (*with a sniff*): I hope I know him better than you. (*Then fussing about the room, setting this and that in place, while* SID *yawns drowsily and blinks his eyes*) Sleeping like a baby—so innocent-looking. You'd think butter wouldn't melt in his mouth. It all goes to show you never can tell by appearances—not even when it's your own child. The idea!

SID (*drowsily*): Oh, Dick's all right, Essie. Stop worrying.

MRS. MILLER (*with a sniff*): Of course, you'd say that. I suppose you'll have him out with you painting the town red the next thing! (*As she is talking,* RICHARD *appears in the doorway from the sitting-room. He shows no ill effects from his experience the night before. In fact, he looks surprisingly healthy. He is dressed in old clothes that look as if they had been hurriedly flung on. His expression is one of hang-dog guilt mingled with a defensive defiance.*)

RICHARD (*with self-conscious unconcern, ignoring his mother*): Hello, Sid.

MRS. MILLER (*whirls on him*): What are you doing here, Young Man? I thought you were asleep! Seems to me you woke up pretty quick—just after your pa left the house!

RICHARD (*sulkily*): I wasn't asleep. I heard you in the room.

MRS. MILLER (*outraged*): Do you mean to say you were deliberately deceiving—

RICHARD: I wasn't deceiving. You didn't ask if I was asleep.

MRS. MILLER: It amounts to the same thing and you know it! It isn't enough your wickedness last night, but now you have to take to lying!

RICHARD: I wasn't lying, Ma. If you'd asked if I was asleep I'd have said no.

MRS. MILLER: I've a good mind to send you straight back to bed and make you stay there!

RICHARD: Ah, what for, Ma? It was only giving me a headache, lying there.

MRS. MILLER: If you've got a headache, I guess you know it doesn't come from that! And imagine me standing there, and feeling sorry for you, like a fool—even having a run-in with your pa because—But you wait till he comes back tonight! If you don't catch it!

RICHARD (*sulkily*): I don't care.

MRS. MILLER: You don't care? You talk as if you weren't sorry for what you did last night!

RICHARD (*defiantly*): I'm not sorry.

MRS. MILLER: Richard! You ought to be ashamed! I'm beginning to think you're hardened in wickedness, that's what!

RICHARD (*with bitter despondency*): I'm not sorry because I don't care a darn what I did, or what's done to me, or anything about anything! I won't do it again—

MRS. MILLER (*seizing on this to relent a bit*): Well, I'm glad to hear you say that, anyway!

RICHARD: But that's not because I think it was wicked or any such old-fogy moral notion, but because it wasn't any fun. It didn't make me happy and funny like it does Uncle Sid—

SID (*drowsily*): What's that? Who's funny?

RICHARD (*ignoring him*): It only made me sadder—and

sick—so I don't see any sense in it.

MRS. MILLER: Now you're talking sense! That's a good boy.

RICHARD: But I'm not sorry I tried it once—curing the soul
by means of the senses, as Oscar Wilde says. (*Then with
despairing pessimism*) But what does it matter what I do
or don't do? Life is all a stupid farce! I'm through with
it! (*With a sinister smile*) It's lucky there aren't any of
General Gabler's pistols around—or you'd see if I'd
stand it much longer!

MRS. MILLER (*worriedly impressed by this threat—but pretending scorn*): I don't know anything about General
Gabler—I suppose that's more of those darned books—
but you're a silly gabbler yourself when you talk that
way!

RICHARD (*darkly*): That's how little you know about me.

MRS. MILLER (*giving in to her worry*): I wish you wouldn't
say those terrible things—about life and pistols! You
don't want to worry me to death, do you?

RICHARD (*reassuringly stoical now*): You needn't worry,
Ma. It was only my despair talking. But I'm not a
coward. I'll face—my fate.

MRS. MILLER (*stands looking at him puzzledly—then gives
it up with a sigh*): Well, all I can say is you're the queer-
est boy I ever did hear of! (*Then solicitously, putting her
hand on his forehead*) How's your headache? Do you
want me to get you some Bromo Seltzer?

RICHARD (*taken down—disgustedly*): No, I don't! Aw, Ma,
you don't understand anything!

MRS. MILLER: Well, I understand this much: It's your liver,
that's what! You'll take a good dose of salts tomorrow
morning, and no nonsense about it! (*Then suddenly*)
My goodness, I wonder what time it's getting to be.
I've got to go upstreet. (*She goes to the front-parlor doorway—then turns*) You stay here, Richard, you hear? Remember, you're not allowed out today—for a punish-

ment. (*She hurries away.* RICHARD *sits in tragic gloom.* SID, *without opening his eyes, speaks to him drowsily.*)

SID: Well, how's my fellow Rum Pot, as good old Dowie calls us? Got a head?

RICHARD (*startled—sheepishly*): Aw, don't go dragging that up, Uncle Sid. I'm never going to be such a fool again, I tell you.

SID (*with drowsy cynicism—not unmixed with bitterness at the end*): Seems to me I've heard someone say that before. Who could it have been, I wonder? Why, if it wasn't Sid Davis! Yes, sir, I've heard him say that very thing a thousand times, must be. But then he's always fooling; you can't take a word he says seriously. He's a card, that Sid is!

RICHARD (*darkly*): I was desperate, Uncle—even if she wasn't worth it. I was wounded to the heart.

SID: I like to the quick better myself—more stylish. (*Then sadly*) But you're right. Love is hell on a poor sucker. Don't I know it? (RICHARD *is disgusted and disdains to reply.* SID'S *chin sinks on his chest and he begins to breathe noisily, fast asleep.* RICHARD *glances at him with aversion. There is a sound of someone on the porch and the screen door is opened and* MILDRED *enters. She smiles on seeing her uncle, then gives a start on seeing* RICHARD.)

MILDRED: Hello! Are you allowed up?

RICHARD: Of course, I'm allowed up.

MILDRED (*comes and sits in her father's chair at right, front, of table*): How did Pa punish you?

RICHARD: He didn't. He went back to the office without seeing me.

MILDRED: Well, you'll catch it later. (*Then rebukingly*) And you ought to. If you'd ever seen how awful you looked last night!

RICHARD: Ah, forget it, can't you?

MILDRED: Well, are you ever going to do it again, that's what I want to know.

RICHARD: What's that to you?

MILDRED (*with suppressed excitement*): Well, if you don't solemnly swear you won't—then I won't give you something I've got for you.

RICHARD: Don't try to kid me. You haven't got anything.

MILDRED: I have, too.

RICHARD: What?

MILDRED: Wouldn't you like to know! I'll give you three guesses.

RICHARD (*with disdainful dignity*): Don't bother me. I'm in no mood to play riddles with kids!

MILDRED: Oh, well, if you're going to get snippy! Anyway you haven't promised yet.

RICHARD (*a prey to keen curiosity now*): I promise. What is it?

MILDRED: What would you like best in the world?

RICHARD: I don't know. What?

MILDRED: And you pretend to be in love! If I told Muriel that!

RICHARD (*breathlessly*): Is it—from her?

MILDRED (*laughing*): Well, I guess it's a shame to keep you guessing. Yes. It is from her. I was walking past her place just now when I saw her waving from their parlor window, and I went up and she said give this to Dick, and she didn't have a chance to say anything else because her mother called her and said she wasn't allowed to have company. So I took it—and here it is. (*She gives him a letter folded many times into a tiny square.* RICHARD *opens it with a trembling eagerness and reads.* MILDRED *watches him curiously—then sighs affectedly*) Gee, it must be nice to be in love like you are —all with one person.

RICHARD (*his eyes shining*): Gee, Mid, do you know what she says—that she didn't mean a word in that other letter. Her old man made her write it. And she loves me and only me and always will, no matter how they punish her!

MILDRED: My! I'd never think she had that much spunk.

RICHARD: Huh! You don't know her! Think I could fall in love with a girl that was afraid to say her soul's her own? I should say not! (*Then more gleefully still*) And she's going to try and sneak out and meet me to-night. She says she thinks she can do it. (*Then suddenly feeling this enthusiasm before* MILDRED *is entirely the wrong note for a cynical pessimist—with an affected bitter laugh*) Ha! I knew darned well she couldn't hold out—that she'd ask to see me again. (*He misquotes cynically*) "Women never know when the curtain has fallen. They always want another act."

MILDRED: Is that so, Smarty?

RICHARD (*as if he were weighing the matter*): I don't know whether I'll consent to keep this date or not.

MILDRED: Well, I know! You're not allowed out, you silly! So you can't!

RICHARD (*dropping all pretense—defiantly*): Can't I, though! You wait and see if I can't! I'll see her tonight if it's the last thing I ever do! I don't care how I'm punished after!

MILDRED (*admiringly*): Goodness! I never thought you had such nerve!

RICHARD: You promise to keep your face shut, Mid—until after I've left—then you can tell Pa and Ma where I've gone—I mean, if they're worrying I'm off like last night.

MILDRED: All right. Only you've got to do something for me when I ask.

RICHARD: 'Course I will. (*Then excitedly*) And say, Mid!

Right now's the best chance for me to get away—while everyone's out! Ma'll be coming back soon and she'll keep watching me like a cat— (*He starts for the back parlor*) I'm going. I'll sneak out the back.

MILDRED (*excitedly*): But what'll you do till nighttime? It's ages to wait.

RICHARD: What do I care how long I wait! (*Intensely sincere now*) I'll think of her—and dream! I'd wait a million years and never mind it—for her! (*He gives his sister a superior scornful glance*) The trouble with you is, you don't understand what love means! (*He disappears through the back parlor.* MILDRED *looks after him admiringly.* SID *puffs and begins to snore peacefully.*)

Curtain

ACT FOUR

SCENE II

SCENE—*A strip of beach along the harbor. At left, a bank of dark earth, running half-diagonally back along the beach, marking the line where the sand of the beach ends and fertile land begins. The top of the bank is grassy and the trailing boughs of willow trees extend out over it and over a part of the beach. At left, front, is a path leading up the bank, between the willows. On the beach, at center, front, a white, flat-bottomed rowboat is drawn up, its bow about touching the bank, the painter trailing up the bank, evidently made fast to the trunk of a willow. Half-way down the sky, at rear, left, the crescent of the new moon casts a soft, mysterious, caressing light over every-*

thing. The sand of the beach shimmers palely. The for-
ward half (left of center) of the rowboat is in the deep
shadow cast by the willow, the stern section is in moon-
light. In the distance, the orchestra of a summer hotel
can be heard very faintly at intervals.

RICHARD *is discovered sitting sideways on the gunwale*
of the rowboat near the stern. He is facing left, watching
the path. He is in a great state of anxious expectancy,
squirming about uncomfortably on the narrow gunwale,
kicking at the sand restlessly, twirling his straw hat, with
a bright-colored band in stripes, around on his finger.

RICHARD (*thinking aloud*): Must be nearly nine. . . . I can
   hear the Town Hall clock strike, it's so still tonight
   . . . Gee, I'll bet Ma had a fit when she found out I'd
   sneaked out . . . I'll catch hell when I get back, but
   it'll be worth it . . . if only Muriel turns up . . . she
   didn't say for certain she could . . . gosh, I wish she'd
   come! . . . am I sure she wrote nine? . . . (*He puts*
   the straw hat on the seat amidships and pulls the folded
   letter out of his pocket and peers at it in the moon-
   light) Yes, it's nine, all right. (*He starts to put the note*
   back in his pocket, then stops and kisses it—then shoves
   it away hastily, sheepish, looking around him shame-
   facedly, as if afraid he were being observed) Aw, that's
   silly . . . no, it isn't either . . . not when you're really
   in love. . . . (*He jumps to his feet restlessly*) Darn it,
   I wish she'd show up! . . . think of something else . . .
   that'll make the time pass quicker . . . where was I this
   time last night? . . . waiting outside the Pleasant Beach
   House . . . Belle . . . ah, forget her! . . . now, when
   Muriel's coming . . . that's a fine time to think of—!
   . . . but you hugged and kissed her . . . not until I was
   drunk, I didn't . . . and then it was all showing off . . .
   darned fool! . . . and I didn't go upstairs with her . . .

even if she was pretty . . . aw, she wasn't pretty . . . she
was all painted up . . . she was just a whore . . . she
was everything dirty . . . Muriel's a million times prettier
anyway . . . Muriel and I will go upstairs . . . when
we're married . . . but that will be beautiful . . . but I
oughtn't even to think of that yet . . . it's not right . . .
I'd never—now . . . and she'd never . . . she's a decent
girl . . . I couldn't love her if she wasn't . . . but after
we're married. . . . (*He gives a little shiver of passionate
longing—then resolutely turns his mind away from these
improper, almost desecrating thoughts*) That damned
barkeep kicking me . . . I'll bet you if I hadn't been
drunk I'd have given him one good punch in the nose,
even if he could have licked me after! . . . (*Then with a
shiver of shamefaced revulsion and self-disgust*) Aw,
you deserved a kick in the pants . . . making such a
darned slob of yourself . . . reciting the Ballad of Reading Gaol to those lowbrows! . . . you must have been a
fine sight when you got home . . . having to be put to
bed and getting sick! . . . Phaw! . . . (*He squirms
disgustedly*) Think of something else, can't you? . . .
recite something . . . see if you remember . . .

> "Nay, let us walk from fire unto fire
> From passionate pain to deadlier delight—
> I am too young to live without desire,
> Too young art thou to waste this summernight—"

. . . gee, that's a peach! . . . I'll have to memorize the
rest and recite it to Muriel the next time. . . . I wish I
could write poetry . . . about her and me. . . . (*He
sighs and stares around him at the night*) Gee, it's
beautiful tonight . . . as if it was a special night . . .
for me and Muriel. . . . Gee, I love tonight. . . . I love
the sand, and the trees, and the grass, and the water
and the sky, and the moon . . . it's all in me and I'm

in it . . . God, it's so beautiful! (*He stands staring at the moon with a rapt face. From the distance the Town Hall clock begins to strike. This brings him back to earth with a start*) There's nine now. . . . (*He peers at the path apprehensively*) I don't see her . . . she must have got caught. . . . (*Almost tearfully*) Gee, I hate to go home and catch hell . . . without having seen her! . . . (*Then calling a manly cynicism to his aid*) Aw, who ever heard of a woman ever being on time. . . . I ought to know enough about life by this time not to expect . . . (*Then with sudden excitement*) There she comes now. . . . Gosh! (*He heaves a huge sigh of relief—then recites dramatically to himself, his eyes on the approaching figure*)

"*And lo my love, mine own soul's heart, more dear
    Than mine own soul, more beautiful than God,
    Who hath my being between the hands of her—*"

(*Then hastily*) Mustn't let her know I'm so tickled. . . . I ought to be mad about that first letter, anyway . . . if women are too sure of you, they treat you like slaves . . . let her suffer, for a change. . . . (*He starts to stroll around with exaggerated carelessness, turning his back on the path, hands in pockets, whistling with insouciance* "*Waiting at the Church.*"

(MURIEL MC COMBER *enters from down the path, left front. She is fifteen, going on sixteen. She is a pretty girl with a plump, graceful little figure, fluffy, light-brown hair, big naïve wondering dark eyes, a round dimpled face, a melting drawly voice. Just now she is in a great thrilled state of timid adventurousness. She hesitates in the shadow at the foot of the path, waiting for* RICHARD *to see her; but he resolutely goes on whistling with back turned, and she has to call him.*)

MURIEL: Oh, Dick.

RICHARD (*turns around with an elaborate simulation of being disturbed in the midst of profound meditation*): Oh, hello. Is it nine already? Gosh, time passes—when you're thinking.

MURIEL (*coming toward him as far as the edge of the shadow—disappointedly*): I thought you'd be waiting right here at the end of the path. I'll bet you'd forgotten I was even coming.

RICHARD (*strolling a little toward her but not too far—carelessly*): No, I hadn't forgotten, honest. But got to thinking about life.

MURIEL: You might think of me for a change, after all the risk I've run to see you! (*Hesitating timidly on the edge of the shadow*) Dick! You come here to me. I'm afraid to go out in that bright moonlight where anyone might see me.

RICHARD (*coming toward her—scornfully*): Aw, there you go again—always scared of life!

MURIEL (*indignantly*): Dick Miller, I do think you've got an awful nerve to say that after all the risks I've run making this date and then sneaking out! You didn't take the trouble to sneak any letter to me, I notice!

RICHARD: No, because after your first letter, I thought everything was dead and past between us.

MURIEL: And I'll bet you didn't care one little bit! (*On the verge of humiliated tears*) Oh, I was a fool ever to come here! I've got a good notion to go right home and never speak to you again! (*She half turns back toward the path.*)

RICHARD (*frightened—immediately becomes terribly sincere—grabbing her hand*): Aw, don't go, Muriel! Please! I didn't mean anything like that, honest, I didn't! Gee, if you knew how broken-hearted I was by that first letter, and how darned happy your second letter made me—!

MURIEL (*happily relieved—but appreciates she has the*

upper hand now and doesn't relent at once): I don't believe you.

RICHARD: You ask Mid how happy I was. She can prove it.

MURIEL: She'd say anything you told her to. I don't care anything about what she'd say. It's you. You've got to swear to me—

RICHARD: I swear!

MURIEL (*demurely*): Well then, all right. I'll believe you.

RICHARD (*his eyes on her face lovingly—genuine adoration in his voice*): Gosh, you're pretty tonight, Muriel! It seems ages since we've been together! If you knew how I've suffered—!

MURIEL: I did, too.

RICHARD (*unable to resist falling into his tragic literary pose for a moment*): The despair in my soul— (*He recites dramatically*) "Something was dead in each of us, And what was dead was Hope!" That was me! My hope of happiness was dead! (*Then with sincere boyish fervor*) Gosh, Muriel, it sure is wonderful to be with you again! (*He puts a timid arm around her awkwardly.*)

MURIEL (*shyly*): I'm glad—it makes you happy. I'm happy, too.

RICHARD: Can't I—won't you let me kiss you—now? Please! (*He bends his face toward hers.*)

MURIEL (*ducking her head away—timidly*): No. You mustn't. Don't—

RICHARD: Aw, why can't I?

MURIEL: Because—I'm afraid.

RICHARD (*discomfited—taking his arm from around her— a bit sulky and impatient with her*): Aw, that's what you always say! You're always so afraid! Aren't you ever going to let me?

MURIEL: I will—sometime.

RICHARD: When?

MURIEL: Soon, maybe.

RICHARD: Tonight, will you?

MURIEL (*coyly*): I'll see.

RICHARD: Promise?

MURIEL: I promise—maybe.

RICHARD: All right. You remember you've promised. (*Then coaxingly*) Aw, don't let's stand here. Come on out and we can sit down in the boat.

MURIEL (*hesitantly*): It's so bright out there.

RICHARD: No one'll see. You know there's never anyone around here at night.

MURIEL (*illogically*): I know there isn't. That's why I thought it would be the best place. But there might be someone.

RICHARD (*taking her hand and tugging at it gently*): There isn't a soul. (MURIEL *steps out a little and looks up and down fearfully.* RICHARD *goes on insistently*) Aw, what's the use of a moon if you can't see it!

MURIEL: But it's only a new moon. That's not much to look at.

RICHARD: But I want to see you. I can't here in the shadow. I want to—drink in—all your beauty.

MURIEL (*can't resist this*): Well, all right—only I can't stay only a few minutes. (*She lets him lead her toward the stern of the boat.*)

RICHARD (*pleadingly*): Aw, you can stay a little while, can't you? Please! (*He helps her in and she settles herself in the stern seat of the boat, facing diagonally left front.*)

MURIEL: A little while. (*He sits beside her*) But I've got to be home in bed again pretending to be asleep by ten o'clock. That's the time Pa and Ma come up to bed, as regular as clockwork, and Ma always looks into my room.

RICHARD: But you'll have oodles of time to do that.

MURIEL (*excitedly*): Dick, you have no idea what I went through to get here tonight! My, but it was exciting! You know Pa's punishing me by sending me to bed at eight sharp, and I had to get all undressed and into bed 'cause at half-past he sends Ma up to make sure I've obeyed, and she came up, and I pretended to be asleep, and she went down again, and I got up and dressed in such a hurry—I must look a sight, don't I?

RICHARD: You do not! You look wonderful!

MURIEL: And then I sneaked down the back stairs. And the pesky old stairs squeaked, and my heart was in my mouth, I was so scared, and then I sneaked out through the back yard, keeping in the dark under the trees, and— My, but it was exciting! Dick, you don't realize how I've been punished for your sake. Pa's been so mean and nasty, I've almost hated him!

RICHARD: And you don't realize what I've been through for you—and what I'm in for—for sneaking out— (*Then darkly*) And for what I did last night—what your letter made me do!

MURIEL (*made terribly curious by his ominous tone*): What did my letter make you do?

RICHARD (*beginning to glory in this*): It's too long a story —and let the dead past bury its dead. (*Then with real feeling*) Only it isn't past, I can tell you! What I'll catch when Pa gets hold of me!

MURIEL: Tell me, Dick! Begin at the beginning and tell me!

RICHARD (*tragically*): Well, after your old—your father left our place I caught holy hell from Pa.

MURIEL: Dick! You mustn't swear!

RICHARD (*somberly*): Hell is the only word that can describe it. And on top of that, to torture me more, he gave me your letter. After I'd read that I didn't want to live any more. Life seemed like a tragic farce.

MURIEL: I'm so awful sorry, Dick—honest I am! But you might have known I'd never write that unless—

RICHARD: I thought your love for me was dead. I thought you'd never loved me, that you'd only been cruelly mocking me—to torture me!

MURIEL: Dick! I'd never! You know I'd never!

RICHARD: I wanted to die. I sat and brooded about death. Finally I made up my mind I'd kill myself.

MURIEL (*excitedly*): Dick! You didn't!

RICHARD: I did, too! If there'd been one of Hedda Gabler's pistols around, you'd have seen if I wouldn't have done it beautifully! I thought, when I'm dead, she'll be sorry she ruined my life!

MURIEL (*cuddling up a little to him*): If you ever had! I'd have died, too! Honest, I would!

RICHARD: But suicide is the act of a coward. That's what stopped me. (*Then with a bitter change of tone*) And anyway, I thought to myself, she isn't worth it.

MURIEL (*huffily*): That's a nice thing to say!

RICHARD: Well, if you meant what was in the letter, you wouldn't have been worth it, would you?

MURIEL: But I've told you Pa—

RICHARD: So I said to myself, I'm through with women; they're all alike!

MURIEL: I'm not.

RICHARD: And I thought, what difference does it make what I do now? I might as well forget her and lead the pace that kills, and drown my sorrows! You know I had eleven dollars saved up to buy you something for your birthday, but I thought, she's dead to me now and why shouldn't I throw it away? (*Then hastily*) I've still got almost five left, Muriel, and I can get you something nice with that.

MURIEL (*excitedly*): What do I care about your old presents? You tell me what you did!

RICHARD (*darkly again*): After it was dark, I sneaked out and went to a low dive I know about.

MURIEL: Dick Miller, I don't believe you ever!

RICHARD: You ask them at the Pleasant Beach House if I didn't! They won't forget me in a hurry!

MURIEL (*impressed and horrified*): You went there? Why, that's a terrible place! Pa says it ought to be closed by the police!

RICHARD (*darkly*): I said it was a dive, didn't I? It's a "secret house of shame." And they let me into a secret room behind the barroom. There wasn't anyone there but a Princeton Senior I know—he belongs to Tiger Inn and he's fullback on the football team—and he had two chorus girls from New York with him, and they were all drinking champagne.

MURIEL (*disturbed by the entrance of the chorus girls*): Dick Miller! I hope you didn't notice—

RICHARD (*carelessly*): I had a highball by myself and then I noticed one of the girls—the one that wasn't with the fullback—looking at me. She had strange-looking eyes. And then she asked me if I wouldn't drink champagne with them and come and sit with her.

MURIEL: She must have been a nice thing! (*Then a bit falteringly*) And did—you?

RICHARD (*with tragic bitterness*): Why shouldn't I, when you'd told me in that letter you'd never see me again?

MURIEL (*almost tearfully*): But you ought to have known Pa made me—

RICHARD: I didn't know that then. (*Then rubbing it in*) Her name was Belle. She had yellow hair—the kind that burns and stings you!

MURIEL: I'll bet it was dyed!

RICHARD: She kept smoking one cigarette after another —but that's nothing for a chorus girl.

MURIEL (*indignantly*): She was low and bad, that's what

she was or she couldn't be a chorus girl, and her smoking cigarettes proves it! (*Then falteringly again*) And then what happened?

RICHARD (*carelessly*): Oh, we just kept drinking champagne—I bought a round—and then I had a fight with the barkeep and knocked him down because he'd insulted her. He was a great big thug but—

MURIEL (*huffily*): I don't see how he could—insult that kind! And why did you fight for her? Why didn't the Princeton fullback who'd brought them there? He must have been bigger than you.

RICHARD (*stopped for a moment—then quickly*): He was too drunk by that time.

MURIEL: And were you drunk?

RICHARD: Only a little then. I was worse later. (*Proudly*) You ought to have seen me when I got home! I was on the verge of delirium tremens!

MURIEL: I'm glad I didn't see you. You must have been awful. I hate people who get drunk. I'd have hated you!

RICHARD: Well, it was all your fault, wasn't it? If you hadn't written that letter—

MURIEL: But I've told you I didn't mean— (*Then faltering but fascinated*) But what happened with that Belle— after—before you went home?

RICHARD: Oh, we kept drinking champagne and she said she'd fallen in love with me at first sight and she came and sat on my lap and kissed me.

MURIEL (*stiffening*): Oh!

RICHARD (*quickly, afraid he has gone too far*): But it was only all in fun, and then we just kept on drinking champagne, and finally I said good night and came home.

MURIEL: And did you kiss her?

RICHARD: No, I didn't.

MURIEL (*distractedly*): You did, too! You're lying and

you know it. You did, too! (*Then tearfully*) And there
I was right at that time lying in bed not able to sleep,
wondering how I was ever going to see you again and
crying my eyes out, while you—! (*She suddenly jumps
to her feet in a tearful fury*) I hate you! I wish you
were dead! I'm going home this minute! I never want to
lay eyes on you again! And this time I mean it! (*She
tries to jump out of the boat but he holds her back. All
the pose has dropped from him now and he is in a
frightened state of contrition.*)

RICHARD (*imploringly*): Muriel! Wait! Listen!

MURIEL: I don't want to listen! Let me go! If you don't
I'll bite your hand!

RICHARD: I won't let you go! You've got to let me explain!
I never—! Ouch! (*For MURIEL has bitten his hand and it
hurts, and, stung by the pain, he lets go instinctively, and
she jumps quickly out of the boat and starts running
toward the path. RICHARD calls after her with bitter despair and hurt*) All right! Go if you want to—if you
haven't the decency to let me explain! I hate you, too!
I'll go and see Belle!

MURIEL (*seeing he isn't following her, stops at the foot of
the path—defiantly*): Well, go and see her—if that's the
kind of girl you like! What do I care? (*Then as he only
stares before him broodingly, sitting dejectedly in the
stern of the boat, a pathetic figure of injured grief*)
You can't explain! What can you explain! You owned
up you kissed her!

RICHARD: I did not. I said she kissed me.

MURIEL (*scornfully, but drifting back a step in his direction*): And I suppose you just sat and let yourself be
kissed! Tell that to the Marines!

RICHARD (*injuredly*): All right! If you're going to call me a
liar every word I say—

MURIEL (*drifting back another step*): I didn't call you a liar. I only meant—it sounds fishy. Don't you know it does?

RICHARD: I don't know anything. I only know I wish I was dead!

MURIEL (*gently reproving*): You oughtn't to say that. It's wicked. (*Then after a pause*) And I suppose you'll tell me you didn't fall in love with her?

RICHARD (*scornfully*): I should say not! Fall in love with that kind of girl! What do you take me for?

MURIEL (*practically*): How do you know what you did if you drank so much champagne?

RICHARD: I kept my head—with her. I'm not a sucker, no matter what you think!

MURIEL (*drifting nearer*): Then you didn't—love her?

RICHARD: I hated her! She wasn't even pretty! And I had a fight with her before I left, she got so fresh. I told her I loved you and never could love anyone else, and for her to leave me alone.

MURIEL: But you said just now you were going to see her—

RICHARD: That was only bluff. I wouldn't—unless you left me. Then I wouldn't care what I did—any more than I did last night. (*Then suddenly defiant*) And what if I did kiss her once or twice? I only did it to get back at you!

MURIEL: Dick!

RICHARD: You're a fine one to blame me—when it was all your fault! Why can't you be fair? Didn't I think you were out of my life forever? Hadn't you written me you were? Answer me that!

MURIEL: But I've told you a million times that Pa—

RICHARD: Why didn't you have more sense than to let him make you write it? Was it my fault you didn't?

MURIEL: It was your fault for being so stupid! You ought to have known he stood right over me and told me each word to write. If I'd refused, it would only have made everything worse. I had to pretend, so I'd get a chance to see you. Don't you see, Silly? And I had sand enough to sneak out to meet you tonight, didn't I? (*He doesn't answer. She moves nearer*) Still I can see how you felt the way you did—and maybe I am to blame for that. So I'll forgive and forget, Dick—if you'll swear to me you didn't even think of loving that—

RICHARD (*eagerly*): I didn't! I swear, Muriel. I couldn't. I love you!

MURIEL: Well, then—I still love you.

RICHARD: Then come back here, why don't you?

MURIEL (*coyly*): It's getting late.

RICHARD: It's not near half-past yet.

MURIEL (*comes back and sits down by him shyly*): All right—only I'll have to go soon, Dick. (*He puts his arm around her. She cuddles up close to him*) I'm sorry —I hurt your hand.

RICHARD: That was nothing. It felt wonderful—even to have you bite!

MURIEL (*impulsively takes his hand and kisses it*): There! That'll cure it. (*She is overcome by confusion at her boldness.*)

RICHARD: You shouldn't—waste that—on my hand. (*Then, tremblingly*) You said—you'd let me—

MURIEL: I said, maybe.

RICHARD: Please, Muriel. You know—I want it so!

MURIEL: Will it wash off—her kisses—make you forget you ever—for always?

RICHARD: I should say so! I'd never remember—anything but it—never want anything but it—ever again.

MURIEL (*shyly lifting her lips*): Then—all right—Dick. (*He kisses her tremblingly and for a moment their lips remain together. Then she lets her head sink on his shoulder and sighs softly)* The moon *is* beautiful, isn't it?

RICHARD *(kissing her hair)*: Not as beautiful as you! Nothing is! *(Then after a pause)* Won't it be wonderful when we're married?

MURIEL: Yes—but it's so long to wait.

RICHARD: Perhaps I needn't go to Yale. Perhaps Pa will give me a job. Then I'd soon be making enough to—

MURIEL: You better do what your pa thinks best—and I'd like you to be at Yale. *(Then patting his face)* Poor you! Do you think he'll punish you awful?

RICHARD *(intensely)*: I don't know and I don't care! Nothing would have kept me from seeing you tonight—not if I'd had to crawl over red-hot coals! *(Then falling back on Swinburne—but with passionate sincerity)* You have my being between the hands of you! You are "my love, mine own soul's heart, more dear than mine own soul, more beautiful than God!"

MURIEL *(shocked and delighted)*: Ssshh! It's wrong to say that.

RICHARD *(adoringly)*: Gosh, but I love you! Gosh, I love you— Darling!

MURIEL: I love you, too—Sweetheart! *(They kiss. Then she lets her head sink on his shoulder again and they both sit in a rapt trance, staring at the moon. After a pause—dreamily)* Where'll we go on our honeymoon, Dick? To Niagara Falls?

RICHARD *(scornfully)*: That dump where all the silly fools go? I should say not! *(With passionate romanticism)* No, we'll go to some far-off wonderful place! *(He calls on Kipling to help him)* Somewhere out on the Long Trail—the trail that is always new—on the road to

Mandalay! We'll watch the dawn come up like thunder
out of China!

MURIEL (*hazily but happily*): That'll be wonderful, won't
it?

Curtain

SCENE III

SCENE—*The sitting-room of the Miller house again—about
10 o'clock the same night.* MILLER *is sitting in his rocker
at left, front, of table, his wife in the rocker at right, front,
of table. Moonlight shines through the screen door at right,
rear. Only the green-shaded reading lamp is lit and by its
light* MILLER, *his specs on, is reading a book while his wife,
sewing basket in lap, is working industriously on a doily.*
MRS. MILLER'S *face wears an expression of unworried content.* MILLER'S *face has also lost its look of harassed preoccupation, although he still is a prey to certain misgivings,
when he allows himself to think of them. Several books are
piled on the table by his elbow, the books that have been
confiscated from* RICHARD.

MILLER (*chuckles at something he reads—then closes the
book and puts it on the table.* MRS. MILLER *looks up
from her sewing*): This Shaw's a comical cuss—even if
his ideas are so crazy they oughtn't to allow them to
be printed. And that Swinburne's got a fine swing to
his poetry—if he'd only choose some other subjects besides loose women.

MRS. MILLER (*smiling teasingly*): I can see where you're

becoming corrupted by those books, too—pretending to read them out of duty to Richard, when your nose has been glued to the page!

MILLER: No, no—but I've got to be honest. There's something to them. That Rubaiyat of Omar Khayyam, now. I read that over again and liked it even better than I had before—parts of it, that is, where it isn't all about boozing.

MRS. MILLER (*has been busy with her own thoughts during this last—with a deep sigh of relief*): My, but I'm glad Mildred told me where Richard went off to. I'd have worried my heart out if she hadn't. But now, it's all right.

MILLER (*frowning a little*): I'd hardly go so far as to say that. Just because we know he's all right tonight doesn't mean last night is wiped out. He's still got to be punished for that.

MRS. MILLER (*defensively*): Well, if you ask me, I think after the way I punished him all day, and the way I know he's punished himself, he's had about all he deserves. I've told you how sorry he was, and how he said he'd never touch liquor again. It didn't make him feel happy like Sid, but only sad and sick, so he didn't see anything in it for him.

MILLER: Well, if he's really got that view of it driven into his skull, I don't know but I'm glad it all happened. That'll protect him more than a thousand lectures—just horse sense about himself. (*Then frowning again*) Still, I can't let him do such things and go scot-free. And then; besides, there's another side to it— (*He stops abruptly.*)

MRS. MILLER (*uneasily*): What do you mean, another side?

MILLER (*hastily*): I mean, discipline. There's got to be some discipline in a family. I don't want him to get the idea he's got a stuffed shirt at the head of the table. No, he's got to be punished, if only to make the lesson stick in his mind, and I'm going to tell him he can't go to Yale, seeing he's so undependable.

MRS. MILLER (*up in arms at once*): Not go to Yale! I guess he can go to Yale! Every man of your means in town is sending his boys to college! What would folks think of you? You let Wilbur go, and you'd have let Lawrence, only he didn't want to, and you're letting Arthur! If our other children can get the benefit of a college education, you're not going to pick on Richard—

MILLER: Hush up, for God's sake! If you'd let me finish what I started to say! I said I'd *tell* him that now—bluff —then later on I'll change my mind, if he behaves himself.

MRS. MILLER: Oh, well, if that's all— (*Then defensively again*) But it's your duty to give him every benefit. He's got an exceptional brain, that boy has! He's proved it by the way he likes to read all those deep plays and books and poetry.

MILLER: But I thought you—(*He stops, grinning helplessly.*)

MRS. MILLER: You thought I what?

MILLER: Never mind.

MRS. MILLER (*sniffs, but thinks it better to let this pass*): You mark my words, that boy's going to turn out to be a great lawyer, or a great doctor, or a great writer, or—

MILLER (*grinning*): You agree he's going to be great, anyway.

MRS. MILLER: Yes, I most certainly have a lot of faith in Richard.

MILLER: Well, so have I, as far as that goes.

MRS. MILLER (*after a pause—judicially*): And as for his being in love with Muriel, I don't see but what it might work out real well. Richard could do worse.

MILLER: But I thought you had no use for her, thought she was stupid.

MRS. MILLER: Well, so I did, but if she's good for Richard and he wants her— (*Then inconsequentially*) Ma used to say you weren't overbright, but she changed her mind when she saw I didn't care if you were or not.

MILLER (*not exactly pleased by this*): Well, I've been bright enough to—

MRS. MILLER (*going on as if he had not spoken*): And Muriel's real cute-looking, I have to admit that. Takes after her mother. Alice Briggs was the prettiest girl before she married.

MILLER: Yes, and Muriel will get big as a house after she's married, the same as her mother did. That's the trouble. A man never can tell what he's letting himself in for— (*He stops, feeling his wife's eyes fixed on him with indignant suspicion.*)

MRS. MILLER (*sharply*): I'm not too fat and don't you say it!

MILLER: Who was talking about you?

MRS. MILLER: And I'd rather have some flesh on my bones than be built like a string bean and bore a hole in a chair every time I sat down—like some people!

MILLER (*ignoring the insult—flatteringly*): Why, no one'd ever call you fat, Essie. You're only plump, like a good figure ought to be.

MRS. MILLER (*childishly pleased—gratefully giving tit for tat*): Well, you're not skinny, either—only slender—and I think you've been putting on weight lately, too. (*Having thus squared matters she takes up her sewing again. A pause. Then* MILLER *asks incredulously.*)

MILLER: You don't mean to tell me you're actually taking this Muriel crush of Richard's seriously, do you? I know it's a good thing to encourage right now but—pshaw, why, Richard'll probably forget all about her before he's away six months, and she'll have forgotten him.

MRS. MILLER: Don't be so cynical. (*Then, after a pause, thoughtfully*) Well, anyway, he'll always have it to remember—no matter what happens after—and that's something.

MILLER: You bet that's something. (*Then with a grin*) You surprise me at times with your deep wisdom.

MRS. MILLER: You don't give me credit for ever having common sense, that's why. (*She goes back to her sewing.*)

MILLER (*after a pause*): Where'd you say Sid and Lily had gone off to?

MRS. MILLER: To the beach to listen to the band. (*She sighs sympathetically*) Poor Lily! Sid'll never change, and she'll never marry him. But she seems to get some queer satisfaction out of fussing over him like a hen that's hatched a duck—though Lord knows I wouldn't in her shoes!

MILLER: Arthur's up with Elsie Rand, I suppose?

MRS. MILLER: Of course.

MILLER: Where's Mildred?

MRS. MILLER: Out walking with her latest. I've forgot who it is. I can't keep track of them. (*She smiles.*)

MILLER (*smiling*): Then, from all reports, we seem to be completely surrounded by love!

MRS. MILLER: Well, we've had our share, haven't we? We don't have to begrudge it to our children. (*Then has a sudden thought*) But I've done all this talking about Muriel and Richard and clean forgot how wild old McComber was against it. But he'll get over that, I suppose.

MILLER (*with a chuckle*): He has already. I ran into him upstreet this afternoon and he was meek as pie. He backed water and said he guessed I was right. Richard had just copied stuff out of books, and kids would be kids, and so on. So I came off my high horse a bit—but not too far—and I guess all that won't bother anyone any more. (*Then rubbing his hands together—with a boyish grin of pleasure*) And I told you about getting that business from Lawson, didn't I? It's been a good day, Essie—a darned good day! (*From the hall beyond the front parlor the sound of the front door being opened and shut is heard.* MRS. MILLER *leans forward to look, pushing her specs up.*)

MRS. MILLER (*in a whisper*): It's Richard.

MILLER (*immediately assuming an expression of becoming gravity*) Hmm. (*He takes off his spectacles and puts them back in their case and straightens himself in his chair.* RICHARD *comes slowly in from the front parlor. He walks like one in a trance, his eyes shining with a dreamy happiness, his spirit still too exalted to be conscious of his surroundings, or to remember the threatened punishment. He carries his straw hat dangling in his hand, quite unaware of its existence.*)

RICHARD (*dreamily, like a ghost addressing fellow shades*): Hello.

MRS. MILLER (*staring at him worriedly*): Hello, Richard.

MILLER (*sizing him up shrewdly*): Hello, Son.

  (RICHARD *moves past his mother and comes to the far corner, left front, where the light is dimmest, and sits down on the sofa, and stares before him, his hat dangling in his hand.*)

MRS. MILLER (*with frightened suspicion now*): Goodness, he acts queer! Nat, you don't suppose he's been—?

MILLER (*with a reassuring smile*): No. It's love, not liquor, this time.

MRS. MILLER (*only partly reassured—sharply*): Richard! What's the matter with you? (*He comes to himself with a start. She goes on scoldingly*) How many times have I told you to hang up your hat in the hall when you come in! (*He looks at his hat as if he were surprised at its existence. She gets up fussily and goes to him*) Here. Give it to me. I'll hang it up for you this once. And what are you sitting over here in the dark for? Don't forget your father's been waiting to talk to you! (*She comes back to the table and he follows her, still half in a dream, and stands by his father's chair.* MRS. MILLER *starts for the hall with his hat.*)

MILLER (*quietly but firmly now*): You better leave Richard and me alone for a while, Essie.

MRS. MILLER (*turns to stare at him apprehensively*): Well —all right. I'll go sit on the piazza. Call me if you want me. (*Then a bit pleadingly*) But you'll remember all I said, Nat, won't you? (MILLER *nods reassuringly. She disappears through the front parlor.* RICHARD, *keenly conscious of himself as the about-to-be-sentenced criminal by this time, looks guilty and a bit defiant, searches his father's expressionless face with uneasy side glances, and steels himself for what is coming.*)

MILLER (*casually, indicating* MRS. MILLER'S *rocker*): Sit down, Richard. (RICHARD *slumps awkwardly into the chair and sits in a self-conscious, unnatural position.* MILLER *sizes him up keenly—then suddenly smiles and asks with quiet mockery*) Well, how are the vine leaves in your hair this evening?

RICHARD (*totally unprepared for this approach—shamefacedly mutters*): I don't know, Pa.

MILLER: Turned out to be poison ivy, didn't they? (*Then kindly*) But you needn't look so alarmed. I'm not going to read you any temperance lecture. That'd bore me more than it would you. And, in spite of your damn foolishness last night, I'm still giving you credit for having brains. So I'm pretty sure anything I could say to you you've already said to yourself.

RICHARD (*his head down—humbly*): I know I was a darned fool.

MILLER (*thinking it well to rub in this aspect—disgustedly*): You sure were—not only a fool but a downright, stupid, disgusting fool! (RICHARD *squirms, his head still lower*) It was bad enough for you to let me and Arthur see you, but to appear like that before your mother and Mildred —! And I wonder if Muriel would think you were so fine if she ever saw you as you looked and acted then. I think she'd give you your walking papers for keeps. And you couldn't blame her. No nice girl wants to give her love to a stupid drunk!

RICHARD (*writhing*): I know, Pa.

MILLER (*after a pause—quietly*): All right. Then that settles—the booze end of it. (*He sizes* RICHARD *up searchingly—then suddenly speaks sharply*) But there is another thing that's more serious. How about that tart you went to bed with at the Pleasant Beach House?

RICHARD (*flabbergasted—stammers*): You know—? But I didn't! If they've told you about her down there, they must have told you I didn't! She wanted me to—but I wouldn't. I gave her the five dollars just so she'd let me out of it. Honest, Pa, I didn't! She made everything seem rotten and dirty—and—I didn't want to do a thing like that to Muriel—no matter how bad I thought she'd treated me—even after I felt drunk, I didn't. Honest!

MILLER: How'd you happen to meet this lady, anyway?

RICHARD: I can't tell that, Pa. I'd have to snitch on someone —and you wouldn't want me to do that.

MILLER (*a bit taken aback*): No. I suppose I wouldn't. Hmm. Well, I believe you—and I guess that settles that. (*Then, after a quick furtive glance at* RICHARD, *he nerves himself for the ordeal and begins with a shamefaced, self-conscious solemnity*) But listen here, Richard, it's about time you and I had a serious talk about—hmm—certain matters pertaining to—and now that the subject's come up of its own accord, it's a good time—I mean, there's no use in procrastinating further—so, here goes. (*But it doesn't go smoothly and as he goes on he becomes more and more guiltily embarrassed and self-conscious and his expressions more stilted.* RICHARD *sedulously avoids even glancing at him, his own embarrassment made tenfold more painful by his father's*) Richard, you have now come to the age when— Well, you're a fully developed man, in a way, and it's only natural for you to have certain desires of the flesh, to put it that way— I mean, pertaining to the opposite sex—certain natural feelings and temptations—that'll want to be gratified—and you'll want to gratify them. Hmm—well, human society being organized as it is, there's only one outlet for—unless you're a scoundrel and go around ruining decent girls— which you're not, of course. Well, there are a certain class of women—always have been and always will be as long as human nature is what it is— It's wrong, maybe, but what can you do about it? I mean, girls like that one you—girls there's something doing with—and lots of 'em are pretty, and it's human nature if you— But that doesn't mean to ever get mixed up with them seriously! You just have what you want and pay 'em and forget it. I know that sounds hard and unfeeling, but we're talking facts and— But don't think I'm encouraging you to— If you can stay away from 'em, all the better—but if—why—hmm— Here's what I'm driving at, Richard. They're apt to be whited sepulchres— I mean, your whole life might be ruined if—so, darn it, you've got to know how to—I mean, there are ways and means— (*Suddenly he can go no farther and winds up helplessly*) But, hell, I suppose you boys talk all this over among yourselves and you know more about it than I do. I'll admit I'm no authority. I never had anything to do with

such women, and it'll be a hell of a lot better for you if
you never do!

RICHARD (*without looking at him*): I'm never going to, Pa.
(*Then shocked indignation coming into his voice*) I
don't see how you could think I could—now—when you
know I love Muriel and am going to marry her. I'd die
before I'd—!

MILLER (*immensely relieved—enthusiastically*): That's the
talk! By God, I'm proud of you when you talk like that!
(*Then hastily*) And now that's all of that. There's nothing more to say and we'll forget it, eh?

RICHARD (*after a pause*): How are you going to punish me,
Pa?

MILLER: I was sort of forgetting that, wasn't I? Well, I'd
thought of telling you you couldn't go to Yale—

RICHARD (*eagerly*): Don't I have to go? Gee, that's great!
Muriel thought you'd want me to. I was telling her I'd
rather you gave me a job on the paper because then she
and I could get married sooner. (*Then with a boyish
grin*) Gee, Pa, you picked a lemon. That isn't any punishment. You'll have to do something besides that.

MILLER (*grimly—but only half concealing an answering
grin*): Then you'll go to Yale and you'll stay there till
you graduate, that's the answer to that! Muriel's got
good sense and you haven't! (RICHARD *accepts this philosophically*) And now we're finished, you better call
your mother. (RICHARD *opens the screen door and calls
"Ma," and a moment later she comes in. She glances
quickly from son to husband and immediately knows
that all is well and tactfully refrains from all questions.*)

MRS. MILLER: My, it's a beautiful night. The moon's way
down low—almost setting. (*She sits in her chair and
sighs contentedly.* RICHARD *remains standing by the door,
staring out at the moon, his face pale in the moonlight.*)

MILLER (*with a nod at* RICHARD, *winking at his wife*): Yes,

I don't believe I've hardly ever seen such a beautiful night—with such a wonderful moon. Have you, Richard?

RICHARD (*turning to them—enthusiastically*): No! It was wonderful—down at the beach— (*He stops abruptly, smiling shyly.*)

MILLER (*watching his son—after a pause—quietly*): I can only remember a few nights that were as beautiful as this—and they were so long ago, when your mother and I were young and planning to get married.

RICHARD (*stares at him wonderingly for a moment, then quickly from his father to his mother and back again, strangely, as if he'd never seen them before—then he looks almost disgusted and swallows as if an acrid taste had come into his mouth—but then suddenly his face is transfigured by a smile of shy understanding and sympathy. He speaks shyly*): Yes, I'll bet those must have been wonderful nights, too. You sort of forget the moon was the same way back then—and everything.

MILLER (*huskily*): You're all right, Richard. (*He gets up and blows his nose.*)

MRS. MILLER (*fondly*): You're a good boy, Richard. (RICHARD *looks dreadfully shy and embarrassed at this. His father comes to his rescue.*)

MILLER: Better get to bed early tonight, Son, hadn't you?

RICHARD: I couldn't sleep. Can't I go out on the piazza and sit for a while—until the moon sets?

MILLER: All right. Then you better say good night now. I don't know about your mother, but I'm going to bed right away. I'm dead tired.

MRS. MILLER: So am I.

RICHARD (*goes to her and kisses her*): Good night, Ma.

MRS. MILLER: Good night. Don't you stay up till all hours now.

RICHARD (*comes to his father and stands awkwardly before him*): Good night, Pa.

MILLER (*puts his arm around him and gives him a hug*): Good night, Richard. (RICHARD *turns impulsively and kisses him—then hurries out the screen door.* MILLER *stares after him—then says huskily*) First time he's done that in years. I don't believe in kissing between fathers and sons after a certain age—seems mushy and silly— but that meant something! And I don't think we'll ever have to worry about his being safe—from himself— again. And I guess no matter what life will do to him, he can take care of it now. (*He sighs with satisfaction and, sitting down in his chair, begins to unlace his shoes*) My darned feet are giving me fits!

MRS. MILLER (*laughing*): Why do you bother unlacing your shoes now, you big goose—when we're going right up to bed?

MILLER (*as if he hadn't thought of that before, stops*): Guess you're right. (*Then getting to his feet—with a grin*) Mind if I don't say my prayers tonight, Essie? I'm certain God knows I'm too darned tired.

MRS. MILLER: Don't talk that way. It's real sinful. (*She gets up—then laughing fondly*) If that isn't you all over! Always looking for an excuse to— You're worse than Tommy! But all right. I suppose tonight you needn't. You've had a hard day. (*She puts her hand on the reading-lamp switch*) I'm going to turn out the light. All ready?

MILLER: Yep. Let her go, Gallagher. (*She turns out the lamp. In the ensuing darkness the faint moonlight shines full in through the screen door. Walking together toward the front parlor they stand full in it for a moment, looking out.* MILLER *puts his arm around her. He says in a low voice*) There he is—like a statue of Love's Young

Dream. (*Then he sighs and speaks with a gentle nostalgic melancholy*) What's it that Rubaiyat says

"*Yet Ah, that Spring should vanish with the Rose!*
That Youth's sweet-scented manuscript should
close!"

(*Then throwing off his melancholy, with a loving smile at her*) Well, Spring isn't everything, is it, Essie? There's a lot to be said for Autumn. That's got beauty, too. And Winter—if you're together.

MRS. MILLER (*simply*): Yes, Nat. (*She kisses him and they move quietly out of the moonlight, back into the darkness of the front parlor.*)

Curtain

A Touch of the Poet

Characters

MICKEY MALOY

JAMIE CREGAN

SARA MELODY

NORA MELODY

CORNELIUS MELODY

DEBORAH (*Mrs. Henry Harford*)

DAN ROCHE

PADDY O'DOWD

PATCH RILEY

NICHOLAS GADSBY

Scenes

SCENE—*The dining room of* MELODY's *Tavern, in a village a few miles from Boston. The tavern is over a hundred years old. It had once been prosperous, a breakfast stop for the stagecoach, but the stage line had been discontinued and for some years now the tavern has fallen upon neglected days.*

The dining room and barroom were once a single spacious room, low-ceilinged, with heavy oak beams and paneled walls—the taproom of the tavern in its prosperous days, now divided into two rooms by a flimsy partition, the barroom being off left. The partition is painted to imitate the old paneled walls but this only makes it more of an eyesore.

At left front, two steps lead up to a closed door opening on a flight of stairs to the floor above. Farther back is the door to the bar. Between these doors hangs a large mirror. Beyond the bar door a small cabinet is fastened to the wall. At rear are four windows. Between the middle two is the street door. At right front is another door, open, giving on a hallway and the main stairway to the second floor, and leading to the kitchen. Farther front at right, there is a high schoolmaster's desk with a stool.

In the foreground are two tables. One, with four chairs, at left center; a larger one, seating six, at right center. At left and right, rear, are two more tables, identical with the ones at right center. All these tables are set with white tablecloths, etc., except the small ones in the foreground at left.

It is around nine in the morning of July 27, 1828. Sunlight shines in through the windows at rear.

MICKEY MALOY *sits at the table at left front, facing right. He is glancing through a newspaper.* MALOY *is twenty-six, with a sturdy physique and an amiable, cunning face, his mouth usually set in a half-leering grin.*

JAMIE CREGAN *peers around the half-open door to the bar. Seeing* MALOY, *he comes in. As obviously Irish as* MALOY, *he is middle-aged, tall, with a lantern-jawed face. There is a scar of a saber cut over one cheekbone. He is dressed neatly but in old, worn clothes. His eyes are bloodshot, his manner sickly, but he grins as he greets* MALOY *sardonically.*

CREGAN: God bless all here—even the barkeep.

MALOY (*With an answering grin.*): Top o' the mornin'.

CREGAN: Top o' me head. (*He puts his hand to his head and groans.*) Be the saints, there's a blacksmith at work on it!

MALOY: Small wonder. You'd the divil's own load when you left at two this mornin'.

CREGAN: I must have. I don't remember leaving. (*He sits at right of table.*) Faix, you're takin' it aisy.

MALOY: There's no trade this time o' day.

CREGAN: It was a great temptation, when I saw no one in the bar, to make off with a bottle. A hair av the dog is what I need, but I've divil a penny in my pantaloons.

MALOY: Have one on the house. (*He goes to the cupboard and takes out a decanter of whiskey and a glass.*)

CREGAN: Thank you kindly. Sure, the good Samaritan was a crool haythen beside you.

MALOY (*Putting the decanter and glass before him.*): It's the same you was drinking last night—his private dew.

He keeps it here for emergencies when he don't want to go in the bar.

CREGAN (*Pours out a big drink.*): Lave it to Con never to be caught dry. (*Raising his glass.*) Your health and inclinations—if they're virtuous! (*He drinks and sighs with relief.*) God bless you, Whiskey, it's you can rouse the dead! Con hasn't been down yet for his morning's morning?

MALOY: No. He won't be till later.

CREGAN: It's like a miracle, me meeting him again. I came to these parts looking for work. It's only by accident I heard talk of a Con Melody and come here to see was it him. Until last night, I'd not seen hide nor hair of him since the war with the French in Spain—after the battle of Salamanca in '12. I was corporal in the Seventh Dragoons and he was major. (*Proudly.*) I got this cut from a saber at Talavera, bad luck to it! —serving under him. He was a captain then.

MALOY: So you told me last night.

CREGAN (*With a quick glance at him.*): Did I now? I must have said more than my prayers, with the lashings of whiskey in me.

MALOY (*With a grin.*): More than your prayers is the truth. (CREGAN *glances at him uneasily.* MALOY *pushes the decanter toward him.*) Take another taste.

CREGAN: I don't like sponging. Sure, my credit ought to be good in this shebeen! Ain't I his cousin?

MALOY: You're forgettin' what himself told you last night as he went up to bed. You could have all the whiskey you could pour down you, but not a penny's worth of credit. This house, he axed you to remember, only gives credit to gentlemen.

CREGAN: Divil mend him!

MALOY (*With a chuckle.*): You kept thinking about his insults after he'd gone out, getting madder and madder.

CREGAN: God pity him, that's like him. He hasn't changed much. (*He pours out a drink and gulps it down—with a cautious look at* MALOY.) If I was mad at Con, and me blind drunk, I must have told you a power of lies.

MALOY (*Winks slyly.*): Maybe they wasn't lies.

CREGAN: If I said any wrong of Con Melody—

MALOY: Arrah, are you afraid I'll gab what you said to him? I won't, you can take my oath.

CREGAN (*His face clearing.*): Tell me what I said and I'll tell you if it was lies.

MALOY: You said his father wasn't of the quality of Galway like he makes out, but a thievin' shebeen keeper who got rich by moneylendin' and squeezin' tenants and every manner of trick. And when he'd enough he married, and bought an estate with a pack of hounds and set up as one of the gentry. He'd hardly got settled when his wife died givin' birth to Con.

CREGAN: There's no lie there.

MALOY: You said none of the gentry would speak to auld Melody, but he had a tough hide and didn't heed them. He made up his mind he'd bring Con up a true gentleman, so he packed him off to Dublin to school, and after that to the College with sloos of money to prove himself the equal of any gentleman's son. But Con found, while there was plenty to drink on him and borrow money, there was few didn't sneer behind his back at his pretensions.

CREGAN: That's the truth, too. But Con wiped the sneer off their mugs when he called one av thim out and put a bullet in his hip. That was his first duel. It gave his pride the taste for revenge and after that he was always lookin' for an excuse to challenge someone.

MALOY: He's done a power av boastin' about his duels, but I thought he was lyin'.

CREGAN: There's no lie in it. It was that brought disgrace

on him in the end, right after he'd been promoted to major. He got caught by a Spanish noble making love to his wife, just after the battle of Salamanca, and there was a duel and Con killed him. The scandal was hushed up but Con had to resign from the army. If it wasn't for his fine record for bravery in battle, they'd have court-martialed him. (*Then guiltily.*) But I'm sayin' more than my prayers again.

MALOY: It's no news about his women. You'd think, to hear him when he's drunk, there wasn't one could resist him in Portugal and Spain.

CREGAN: If you'd seen him then, you wouldn't wonder. He was as strong as an ox, and on a thoroughbred horse, in his uniform, there wasn't a handsomer man in the army. And he had the chance he wanted in Portugal and Spain where a British officer was welcome in the gentry's houses. At home, the only women he'd known was whores. (*He adds hastily.*) Except Nora, I mean. (*Lowering his voice.*) Tell me, has he done any rampagin' wid women here?

MALOY: He hasn't. The damned Yankee gentry won't let him come near them, and he considers the few Irish around here to be scum beneath his notice. But once in a while there'll be some Yankee stops overnight wid his wife or daughter and then you'd laugh to see Con, if he thinks she's gentry, sidlin' up to her, playin' the great gentleman and makin' compliments, and then boasting afterward he could have them in bed if he'd had a chance at it, for all their modern Yankee airs.

CREGAN: And maybe he could. If you'd known him in the auld days, you'd nivir doubt any boast he makes about fightin' and women, and gamblin' or any kind av craziness. There nivir was a madder divil.

MALOY (*Lowering his voice.*): Speakin' av Nora, you nivir mentioned her last night, but I know all about it without you telling me. I used to have my room here, and there's nights he's madder drunk than most when he throws it in her face he had to marry her because— Mind you, I'm not saying anything against poor Nora. A sweeter woman never lived. And I know you know all about it.

CREGAN (*Reluctantly.*): I do. Wasn't I raised on his estate?

MALOY: He tells her it was the priests tricked him into marrying her. He hates priests.

CREGAN: He's a liar, then. He may like to blame it on them but it's little Con Melody cared what they said. Nothing ever made him do anything, except himself. He married her because he'd fallen in love with her, but he was ashamed of her in his pride at the same time because her folks were only ignorant peasants on his estate, as poor as poor. Nora was as pretty a girl as you'd find in a year's travel, and he'd come to be bitter lonely, with no woman's company but the whores was helpin' him ruin the estate. (*He shrugs his shoulders.*) Well, anyways, he married her and then went off to the war, and left her alone in the castle to have her child, and nivir saw her again till he was sent home from Spain. Then he raised what money he still was able, and took her and Sara here to America where no one would know him.

MALOY (*Thinking this over for a moment.*): It's hard for me to believe he ever loved her. I've seen the way he treats her now. Well, thank you for telling me, and I take my oath I'll nivir breathe a word of it—for Nora's sake, not his.

CREGAN (*Grimly.*): You'd better kape quiet for fear of him, too. If he's one-half the man he was, he could bate the lights out of the two av us.

MALOY: He's strong as a bull still for all the whiskey he's drunk. (*He pushes the bottle toward* CREGAN.) Have another taste. (CREGAN *pours out a drink.*) Drink hearty.

CREGAN: Long life. (*He drinks.* MALOY *puts the decanter*

*and glass back on the cupboard. A girl's voice is heard
from the hall at right.* CREGAN *jumps up—hastily.*) That's
Sara, isn't it? I'll get out. She'll likely blame me for Con
getting so drunk last night. I'll be back after Con is
down. (*He goes out.* MALOY *starts to go in the bar, as if
he too wanted to avoid* SARA. *Then he sits down defiantly.*)

MALOY: Be damned if I'll run from her. (*He takes up the
paper as* SARA MELODY *comes in from the hall at right.*)

(SARA *is twenty, an exceedingly pretty girl with a mass
of black hair, fair skin with rosy cheeks, and beautiful,
deep-blue eyes. There is a curious blending in her of
what are commonly considered aristocratic and peasant
characteristics. She has a fine forehead. Her nose is thin
and straight. She has small ears set close to her well-
shaped head, and a slender neck. Her mouth, on the
other hand, has a touch of coarseness and sensuality
and her jaw is too heavy. Her figure is strong and
graceful, with full, firm breasts and hips, and a slender
waist. But she has large feet and broad, ugly hands
with stubby fingers. Her voice is soft and musical, but
her speech has at times a self-conscious, stilted quality
about it, due to her restraining a tendency to lapse into
brogue. Her everyday working dress is of cheap material, but she wears it in a way that gives a pleasing
effect of beauty unadorned.*)

SARA (*With a glance at* MALOY, *sarcastically.*): I'm sorry to
interrupt you when you're so busy, but have you your
bar book ready for me to look over?

MALOY (*Surlily.*): I have. I put it on your desk.

SARA: Thank you. (*She turns her back on him, sits at the
desk, takes a small account book from it, and begins
checking figures.*)

MALOY (*Watches her over his paper.*): If it's profits you're
looking for, you won't find them—not with all the drinks

himself's been treating to. (*She ignores this. He becomes resentful.*) You've got your airs of a grand lady this morning, I see. There's no talkin' to you since you've been playin' nurse to the young Yankee upstairs. (*She makes herself ignore this, too.*) Well, you've had your cap set for him ever since he came to live by the lake, and now's your chance, when he's here sick and too weak to defend himself.

SARA (*Turns on him—with quiet anger.*): I warn you to mind your own business, Mickey, or I'll tell my father of your impudence. He'll teach you to keep your place, and God help you.

MALOY (*Doesn't believe this threat but is frightened by the possibility.*): Arrah, don't try to scare me. I know you'd never carry tales to him. (*Placatingly.*) Can't you take a bit of teasing, Sara?

SARA (*Turns back to her figuring.*): Leave Simon out of your teasing.

MALOY: Oho, he's Simon to you now, is he? Well, well. (*He gives her a cunning glance.*) Maybe, if you'd come down from your high horse, I could tell you some news.

SARA: You're worse than an old woman for gossip. I don't want to hear it.

MALOY: When you was upstairs at the back taking him his breakfast, there was a grand carriage with a nigger coachman stopped at the corner and a Yankee lady got out and came in here. I was sweeping and Nora was scrubbing the kitchen. (SARA *has turned to him, all attention now.*) She asked me what road would take her near the lake—

SARA (*Starts.*): Ah.

MALOY: So I told her, but she didn't go. She kept looking around, and said she'd like a cup of tea, and where was the waitress. I knew she must be connected someway with Harford or why would she want to go to the lake, where no one's ever lived but him. She didn't want tea at all, but only an excuse to stay.

SARA (*Resentfully.*): So she asked for the waitress, did she? I hope you told her I'm the owner's daughter, too.

MALOY: I did. I don't like Yankee airs any more than you. I was short with her. I said you was out for a walk, and the tavern wasn't open yet, anyway. So she went out and drove off.

SARA (*Worriedly now.*): I hope you didn't insult her with your bad manners. What did she look like, Mickey?

MALOY: Pretty, if you like that kind. A pale, delicate wisp of a thing with big eyes.

SARA: That fits what he's said of his mother. How old was she?

MALOY: It's hard to tell, but she's too young for his mother, I'd swear. Around thirty, I'd say. Maybe it's his sister.

SARA: He hasn't a sister.

MALOY (*Grinning.*): Then maybe she's an old sweetheart looking for you to scratch your eyes out.

SARA: He's never had a sweetheart.

MALOY (*Mockingly.*): Is that what he tells you, and you believe him? Faix, you must be in love!

SARA (*Angrily.*): Will you mind your own business? I'm not such a fool! (*Worried again.*) Maybe you ought to have told her he's here sick to save her the drive in the hot sun and the walk through the woods for nothing.

MALOY: Why would I tell her, when she never mentioned him?

SARA: Yes, it's her own fault. But— Well, there's no use thinking of it now—or bothering my head about her, anyway, whoever she was. (*She begins checking figures again. Her mother appears in the doorway at right.*)

(NORA MELODY *is forty, but years of overwork and worry have made her look much older. She must have been as pretty as a girl as* SARA *is now. She still*

*has the beautiful eyes her daughter has inherited. But
she has become too worn out to take care of her appearance. Her black hair, streaked with gray, straggles in
untidy wisps about her face. Her body is dumpy, with
sagging breasts, and her old clothes are like a bag
covering it, tied around the middle. Her red hands are
knotted by rheumatism. Cracked working shoes, run
down at the heel, are on her bare feet. Yet in spite of
her slovenly appearance there is a spirit which shines
through and makes her lovable, a simple sweetness and
charm, something gentle and sad and, somehow, daunt-
less.)*

MALOY (*Jumps to his feet, his face lighting up with affection.*) : God bless you, Nora, you're the one I was waitin'
to see. Will you keep an eye on the bar while I run to
the store for a bit av 'baccy?

SARA (*Sharply.*) : Don't do it, Mother.

NORA (*Smiles—her voice is soft, with a rich brogue.*) : Why
wouldn't I? "Don't do it, Mother."

MALOY : Thank you, Nora. (*He goes to the door at rear
and opens it, burning for a parting shot at* SARA.) And
the back o' my hand to you, your Ladyship! (*He goes
out, closing the door.*)

SARA : You shouldn't encourage his laziness. He's always
looking for excuses to shirk.

NORA : Ah, nivir mind, he's a good lad. (*She lowers herself
painfully on the nearest chair at the rear of the table at
center front.*) Bad cess to the rheumatism. It has me
destroyed this mornin'.

SARA (*Still checking figures in the book—gives her mother
an impatient but at the same time worried glance. Her
habitual manner toward her is one of mingled love and
pity and exasperation.*) : I've told you a hundred times to
see the doctor.

NORA: We've no money for doctors. They're bad luck, anyway. They bring death with them. (*A pause.* NORA *sighs.*) Your father will be down soon. I've some fine fresh eggs for his breakfast.

SARA (*Her face becomes hard and bitter.*): He won't want them.

NORA (*Defensively.*): You mean he'd a drop too much taken last night? Well, small blame to him, he hasn't seen Jamie since—

SARA: *Last* night? What night hasn't he?

NORA: Ah, don't be hard on him. (*A pause—worriedly.*) Neilan sent round a note to me about his bill. He says we'll have to settle by the end of the week or we'll get no more groceries. (*With a sigh.*) I can't blame him. How we'll manage, I dunno. There's the intrist on the mortgage due the first. But that I've saved, God be thanked.

SARA (*Exasperatedly.*): If you'd only let me take charge of the money.

NORA (*With a flare of spirit.*): I won't. It'd mean you and himself would be at each other's throats from dawn to dark. It's bad enough between you as it is.

SARA: Why didn't you pay Neilan the end of last week? You told me you had the money put aside.

NORA: So I did. But Dickinson was tormentin' your father with his feed bill for the mare.

SARA (*Angrily.*): I might have known! The mare comes first, if she takes the bread out of our mouths! The grand gentleman must have his thoroughbred to ride out in state!

NORA (*Defensively.*): Where's the harm? She's his greatest pride. He'd be heartbroken if he had to sell her.

SARA: Oh, yes, I know well he cares more for a horse than for us!

NORA: Don't be saying that. He has great love for you, even if you do be provokin' him all the time.

SARA: Great love for me! Arrah, God pity you, Mother!

NORA (*Sharply.*): Don't put on the brogue, now. You know how he hates to hear you. And I do, too. There's no excuse not to cure yourself. Didn't he send you to school so you could talk like a gentleman's daughter?

SARA (*Resentfully, but more careful of her speech.*): If he did, I wasn't there long.

NORA: It was you insisted on leavin'.

SARA: Because if he hadn't the pride or love for you not to live on your slaving your heart out, I had that pride and love!

NORA (*Tenderly.*): I know, Acushla. I know.

SARA (*With bitter scorn.*): We can't afford a waitress, but he can afford to keep a thoroughbred mare to prance around on and show himself off! And he can afford a barkeep when, if he had any decency, he'd do his part and tend the bar himself.

NORA (*Indignantly.*): Him, a gentleman, tend bar!

SARA: A gentleman! Och, Mother, it's all right for the two of us, out of our own pride, to pretend to the world we believe that lie, but it's crazy for you to pretend to me.

NORA (*Stubbornly.*): It's no lie. He *is* a gentleman. Wasn't he born rich in a castle on a grand estate and educated in college, and wasn't he an officer in the Duke of Wellington's army—

SARA: All right, Mother. You can humor his craziness, but he'll never make me pretend to him I don't know the truth.

NORA: Don't talk as if you hated him. You ought to be shamed—

SARA: I do hate him for the way he treats you. I heard him again last night, raking up the past, and blaming his ruin on his having to marry you.

NORA (*Protests miserably.*): It was the drink talkin', not him.

SARA (*Exasperated.*): It's you ought to be ashamed, for not having more pride! You bear all his insults as meek as a lamb! You keep on slaving for him when it's that has made you old before your time! (*Angrily.*) You can't much longer, I tell you! He's getting worse. You'll have to leave him.

NORA (*Aroused.*): I'll never! Howld your prate!

SARA: You'd leave him today, if you had any pride!

NORA: I've pride in my love for him! I've loved him since the day I set eyes on him, and I'll love him till the day I die! (*With a strange superior scorn.*) It's little you know of love, and you never will, for there's the same divil of pride in you that's in him, and it'll kape you from ivir givin' all of yourself, and that's what love is.

SARA: I could give all of myself if I wanted to, but—

NORA: If! Wanted to! Faix, it proves how little of love you know when you prate about if's and want-to's. It's when you don't give a thought for all the if's and want-to's in the world! It's when, if all the fires of hell was between you, you'd walk in them gladly to be with him, and sing with joy at your own burnin', if only his kiss was on your mouth! That's love, and I'm proud I've known the great sorrow and joy of it!

SARA (*Cannot help being impressed—looks at her mother with wondering respect.*): You're a strange woman, Mother. (*She kisses her impulsively.*) And a grand woman! (*Defiant again, with an arrogant toss of her head.*) I'll love—but I'll love where it'll gain me freedom and not put me in slavery for life.

NORA: There's no slavery in it when you love! (*Suddenly her exultant expression crumbles and she breaks down.*) For the love of God, don't take the pride of my love from me, Sara, for without it what am I at all but an ugly, fat woman gettin' old and sick!

SARA: (*Puts her arm around her—soothingly.*) Hush, Mother. Don't mind me. (*Briskly, to distract her mother's mind.*) I've got to finish the bar book. Mickey can't put two and two together without making five. (*She goes to the desk and begins checking figures again.*)

NORA (*Dries her eyes—after a pause she sighs worriedly.*): I'm worried about your father. Father Flynn stopped me on the road yesterday and tould me I'd better warn him not to sneer at the Irish around here and call thim scum, or he'll get in trouble. Most of thim is in a rage at him because he's come out against Jackson and the Democrats and says he'll vote with the Yankees for Quincy Adams.

SARA (*Contemptuously.*): Faith, they can't see a joke, then, for it's a great joke to hear him shout against mob rule, like one of the Yankee gentry, when you know what he came from. And after the way the Yanks swindled him when he came here, getting him to buy this inn by telling him a new coach line was going to stop here. (*She laughs with bitter scorn.*) Oh, he's the easiest fool ever came to America! It's that I hold against him as much as anything, that when he came here the chance was before him to make himself all his lies pretended to be. He had education above most Yanks, and he had money enough to start him, and this is a country where you can rise as high as you like, and no one but the fools who envy you care what you rose from, once you've the money and the power goes with it. (*Passionately.*) Oh, if I was a man with the chance he had, there wouldn't be a dream I'd not make come true! (*She looks at her mother, who is staring at the floor dejectedly and hasn't been listening. She is exasperated for a second—then she smiles pity-*

ingly.) You're a fine one to talk to, Mother. Wake up. What's worrying you now?

NORA: Father Flynn tould me again I'd be damned in hell for lettin' your father make a haythen of me and bring you up a haythen, too.

SARA (*With an arrogant toss of her head.*): Let Father Flynn mind his own business, and not frighten you with fairy tales about hell.

NORA: It's true, just the same.

SARA: True, me foot! You ought to tell the good Father we aren't the ignorant shanty scum he's used to dealing with. (*She changes the subject abruptly—closing* MICKEY's *bar book.*) There. That's done. (*She puts the book in the desk.*) I'll take a walk to the store and have a talk with Neilan. Maybe I can blarney him to let the bill go another month.

NORA (*Gratefully.*): Oh, you can. Sure, you can charm a bird out of a tree when you want to. But I don't like you beggin' to a Yankee. It's all right for me but I know how you hate it.

SARA (*Puts her arms around her mother—tenderly.*): I don't mind at all, if I can save you a bit of the worry that's killing you. (*She kisses her.*) I'll change to my Sunday dress so I can make a good impression.

NORA (*With a teasing smile.*): I'm thinkin' it isn't on Neilan alone you want to make an impression. You've changed to your Sunday best a lot lately.

SARA (*Coquettishly.*): Aren't you the sly one! Well, maybe you're right.

NORA: How was he when you took him his breakfast?

SARA: Hungry, and that's a good sign. He had no fever last night. Oh, he's on the road to recovery now, and it won't be long before he'll be back in his cabin by the lake.

NORA: I'll never get it clear in my head what he's been doing there the past year, living like a tramp or a tinker, and him a rich gentleman's son.

SARA (*With a tender smile.*): Oh, he isn't like his kind, or like anyone else at all. He's a born dreamer with a raft of great dreams, and he's very serious about them. I've told you before he wanted to get away from his father's business, where he worked for a year after he graduated from Harvard College, because he didn't like being in trade, even if it is a great company that trades with the whole world in its own ships.

NORA (*Approvingly.*): That's the way a true gentleman would feel—

SARA: He wanted to prove his independence by living alone in the wilds, and build his own cabin, and do all the work, and support himself simply, and feel one with Nature, and think great thoughts about what life means, and write a book about how the world can be changed so people won't be greedy to own money and land and get the best of each other but will be content with little and live in peace and freedom together, and it will be like heaven on earth. (*She laughs fondly—and a bit derisively.*) I can't remember all of it. It seems crazy to me, when I think of what people are like. He hasn't written any of it yet, anyway—only the notes for it. (*She smiles coquettishly.*) All he's written the last few months are love poems.

NORA: That's since you began to take long walks by the lake. (*She smiles.*) It's you are the sly one.

SARA (*Laughing.*): Well, why shouldn't I take walks on our own property? (*Her tone changes to a sneer.*) The land our great gentleman was swindled into buying when he came here with grand ideas of owning an American estate! —a bit of farm land no one would work any more, and the rest all wilderness! You couldn't give it away.

NORA (*Soothingly.*): Hush, now. (*Changing the subject.*) Well, it's easy to tell young Master Harford has a touch av the poet in him— (*She adds before she thinks.*) the same as your father.

SARA (*Scornfully.*): God help you, Mother! Do you think Father's a poet because he shows off reciting Lord Byron?

NORA (*With an uneasy glance at the door at left front.*): Whist, now. Himself will be down any moment. (*Changing the subject.*) I can see the Harford lad is falling in love with you.

SARA (*Her face lights up triumphantly.*): Falling? He's fallen head over heels. He's so timid, he hasn't told me yet, but I'll get him to soon.

NORA: I know you're in love with him.

SARA (*Simply.*): I am, Mother. (*She adds quickly.*) But not too much. I'll not let love make me any man's slave. I want to love him just enough so I can marry him without cheating him, or myself. (*Determinedly.*) For I'm going to marry him, Mother. It's my chance to rise in the world and nothing will keep me from it.

NORA (*Admiringly.*): Musha, but you've boastful talk! What about his fine Yankee family? His father'll likely cut him off widout a penny if he marries a girl who's poor and Irish.

SARA: He may at first, but when I've proved what a good wife I'll be— He can't keep Simon from marrying me. I know that. Simon doesn't care what his father thinks. It's only his mother I'm afraid of. I can tell she's had great influence over him. She must be a queer creature, from all he's told me. She's very strange in her ways. She never goes out at all but stays home in their mansion, reading books, or in her garden. (*She pauses.*) Did you notice a carriage stop here this morning, Mother?

NORA (*Preoccupied—uneasily.*): Don't count your chickens

before they're hatched. Young Harford seems a dacent lad. But maybe it's not marriage he's after.

SARA (*Angrily.*): I won't have you wronging him, Mother. He has no thought— (*Bitterly.*) I suppose you're bound to suspect— (*She bites her words back, ashamed.*) Forgive me, Mother. But it's wrong of you to think badly of Simon. (*She smiles.*) You don't know him. Faith, if it came to seducing, it'd be me that'd have to do it. He's that respectful you'd think I was a holy image. It's only in his poems, and in the diary he keeps— I had a peek in it one day I went to tidy up the cabin for him. He's terribly ashamed of his sinful inclinations and the insult they are to my purity. (*She laughs tenderly.*)

NORA (*Smiling, but a bit shocked.*): Don't talk so bould. I don't know if it's right, you to be in his room so much, even if he is sick. There's a power av talk about the two av you already.

SARA: Let there be, for all I care! Or all Simon cares, either. When it comes to not letting others rule him, he's got a will of his own behind his gentleness. Just as behind his poetry and dreams I feel he has it in him to do anything he wants. So even if his father cuts him off, with me to help him we'll get on in the world. For I'm no fool, either.

NORA: Glory be to God, you have the fine opinion av yourself!

SARA (*Laughing.*): Haven't I, though! (*Then bitterly.*) I've had need to have, to hold my head up, slaving as a waitress and chambermaid so my father can get drunk every night like a gentleman!

(*The door at left front is slowly opened and* CORNELIUS MELODY *appears in the doorway above the two steps. He and* SARA *stare at each other. She stiffens into hostility and her mouth sets in scorn. For a second his eyes waver and he looks guilty. Then his face be-*

comes expressionless. *He descends the steps and bows
—pleasantly.*)

MELODY: Good morning, Sara.

SARA (*Curtly.*): Good morning. (*Then, ignoring him.*) I'm
going up and change my dress, Mother. (*She goes out
right.*)

(CORNELIUS MELODY *is forty-five, tall, broad-shouldered,
deep-chested, and powerful, with long muscular arms,
big feet, and large hairy hands. His heavy-boned body
is still firm, erect, and soldierly. Beyond shaky nerves,
it shows no effects of hard drinking. It has a bull-like,
impervious strength, a tough peasant vitality. It is his
face that reveals the ravages of dissipation—a ruined
face, which was once extraordinarily handsome in a
reckless, arrogant fashion. It is still handsome—the
face of an embittered Byronic hero, with a finely
chiseled nose over a domineering, sensual mouth set in
disdain, pale, hollow-cheeked, framed by thick, curly
iron-gray hair. There is a look of wrecked distinction
about it, of brooding, humiliated pride. His bloodshot
gray eyes have an insulting cold stare which antici-
pates insult. His manner is that of a polished gentleman. Too much so. He overdoes it and one soon feels
that he is overplaying a role which has become more
real than his real self to him. But in spite of this, there
is something formidable and impressive about him. He
is dressed with foppish elegance in old, expensive, finely
tailored clothes of the style worn by English aristocracy
in Peninsular War days.*)

MELODY (*Advancing into the room—bows formally to his
wife.*): Good morning, Nora. (*His tone condescends. It
addresses a person of inferior station.*)

NORA (*Stumbles to her feet—timidly.*): Good mornin', Con.
I'll get your breakfast.

MELODY: No. Thank you. I want nothing now.

NORA (*Coming toward him.*): You look pale. Are you sick, Con, darlin'?

MELODY: No.

NORA (*Puts a timid hand on his arm.*): Come and sit down. (*He moves his arm away with instinctive revulsion and goes to the table at center front, and sits in the chair she had occupied.* NORA *hovers round him.*) I'll wet a cloth in cold water to put round your head.

MELODY: No! I desire nothing—except a little peace in which to read the news. (*He picks up the paper and holds it so it hides his face from her.*)

NORA (*Meekly.*): I'll lave you in peace. (*She starts to go to the door at right but turns to stare at him worriedly again. Keeping the paper before his face with his left hand, he reaches out with his right and pours a glass of water from the carafe on the table. Although he cannot see his wife, he is nervously conscious of her. His hand trembles so violently that when he attempts to raise the glass to his lips the water sloshes over his hand and he sets the glass back on the table with a bang. He lowers the paper and explodes nervously.*)

MELODY: For God's sake, stop your staring!

NORA: I— I was thinkin' you'd feel better if you'd a bit av food in you.

MELODY: I told you once— ! (*Controlling his temper.*) I am not hungry, Nora. (*He raises the paper again. She sighs, her hands fiddling with her apron. A pause.*)

NORA (*Dully.*): Maybe it's a hair av the dog you're needin'.

MELODY (*As if this were something he had been waiting to hear, his expression loses some of its nervous strain. But he replies virtuously.*): No, damn the liquor. Upon my conscience, I've about made up my mind I'll have no more of it. Besides, it's a bit early in the day.

NORA: If it'll give you an appetite—

MELODY: To tell the truth, my stomach is out of sorts. (*He licks his lips.*) Perhaps a drop wouldn't come amiss. (NORA *gets the decanter and glass from the cupboard and sets them before him. She stands gazing at him with a resigned sadness.* MELODY, *his eyes on the paper, is again acutely conscious of her. His nerves cannot stand it. He throws his paper down and bursts out in bitter anger.*) Well? I know what you're thinking! Why haven't you the courage to say it for once? By God, I'd have more respect for you! I hate the damned meek of this earth! By the rock of Cashel, I sometimes believe you have always deliberately encouraged me to— It's the one point of superiority you can lay claim to, isn't it?

NORA (*Bewilderedly—on the verge of tears.*): I don't— It's your comfort— I can't bear to see you—

MELODY (*His expression changes and a look of real affection comes into his eyes. He reaches out a shaking hand to pat her shoulder with an odd, guilty tenderness. He says quietly and with genuine contrition.*): Forgive me, Nora. That was unpardonable. (*Her face lights up. Abruptly he is ashamed of being ashamed. He looks away and grabs the decanter. Despite his trembling hand he manages to pour a drink and get it to his mouth and drain it. Then he sinks back in his chair and stares at the table, waiting for the liquor to take effect. After a pause he sighs with relief.*) I confess I needed that as medicine. I begin to feel more myself. (*He pours out another big drink and this time his hand is steadier, and he downs it without much difficulty. He smacks his lips.*) By the Immortal, I may have sunk to keeping an inn but at least I've a conscience in my trade. I keep liquor a gentleman can drink. (*He starts looking over the paper again—scowls at something—disdainfully, emphasizing his misquote of the line from Byron.*) "There shall he rot—Ambition's *dis*honored fool!" The paper is full of the latest swindling lies of that idol of the riffraff, Andrew Jackson. Contemptible, drunken scoundrel! But he will be the next President, I predict, for all we others can do to prevent. There is a cursed destiny in these decadent times. Everywhere the scum rises to the top. (*His eyes fasten on the date and suddenly he strikes the table with his fist.*) Today is the 27th! By God, and I would have forgotten!

NORA: Forgot what?

MELODY: The anniversary of Talavera!

NORA (*Hastily.*): Oh, ain't I stupid not to remember.

MELODY (*Bitterly.*): I had forgotten myself and no wonder. It's a far cry from this dunghill on which I rot to that glorious day when the Duke of Wellington—Lord Wellesley, then—did me the honor before all the army to commend my bravery. (*He glances around the room with loathing.*) A far cry, indeed! It would be better to forget!

NORA (*Rallying him.*): No, no, you mustn't. You've never missed celebratin' it and you won't today. I'll have a special dinner for you like I've always had.

MELODY (*With a quick change of manner—eagerly.*): Good, Nora. I'll invite Jamie Cregan. It's a stroke of fortune he is here. He served under me at Talavera, as you know. A brave soldier, if he isn't a gentleman. You can place him on my right hand. And we'll have Patch Riley to make music, and O'Dowd and Roche. If they are rabble, they're full of droll humor at times. But put them over there. (*He points to the table at left front.*) I may tolerate their presence out of charity, but I'll not sink to dining at the same table.

NORA: I'll get your uniform from the trunk, and you'll wear it for dinner like you've done each year.

MELODY: Yes, I must confess I still welcome an excuse to wear it. It makes me feel at least the ghost of the man I was then.

NORA: You're so handsome in it still, no woman could take her eyes off you.

MELODY (*With a pleased smile.*): I'm afraid you've blarney on your tongue this morning, Nora. (*Then boastfully.*) But it's true, in those days in Portugal and Spain— (*He stops a little shamefacedly, but* NORA *gives no sign of offense. He takes her hand and pats it gently—avoiding her eyes.*) You have the kindest heart in the world, Nora. And I— (*His voice breaks.*)

NORA (*Instantly on the verge of grateful tears.*): Ah, who wouldn't, Con darlin', when you— (*She brushes a hand across her eyes—hastily.*) I'll go to the store and get something tasty. (*Her face drops as she remembers.*) But, God help us, where's the money?

MELODY (*Stiffens—haughtily.*): Money? Since when has my credit not been good?

NORA (*Hurriedly.*): Don't fret, now. I'll manage. (*He returns to his newspaper, disdaining further interest in money matters.*)

MELODY: Ha. I see work on the railroad at Baltimore is progressing. (*Lowering his paper.*) By the Eternal, if I had not been a credulous gull and let the thieving Yankees swindle me of all I had when we came here, that's how I would invest my funds now. And I'd become rich. This country, with its immense territory cannot depend solely on creeping canal boats, as short-sighted fools would have us believe. We must have railroads. Then you will see how quickly America will become rich and great! (*His expression changes to one of bitter hatred.*) Great enough to crush England in the next war between them, which I know is inevitable! Would I could live to celebrate that victory! If I have one regret for the past—and there are few things in it that do not call for bitter regret—it is that I shed my blood for a country that thanked me with disgrace. But I will be avenged. This country—my country, now—will drive the English from the face of the earth their shameless perfidy has dishonored!

NORA: Glory be to God for that! And we'll free Ireland!

MELODY (*Contemptuously.*): Ireland? What benefit would freedom be to her unless she could be freed from the Irish? (*Then irritably.*) But why do I discuss such things with you?

NORA (*Humbly.*): I know. I'm ignorant.

MELODY: Yet I tried my best to educate you, after we came to America—until I saw it was hopeless.

NORA: You did, surely. And I tried, too, but—

MELODY: You won't even cure yourself of that damned peasant's brogue. And your daughter is becoming as bad.

NORA: She only puts on the brogue to tease you. She can speak as fine as any lady in the land if she wants.

MELODY (*Is not listening—sunk in bitter brooding.*): But, in God's name, who am I to reproach anyone with anything? Why don't you tell me to examine my own conduct?

NORA: You know I'd never.

MELODY (*Stares at her—again he is moved—quietly.*): No. I know you would not, Nora. (*He looks away—after a pause.*) I owe you an apology for what happened last night.

NORA: Don't think of it.

MELODY (*With assumed casualness.*): Faith, I'd a drink too many, talking over old times with Jamie Cregan.

NORA: I know.

MELODY: I am afraid I may have— The thought of old times — I become bitter. But you understand, it was the liquor talking, if I said anything to wound you.

NORA: I know it.

MELODY (*Deeply moved, puts his arm around her.*): You're a sweet, kind woman, Nora—too kind. (*He kisses her.*)

NORA (*With blissful happiness.*): Ah, Con darlin', what do I care what you say when the black thoughts are on you? Sure, don't you know I love you?

MELODY (*A sudden revulsion of feeling convulses his face. He bursts out with disgust, pushing her away from him.*): For God's sake, why don't you wash your hair? It turns my stomach with its stink of onions and stew! (*He reaches for the decanter and shakingly pours a drink. NORA looks as if he had struck her.*)

NORA (*Dully.*): I do be washin' it often to plaze you. But when you're standin' over the stove all day, you can't help—

MELODY: Forgive me, Nora. Forget I said that. My nerves are on edge. You'd better leave me alone.

NORA (*Her face brightening a little.*): Will you ate your breakfast now? I've fine fresh eggs—

MELODY (*Grasping at this chance to get rid of her—impatiently.*): Yes! In a while. Fifteen minutes, say. But leave me alone now. (*She goes out right. MELODY drains his drink. Then he gets up and paces back and forth, his hands clasped behind him. The third drink begins to work and his face becomes arrogantly self-assured. He catches his reflection in the mirror on the wall at left and stops before it. He brushes a sleeve fastidiously, adjusts the set of his coat, and surveys himself.*) Thank God, I still bear the unmistakable stamp of an officer and a gentleman. And so I will remain to the end, in spite of all fate can do to crush my spirit! (*He squares his shoulders defiantly. He stares into his eyes in the glass and recites from Byron's "Childe Harold," as if it were an incantation by which he summons pride to justify his life to himself.*)

"I have not loved the World, nor the World me;
   I have not flattered its rank breath, nor bowed

> *To its idolatries a patient knee,*
> *Nor coined my cheek to smiles,—nor cried aloud*
> *In worship of an echo: in the crowd*
> *They could not deem me one of such—I stood*
> *Among them, but not of them . . ."*

(*He pauses, then repeats.*) "Among them, but not of them." By the Eternal, that express it! Thank God for you, Lord Byron—poet and nobleman who made of his disdain immortal music! (SARA *appears in the doorway at right. She has changed to her Sunday dress, a becoming blue that brings out the color of her eyes. She draws back for a moment—then stands watching him contemptuously.* MELODY *senses her presence. He starts and turns quickly away from the mirror. For a second his expression is guilty and confused, but he immediately assumes an air of gentlemanly urbanity and bows to her.*) Ah, it's you, my dear. Are you going for a morning stroll? You've a beautiful day for it. It will bring fresh roses to your cheeks.

SARA: I don't know about roses, but it will bring a blush of shame to my cheeks. I have to beg Neilan to give us another month's credit, because you made Mother pay the feed bill for your fine thoroughbred mare! (*He gives no sign he hears this. She adds scathingly.*) I hope you saw something in the mirror you could admire!

MELODY (*In a light tone.*): Faith, I suppose I must have looked a vain peacock, preening himself, but you can blame the bad light in my room. One cannot make a decent toilet in that dingy hole in the wall.

SARA: You have the best room in the house, that we ought to rent to guests.

MELODY: Oh, I've no complaints. I was merely explaining my seeming vanity.

SARA: Seeming!

MELODY (*Keeping his tone light.*): Faith, Sara, you must have risen the wrong side of the bed this morning, but it takes two to make a quarrel and I don't feel quarrelsome. Quite the contrary. I was about to tell you how exceedingly charming and pretty you look, my dear.

SARA (*With a mocking, awkward, servant's curtsy—in broad brogue.*): Oh, thank ye, yer Honor.

MELODY: Every day you resemble your mother more, as she looked when I first knew her.

SARA: Musha, but it's you have the blarneyin' tongue, God forgive you!

MELODY (*In spite of himself, this gets under his skin— angrily.*): Be quiet! How dare you talk to me like a common, ignorant— You're my daughter, damn you. (*He controls himself and forces a laugh.*) A fair hit! You're a great tease, Sara. I shouldn't let you score so easily. Your mother warned me you only did it to provoke me. (*Unconsciously he reaches out for the decanter on the table—then pulls his hand back.*)

SARA (*Contemptuously—without brogue now.*): Go on and drink. Surely you're not ashamed before me, after all these years.

MELODY (*Haughtily.*): Ashamed? I don't understand you. A gentleman drinks as he pleases—provided he can hold his liquor as he should.

SARA: A gentleman!

MELODY (*Pleasantly again.*): I hesitated because I had made a good resolve to be abstemious today. But if you insist— (*He pours a drink—a small one—his hand quite steady now.*) To your happiness, my dear. (*She stares at him scornfully. He goes on graciously.*) Will you do me the favor to sit down? I have wanted a quiet chat with you for some time. (*He holds out a chair for her at rear of table at center.*)

SARA (*Eyes him suspiciously—then sits down.*): What is it you want?

MELODY (*With a playfully paternal manner.*): Your happiness, my dear, and what I wish to discuss means happiness to you, unless I have grown blind. How is our patient, young Simon Harford, this morning?

SARA (*Curtly.*): He's better.

MELODY: I am delighted to hear it. (*Gallantly.*) How could he help but be with such a charming nurse? (*She stares at him coldly. He goes on.*) Let us be frank. Young Simon is in love with you. I can see that with half an eye—and, of course, you know it. And you return his love, I surmise.

SARA: Surmise whatever you please.

MELODY: Meaning you do love him? I am glad, Sara. (*He becomes sentimentally romantic.*) Requited love is the greatest blessing life can bestow on us poor mortals; and first love is the most blessed of all. As Lord Byron has it (*He recites.*)

> "But sweeter still than this, than these, than all,
> Is first and passionate Love—it stands alone,
> Like Adam's recollection of his fall . . ."

SARA (*Interrupts him rudely.*): Was it to listen to you recite Byron—?

MELODY (*Concealing discomfiture and resentment—pleasantly.*): No. What I was leading up to is that you have my blessing, if that means anything to you. Young Harford is, I am convinced, an estimable youth. I have enjoyed my talks with him. It has been a privilege to be able to converse with a cultured gentleman again. True, he is a bit on the sober side for one so young, but by way of compensation, there is a romantic touch of the poet behind his Yankee phlegm.

SARA: It's fine you approve of him!

MELODY: In your interest I have had some enquiries made about his family.

SARA (*Angered—with taunting brogue.*): Have you, indade? Musha, that's cute av you! Was it auld Patch Riley, the Piper, made them? Or was it Dan Roche or Paddy O'Dowd, or some other drunken sponge—

MELODY (*As if he hadn't heard—condescendingly.*): I find his people will pass muster.

SARA: Oh, do you? That's nice!

MELODY: Apparently, his father is a gentleman—that is, by Yankee standards, insofar as one in trade can lay claim to the title. But as I've become an American citizen myself, I suppose it would be downright snobbery to hold to old-world standards.

SARA: Yes, wouldn't it be!

MELODY: Though it is difficult at times for my pride to remember I am no longer the master of Melody Castle and an estate of three thousand acres of as fine pasture and woodlands as you'd find in the whole United Kingdom, with my stable of hunters, and—

SARA (*Bitterly.*): Well, you've a beautiful thoroughbred mare now, at least—to prove you're still a gentleman!

MELODY (*Stung into defiant anger.*): Yes, I've the mare! And by God, I'll keep her if I have to starve myself so she may eat.

SARA: You mean, make Mother slave to keep her for you, even if she has to starve!

MELODY (*Controls his anger—and ignores this.*): But what was I saying? Oh, yes, young Simon's family. His father will pass muster, but it's through his mother, I believe, he comes by his really good blood. My information is, she springs from generations of well-bred gentlefolk.

SARA: It would be a great pride to her, I'm sure, to know you found her suitable!

MELODY: I suppose I may expect the young man to request

an interview with me as soon as he is up and about again?

SARA: To declare his honorable intentions and ask you for my hand, is that what you mean?

MELODY: Naturally. He is a man of honor. And there are certain financial arrangements Simon's father or his legal representative will wish to discuss with me. The amount of your settlement has to be agreed upon.

SARA (*Stares at him as if she could not believe her ears.*): My settlement! Simon's father! God pity you—!

MELODY (*Firmly.*): Your settlement, certainly. You did not think, I hope, that I would give you away without a penny to your name as if you were some poverty-stricken peasant's daughter? Please remember I have my own position to maintain. Of course, it is a bit difficult at present. I am temporarily hard pressed. But perhaps a mortgage on the inn—

SARA: It's mortgaged to the hilt already, as you very well know.

MELODY: If nothing else, I can always give my note at hand for whatever amount—

SARA: You can give it, sure enough! But who'll take it?

MELODY: Between gentlemen, these matters can always be arranged.

SARA: God help you, it must be a wonderful thing to live in a fairy tale where only dreams are real to you. (*Then sharply.*) But you needn't waste your dreams worrying about my affairs. I'll thank you not to interfere. Attend to your drinking and leave me alone. (*He gives no indication that he has heard a word she has said. She stares at him and a look almost of fear comes into her eyes. She bursts out with a bitter exasperation in which there is a strong undercurrent of entreaty.*) Father! Will you never let yourself wake up—not even now when you're sober, or nearly? Is it stark mad you've gone, so you can't tell any more what's dead and a lie, and what's the living truth?

MELODY (*His face is convulsed by a spasm of pain as if something vital had been stabbed in him—with a cry of tortured appeal.*): Sara! (*But instantly his pain is transformed into rage. He half rises from his chair threateningly.*) Be quiet, damn you! How dare you—! (*She shrinks away and rises to her feet. He forces control on himself and sinks back in his chair, his hands gripping the arms.*)

(*The street door at rear is flung open and* DAN ROCHE, PADDY O'DOWD, *and* PATCH RILEY *attempt to pile in together and get jammed for a moment in the doorway. They all have hangovers, and* ROCHE *is talking boisterously.* DAN ROCHE *is middle-aged, squat, bowlegged, with a potbelly and short arms lumpy with muscle. His face is flat with a big mouth, protruding ears, and red-rimmed little pig's eyes. He is dressed in dirty, patched clothes.* PADDY O'DOWD *is thin, round-shouldered, flat-chested, with a pimply complexion, bulgy eyes, and a droopy mouth. His manner is oily and fawning, that of a born sponger and parasite. His clothes are those of a cheap sport.* PATCH RILEY *is an old man with a thatch of dirty white hair. His washed-out blue eyes have a wandering, half-witted expression. His skinny body is clothed in rags and there is nothing under his tattered coat but his bare skin. His mouth is sunken in, toothless. He carries an Irish bagpipe under his arm.*)

ROCHE (*His back is half turned as he harangues* O'DOWD *and* RILEY, *and he does not see* MELODY *and* SARA.): And I says, it's Andy Jackson will put you in your place, and all the slave-drivin' Yankee skinflints like you! Take your damned job, I says, and—

O'DOWD (*Warningly, his eyes on* MELODY.): Whist! Whist!

Hold your prate! (ROCHE *whirls around to face* MELODY, *and his aggressiveness oozes from him, changing to a hangdog apprehension. For* MELODY *has sprung to his feet, his eyes blazing with an anger which is increased by the glance of contempt* SARA *cast from him to the three men.* O'DOWD *avoids* MELODY'S *eyes, busies himself in closing the door.* PATCH RILEY *stands gazing at* SARA *with a dreamy, admiring look, lost in a world of his own fancy, oblivious to what is going on.*)

ROCHE (*Placatingly.*): Good mornin' to ye, Major.

O'DOWD (*Fawning.*): Good mornin', yer Honor.

MELODY: How dare you come tramping in here in that manner! Have you mistaken this inn for the sort of dirty shebeen you were used to in the old country where the pigs ran in and out the door?

O'DOWD: We ask pardon, yer Honor.

MELODY (*To* ROCHE—*an impressive menace in his tone.*): You, Paddy. Didn't I forbid you ever to mention that scoundrel Jackson's name in my house or I'd horsewhip the hide off your back? (*He takes a threatening step toward him.*) Perhaps you think I cannot carry out that threat.

ROCHE (*Backs away frightenedly.*): No, no, Major. I forgot — Good mornin' to ye, Miss.

O'DOWD: Good mornin', Miss Sara. (*She ignores them.* PATCH RILEY *is still gazing at her with dreamy admiration, having heard nothing, his hat still on his head.* O'DOWD *officiously snatches it off for him—rebukingly.*) Where's your wits, Patch? Didn't ye hear his Honor?

RILEY (*Unheeding—addresses* SARA.): Sure it's you, God bless you, looks like a fairy princess as beautiful as a rose in the mornin' dew. I'll raise a tune for you. (*He starts to arrange his pipes.*

SARA (*Curtly.*): I want none of your tunes. (*Then, seeing the look of wondering hurt in the old man's eyes, she adds kindly.*) That's sweet of you, Patch. I know you'd raise a beautiful tune, but I have to go out. (*Consoled, the old man smiles at her gratefully.*)

MELODY: Into the bar, all of you, where you belong! I told you not to use this entrance! (*With disdainful tolerance.*) I suppose it's a free drink you're after. Well, no one can say of me that I turned away anyone I knew thirsty from my door.

O'DOWD: Thank ye, yer Honor. Come along, Dan. (*He takes* RILEY'S *arm.*) Come on, Patch. (*The three go into the bar and* O'DOWD *closes the door behind them.*)

SARA (*In derisive brogue.*): Sure, it's well trained you've got the poor retainers on your American estate to respect the master! (*Then as he ignores her and casts a furtive glance at the door to the bar, running his tongue over his dry lips, she says acidly, with no trace of brogue.*) Don't let me keep you from joining the gentlemen! (*She turns her back on him and goes out the street door at rear.*)

MELODY (*His face is again convulsed by a spasm of pain— pleadingly.*): Sara!

(NORA *enters from the hall at right, carrying a tray with toast, eggs, bacon, and tea. She arranges his breakfast on the table at front center, bustling garrulously.*)

NORA: Have I kept you waitin'? The divil was in the toast. One lot burned black as a naygur when my back was turned. But the bacon is crisp, and the eggs not too soft, the way you like them. Come and sit down now. (MELODY *does not seem to hear her. She looks at him worriedly.*) What's up with you, Con? Don't you hear me?

O'DOWD (*Pokes his head in the door from the bar.*): Mickey won't believe you said we could have a drink, yer Honor, unless ye tell him.

MELODY (*Licking his lips.*): I'm coming. (*He goes to the bar door.*)

NORA: Con! Have this in your stomach first! It'll all get cauld.

MELODY (*Without turning to her—in his condescendingly polite tone.*): I find I am not the least hungry, Nora. I regret your having gone to so much trouble. (*He goes into the bar, closing the door behind him.* NORA *slumps on a chair at the rear of the table and stares at the breakfast with a pitiful helplessness. She begins to sob quietly.*)

Curtain

Act Two

SCENE—*Same as Act One. About half an hour has elapsed. The barroom door opens and* MELODY *comes in. He has had two more drinks and still no breakfast, but this has had no outward effect except that his face is paler and his manner more disdainful. He turns to give orders to the spongers in the bar.*

MELODY: Remember what I say. None of your loud brawling. And you, Riley, keep your bagpipe silent, or out you go. I wish to be alone in quiet for a while with my memories. When Corporal Cregan returns, Mickey, send him in to me. He, at least, knows Talavera is not the name of a new brand of whiskey. (*He shuts the door contemptuously on* MICKEY's "Yes, Major" *and the obedient murmur of the others. He sits at rear of the table at left front. At first, he poses to himself, striking an attitude—a Byronic hero, noble, embittered, disdainful, defying his tragic fate, brooding over past glories. But he has no audience and he cannot keep it up. His shoulders sag and he stares at the table top, hopelessness and defeat bringing a trace of real tragedy to his ruined, handsome face.*)

(*The street door is opened and* SARA *enters. He does not hear the click of the latch, or notice her as she comes forward. Fresh from the humiliation of cajoling the storekeeper to extend more credit, her eyes are bitter. At sight of her father they become more so. She moves toward the door at right, determined to ignore him, but something unusual in his attitude strikes her and she stops to regard him searchingly. She starts to say something bitter—stops—finally, in spite of herself, she asks with a trace of genuine pity in her voice.*)

SARA: What's wrong with you, Father? Are you really sick or is it just— (*He starts guiltily, ashamed of being caught in such a weak mood.*)

MELODY (*Gets to his feet politely and bows.*): I beg your pardon, my dear. I did not hear you come in. (*With a deprecating smile.*) Faith, I was far away in spirit, lost in memories of a glorious battle in Spain, nineteen years ago today.

SARA (*Her face hardens.*): Oh. It's the anniversary of Talavera, is it? Well, I know what that means—a great day for the spongers and a bad day for this inn!

MELODY (*Coldly.*): I don't understand you. Of course I shall honor the occasion.

SARA: You needn't tell me. I remember the other celebrations—and this year, now Jamie Cregan has appeared, you've an excuse to make it worse.

MELODY: Naturally, an old comrade in arms will be doubly welcome—

SARA: Well, I'll say this much. From the little I've seen of him, I'd rather have free whiskey go down his gullet than the others'. He's a relation, too.

MELODY (*Stiffly.*): Merely a distant cousin. That has no bearing. It's because Corporal Cregan fought by my side—

SARA: I suppose you've given orders to poor Mother to cook a grand feast for you, as usual, and you'll wear your beautiful uniform, and I'll have the honor of waiting on table. Well, I'll do it just this once more for Mother's sake, or she'd have to, but it'll be the last time. (*She*

turns her back on him and goes to the door at right.)
You'll be pleased to learn your daughter had almost to
beg on her knees to Neilan before he'd let us have another month's credit. He made it plain it was to Mother
he gave it because he pities her for the husband she's
got. But what do you care about that, as long as you and
your fine thoroughbred mare can live in style! (MELODY
*is shaken for a second. He glances toward the bar
as if he longed to return there to escape her. Then he
gets hold of himself. His face becomes expressionless. He
sits in the same chair and picks up the paper, ignoring
her. She starts to go out just as her mother appears in
the doorway.* NORA *is carrying a glass of milk.*)

NORA: Here's the milk the doctor ordered for the young
gentleman. It's time for it, and I knew you'd be going
upstairs.

SARA (*Takes the milk.*): Thank you, Mother. (*She nods
scornfully toward her father.*) I've just been telling him I
begged another month's credit from Neilan, so he needn't
worry.

NORA: Ah, thank God for that. Neilan's a kind man.

MELODY (*Explodes.*): Damn his kindness! By the Eternal,
if he'd refused, I'd have—! (*He controls himself, meeting* SARA'S *contemptuous eyes. He goes on quietly, a bitter, sneering antagonism underneath.*) Don't let me detain you, my dear. Take his milk to our Yankee guest,
as your mother suggests. Don't miss any chance to play
the ministering angel. (*Vindictively.*) Faith, the poor
young devil hasn't a chance to escape with you two
scheming peasants laying snares to trap him!

SARA: That's a lie! And leave Mother out of your insults!

MELODY: And if all other tricks fail, there's always one last
trick to get him through his honor!

SARA (*Tensely.*): What trick do you mean? (*NORA grabs
her arm.*)

NORA: Hould your prate, now! Why can't you leave him be? It's your fault, for provoking him.

SARA (*Quietly.*): All right, Mother. I'll leave him to look in the mirror, like he loves to, and remember what he said, and be proud of himself. (MELODY *winces.* SARA *goes out right.*)

MELODY (*After a pause—shakenly.*): I— She mistook my meaning— It's as you said. She goads me into losing my temper, and I say things—

NORA (*Sadly.*): I know what made you say it. You think maybe she's like I was, and you can't help remembering my sin with you.

MELODY (*Guiltily vehement.*): No! No! I tell you she mistook my meaning, and now you— (*Then exasperatedly.*) Damn your priests' prating about your sin! (*With a strange, scornful vanity.*) To hear you tell it, you'd think it was you who seduced me! That's likely, isn't it? —remembering the man I was then!

NORA: I remember well. Sure, you was that handsome, no woman could resist you. And you are still.

MELODY (*Pleased.*): None of your blarney, Nora. (*With Byronic gloom.*) I am but a ghost haunting a ruin. (*Then gallantly but without looking at her.*) And how about you in those days? Weren't you the prettiest girl in all Ireland? (*Scornfully.*) And be damned to your lying, pious shame! You had no shame then, I remember. It was love and joy and glory in you and you were proud!

NORA (*Her eyes shining.*): I'm still proud and will be to the day I die!

MELODY (*Gives her an approving look which turns to distaste at her appearance—looks away irritably.*): Why do you bring up the past? I do not wish to discuss it.

NORA (*After a pause—timidly.*): All the same, you shouldn't talk to Sara as if you thought she'd be up to anything to catch young Harford.

MELODY: I did not think that! She is my daughter—

NORA: She is surely. And he's a dacent lad. (*She smiles a bit scornfully.*) Sure, from all she's told me, he's that shy he's never dared even to kiss her hand!

MELODY (*With more than a little contempt.*): I can well believe it. When it comes to making love the Yankees are clumsy, fish-blooded louts. They lack savoir-faire. They have no romantic fire! They know nothing of women. (*He snorts disdainfully.*) By the Eternal, when I was his age— (*Then quickly.*) Not that I don't approve of young Harford, mind you. He is a gentleman. When he asks me for Sara's hand I will gladly give my consent, provided his father and I can agree on the amount of her settlement.

NORA (*Hastily.*): Ah, there's no need to think of that yet. (*Then lapsing into her own dream.*) Yes, she'll be happy because she loves him dearly, a lot more than she admits. And it'll give her a chance to rise in the world. We'll see the day when she'll live in a grand mansion, dressed in silks and satins, and riding in a carriage with coachman and footman.

MELODY: I desire that as much as you do, Nora. I'm done— finished—no future but the past. But my daughter has the looks, the brains—ambition, youth— She can go far. (*Then sneeringly.*) That is, if she can remember she's a gentlewoman and stop acting like a bogtrotting peasant wench! (*He hears* SARA *returning downstairs.*) She's coming back. (*He gets up—bitterly.*) As the sight of me seems to irritate her, I'll go in the bar a while. I've had my fill of her insults for one morning. (*He opens the bar door. There is a chorus of eager, thirsty welcome from inside. He goes in, closing the door.* SARA *enters from*

*right. Her face is flushed and her eyes full of dreamy hap-
piness.*)

NORA (*Rebukingly.*): Himself went in the bar to be out of
reach of your tongue. A fine thing! Aren't you ashamed
you haven't enough feeling not to torment him, when
you know it's the anniversary—

SARA: All right, Mother. Let him take what joy he can out
of the day. I'll even help you get his uniform out of the
trunk in the attic and brush and clean it for you.

NORA: Ah, God bless you, that's the way— (*Then, astonished at this unexpected docility.*) Glory be, but you've
changed all of a sudden. What's happened to you?

SARA: I'm so happy now—I can't feel bitter against anyone.
(*She hesitates—then shyly.*) Simon kissed me. (*Having
said this, she goes on triumphantly.*) He got his courage
up at last, but it was me made him. I was freshening up
his pillows and leaning over him, and he couldn't help
it, if he was human. (*She laughs tenderly.*) And then
you'd have laughed to see him. He near sank through
the bed with shame at his boldness. He began apologizing
as if he was afraid I'd be so insulted I'd never speak to
him again.

NORA (*Teasingly.*): And what did you do? I'll wager you
wasn't as brazen as you pretend.

SARA (*Ruefully.*): It's true, Mother. He made me as bashful as he was. I felt a great fool.

NORA: And was that all? Sure, kissing is easy. Didn't he
ask you if you'd marry—?

SARA: No. (*Quickly.*) But it was my fault he didn't. He
was trying to be brave enough. All he needed was a
word of encouragement. But I stood there, dumb as a
calf, and when I did speak it was to say I had to come
and help you, and the end was I ran from the room,
blushing as red as a beet— (*She comes to her mother.*
NORA *puts her arms around her.* SARA *hides her face on*

her shoulder, on the verge of tears.) Oh, Mother, ain't it crazy to be such a fool?

NORA: Well, when you're in love—

SARA (*Breaking away from her—angrily.*): That's just it! I'm too much in love and I don't want to be! I won't let my heart rule my head and make a slave of me! (*Suddenly she smiles confidently.*) Ah well, he loves me as much, and more, I know that, and the next time I'll keep my wits. (*She laughs happily.*) You can consider it as good as done, Mother. I'm Mrs. Simon Harford, at your pleasure. (*She makes a sweeping bow.*)

NORA (*Smiling.*): Arrah, none of your airs and graces with me! Help me, now, like you promised, and we'll get your father's uniform out of the trunk. It won't break your back in the attic, like it does me.

SARA (*Gaily puts her arm around her mother's waist.*): Come along then.

NORA (*As they go out right.*): I disremember which trunk —and you'll have to help me find the key.

(*There is a pause. Then the bar door is opened and* MELODY *enters again in the same manner as he did at the beginning of the act. There is the same sound of voices from the bar but this time* MELODY *gives no parting orders but simply shuts the door behind him. He scowls with disgust.*)

MELODY: Cursed ignorant cattle. (*Then with a real, lonely yearning.*) I wish Jamie Cregan would come. (*Bitterly.*) Driven from pillar to post in my own home! Everywhere ignorance—or the scorn of my own daughter! (*Then defiantly.*) But by the Eternal God, no power on earth, nor in hell itself, can break me! (*His eyes are drawn irresistibly to the mirror. He moves in front of it, seeking the satisfying reassurance of his reflection there. What follows is an exact repetition of his scene before the mirror in Act One. There is the same squaring of his shoul-*

ders, arrogant lifting of his head, and then the favorite
quote from Byron, recited aloud to his own image.)

> "I have not loved the World, nor the World me;
> I have not flattered its rank breath, nor bowed
> To its idolatries a patient knee,
> Nor coined my cheek to smiles,—nor cried aloud
> In the worship of an echo: in the crowd
> They could not deem me one of such—I stood
> Among them, but not of them . . ."

(He stands staring in the mirror and does not hear
the latch of the street door click. The door opens and
DEBORAH (Mrs. Henry Harford), SIMON'S mother, enters, closing the door quietly behind her. MELODY continues to be too absorbed to notice anything. For a
moment, blinded by the sudden change from the
bright glare of the street, she does not see him. When
she does, she stares incredulously. Then she smiles
with an amused and mocking relish.)

(DEBORAH is forty-one, but looks to be no more than
thirty. She is small, a little over five feet tall, with a
fragile, youthful figure. One would never suspect that
she is the middle-aged mother of two grown sons. Her
face is beautiful—that is, it is beautiful from the standpoint of the artist with an eye for bone structure and
unusual character. It is small, with high cheekbones,
wedge-shaped, narrowing from a broad forehead to a
square chin, framed by thick, wavy, red-brown hair.
The nose is delicate and thin, a trifle aquiline. The
mouth, with full lips and even, white teeth, is too
large for her face. So are the long-lashed, green-flecked
brown eyes, under heavy, angular brows. These would
appear large in any face, but in hers they seem enormous and are made more startling by the pallor of her
complexion. She has tiny, high-arched feet and thin,

tapering hands. Her slender, fragile body is dressed in white with calculated simplicity. About her whole personality is a curious atmosphere of deliberate detachment, the studied aloofness of an ironically amused spectator. Something perversely assertive about it too, as if she consciously carried her originality to the point of whimsical eccentricity.)

DEBORAH: I beg your pardon. (MELODY *jumps and whirls around. For a moment his face has an absurdly startled, stupid look. He is shamed and humiliated and furious at being caught for the second time in one morning before the mirror. His revenge is to draw himself up haughtily and survey her insolently from head to toe. But at once, seeing she is attractive and a lady, his manner changes. Opportunity beckons and he is confident of himself, put upon his mettle. He bows, a gracious, gallant gentleman. There is seductive charm in his welcoming smile and in his voice.)*

MELODY: Good morning, Mademoiselle. It is an honor to welcome you to this unworthy inn. (*He draws out a chair at rear of the larger table in the foreground—bowing again.*) If I may presume. You will find it comfortable here, away from the glare of the street.

DEBORAH (*Regards him for a second puzzledly. She is impressed in spite of herself by his bearing and distinguished, handsome face.*): Thank you. (*She comes forward.* MELODY *makes a gallant show of holding her chair and helping her be seated. He takes in all her points with sensual appreciation. It is the same sort of pleasure a lover of horseflesh would have in the appearance of a thoroughbred horse. Meanwhile he speaks with caressing courtesy.*)

MELODY: Mademoiselle— (*He sees her wedding ring.*) Pray forgive me, I see it is Madame— Permit me to say again, how great an honor I will esteem it to be of any service.

(*He manages, as he turns away, as if by accident to brush his hand against her shoulder. She is startled and caught off guard. She shrinks and looks up at him. Their eyes meet and at the nakedly physical appraisement she sees in his, a fascinated fear suddenly seizes her. But at once she is reassured as he shifts his gaze, satisfied by her re-actions to his first attack, and hastens to apologize.*) I beg your pardon, Madame. I am afraid my manners have grown clumsy with disuse. It is not often a lady comes here now. This inn, like myself, has fallen upon unlucky days.

DEBORAH (*Curtly ignoring this.*) : I presume you are the inn-keeper, Melody?

MELODY (*A flash of anger in his eyes—arrogantly.*) : I am *Major* Cornelius Melody, one time of His Majesty's Seventh Dragoons, at your service. (*He bows with chill formality.*)

DEBORAH (*Is now an amused spectator again—apologeti-cally.*) : Oh. Then it is I who owe you an apology, Major Melody.

MELODY (*Encouraged—gallantly.*) : No, no, dear lady, the fault is mine. I should not have taken offense. (*With the air of one frankly admitting a praiseworthy weakness.*) Faith, I may as well confess my besetting weakness is that of all gentlemen who have known better days. I have a pride unduly sensitive to any fancied slight.

DEBORAH (*Playing up to him now.*) : I assure you, sir, there was no intention on my part to slight you.

MELODY (*His eyes again catch hers and hold them—his tone insinuatingly caressing.*) : You are as gracious as you are beautiful, Madame. (DEBORAH's *amusement is gone. She is again confused and, in spite of herself, frightened and fascinated.* MELODY *proceeds with his attack, full of con-fidence now, the successful seducer of old. His voice takes on a calculated melancholy cadence. He becomes a*

*romantic, tragic figure, appealing for a woman's under-
standing and loving compassion.*) I am a poor fool,
Madame. I would be both wiser and happier if I could
reconcile myself to being the proprietor of a tawdry
tavern, if I could abjure pride and forget the past. Today of all days it is hard to forget, for it is the anniversary of the battle of Talavera. The most memorable
day of my life, Madame. It was on that glorious field I
had the honor to be commended for my bravery by the
great Duke of Wellington, himself—Sir Arthur Wellesley, then. So I am sure you can find it in your heart to
forgive— (*His tone more caressing.*) One so beautiful
must understand the hearts of men full well, since so
many must have given their hearts to you. (*A coarse passion comes into his voice.*) Yes, I'll wager my all against
a penny that even among the fish-blooded Yankees
there's not a man whose heart doesn't catch flame from
your beauty! (*He puts his hand over one of her hands
on the table and stares into her eyes ardently.*) As mine
does now!

DEBORAH (*Feeling herself borne down weakly by the sheer
force of his physical strength, struggles to release her
hand. She stammers, with an attempt at lightness.*): Is
this—what the Irish call blarney, sir?

MELODY (*With a fierce, lustful sincerity.*): No! I take my
oath by the living God, I would charge a square of Napoleon's Old Guard singlehanded for one kiss of your
lips. (*He bends lower, while his eyes hold hers. For a
second it seems he will kiss her and she cannot help herself. Then abruptly the smell of whiskey on his breath
brings her to herself, shaken with disgust and coldly
angry. She snatches her hand from his and speaks with
withering contempt.*)

DEBORAH: Pah! You reek of whiskey! You are drunk, sir!
You are insolent and disgusting! I do not wonder your

inn enjoys such meager patronage, if you regale all your guests of my sex with this absurd performance! (MELODY *straightens up with a jerk, taking a step back as though he had been slapped in the face.* DEBORAH *rises to her feet, ignoring him disdainfully. At this moment* SARA *and her mother enter through the doorway at right. They take in the scene at a glance.* MELODY *and* DEBORAH *do not notice their entrance.*

NORA (*Half under her breath.*): Oh, God help us!

SARA (*Guesses at once this must be the woman* MICKEY *had told her about. She hurries toward them quickly, trying to hide her apprehension and anger and shame at what she knows must have happened.*): What is it, Father? What does the lady wish? (*Her arrival is a further blow for* MELODY, *seething now in a fury of humiliated pride.* DEBORAH *turns to face* SARA.)

DEBORAH (*Coolly self-possessed—pleasantly.*): I came here to see you, Miss Melody, hoping you might know the present whereabouts of my son, Simon. (*This is a bombshell for* MELODY.)

MELODY (*Blurts out with no apology in his tone but angrily, as if she had intentionally made a fool of him.*): You're his mother? In God's name, Madame, why didn't you say so!

DEBORAH (*Ignoring him—to* SARA.): I've been out to his hermit's cabin, only to find the hermit flown.

SARA (*Stammers.*): He's here, Mrs. Harford—upstairs in bed. He's been sick—

DEBORAH: Sick? You don't mean seriously?

SARA (*Recovering a little from her confusion.*): Oh, he's over it now, or almost. It was only a spell of chills and fever he caught from the damp of the lake. I found him there shivering and shaking and made him come here where there's a doctor handy and someone to nurse him.

DEBORAH (*Pleasantly.*): The someone being you, Miss Melody?

SARA: Yes, me and—my mother and I.

DEBORAH (*Graciously.*): I am deeply grateful to you and your mother for your kindness.

NORA (*Who has remained in the background, now comes forward—with her sweet, friendly smile.*): Och, don't be thankin' us, ma'am. Sure, your son is a gentle, fine lad, and we all have great fondness for him. He'd be welcome here if he never paid a penny— (*She stops embarrassedly, catching a disapproving glance from* SARA. DEBORAH *is repelled by* NORA's *slovenly appearance, but she feels her simple charm and gentleness, and returns her smile.*)

SARA (*With embarrassed stiffness.*): This is my mother, Mrs. Harford. (DEBORAH *inclines her head graciously.* NORA *instinctively bobs in a peasant's curtsy to one of the gentry.* MELODY, *snubbed and seething, glares at her.*)

NORA: I'm pleased to make your acquaintance, ma'am.

MELODY: Nora! For the love of God, stop— (*Suddenly he is able to become the polished gentleman again—considerately and even a trifle condescendingly.*) I am sure Mrs. Harford is waiting to be taken to her son. Am I not right, Madame? (DEBORAH *is so taken aback by his effrontery that for a moment she is speechless. She replies coldly, obviously doing so only because she does not wish to create further embarrassment.*)

DEBORAH: That is true, sir. (*She turns her back on him.*) If you will be so kind, Miss Melody. I've wasted so much of the morning and I have to return to the city. I have only time for a short visit—

SARA: Just come with me, Mrs. Harford. (*She goes to the door at right, and steps aside to let* DEBORAH *precede her.*) What a pleasant surprise this will be for Simon. He'd have written you he was sick, but he didn't want to worry you. (*She follows* DEBORAH *into the hall.*)

MELODY: Damned fool of a woman! If I'd known— No, be damned if I regret! Cursed Yankee upstart! (*With a sneer.*) But she didn't fool me with her insulted airs! I've known too many women— (*In a rage.*) "Absurd performance," was it? God damn her!

NORA (*Timidly.*): Don't be cursing her and tormenting yourself. She seems a kind lady. She won't hold it against you, when she stops to think, knowing you didn't know who she is.

MELODY (*Tensely.*): Be quiet!

NORA: Forget it now, do, for Sara's sake. Sure, you wouldn't want anything to come between her and the lad. (*He is silent. She goes on comfortingly.*) Go on up to your room now and you'll find something to take your mind off. Sara and I have your uniform brushed and laid out on the bed.

MELODY (*Harshly.*): Put it back in the trunk! I don't want it to remind me— (*With humiliated rage again.*) By the Eternal, I'll wager she believed what I told her of Talavera and the Great Duke honoring me was a drunken liar's boast!

NORA: No, she'd never, Con. She couldn't.

MELODY (*Seized by an idea.*): Well, seeing would be believing, eh, my fine lady? Yes, by God, that will prove to her— (*He turns to* NORA, *his self-confidence partly restored.*) Thank you for reminding me of my duty to Sara. You are right. I do owe it to her interests to forget my anger and make a formal apology to Simon's mother for our little misunderstanding. (*He smiles condescendingly.*) Faith, as a gentleman, I should grant it is a pretty woman's privilege to be always right even when she is wrong. (*He goes to the door at extreme left front and opens it.*) If the lady should come back, kindly keep her here on some excuse until I return. (*This is a command. He disappears, closing the door behind him.*)

NORA (*Sighs.*): Ah well, it's all right. He'll be on his best behavior now, and he'll feel proud again in his uniform. (*She sits at the end of center table right and relaxes wearily. A moment later* SARA *enters quickly from right and comes to her.*)

SARA: Where's Father?

NORA: I got him to go up and put on his uniform. It'll console him.

SARA (*Bitterly.*): Console *him*? It's me ought to be consoled for having such a great fool for a father!

NORA: Hush now! How could he know who—?

SARA (*With a sudden reversal of feeling—almost vindictively.*): Yes, it serves her right. I suppose she thinks she's such a great lady anyone in America would pay her respect. Well, she knows better now. And she didn't act as insulted as she might. Maybe she liked it, for all her pretenses. (*Again with an abrupt reversal of feeling.*) Ah, how can I talk such craziness! Him and his drunken love-making! Well, he got put in his place, and aren't I glad! He won't forget in a hurry how she snubbed him, as if he was no better than dirt under her feet!

NORA: She didn't. She had the sense to see he'd been drinking and not to mind him.

SARA (*Dully.*): Maybe. But isn't that bad enough? What woman would want her son to marry the daughter of a man like— (*She breaks down.*) Oh, Mother, I was feeling so happy and sure of Simon, and now— Why did she have to come today? If she'd waited till tomorrow, even, I'd have got him to ask me to marry him, and once he'd done that no power on earth could change him.

NORA: If he loves you no power can change him, anyway. (*Proudly.*) Don't I know! (*Reassuringly.*) She's his mother, and she loves him and she'll want him to be happy, and she'll see he loves you. What makes you think she'll try to change him?

SARA: Because she hates me, Mother—for one reason.

NORA: She doesn't. She couldn't.

SARA: She does. Oh, she acted as nice as nice, but she didn't fool me. She's the kind would be polite to the hangman, and her on the scaffold. (*She lowers her voice.*) It isn't just to pay Simon a visit she came. It's because Simon's father got a letter telling him about us, and he showed it to her.

NORA: Who did a dirty trick like that?

SARA: It wasn't signed, she said. I suppose someone around here that hates Father—and who doesn't?

NORA: Bad luck to the blackguard, whoever it was!

SARA: She said she'd come to warn Simon his father is wild with anger and he's gone to see his lawyer— But that doesn't worry me. It's only her influence I'm afraid of.

NORA: How do you know about the letter?

SARA (*Avoiding her eyes.*): I sneaked back to listen outside the door.

NORA: Shame on you! You should have more pride!

SARA: I was ashamed, Mother, after a moment or two, and I came away. (*Then defiantly.*) No, I'm not ashamed. I wanted to learn what tricks she might be up to, so I'll be able to fight them. I'm not ashamed at all. I'll do anything to keep him. (*Lowering her voice.*) She started talking the second she got in the door. She had only a few minutes because she has to be home before dinner so her husband won't suspect she came here. He's forbidden her to see Simon ever since Simon came out here to live.

NORA: Well, doesn't her coming against her husband's orders show she's on Simon's side?

SARA: Yes, but it doesn't show she wants him to marry me. (*Impatiently.*) Don't be so simple, Mother. Wouldn't she

tell Simon that anyway, even if the truth was her husband sent her to do all she could to get him away from
me?

NORA: Don't look for trouble before it comes. Wait and see,
now. Maybe you'll find—

SARA: I'll find what I said, Mother—that she hates me.
(*Bitterly.*) Even if she came here with good intentions,
she wouldn't have them now, after our great gentleman
has insulted her. Thank God, if he's putting on his uniform, he'll be hours before the mirror, and she'll be gone
before he can make a fool of himself again. (NORA *starts
to tell her the truth—then thinks better of it.* SARA *goes
on, changing her tone.*) But I'd like her to see him in his
uniform, at that, if he was sober. She'd find she couldn't
look down on him— (*Exasperatedly.*) Och! I'm as crazy
as he is. As if she hadn't the brains to see through him.

NORA (*Wearily.*): Leave him be, for the love of God.

SARA (*After a pause—defiantly.*): Let her try whatever
game she likes. I have brains too, she'll discover. (*Then
uneasily.*) Only, like Simon's told me, I feel she's strange
and queer behind her lady's airs, and it'll be hard to tell
what she's really up to. (*They both hear a sound from
upstairs.*) That's her, now. She didn't waste much time.
Well, I'm ready for her. Go in the kitchen, will you,
Mother? I want to give her the chance to have it out
with me alone. (NORA *gets up—then, remembering* MEL-
ODY'*s orders, glances toward the door at left front uneasily and hesitates.* SARA *says urgently.*) Don't you hear
me? Hurry, Mother! (NORA *sighs and goes out quickly,
right.* SARA *sits at rear of the center table and waits, drawing herself up in an unconscious imitation of her father's
grand manner.* DEBORAH *appears in the doorway at right.
There is nothing in her expression to betray any emotion
resulting from her interview with her son. She smiles
pleasantly at* SARA, *who rises graciously from her chair.*)

DEBORAH (*Coming to her.*): I am glad to find you here, Miss Melody. It gives me another opportunity to express my gratitude for your kindness to my son during his illness.

SARA: Thank you, Mrs. Harford. My mother and I have been only too happy to do all we could. (*She adds defiantly.*) We are very fond of Simon.

DEBORAH (*A glint of secret amusement in her eyes.*): Yes, I feel you are. And he has told me how fond he is of you. (*Her manner becomes reflective. She speaks rapidly in a remote, detached way, lowering her voice unconsciously as if she were thinking aloud to herself.*) This is the first time I have seen Simon since he left home to seek self-emancipation at the breast of Nature. I find him not so greatly changed as I had been led to expect from his letters. Of course, it is some time since he has written. I had thought his implacably honest discovery that the poetry he hoped the pure freedom of Nature would inspire him to write is, after all, but a crude imitation of Lord Byron's would have more bitterly depressed his spirit. (*She smiles.*) But evidently he has found a new romantic dream by way of recompense. As I might have known he would. Simon is an inveterate dreamer—a weakness he inherited from me, I'm afraid, although I must admit the Harfords have been great dreamers, too, in their way. Even my husband has a dream—a conservative, material dream, naturally. I have just been reminding Simon that his father is rigidly unforgiving when his dream is flouted, and very practical in his methods of defending it. (*She smiles again.*) My warning was the mechanical gesture of a mother's duty, merely. I realized it would have no effect. He did not listen to what I said. For that matter, neither did I. (*She laughs a little detached laugh, as if she were secretly amused.*)

SARA (*Stares at her, unable to decide what is behind all this and how she should react—with an undercurrent of resentment.*): I don't think Simon imitates Lord Byron. I hate Lord Byron's poetry. And I know there's a true poet in Simon.

DEBORAH (*Vaguely surprised—speaks rapidly again.*): Oh, in feeling, of course. It is natural you should admire that in him—now. But I warn you it is a quality difficult for a woman to keep on admiring in a Harford, judging from what I know of the family history. Simon's great-grandfather, Jonathan Harford, had it. He was killed at Bunker Hill, but I suspect the War for Independence was merely a symbolic opportunity for him. His was a personal war, I am sure—for pure freedom. Simon's grandfather, Evan Harford, had the quality too. A fanatic in the cause of pure freedom, he became scornful of our Revolution. It made too many compromises with the ideal to free him. He went to France and became a rabid Jacobin, a worshiper of Robespierre. He would have liked to have gone to the guillotine with his incorruptible Redeemer, but he was too unimportant. They simply forgot to kill him. He came home and lived in a little temple of Liberty he had built in a corner of what is now my garden. It is still there. I remember him well. A dry, gentle, cruel, indomitable, futile old idealist who used frequently to wear his old uniform of the French Republican National Guard. He died wearing it. But the point is, you can have no idea what revengeful hate the Harford pursuit of freedom imposed upon the women who shared their lives. The three daughters-in-law of Jonathan, Evan's half-sisters, had to make a large, greedy fortune out of privateering and the Northwest trade, and finally were even driven to embrace the profits of the slave trade—as a triumphant climax, you understand, of their long battle to escape the enslavement of freedom by

enslaving it. Evan's wife, of course, was drawn into this
conflict, and became their tool and accomplice. They
even attempted to own me, but I managed to escape because there was so little of me in the flesh that aged,
greedy fingers could clutch. I am sorry they are dead
and cannot know you. They would approve of you, I
think. They would see that you are strong and ambitious
and determined to take what you want. They would
have smiled like senile, hungry serpents and welcomed
you into their coils. (*She laughs.*) Evil old witches! De-
testable, but I could not help admiring them—pitying
them, too—in the end. We had a bond in common. They
idolized Napoleon. They used to say he was the only
man they would ever have married. And I used to dream
I was Josephine—even after my marriage, I'm afraid.
The Sisters, as everyone called them, and all of the family accompanied my husband and me on our honeymoon
—to Paris to witness the Emperor's coronation. (*She
pauses, smiling at her memories.*)

SARA (*Against her will, has become a bit hypnotized by
DEBORAH's rapid, low, musical flow of words, as she strains
to grasp the implication for her. She speaks in a low, confidential tone herself, smiling naturally.*) : I've always ad-
mired him too. It's one of the things I've held against my
father, that he fought against him and not for him.

DEBORAH (*Starts, as if awakening—with a pleasant smile.*) :
Well, Miss Melody, this is tiresome of me to stand here
giving you a discourse on Harford family history. I
don't know what you must think of me—but doubtless
Simon has told you I am a bit eccentric at times. (*She
glances at* SARA's *face—amusedly.*) Ah, I can see he has.
Then I am sure you will make allowances. I really do
not know what inspired me—except perhaps, that I wish
to be fair and warn you, too.

SARA (*Stiffens.*) : Warn me about what, Mrs. Harford?

DEBORAH: Why, that the Harfords never part with their dreams even when they deny them. They cannot. That is the family curse. For example, this book Simon plans to write to denounce the evil of greed and possessive ambition, and uphold the virtue of freeing oneself from the lust for power and saving our souls by being content with little. I cannot imagine you taking that seriously. (*She again flashes a glance at* SARA.) I see you do not. Neither do I. I do not even believe Simon will ever write this book on paper. But I warn you it is already written on his conscience and— (*She stops with a little disdaining laugh.*) I begin to resemble Cassandra with all my warnings. And I continue to stand here boring you with words. (*She holds out her hand graciously.*) Goodbye, Miss Melody.

SARA (*Takes her hand mechanically.*): Goodbye, Mrs. Harford. (DEBORAH *starts for the door at rear.* SARA *follows her, her expression confused, suspicious, and at the same time hopeful. Suddenly she blurts out impulsively.*) Mrs. Harford, I—

DEBORAH (*Turns on her, pleasantly.*): Yes, Miss Melody? (*But her eyes have become blank and expressionless and discourage any attempt at further contact.*)

SARA (*Silenced—with stiff politeness.*): Isn't there some sort of cooling drink I could get you before you go? You must be parched after walking from the road to Simon's cabin and back on this hot day.

DEBORAH: Nothing, thank you. (*Then talking rapidly again in her strange detached way.*) Yes, I did find my walk alone in the woods a strangely overpowering experience. Frightening—but intoxicating, too. Such a wild feeling of release and fresh enslavement. I have not ventured from my garden in many years. There, Nature is tamed, constrained to obey and adorn. I had forgotten how compelling the brutal power of primitive, possessive Nature can be—when suddenly one is attacked by it. (*She smiles.*) It has been a most confusing morning for a tired, middle-aged matron, but I flatter myself I have preserved a philosophic poise, or should I say, pose, as well as may be. Nevertheless, it will be a relief to return to my garden and books and meditations and listen indifferently again while the footsteps of life pass and recede along the street beyond the high wall. I shall never venture forth again to do my duty. It is a noble occupation, no doubt, for those who can presume they know what their duty to others is; but I— (*She laughs.*) Mercy, here I am chattering on again. (*She turns to the door.*) Cato will be provoked at me for keeping him waiting. I've already caused his beloved horses to be half-devoured by flies. Cato is our black coachman. He also is fond of Simon, although since Simon became emancipated he has embarrassed Cato acutely by shaking his hand whenever they meet. Cato was always a self-possessed free man even when he was a slave. It astonishes him that Simon has to prove that he—I mean Simon—is free. (*She smiles.*) Goodbye again, Miss Melody. This time I really am going. (SARA *opens the door for her. She walks past* SARA *into the street, turns left, and, passing before the two windows, disappears.* SARA *closes the door and comes back slowly to the head of the table at center. She stands thinking, her expression puzzled, apprehensive, and resentful.* NORA *appears in the doorway at right.*)

NORA: God forgive you, Sara, why did you let her go? Your father told me—

SARA: I can't make her out, Mother. You'd think she didn't care, but she does care. And she hates me. I could feel it. But you can't tell— She's crazy, I think. She talked on and on as if she couldn't stop—queer blather about Simon's ancestors, and herself, and Napoleon, and Nature, and her garden and freedom, and God knows what

—but letting me know all the time she had a meaning behind it, and was warning and threatening me. Oh, she may be daft in some ways, but she's no fool. I know she didn't let Simon guess she'd rather have him dead than married to me. Oh, no, I'm sure she told him if he was sure he loved me and I meant his happiness— But then she'd say he ought to wait and prove he's sure—anything to give her time. She'd make him promise to wait. Yes, I'll wager that's what she's done!

NORA (*Who has been watching the door at left front, preoccupied by her own worry—frightenedly*.): Your father'll be down any second. I'm going out in the garden. (*She grabs* SARA's *arm*.) Come along with me, and give him time to get over his rage.

SARA (*Shakes off her hand—exasperatedly*.): Leave me be, Mother. I've enough to worry me without bothering about him. I've got to plan the best way to act when I see Simon. I've got to be as big a liar as she was. I'll have to pretend I liked her and I'd respect whatever advice she gave him. I mustn't let him see— But I won't go to him again today, Mother. You can take up his meals and his milk, if you will. Tell him I'm too busy. I want to get him anxious and afraid maybe I'm mad at him for something, that maybe his mother said something. If he once has the idea maybe he's lost me—that ought to help, don't you think, Mother?

NORA (*Sees the door at left front begin to open—in a whisper*.): Oh, God help me! (*She turns in panicky flight and disappears through the doorway, right*.)

(*The door at left front slowly opens—slowly because* MELODY, *hearing voices in the room and hoping* DEBORAH *is there, is deliberately making a dramatic entrance. And in spite of its obviousness, it is effective. Wearing the brilliant scarlet full-dress uniform of a major in one of Wellington's dragoon regiments, he*

*looks extraordinarily handsome and distinguished—
a startling, colorful, romantic figure, possessing now
a genuine quality he has not had before, the quality
of the formidably strong, disdainfully fearless cavalry
officer he really had been. The uniform has been preserved with the greatest care. Each button is shining
and the cloth is spotless. Being in it has notably restored his self-confident arrogance. Also, he has done
everything he can to freshen up his face and hide any
effect of his morning's drinks. When he discovers
*DEBORAH *is not in the room, he is mildly disappointed
and, as always when he first confronts *SARA *alone, he
seems to shrink back guiltily within himself. *SARA*'s
face hardens and she gives no sign of knowing he is
there. He comes slowly around the table at left front,
until he stands at the end of the center table facing her.
She still refuses to notice him and he is forced to speak.
He does so with the air of one who condescends to be
amused by his own foibles.*

MELODY: I happened to go to my room and found you and
your mother had laid out my uniform so invitingly that
I could not resist the temptation to put it on at once instead of waiting until evening.

SARA (*Turns on him. In spite of herself she is so struck by
his appearance that the contempt is forced back and she
can only stammer a bit foolishly.*): Yes, I—I see you did.
(*There is a moment's pause. She stares at him fascinatedly
—then blurts out with impulsive admiration.*) You look
grand and handsome, Father.

MELODY (*As pleased as a child.*): Why, it is most kind of
you to say that, my dear Sara. (*Preening himself.*) I flatter myself I do not look too unworthy of the man I
was when I wore this uniform with honor.

SARA (*An appeal forced out of her that is both pleading and
a bitter reproach.*): Oh, Father, why can't you ever be

the thing you can seem to be? (*A sad scorn comes into her voice.*) The man you were. I'm sorry I never knew that soldier. I think he was the only man who wasn't just a dream.

MELODY (*His face becomes a blank disguise—coldly.*): I don't understand you. (*A pause. He begins to talk in an arrogantly amused tone.*) I suspect you are still holding against me my unfortunate blunder with your future mother-in-law. I would not blame you if you did. (*He smiles.*) Faith, I did put my foot in it. (*He chuckles.*) The devil of it is, I can never get used to these Yankee ladies. I do them the honor of complimenting them with a bit of harmless flattery and, lo and behold, suddenly my lady acts as if I had insulted her. It must be their damned narrow Puritan background. They can't help seeing sin hiding under every bush, but this one need not have been alarmed. I never had an eye for skinny, pale snips of women— (*Hastily.*) But what I want to tell you is I am sorry it happened, Sara, and I will do my best, for the sake of your interests, to make honorable amends. I shall do the lady the honor of tendering her my humble apologies when she comes downstairs. (*With arrogant vanity.*) I flatter myself she will be graciously pleased to make peace. She was not as outraged by half as her conscience made her pretend, if I am any judge of feminine frailty.

SARA (*Who has been staring at him with scorn until he says this last—impulsively, with a sneer of agreement.*): I'll wager she wasn't for all her airs. (*Then furious at herself and him.*) Ah, will you stop telling me your mad dreams! (*Controlling herself—coldly.*) You'll have no chance to make bad worse by trying to fascinate her with your beautiful uniform. She's gone.

MELODY (*Stunned.*): Gone? (*Furiously.*) You're lying, damn you!

SARA: I'm not. She left ten minutes ago, or more.

MELODY (*Before he thinks.*): But I told your mother to keep her here until— (*He stops abruptly.*)

SARA: So that's why Mother is so frightened. Well, it was me let her go, so don't take out your rage on poor Mother.

MELODY: Rage? My dear Sara, all I feel is relief. Surely you can't believe I could have looked forward to humbling my pride, even though it would have furthered your interests.

SARA: Furthered my interests by giving her another reason to laugh up her sleeve at your pretenses? (*With angry scorn, lapsing into broad brogue.*) Arrah, God pity you! (*She turns her back on him and goes off, right.* MELODY *stands gripping the back of the chair at the foot of the table in his big, powerful hands in an effort to control himself. There is a crack as the chair back snaps in half. He stares at the fragments in his hands with stupid surprise. The door to the bar is shoved open and* MICKEY *calls in.*)

MALOY: Here's Cregan back to see you, Major.

MELODY (*Startled, repeats stupidly.*): Cregan? (*Then his face suddenly lights up with pathetic eagerness and his voice is full of welcoming warmth as he calls.*) Jamie! My old comrade in arms! (*As* CREGAN *enters, he grips his hand.*) By the Powers, I'm glad you're here, Jamie. (CREGAN *is surprised and pleased by the warmth of his welcome.* MELODY *draws him into the room.*) Come: Sit down. You'll join me in a drink, I know. (*He gets* CREGAN *a glass from the cupboard. The decanter and* MELODY's *glass are already on the table.*)

CREGAN (*Admiringly.*): Be God, it's the old uniform, no less, and you look as fine a figure in it as ever you did in Spain. (*He sits at right of table at left front as* MELODY *sits at rear.*)

MELODY (*Immensely pleased—deprecatingly*.): Hardly, Jamie—but not a total ruin yet, I hope. I put it on in honor of the day. I see you've forgotten. For shame, you dog, not to remember Talavera.

CREGAN (*Excitedly*.): Talavera, is it? Where I got my saber cut. Be the mortal, I remember it, and you've a right to celebrate. You was worth any ten men in the army that day! (MELODY *has shoved the decanter toward him. He pours a drink*.)

MELODY (*This compliment completely restores him to his arrogant self*.): Yes, I think I may say I did acquit myself with honor. (*Patronizingly*.) So, for that matter, did you. (*He pours a drink and raises his glass*.) To the day and your good health, Corporal Cregan.

CREGAN (*Enthusiastically*.): To the day and yourself, God bless you, Con! (*He tries to touch brims with* MELODY's *glass, but* MELODY *holds his glass away and draws himself up haughtily*.)

MELODY (*With cold rebuke*.): I said, to the day and your good health, *Corporal Cregan*.

CREGAN (*For a second is angry—then he grins and mutters admiringly*.): Be God, it's you can bate the world and nevèr let it change you! (*Correcting his toast with emphasis*.) To the day and yourself, *Major Melody*.

MELODY (*Touches his glass to* CREGAN's—*graciously condescending*.): Drink hearty, Corporal. (*They drink*.)

Curtain

Act Three

SCENE—*The same. The door to the bar is closed. It is around eight that evening and there are candles on the center table.* MELODY *sits at the head of this table. In his brilliant uniform he presents more than ever an impressively colorful figure in the room, which appears smaller and dingier in the candlelight.* CREGAN *is in the chair on his right. The other chairs at this table are unoccupied.* RILEY, O'DOWD, *and* ROCHE *sit at the table at left front.* RILEY *is at front, but his chair is turned sideways so he faces right.* O'DOWD *has the chair against the wall, facing right, with* ROCHE *across the table from him, his back to* MELODY. *All five are drunk,* MELODY *more so than any of them, but except for the glazed glitter in his eyes and his deathly pallor, his appearance does not betray him. He is holding his liquor like a gentleman.*

CREGAN *is the least drunk.* O'DOWD *and* ROCHE *are boisterous. The effect of the drink on* RILEY *is merely to sink him deeper in dreams. He seems oblivious to his surroundings.*

An empty and half-empty bottle of port are on the table before MELODY *and* CREGAN, *and their glasses are full. The three at the table have a decanter of whiskey.*

SARA, *wearing her working dress and an apron, is removing dishes and the remains of the dinner. Her face is set. She is determined to ignore them, but there is angry disgust in her eyes.* MELODY *is arranging forks, knives, spoons, saltcellar, etc., in a plan of battle on the table before him.* CREGAN *watches him.* PATCH RILEY *gives a few tuning-up quavers on his pipes.*

MELODY: Here's the river Tagus. And here, Talavera. This would be the French position on a rise of ground with the plain between our lines and theirs. Here is our redoubt with the Fourth Division and the Guards. And here's our cavalry brigade in a valley toward our left, if you'll remember, Corporal Cregan.

CREGAN (*Excitedly.*): Remember? Sure I see it as clear as yesterday!

RILEY (*Bursts into a rollicking song, accompanying himself on the pipes, his voice the quavering ghost of a tenor but still true—to the tune of "Baltiorum.")* :

"She'd a pig and boneens,
She'd a bed and a dresser,
And a nate little room
For the father confessor;
With a cupboard and curtains, and something,
                                    I'm towld,
That his riv'rance liked when the weather was cowld.
And it's hurroo, hurroo! Biddy O'Rafferty!"

(ROCHE *and* O'DOWD *roar after him, beating time on the table with their glasses—"Hurroo, hurroo! Biddy O'Rafferty!"—and laugh drunkenly.* CREGAN, *too, joins in this chorus.* MELODY *frowns angrily at the interruption, but at the end he smiles with lordly condescension, pleased by the irreverence of the song.*)

O'DOWD (*After a cunning glance at* MELODY's *face to see what his reaction is—derisively.*): Och, lave it to the priests, divil mend thim! Ain't it so, Major?

MELODY: Ay, damn them all! A song in the right spirit, Piper. Faith, I'll have you repeat it for my wife's benefit when she joins us. She still has a secret fondness for priests. And now, less noise, you blackguards. Corporal Cregan and I cannot hear each other with your brawling.

O'DOWD (*Smirkingly obedient.*): Quiet it is, yer Honor. Be quiet, Patch. (*He gives the old man, who is lost in dreams, a shove that almost knocks him off his chair.* RILEY *stares at him bewilderedly.* O'DOWD *and* ROCHE *guffaw.*)

MELODY (*Scowls at them, then turns to* CREGAN.): Where was I, Corporal? Oh, yes, we were waiting in the valley. We heard a trumpet from the French lines and saw them forming for the attack. An aide-de-camp galloped down the hill to us—

SARA (*Who has been watching him disdainfully, reaches out to take his plate—rudely in mocking brogue.*): I'll have your plate, av ye plaze, Major, before your gallant dragoons charge over it and break it.

MELODY (*Holds his plate on the table with one hand so she cannot take it, and raises his glass of wine with the other —ignoring her.*): Wet your lips, Corporal. Talavera was a devilish thirsty day, if you'll remember. (*He drinks.*)

CREGAN (*Glances uneasily at* SARA.): It was that. (*He drinks.*)

MELODY (*Smacking his lips.*): Good wine, Corporal. Thank God, I still have wine in my cellar fit for a gentleman.

SARA (*Angrily.*): Are you going to let me take your plate?

MELODY (*Ignoring her.*): No, I have no need to apologize for the wine. Nor for the dinner, for that matter. Nora is a good cook when she forgets her infernal parsimony and buys food that one can eat without disgust. But I do owe you an apology for the quality of the service. I have tried to teach the waitress not to snatch plates from the table as if she were feeding dogs in a kennel but she cannot learn. (*He takes his hand from the plate—to* SARA.) There. Now let me see you take it properly. (*She*

*stares at him for a moment, speechless with anger—
then snatches the plate from in front of him.*)

CREGAN (*Hastily recalls* MELODY *to the battlefield.*): You
were where the aide-de-camp galloped up to us, Major.
It was then the French artillery opened on us. (SARA
goes out right, carrying a tray laden with plates.)

MELODY: We charged the columns on our left—here— (*He
marks the tablecloth.*) that were pushing back the Guards.
I'll never forget the blast of death from the French
squares. And then their chasseurs and lancers were on
us! By God, it's a miracle any of us came through!

CREGAN: You wasn't touched except you'd a bullet through
your coat, but I had this token on my cheek to remember
a French saber by.

MELODY: Brave days, those! By the Eternal, then one lived!
Then one forgot! (*He stops—when he speaks again it is
bitterly.*) Little did I dream then the disgrace that was to
be my reward later on.

CREGAN (*Consolingly.*): Ah well, that's the bad luck of
things. You'd have been made a colonel soon, if you'd
left the Spanish woman alone and not fought that duel.

MELODY (*Arrogantly threatening.*): Are you presuming
to question my conduct in that affair, Corporal Cregan?

CREGAN (*Hastily.*): Sorra a bit! Don't mind me, now.

MELODY (*Stiffly.*): I accept your apology. (*He drinks the
rest of his wine, pours another glass, then stares moodily
before him.* CREGAN *drains his glass and refills it.*)

O'DOWD (*Peering past* ROCHE *to watch* MELODY, *leans across
to* ROCHE—*in a sneering whisper.*): Ain't he the lunatic,
sittin' like a play-actor in his red coat, lyin' about his
battles with the French!

ROCHE (*Sullenly—but careful to keep his voice low.*): He'd
ought to be shamed he ivir wore the bloody red av
England, God's curse on him!

O'DOWD: Don't be wishin' him harm, for it's thirsty we'd be
without him. Drink long life to him, and may he always
be as big a fool as he is this night! (*He sloshes whiskey
from the decanter into both their glasses.*)

ROCHE (*With a drunken leer.*): Thrue for you! I'll toast
him on that. (*He twists round to face* MELODY, *holds up
his glass and bawls.*) To the grandest gintleman ivir come
from the shores av Ireland! Long life to you, Major!

O'DOWD: Hurroo! Long life, yer Honor!

RILEY (*Awakened from his dream, mechanically raises his
glass.*): And to all that belong to ye.

MELODY (*Startled from his thoughts, becomes at once the
condescending squire—smiling tolerantly.*): I said, less
noise, you dogs. All the same, I thank you for your toast.
(*They drink. A pause. Abruptly* MELODY *begins to recite
from Byron. He reads the verse well, quietly, with a bitter
eloquence.*)

> "But midst the crowd, the hum, the shock of men,
>   To hear, to see, to feel, and to possess,
>   And roam along, the World's tired denizen,
>   With none who bless us, none whom we can bless;
>   Minions of Splendour shrinking from distress!
>   None that, with kindred consciousness endued,
>   If we were not, would seem to smile the less,
>   Of all that flattered—followed—sought, and sued;
>   This is to be alone—This, this is Solitude!"

(*He stops and glances from one face to another. Their
expressions are all blank. He remarks with insulting
derisiveness.*) What? You do not understand, my lads?
Well, all the better for you. So may you go on fooling
yourselves that I am fooled in you. (*Then with a quick
change of mood, heartily.*) Give us a hunting song, Patch.
You've not forgotten "Modideroo," I'll be bound.

RILEY (*Roused to interest immediately.*): Does a duck

forget wather? I'll show ye! (*He begins the preliminary quavers on his pipes.*)

o'dowd: Modideroo!

roche: Hurroo!

riley (*Accompanying himself, sings with wailing melancholy the first verse that comes to his mind of an old hunting song.*):

> *"And the fox set him down and looked about,*
> *And many were feared to follow;*
> *'Maybe I'm wrong,' says he, 'but I doubt*
> *That you'll be as gay tomorrow.*
> *For loud as you cry, and high as you ride,*
> *And little you feel my sorrow,*
> *I'll be free on the mountainside*
> *While you'll lie low tomorrow.'*
> *Oh, Modideroo, aroo, aroo!"*

(melody, *excited now, beats time on the table with his glass along with* cregan, roche, *and* o'dowd, *and all bellow the refrain,* "Oh, Modideroo, aroo, aroo!")

melody (*His eyes alight, forgetting himself, a strong lilt of brogue coming into his voice.*): Ah, that brings it back clear as life! Melody Castle in the days that's gone! A wind from the south, and a sky gray with clouds—good weather for the hounds. A true Irish hunter under me that knows and loves me and would raise to a jump over hell if I gave the word! To hell with men, I say!—and women, too!—with their cowardly hearts rotten and stinking with lies and greed and treachery! Give me a horse to love and I'll cry quits to men! And then away, with the hounds in full cry, and after them! Off with divil a care for your neck, over ditches and streams and stone walls and fences, the fox doubling up the mountainside through the furze and the heather—! (sara *has entered from right as he begins this longing invocation of old hunting days. She stands behind his chair, listening contemptuously. He suddenly feels her presence and turns his head. When he catches the sneer in her eyes, it is as if cold water were dashed in his face. He addresses her as if she were a servant.*) Well? What is it? What are you waiting for now?

SARA (*Roughly, with coarse brogue.*): What would I be waitin' for but for you to get through with your blather about lovin' horses, and give me a chance to finish my work? Can't you—and the other gintlemen—finish gettin' drunk in the bar and lave me clear the tables? (O'DOWD *conceals a grin behind his hand;* ROCHE *stifles a malicious guffaw.*)

CREGAN (*With an apprehensive glance at* MELODY, *shakes his head at her admonishingly.*): Now, Sara, be aisy. (*But* MELODY *suppresses any angry reaction. He rises to his feet, a bit stiffly and carefully, and bows.*)

MELODY (*Coldly.*): I beg your pardon if we have interfered with your duties. (*To* O'DOWD *and his companions.*) Into the bar, you louts!

O'DOWD: The bar it is, sorr. Come, Dan. Wake up, Patch. (*He pokes the piper. He and* ROCHE *go into the bar, and* RILEY *stumbles vaguely after them.* CREGAN *waits for* MELODY.)

MELODY: Go along, Corporal. I'll join you presently. I wish to speak to my daughter.

CREGAN: All right, Major. (*He again shakes his head at* SARA, *as if to say, don't provoke him. She ignores him. He goes into the bar, closing the door behind him. She stares at her father with angry disgust.*)

SARA: You're drunk. If you think I'm going to stay here and listen to—

MELODY (*His face expressionless, draws out his chair at the head of the center table for her—politely.*): Sit down, my dear.

SARA: I won't. I have no time. Poor Mother is half dead on her feet. I have to help her. There's a pile of dishes to wash after your grand anniversary feast! (*With bitter anger.*) Thank God it's over, and it's the last time you'll ever take satisfaction in having me wait on table for drunken scum like O'Dowd and—

MELODY (*Quietly.*): A daughter who takes satisfaction in letting even the scum see that she hates and despises her father! (*He shrugs his shoulders.*) But no matter. (*Indicating the chair again.*) Won't you sit down, my dear?

SARA: If you ever dared face the truth, you'd hate and despise yourself! (*Passionately.*) All I pray to God is that someday when you're admiring yourself in the mirror something will make you see at last what you really are! That will be revenge in full for all you've done to Mother and me! (*She waits defiantly, as if expecting him to lose his temper and curse her. But* MELODY *acts as if he had not heard her.*)

MELODY (*His face expressionless, his manner insistently bland and polite.*): Sit down, my dear. I will not detain you long, and I think you will find what I have to tell you of great interest. (*She searches his face, uneasy now, feeling a threat hidden behind his cold, quiet, gentlemanly tone. She sits down and he sits at rear of table, with an empty chair separating them.*)

SARA: You'd better think well before you speak, Father. I know the devil that's in you when you're quiet like this with your brain mad with drink.

MELODY: I don't understand you. All I wish is to relate something which happened this afternoon.

SARA (*Giving way to bitterness at her humiliation again—sneeringly.*): When you went riding on your beautiful thoroughbred mare while Mother and I were sweating and suffocating in the heat of the kitchen to prepare your Lordship's banquet? Sure, I hope you didn't show off

and jump your beauty over a fence into somebody's
garden, like you've done before, and then have to pay
damages to keep out of jail!

MELODY (*Roused by mention of his pet—disdainfully.*):
The damned Yankee yokels should feel flattered that she
deigns to set her dainty hooves in their paltry gardens!
She's a truer-born, well-bred lady than any of their women
—than the one who paid us a visit this morning, for
example.

SARA: Mrs. Harford was enough of a lady to put you in
your place and make a fool of you.

MELODY (*Seemingly unmoved by this taunt—calmly.*): You
are very simple-minded, my dear, to let yourself be
taken in by such an obvious bit of clever acting. Naturally, the lady was a bit discomposed when she heard
you and your mother coming, after she had just allowed
me to kiss her. She had to pretend—

SARA (*Eagerly.*): She let you kiss her? (*Then disgustedly.*)
It's a lie, but I don't doubt you've made yourself think
it's the truth by now. (*Angrily.*) I'm going. I don't
want to listen to the whiskey in you boasting of what
never happened—as usual! (*She puts her hands on the
table and starts to rise.*)

MELODY (*With a quick movement pins hers down with one
of his.*): Wait! (*A look of vindictive cruelty comes into
his eyes—quietly.*) Why are you so jealous of the mare,
I wonder? Is it because she has such slender ankles and
dainty feet? (*He takes his hand away and stares at her
hands—with disgust, commandingly.*) Keep your thick
wrists and ugly, peasant paws off the table in my
presence, if you please! They turn my stomach! I advise
you never to let Simon get a good look at them—

SARA (*Instinctively jerks her hands back under the table
guiltily. She stammers.*): You—you cruel devil! I knew
you'd—

MELODY (*For a second is ashamed and really contrite.*):
Forgive me, Sara. I didn't mean—the whiskey talking
—as you said. (*He adds in a forced tone, a trace of
mockery in it.*) An absurd taunt, when you really have
such pretty hands and feet, my dear. (*She jumps to her
feet, so hurt and full of hatred her lips tremble and she
cannot speak. He speaks quietly.*) Are you going? I was
about to tell you of the talk I had this afternoon with
young Harford. (*She stares at him in dismay. He goes on
easily.*) It was after I returned from my ride. I cantered
the mare by the river and she pulled up lame. So I
dismounted and led her back to the barn. No one noticed
my return and when I went upstairs it occurred to me I
would not find again such an opportunity to have a frank
chat with Harford—free from interruptions. (*He pauses,
as if he expects her to be furious, but she remains tensely
silent, determined not to let him know her reaction.*)
I did not beat about the bush. I told him he must appreciate, as a gentleman, it was my duty as your father to
demand he lay his cards on the table. I said he must
realize that even before you began nursing him here
and going alone to his bedroom, there was a deal of
gossip about your visits to his cabin, and your walks in
the woods with him. I put it to him that such an intimacy
could not continue without gravely compromising your
reputation.

SARA (*Stunned—weakly.*): God forgive you! And what did
he say?

MELODY: What could he say? He is a man of honor. He
looked damn embarrassed and guilty for a moment,
but when he found his tongue, he agreed with me most
heartily. He said his mother had told him the same thing.

SARA: Oh, she did, did she? I suppose she did it to find out
by watching him how far—

MELODY (*Coldly.*): Well, why not? Naturally, it was her

duty as his mother to discover all she could about you. She is a woman of the world. She would be bound to suspect that you might be his mistress.

SARA (*Tensely*.): Oh, would she!

MELODY: But that's beside the point. The point is, my bashful young gentleman finally blurted out that he wanted to marry you.

SARA (*Forgetting her anger—eagerly*.): He told you that?

MELODY: Yes, and he said he had told his mother, and she had said all she wanted was his happiness but she felt in fairness to you and to himself—and I presume she also meant to both families concerned—he should test his love and yours by letting a decent interval of time elapse before your marriage. She mentioned a year, I believe.

SARA (*Angrily*.): Ah! Didn't I guess that would be her trick!

MELODY (*Lifting his eyebrows—coldly*.): Trick? In my opinion, the lady displayed more common sense and knowledge of the world than I thought she possessed. The reasons she gave him are sound and show a consideration for your good name which ought to inspire gratitude in you and not suspicion.

SARA: Arrah, don't tell me she's made a fool of you again! A lot of consideration she has for me!

MELODY: She pointed out to him that if you were the daughter of some family in their own little Yankee clique, there would be no question of a hasty marriage, and so he owed it to you—

SARA: I see. She's the clever one!

MELODY: Another reason was—and here your Simon stammered so embarrassedly I had trouble making him out —she warned him a sudden wedding would look damnably suspicious and start a lot of evil-minded gossip.

SARA (*Tensely.*): Oh, she's clever, all right! But I'll beat her.

MELODY: I told him I agreed with his mother. It is obvious that were there a sudden wedding without a suitable period of betrothal, everyone would believe—

SARA: I don't care what they believe! Tell me this! Did she get him to promise her he'd wait? (*Before he can answer —bitterly.*) But of course she did! She'd never have left till she got that out of him!

MELODY (*Ignores this.*): I told him I appreciated the honor he did me in asking for your hand, but he must understand that I could not commit myself until I had talked to his father and was assured the necessary financial arrangements could be concluded to our mutual satisfaction. There was the amount of settlement to be agreed upon, for instance.

SARA: That dream, again! God pity you! (*She laughs helplessly and a bit hysterically.*) And God help Simon. He must have thought you'd gone out of your mind! What did he say?

MELODY: He said nothing, naturally. He is well bred and he knows this is a matter he must leave to his father to discuss. There is also the equally important matter of how generous an allowance Henry Harford is willing to settle on his son. I did not mention this to Simon, of course, not wishing to embarrass him further with talk of money.

SARA: Thank God for that, at least! (*She giggles hysterically.*)

MELODY (*Quietly.*): May I ask what you find so ridiculous in an old established custom? Simon is an elder son, the heir to his father's estate. No matter what their differences in the past may have been, now that Simon has decided to marry and settle down his father will wish to do the fair thing by him. He will realize, too, that although there is no more honorable calling than that of poet and philosopher, which his son has chosen to pursue, there is no decent living to be gained by its practice. So naturally he will settle an allowance on Simon, and I shall insist it be a generous one, befitting your position as my daughter. I will tolerate no niggardly trader's haggling on his part.

SARA (*Stares at him fascinatedly, on the edge of helpless, hysterical laughter.*): I suppose it would never occur to you that old Harford might not think it an honor to have his son marry your daughter.

MELODY (*Calmly.*): No, it would never occur to me—and if it should occur to him, I would damned soon disabuse his mind. Who is he but a money-grubbing trader? I would remind him that I was born in a castle and there was a time when I possessed wealth and position, and an estate compared to which any Yankee upstart's home in this country is but a hovel stuck in a cabbage patch. I would remind him that you, my daughter, were born in a castle!

SARA (*Impulsively, with a proud toss of her head.*): Well, that's no more than the truth. (*Then furious with herself and him.*) Och, what crazy blather! (*She springs to her feet.*) I've had enough of your mad dreams!

MELODY: Wait! I haven't finished yet. (*He speaks quietly, but as he goes on there is an increasing vindictiveness in his tone.*) There was another reason why I told young Harford I could not make a final decision. I wished time to reflect on a further aspect of this proposed marriage. Well, I have been reflecting, watching you and examining your conduct, without prejudice, trying to be fair to you and make every possible allowance— (*He pauses.*) Well, to be brutally frank, my dear, all I can see in you is a common, greedy, scheming, cunning peasant girl, whose only thought is money and who has shamelessly thrown herself at a young man's head because his family happens to possess a little wealth and position.

SARA (*Trying to control herself.*): I see your game, Father. I told you when you were drunk like this— But this time, I won't give you the satisfaction— (*Then she bursts out angrily.*) It's a lie! I love Simon, or I'd never—

MELODY (*As if she hadn't spoken.*): So, I have about made up my mind to decline for you Simon Harford's request for your hand in marriage.

SARA (*Jeers angrily now.*): Oh, you have, have you? As if I cared a damn what you—!

MELODY: As a gentleman, I feel I have a duty, in honor, to Simon. Such a marriage would be a tragic misalliance for him—and God knows I know the sordid tragedy of such a union.

SARA: It's Mother has had the tragedy!

MELODY: I hold young Harford in too high esteem. I cannot stand by and let him commit himself irrevocably to what could only bring him disgust and bitterness, and ruin to all his dreams.

SARA: So I'm not good enough for him, you've decided now?

MELODY: That is apparent from your every act. No one, no matter how charitably inclined, could mistake you for a lady. I have tried to make you one. It was an impossible task. God Himself cannot transform a sow's ear into a silk purse!

SARA (*Furiously.*): Father!

MELODY: Young Harford needs to be saved from himself. I can understand his physical infatuation. You are pretty. So was your mother pretty once. But marriage is another matter. The man who would be the ideal husband for you, from a standpoint of conduct and character, is Mickey Maloy, my bartender, and I will be happy to give him my parental blessing—

SARA: Let you stop now, Father!

MELODY: You and he would be congenial. You can match tongues together. He's a healthy animal. He can give you a raft of peasant brats to squeal and fight with the pigs on the mud floor of your hovel.

SARA: It's the dirty hut in which your father was born and raised you're remembering, isn't it?

MELODY (*Stung to fury, glares at her with hatred. His voice quivers but is deadly quiet.*): Of course, if you trick Harford into getting you with child, I could not refuse my consent. (*Letting go, he bangs his fist on the table.*) No, by God, even then, when I remember my own experience, I'll be damned if I could with a good conscience advise him to marry you!

SARA (*Glaring back at him with hatred.*): You drunken devil! (*She makes a threatening move toward him, raising her hand as if she were going to slap his face—then she controls herself and speaks with quiet, biting sarcasm.*) Consent or not, I want to thank you for your kind fatherly advice on how to trick Simon. I don't think I'll need it but if the worst comes to the worst I promise you I'll remember—

MELODY (*Coldly, his face expressionless.*): I believe I have said all I wished to say to you. (*He gets up and bows stiffly.*) If you will excuse me, I shall join Corporal Cregan. (*He goes to the bar door.* SARA *turns and goes quietly out right, forgetting to clear the few remaining dishes on the center table. His back turned, he does not see her go. With his hand on the knob of the bar door, he hesitates. For a second he breaks—torturedly.*) Sara! (*Then quietly.*) There are things I said which I regret—even now. I—I trust you will overlook— As your mother knows, it's the liquor talking, not— I must admit that, due to my celebrating the anniversary, my brain is a bit addled by whiskey—as you said. (*He waits, hoping for a word of forgiveness. Finally, he glances over his shoulder. As he discovers she is not there and has not heard him, for a second he crumbles, his soldierly erectness sags and his face falls. He looks sad and hopeless and bitter and old, his eyes wandering dully. But, as in the two preceding acts, the mirror attracts him, and as he moves from the bar door to stand before it he assumes his arrogant, Byronic pose again. He repeats in each detail his pantomime before the mirror. He speaks proudly.)* My-self to the bitter end! No weakening, so help me God! *(There is a knock on the street door but he does not hear it. He starts his familiar incantation quotes from Byron.)*

"I have not loved the World, nor the World me;
I have not flattered its rank breath, nor bowed
To its idolatries a patient knee . . ."

(The knock on the door is repeated more loudly. MELODY *starts guiltily and steps quickly away from the mirror. His embarrassment is transformed into resentful anger. He calls.)* Come in, damn you! Do you expect a lackey to open the door for you? *(The door opens and* NICHOLAS GADSBY *comes in.* GADSBY *is in his late forties, short, stout, with a big, bald head, round, florid face, and small, blue eyes. A rigidly conservative, best-family attorney, he is stiffly correct in dress and manner, dryly portentous in speech, and extremely conscious of his professional authority and dignity. Now, however, he is venturing on unfamiliar ground and is by no means as sure of himself as his manner indicates. The unexpected vision of* MELODY *in his uniform startles him and for a second he stands, as close to gaping as he can be, impressed by* MELODY'S *handsome distinction.* MELODY, *in his turn, is surprised. He had not thought the intruder would be a gentleman. He unbends, although his tone is still a bit curt. He bows a bit stiffly, and* GADSBY *finds himself returning the bow.)*

Your pardon, sir. When I called, I thought it was one of the damned riffraff mistaking the barroom door. Pray be seated, sir. (GADSBY *comes forward and takes the chair at the head of the center table, glancing at the few dirty dishes on it with distaste.* MELODY *says.*) Your pardon again, sir. We have been feasting late, which accounts for the disarray. I will summon a servant to inquire your pleasure.

GADSBY (*Beginning to recover his aplomb—shortly.*): Thank you, but I want nothing, sir. I came here to seek a private interview with the proprietor of this tavern, by name, Melody. (*He adds a bit hesitantly.*) Are you, by any chance, he?

MELODY (*Stiffens arrogantly.*): I am not, sir. But if you wish to see Major Cornelius Melody, one time of His Majesty's Seventh Dragoons, who served with honor under the Duke of Wellington in Spain, I am he.

GADSBY (*Dryly.*): Very well, sir. Major Melody, then.

MELODY (*Does not like his tone—insolently sarcastic.*): And whom have I the *honor* of addressing? (*As* GADSBY *is about to reply,* SARA *enters from right, having remembered the dishes.* MELODY *ignores her as he would a servant.* GADSBY *examines her carefully as she gathers up the dishes. She notices him staring at her and gives him a resentful, suspicious glance. She carries the dishes out, right, to the kitchen, but a moment later she can be seen just inside the hall at right, listening. Meanwhile, as soon as he thinks she has gone,* GADSBY *speaks.*)

GADSBY (*With affected casualness.*): A pretty young woman. Is she your daughter, sir? I seemed to detect a resemblance—

MELODY (*Angrily.*): No! Do I look to you, sir, like a man who would permit his daughter to work as a waitress? Resemblance to me? You must be blind, sir. (*Coldly.*)

I am still waiting for you to inform me who you are and why you should wish to see me.

GADSBY (*Hands him a card—extremely nettled by* MELODY's *manner—curtly.*): My card, sir.

MELODY (*Glances at the card.*): Nicholas Gadsby. (*He flips it aside disdainfully.*) Attorney, eh? The devil take all your tribe, say I. I have small liking for your profession, sir, and I cannot imagine what business you can have with me. The damned thieves of the law did their worst to me many years ago in Ireland. I have little left to tempt you. So I do not see— (*Suddenly an idea comes to him. He stares at* GADSBY, *then goes on in a more friendly tone.*) That is, unless— Do you happen by any chance to represent the father of young Simon Harford?

GADSBY (*Indignant at* MELODY's *insults to his profession—with a thinly veiled sneer.*): Ah, then you were expecting— That makes things easier. We need not beat about the bush. I do represent Mr. Henry Harford, sir.

MELODY (*Thawing out, in his total misunderstanding of the situation.*): Then accept my apologies, sir, for my animadversions against your profession. I am afraid I may be prejudiced. In the army, we used to say we suffered more casualties from your attacks at home than the French ever inflicted. (*He sits down on the chair on* GADSBY's *left, at rear of table—remarking with careless pride.*) A word of explanation as to why you find me in uniform. It is the anniversary of the battle of Talavera, sir, and—

GADSBY (*Interrupts dryly.*): Indeed, sir? But I must tell you my time is short. With your permission, we will proceed at once to the matter in hand.

MELODY (*Controlling his angry discomfiture—coldly.*): I think I can hazard a guess as to what that matter is. You have come about the settlement?

GADSBY (*Misunderstanding him, replies in a tone almost openly contemptuous.*): Exactly, sir. Mr. Harford was of the opinion, and I agreed with him, that a settlement would be foremost in your mind.

MELODY (*Scowls at his tone but, as he completely misunderstands* GADSBY'S *meaning, he forces himself to bow politely.*): It does me honor, sir, that Mr. Harford appreciates he is dealing with a gentleman and has the breeding to know how these matters are propertly arranged. (GADSBY *stares at him, absolutely flabbergasted by what he considers a piece of the most shameless effrontery.* MELODY *leans toward him confidentially.*) I will be frank with you, sir. The devil of it is, this comes at a difficult time for me. Temporary, of course, but I cannot deny I am pinched at the moment—devilishly pinched. But no matter. Where my only child's happiness is at stake, I am prepared to make every possible effort. I will sign a note of hand, no matter how ruinous the interest demanded by the scoundrelly moneylenders. By the way, what amount does Mr. Harford think proper? Anything in reason—

GADSBY (*Listening in utter confusion, finally gets the idea* MELODY *is making him the butt of a joke—fuming.*): I do not know what you are talking about, sir, unless you think to make a fool of me! If this is what is known as Irish wit—

MELODY (*Bewildered for a second—then in a threatening tone.*): Take care, sir, and watch your words or I warn you you will repent them, no matter whom you represent! No damned pettifogging dog can insult me with impunity! (*As* GADSBY *draws back apprehensively, he adds with insulting disdain.*) As for making a fool of you, sir, I would be the fool if I attempted to improve on God's handiwork!

GADSBY (*Ignoring the insults, forces a placating tone.*): I wish no quarrel with you, sir. I cannot for the life of me see— I fear we are dealing at cross-purposes. Will you tell me plainly what you mean by your talk of settlement?

MELODY: Obviously, I mean the settlement I am prepared to make on my daughter. (*As* GADSBY *only looks more dumfounded, he continues sharply*.) Is not your purpose in coming here to arrange, on Mr. Harford's behalf, for the marriage of his son with my daughter?

GADSBY: Marriage? Good God, no! Nothing of the kind!

MELODY (*Dumfounded*.): Then what have you come for?

GADSBY (*Feeling he has now the upper hand—sharply*.): To inform you that Mr. Henry Harford is unalterably opposed to any further relationship between his son and your daughter, whatever the nature of that relationship in the past.

MELODY (*Leans forward threateningly*.): By the Immortal, sir, if you dare insinuate—!

GADSBY (*Draws back again, but he is no coward and is determined to carry out his instructions*.): I insinuate nothing, sir. I am here on Mr. Harford's behalf, to make you an offer. That is what I thought you were expecting when you mentioned a settlement. Mr. Harford is prepared to pay you the sum of three thousand dollars— provided, mark you, that you and your daughter sign an agreement I have drawn up which specifies that you relinquish all claims, of whatever nature. And also provided you agree to leave this part of the country at once with your family. Mr. Harford suggests it would be advisable that you go West—to Ohio, say.

MELODY (*So overcome by a rising tide of savage, humiliated fury, he can only stammer hoarsely*.): So Henry Harford does me the honor—to suggest that, does he?

GADSBY (*Watching him uneasily, attempts a reasonable, persuasive tone*.): Surely you could not have spoken seriously when you talked of marriage. There is such a dif-

ference in station. The idea is preposterous. If you knew
Mr. Harford, you would realize he would never coun-
tenance—

MELODY (*His pent-up rage bursts out—smashing his fist on
the table.*): Know him? By the Immortal God, I'll know
him soon! And he'll know me! (*He springs to his feet.*)
But first, you Yankee scum, I'll deal with you! (*He draws
back his fist to smash* GADSBY *in the face, but* SARA *has run
from the door at right and she grabs his arm. She is almost as furious as he is and there are tears of humiliated
pride in her eyes.*)

SARA: Father! Don't! He's only a paid lackey. Where is
your pride that you'd dirty your hands on the like of
him? (*While she is talking the door from the bar opens
and* ROCHE, O'DOWD, *and* CREGAN *crowd into the room.*
MICKEY *stands in the doorway.* NORA *follows* SARA *in from
right.*)

ROCHE (*With drunken enthusiasm.*): It's a fight! For the
love of God, clout the damned Yankee, Major!

MELODY (*Controls himself—his voice shaking.*): You are
right, Sara. It would be beneath me to touch such a vile
lickspittle. But he won't get off scot-free. (*Sharply, a
commander ordering his soldiers.*) Here you, Roche and
O'Dowd! Get hold of him! (*They do so with enthusiasm
and yank* GADSBY *from his chair.*)

GADSBY: You drunken ruffians! Take your hands off me!

MELODY (*Addressing him—in his quiet, threatening tone
now.*): You may tell the swindling trader, Harford, who
employs you that he'll hear from me! (*To* ROCHE *and*
O'DOWD.) Throw this thing out! Kick it down to the
crossroads!

ROCHE: Hurroo! (*He and* O'DOWD *run* GADSBY *to the door at
rear.* CREGAN *jumps ahead, grinning, and opens the door
for them.*)

GADSBY (*Struggling futilely as they rush him through the*

door.): You scoundrels! Take your hands off me! Take
— (MELODY *looks after them. The two women watch him,*
NORA *frightened,* SARA *with a strange look of satisfied
pride.*)

CREGAN (*In the doorway, looking out—laughing.*): Oh, it'd
do your heart good, Con, to see the way they're kicking
his butt down the street! (*He comes in and shuts the
door.*)

MELODY (*His rage welling again, as his mind dwells on his
humiliation—starting to pace up and down.*): It's with
his master I have to deal, and, by the Powers, I'll deal
with him! You'll come with me, Jamie. I'll want you for
a witness. He'll apologize to me—more than that, he'll
come back here this very night and apologize publicly to
my daughter, or else he meets me in the morning! By
God, I'll face him at ten paces or across a handkerchief!
I'll put a bullet through him, so help me, Christ!

NORA (*Breaks into a dirgelike wail.*): God forgive you,
Con, is it a duel again—murtherin' or gettin' murthered?

MELODY: Be quiet, woman! Go back to your kitchen! Go,
do you hear me! (NORA *turns obediently toward the door
at right, beginning to cry.*)

SARA (*Puts an arm around her mother. She is staring at
MELODY apprehensively now.*): There, Mother, don't
worry. Father knows that's all foolishness. He's only
talking. Go on now in the kitchen and sit down and
rest, Mother. (NORA *goes out right.* SARA *closes the door
after her and comes back.*)

MELODY (*Turns on her with bitter anger.*): Only talking,
am I? It's the first time in my life I ever heard anyone
say Con Melody was a coward! It remains for my own
daughter—!

SARA (*Placatingly.*): I didn't say that, Father. But can't you
see—you're not in Ireland in the old days now. The
days of duels are long past and dead, in this part of

America anyway. Harford will never fight you. He—

MELODY: He won't, won't he? By God, I make him! I'll
take a whip. I'll drag him out of his house and lash him
down the street for all his neighbors to see! He'll apologize, or he'll fight, or I'll brand him a craven before the
world!

SARA (*Frightened now.*): But you'll never be let see him!
His servants will keep you out! He'll have the police ar-
rest you, and it'll be in the papers about another drunken
Mick raising a crazy row! (*She appeals to* CREGAN.) Tell
him I'm telling the truth, Jamie. You've still got some
sober sense in you. Maybe he'll listen to you.

CREGAN (*Glances at* MELODY *uneasily.*): Maybe Sara's right,
Major.

MELODY: When I want your opinion, I'll ask for it! (*Sneeringly.*) Of course, if you've become such a coward you're
afraid to go with me—

CREGAN (*Stung.*): Coward, is ut? I'll go, and be damned to
you!

SARA: Jamie, you fool! Oh, it's like talking to crazy men!
(*She grabs her father's arm—pleadingly.*) Don't do it,
Father, for the love of God! Have I ever asked you
anything? Well, I ask you to heed me now! I'll beg you
on my knees, if you like! Isn't it me you'd fight about,
and haven't I a right to decide? You punished that lawyer for the insult. You had him thrown out of here like
a tramp. Isn't that your answer to old Harford that insults him? It's for him to challenge you, if he dares,
isn't it? Why can't you leave it at that and wait—

MELODY (*Shaking off her hand—angrily.*): You talk like a
scheming peasant! It's a question of my honor!

SARA: No! It's a question of my happiness, and I won't
have your mad interfering—! (*Desperately forcing herself to reason with him again.*) Listen, Father! If you'll
keep out of it, I'll show you how I'll make a fool of old

Harford! Simon won't let anything his father does keep him from marrying me. His mother is the only one who might have the influence over him to come between us. She's only watching for a good excuse to turn Simon against marrying me, and if you go raising a drunken row at their house, and make a public scandal, shouting you want to murder his father, can't you see what a chance that will give her?

MELODY (*Raging.*): That damned, insolent Yankee bitch! She's all the more reason. Marry, did you say? You dare to think there can be any question now of your marrying the son of a man who has insulted my honor—and yours?

SARA (*Defiantly.*): Yes, I dare to think it! I love Simon and I'm going to marry him!

MELODY: And I say you're not! If he wasn't sick, I'd— But I'll get him out of here tomorrow! I forbid you ever to see him again! If you dare disobey me I'll—! (*Beginning to lose all control of himself.*) If you dare defy me—for the sake of the dirty money you think you can beg from his family, if you're his wife—!

SARA (*Fiercely.*): You lie! (*Then with quiet intensity.*) Yes. I defy you or anyone who tries to come between us!

MELODY: You'd sell your pride as my daughter—! (*His face convulsed by fury.*) You filthy peasant slut! You whore! I'll see you dead first—! By the living God, I'd kill you myself! (*He makes a threatening move toward her.*)

SARA (*Shrinks back frightenedly.*): Father! (*Then she stands and faces him defiantly.*)

CREGAN (*Steps between them.*): Con! In the name of God! (MELODY's *fit of insane fury leaves him. He stands panting for breath, shuddering with the effort to regain some sort of poise.* CREGAN *speaks, his only thought to get him away from* SARA.) If we're going after old Harford, Major, we'd better go. That thief of a lawyer will warn him—

MELODY (*Seizing on this—hoarsely.*): Yes, let's go. Let's go, Jamie. Come along, Corporal. A stirrup cup, and we'll be off. If the mare wasn't lame, I'd ride alone—but we can get a rig at the livery stable. Don't let me forget to stop at the barn for my whip. (*By the time he finishes speaking, he has himself in hand again and his ungovernable fury has gone. There is a look of cool, menacing vengefulness in his face. He turns toward the bar door.*)

SARA (*Helplessly.*): Father! (*Desperately, as a last, frantic threat.*) You'll force me to go to Simon—and do what you said! (*If he hears this, he gives no sign of it. He strides into the bar.* CREGAN *follows him, closing the door.* SARA *stares before her, the look of defiant desperation hardening on her face. The street door is flung open and* O'DOWD *and* ROCHE *pile in, laughing uproariously.*)

ROCHE: Hurroo!

O'DOWD: The army is back, Major, with the foe flying in retreat. (*He sees* MELODY *is not there—to* SARA.) Where's himself? (SARA *appears not to see or hear him.*)

ROCHE (*After a quick glance at her.*): Lave her be. He'll be in the bar. Come on. (*He goes to the bar.*)

O'DOWD (*Following him, speaks over his shoulder to* SARA.): You should have seen the Yank! His coachman had to help him in his rig at the corner—and Roche gave the coachman a clout too, for good measure! (*He disappears, laughing, slamming the door behind him.* NORA *opens the door at right and looks in cautiously. Seeing* SARA *alone, she comes in.*)

NORA: Sara. (*She comes over to her.*) Sara. (*She takes hold of her arm—whispers uneasily.*) Where's himself?

SARA (*Dully.*): I couldn't stop him.

NORA: I could have told you you was wastin' breath. (*With a queer pride.*) The divil himself couldn't kape Con Melody from a duel! (*Then mournfully.*) It's like the auld

times come again, and the same worry and sorrow. Even
in the days before ivir I'd spoke a word to him, or done
more than make him a bow when he'd ride past on his
hunter, I used to lie awake and pray for him when I'd
hear he was fightin' a duel in the mornin'. (*She smiles
a shy, gentle smile.*) I was in love with him even then.
(SARA *starts to say something bitter but what she sees in
her mother's face stops her.* NORA *goes on, with a feeble
attempt at boastful confidence.*) But I'll not worry this
time, and let you not, either. There wasn't a man in
Galway was his equal with a pistol, and what chance
will this auld stick av a Yankee have against him?
(*There is a noise of boisterous farewells from the bar
and the noise of an outer door shutting.* NORA *starts.*)
That's him leavin'! (*Her mouth pulls down pitiably. She
starts for the bar with a sob.*) Ah, Con darlin', don't—!
(*She stops, shaking her head helplessly.*) But what's the
good? (*She sinks on a chair with a weary sigh.*)

SARA (*Bitterly, aloud to herself more than to her mother.*):
No good. Let him go his way—and I'll go mine.
(*Tensely.*) I won't let him destroy my life with his madness, after all the plans I've made and the dreams I've
dreamed. I'll show him I can play at the game of gentleman's honor too! (NORA *has not listened. She is sunk in
memories of old fears and her present worry about the
duel.* SARA *hesitates—then, keeping her face turned away
from her mother, touches her shoulder.*) I'm going upstairs to bed, Mother.

NORA (*Starts—then indignantly.*): To bed, is it? You can
think of sleepin' when he's—

SARA: I didn't say sleep, but I can lie down and try to rest.
(*Still avoiding looking at her mother.*) I'm dead tired,
Mother.

NORA (*Tenderly solicitous now, puts an arm around her.*):
You must be, darlin'. It's been the divil's own day for

you, with all— (*With sudden remorse.*) God forgive me, darlin'. I was forgettin' about you and the Harford lad. (*Miserably.*) Oh, God help us! (*Suddenly with a flash of her strange, fierce pride in the power of love.*) Never mind! If there's true love between you, you'll not let a duel or anything in the world kape you from each other, whatever the cost! Don't I know!

SARA (*Kisses her impulsively, then looks away again.*): You're going to sit up and wait down here?

NORA: I am. I'd be destroyed with fear lying down in the dark. Here, the noise of them in the bar kapes up my spirits, in a way.

SARA: Yes, you'd better stay here. Good night, Mother.

NORA: Good night, darlin'. (SARA *goes out at right, closing the door behind her.*)

Curtain

Act Four

SCENE—*The same. It is around midnight. The room is in darkness except for one candle on the table, center. From the bar comes the sound of PATCH RILEY'S pipes playing a reel and the stamp of dancing feet.*

NORA *sits at the foot of the table at center. She is hunched up in an old shawl, her arms crossed over her breast, hugging herself as if she were cold. She looks on the verge of collapse from physical fatigue and hours of worry. She starts as the door from the bar is opened. It is MICKEY. He closes the door behind him, shutting out an uproar of music and drunken voices. He has a decanter of whiskey and a glass in his hand. He has been drinking, but is not drunk.*

NORA (*Eagerly.*): There's news of himself?

MALOY (*Putting the decanter and glass on the table.*): Sorra a bit. Don't be worryin' now. Sure, it's not so late yet.

NORA (*Dully.*): It's aisy for you to say—

MALOY: I came in to see how you was, and bring you a taste to put heart in you. (*As she shakes her head.*) Oh, I know you don't indulge, but I've known you once in a while, and you need it this night. (*As she again shakes her head—with kindly bullying.*) Come now, don't be stubborn. I'm the doctor and I highly recommend a drop to drive out black thoughts and rheumatism.

NORA: Well—maybe—a taste, only.

MALOY: That's the talkin'. (*He pours a small drink and hands it to her.*) Drink hearty, now.

NORA (*Takes a sip, then puts the glass on the table and pushes it away listlessly.*): I've no taste for anything. But I thank you for the thought. You're a kind lad, Mickey.

MALOY: Here's news to cheer you. The word has got round among the boys, and they've all come in to wait for Cregan and himself. (*With enthusiasm.*) There'll be more money taken over the bar than any night since this shebeen started!

NORA: That's good.

MALOY: If they do hate Con Melody, he's Irish, and they hate the Yanks worse. They're all hopin' he's bate the livin' lights out of Harford.

NORA (*With belligerent spirit.*): And so he has, I know that!

MALOY (*Grins.*): That's the talk. I'm glad to see you roused from your worryin'. (*Turning away.*) I'd better get back. I left O'Dowd to tend bar and I'll wager he has three drinks stolen already. (*He hesitates.*) Sara's not been down?

NORA: No.

MALOY (*Resentfully.*): It's a wonder she wouldn't have more thought for you than to lave you sit up alone.

NORA (*Stiffens defensively.*): I made her go to bed. She was droppin' with tiredness and destroyed with worry. She must have fallen asleep, like the young can. None of your talk against Sara, now!

MALOY (*Starts an exasperated retort.*): The divil take— (*He stops and grins at her with affection.*) There's no batin' you, Nora. Sure, it'd be the joy av me life to have a mother like you to fight for me—or, better still, a wife like you.

NORA (*A sweet smile of pleased coquetry lights up her*

drawn face.): Arrah, save your blarney for the young girls!

MALOY: The divil take young girls. You're worth a hundred av thim.

NORA (*With a toss of her head.*): Get along with you! (MICKEY *grins with satisfaction at having cheered her up and goes in the bar, closing the door. As soon as he is gone, she sinks back into apprehensive brooding.*)

(SARA *appears silently in the doorway at right. She wears a faded old wrapper over her nightgown, slippers on her bare feet. Her hair is down over her shoulders, reaching to her waist. There is a change in her. All the bitterness and defiance have disappeared from her face. It looks gentle and calm and at the same time dreamily happy and exultant. She is much prettier than she has ever been before. She stands looking at her mother, and suddenly she becomes shy and uncertain—as if, now that she'd come this far, she had half a mind to retreat before her mother discovered her. But NORA senses her presence and looks up.*)

NORA (*Dully.*): Ah, it's you, darlin'! (*Then gratefully.*) Praise be, you've come at last! I'm sick with worry and I've got to the place where I can't bear waitin' alone, listenin' to drunks dancin' and celebratin'. (SARA *comes to her.* NORA *breaks. Tears well from her eyes.*) It's cruel, it is! There's no heart or thought for himself in divil a one av thim. (*She starts to sob.* SARA *hugs her and kisses her cheek gently. But she doesn't speak. It is as if she were afraid her voice would give her away.* NORA *stops sobbing. Her mood changes to resentment and she speaks as if* SARA *had spoken.*) Don't tell me not to worry. You're as bad as Mickey. The Yankee didn't apologize or your father'd been back here long since. It's a duel, that's certain, and he must have taken a room in the city so he'll be near the ground. I hope he'll sleep, but I'm feared he'll stay up drinkin', and at the dawn he'll have had too much to shoot his best and maybe— (*Then defiantly self-reassuringly.*) Arrah, I'm the fool! It's himself can keep his head clear and his eyes sharp, no matter what he's taken! (*Pushing* SARA *away—with nervous peevishness.*) Let go of me. You've hardened not to care. I'd rather stay alone. (*She grabs* SARA'*s hand.*) No. Don't heed me. Sit down, darlin'. (SARA *sits down on her left at rear of table. She pats her mother's hand, but remains silent, her expression dreamily happy, as if she heard* NORA'*s words but they had no meaning for her.* NORA *goes on worriedly again.*) But if he's staying in the city, why hasn't he sent Jamie Cregan back for his duelin' pistols? I know he'd nivir fight with any others. (*Resentful now at* MELODY.) Or you'd think he'd send Jamie or someone back with a word for me. He knows well how tormented I'd be waiting. (*Bitterly.*) Arrah, don't talk like a loon! Has he ever cared for anyone except himself and his pride? Sure, he'd never stoop to think of me, the grand gentleman in his red livery av bloody England! His pride, indade! What is it but a lie? What's in his veins, God pity him, but the blood of thievin' auld Ned Melody who kept a dirty shebeen? (*Then is horrified at herself as if she had blasphemed.*) No! I won't say it! I've nivir! It would break his heart if he heard me! I'm the only one in the world he knows nivir sneers at his dreams! (*Working herself to rebellion again.*) All the same, I won't stay here the rist of the night worryin' my heart out for a man who—it isn't only fear over the duel. It's because I'm afraid it's God's punishment, all the sorrow and trouble that's come on us, and I have the black tormint in my mind that it's the fault of the mortal sin I did with him unmarried, and the promise he made me make to leave the Church that's kept me from ever confessin' to a priest. (*She pauses—dully.*) Go to a doctor, you say, to cure the rheumatism. Sure, what's rheumatism but a pain in your body? I could bear ten of it. It's the pain of guilt in my soul. Can a doctor's medicine cure that? No, only a priest of Almighty God— (*With a roused rebellion again.*) It would serve Con right if I took the chance now and broke my promise and woke up the priest to hear my confession and give me God's forgiveness that'd bring my soul peace and comfort so I wouldn't feel the three of us were damned. (*Yearningly.*) Oh, if I only had the courage! (*She rises suddenly from her chair—with brave defiance.*) I'll do it, so I will! I'm going to the priest's, Sara. (*She starts for the street door—gets halfway to it and stops.*)

SARA (*A strange, tenderly amused smile on her lips—teasingly.*): Well, why don't you go, Mother?

NORA (*Defiantly.*): Ain't I goin'? (*She takes a few more steps toward the door—stops again—she mutters beatenly.*) God forgive me, I can't. What's the use pretendin'?

SARA (*As before.*): No use at all, Mother. I've found that out.

NORA (*As if she hadn't heard, comes back slowly.*): He'd feel I'd betrayed him and my word and my love for him —and for all his scorn, he knows my love is all he has in the world to comfort him. (*Then spiritedly, with a proud toss of her head.*) And it's my honor, too! It's not for his sake at all! Divil mend him, he always prates as if he had all the honor there is, but I've mine, too, as proud as his. (*She sits down in the same chair.*)

SARA (*Softly.*): Yes, the honor of her love to a woman. I've learned about that too, Mother.

NORA (*As if this were the first time she was really conscious of SARA speaking, and even now had not heard what she said—irritably.*): So you've found your tongue, have you? Thank God. You're cold comfort, sitting silent like a statue, and me making talk to myself. (*Regarding her as if she hadn't really seen her before—resentfully.*) Musha but it's pleased and pretty you look, as if there wasn't a care in the world, while your poor father—

SARA (*Dreamily amused, as if this no longer had any importance or connection with her.*): I know it's no use telling you there won't be any duel, Mother, and it's crazy to give it a thought. You're living in Ireland long ago, like Father. But maybe you'll take Simon's word for it, if you won't mine. He said his father would be paralyzed with indignation just at the thought he'd ever fight a duel. It's against the law.

NORA (*Scornfully.*): Och, who cares for the law? He must be a coward. (*She looks relieved.*) Well, if the young lad said that, maybe it's true.

SARA: Of course it's true, Mother.

NORA: Your father'd be satisfied with Harford's apology and that'd end it.

SARA (*Helplessly.*): Oh, Mother! (*Then quickly.*) Yes, I'm sure it ended hours ago.

NORA (*Intent on her hope.*): And you think what's keeping him out is he and Jamie would take a power av drinks to celebrate.

SARA: They'd drink, that's sure, whatever happened. (*She adds dreamily.*) But that doesn't matter now at all.

NORA (*Stares at her—wonderingly.*): You've a queer way of talking, as if you'd been asleep and was still half in a dream.

SARA: In a dream right enough, Mother, and it isn't half of me that's in it but all of me, body and soul. And it's a dream that's true, and always will be to the end of life, and I'll never wake from it.

NORA: Sure, what's come over you at all?

SARA (*Gets up impulsively and comes around in back of her mother's chair and slips to her knees and puts her arms about her—giving her a hug.*): Joy. That's what's come over me. I'm happy, Mother. I'm happy because I know now Simon is mine, and no one can ever take him from me.

NORA (*At first her only reaction is pleased satisfaction.*): God be thanked! It was a great sorrow tormentin' me that the duel would come between you. (*Defiantly.*) Honor or not, why should the children have their lives and their love destroyed!

SARA: I was a great fool to fear his mother could turn him against me, no matter what happened.

NORA: You've had a talk with the lad?

SARA: I have. That's where I've been.

NORA: You've been in his room ever since you went up?

SARA: Almost. After I'd got upstairs it took me a while to get up my courage.

NORA (*Rebukingly.*): All this time—in the dead of the night!

SARA (*Teasingly.*): I'm his nurse, aren't I? I've a right.

NORA: That's no excuse!

SARA (*Her face hardening.*): Excuse? I had the best in the world. Would you have me do nothing to save my happiness and my chance in life, when I thought there was danger they'd be ruined forever? Don't you want me to have love and be happy, Mother?

NORA (*Melting.*): I do, darlin'. I'd give my life— (*Then rebuking again.*) Were you the way you are, in only a nightgown and wrapper?

SARA (*Gaily.*): I was—and Simon liked my costume, if you don't, although he turned red as a beet when I came in.

NORA: Small wonder he did! Shame on you!

SARA: He was trying to read a book of poetry, but he couldn't he was that worried hoping I'd come to say goodnight, and being frightened I wouldn't. (*She laughs tenderly.*) Oh, it was the cutest thing I've ever done,

Mother, not to see him at all since his mother left. He kept waiting for me and when I didn't come, he got scared to death that his kissing me this morning had made me angry. So he was wild with joy to see me—

NORA: In your bare legs with only your nightgown and wrapper to cover your nakedness! Where's your modesty?

SARA (*Gaily teasing.*): I had it with me, Mother, though I'd tried hard to leave it behind. I got as red as he was. (*She laughs.*) Oh, Mother, it's a great joke on me. Here I'd gone to his room with my mind made up to be as bold as any street woman and tempt him because I knew his honor would make him marry me right away if— (*She laughs.*) And then all I could do was stand and gape at him and blush!

NORA Oh. (*Rebukingly.*) I'm glad you had the dacency to blush.

SARA: It was Simon spoke first, and once he started, all he'd been holding back came out. The waiting for me, and the fear he'd had made him forget all his shyness, and he said he loved me and asked me to marry him the first day we could. Without knowing how it happened, there I was with his arms around me and mine around him and his lips on my lips and it was heaven, Mother.

NORA (*Moved by the shining happiness in* SARA'S *face.*): God bless the two av you.

SARA: Then I was crying and telling him how afraid I'd been his mother hated me, Father's madness about the duel would give her a good chance to come between us; Simon said no one could ever come between us and his mother would never try to, now she knew he loved me, which was what she came over to find out. He said all she wanted was for him to be free to do as he pleased, and she only suggested he wait a year, she didn't make him promise. And Simon said I was foolish to think she would take the duel craziness serious. She'd only

be amused at the joke it would be on his father, after he'd
been so sure he could buy us off, if he had to call the
police to save him.

NORA (*Aroused at the mention of police.*): Call the police,
is it? The coward!

SARA (*Goes on, unheedingly.*): Simon was terribly angry
at his father for that. And at Father too when I told
how he threatened he'd kill me. But we didn't talk of
it much. We had better things to discuss. (*She smiles
tenderly.*)

NORA (*Belligerently.*): A lot Con Melody cares for police,
and him in a rage! Not the whole dirty force av thim
will dare interfere with him!

SARA (*Goes on as if she hadn't heard.*): And then Simon
told me how scared he'd been I didn't love him and
wouldn't marry him. I was so beautiful, he said, and he
wasn't handsome at all. So I kissed him and told him
he was the handsomest in the world, and he is. And he
said he wasn't worthy because he had so little to offer,
and was a failure at what he'd hoped he could be, a poet.
So I kissed him and told him he was too a poet, and
always would be, and it was what I loved most about
him.

NORA: The police! Let one av thim lay his dirty hand on
Con Melody, and he'll knock him senseless with one
blow.

SARA: Then Simon said how poor he was, and he'd never
accept a penny from his father, even if he offered it. And
I told him never mind, that if we had to live in a hut, or
sleep in the grass of a field without a roof to our heads,
and work our hands to the bone, or starve itself, I'd be in
heaven and sing with the joy of our love! (*She looks up
at her mother.*) And I meant it, Mother! I meant every
word of it from the bottom of my heart!

NORA (*Answers vaguely from her preoccupation with the*

police—patting SARA's *hair mechanically*.): Av course you did, darlin'.

SARA: But he kissed me and said it wouldn't be as bad as that, he'd been thinking and he'd had an offer from an old college friend who'd inherited a cotton mill and who wants Simon to be equal partners if he'll take complete charge of it. It's only a small mill and that's what tempts Simon. He said maybe I couldn't believe it but he knows from his experience working for his father he has the ability for trade, though he hates it, and he could easily make a living for us from this mill—just enough to be comfortable, and he'd have time over to write his book, and keep his wisdom, and never let himself become a slave to the greed for more than enough that is the curse of mankind. Then he said he was afraid maybe I'd think it was weakness in him, not wisdom, and could I be happy with enough and no more. So I kissed him and said all I wanted in life was his love, and whatever meant happiness to him would be my only ambition. (*She looks up at her mother again—exultantly*.) And I meant it, Mother! With all my heart and soul!

NORA (*As before, patting her hair*.): I know, darlin'.

SARA: Isn't that a joke on me, with all my crazy dreams of riches and a grand estate and me a haughty lady riding around in a carriage with coachman and footman! (*She laughs at herself*.) Wasn't I the fool to think that had any meaning at all when you're in love? You were right, Mother. I knew nothing of love, or the pride a woman can take in giving everything—the pride in her own love! I was only an ignorant, silly girl boasting, but I'm a woman now, Mother, and I know.

NORA (*As before, mechanically*.): I'm sure you do, darlin'. (*She mutters fumingly to herself*.) Let the police try it! He'll whip them back to their kennels, the dirty curs!

SARA (*Lost in her happiness*.): And then we put out the

light and talked about how soon we'd get married, and how happy we'd be the rest of our lives together, and we'd have children—and he forgot whatever shyness was left in the dark and said he meant all the bold things he'd written in the poems I'd seen. And I confessed that I was up to every scheme to get him, because I loved him so much there wasn't anything I wouldn't do to make sure he was mine. And all the time we were kissing each other, wild with happiness. And— (*She stops abruptly and looks down guiltily.*)

NORA (*As before.*): Yes, darlin', I know.

SARA (*Guiltily, keeping her eyes down.*): You—know, Mother?

NORA (*Abruptly comes out of her preoccupation, startled and uneasy.*): I know what? What are you sayin'? Look up at me! (*She pulls* SARA's *head back so she can look down in her face—falteringly.*) I can see— You let him! You wicked, sinful girl!

SARA (*Defiantly and proudly.*): There was no letting about it, only love making the two of us!

NORA (*Helplessly resigned already but feeling it her duty to rebuke.*): Ain't you ashamed to boast—?

SARA: No! There was no shame in it! (*Proudly.*) Ashamed? You know I'm not! Haven't you told me of the pride in your love? Were you ashamed?

NORA (*Weakly.*): I was. I was dead with shame.

SARA: You were not! You were proud like me!

NORA: But it's a mortal sin. God will punish you—

SARA: Let Him! If He'd say to me, for every time you kiss Simon you'll have a thousand years in hell, I wouldn't care, I'd wear out my lips kissing him!

NORA (*Frightenedly.*): Whist, now! He might hear you.

SARA: Wouldn't you have said the same—?

NORA (*Distractedly.*): Will you stop! Don't torment me with your sinful questions! I won't answer you!

SARA (*Hugging her.*): All right. Forgive me, Mother. (*A pause—smilingly.*) It was Simon who felt guilty and repentant. If he'd had his way, he'd be out of bed now, and the two of us would be walking around in the night, trying to wake up someone who could marry us. But I was so drunk with love, I'd lost all thought or care about marriage. I'd got to the place where all you know or care is that you belong to love, and you can't call your soul your own any more, let alone your body, and you're proud you've given them to love. (*She pauses—then teasing lovingly.*) Sure, I've always known you're the sweetest woman in the world, Mother, but I never suspected you were a wise woman too, until I knew tonight the truth of what you said this morning, that a woman can forgive whatever the man she loves could do and still love him, because it was through him she found the love in herself; that, in one way, he doesn't count at all, because it's love, your own love, you love in him, and to keep that your pride will do anything. (*She smiles with a self-mocking happiness.*) It's love's slaves we are, Mother, not men's—and wouldn't it shame their boasting and vanity if we ever let them know our secret? (*She laughs—then suddenly looks guilty.*) But I'm talking great nonsense. I'm glad Simon can't hear me. (*She pauses.* NORA *is worrying and hasn't listened.* SARA *goes on.*) Yes, I can even understand now—a little anyway— how you can still love Father and be proud of it, in spite of what he is.

NORA (*At the mention of* MELODY, *comes out of her brooding.*): Hush, now! (*Miserably.*) God help us, Sara, why doesn't he come, what's happened to him?

SARA (*Gets to her feet exasperatedly.*): Don't be a fool, Mother. (*Bitterly.*) Nothing's happened except he's made a public disgrace of himself, for Simon's mother to sneer at. If she wanted revenge on him, I'm sure she's had her

fill of it. Well, I don't care. He deserves it. I warned him
and I begged him, and got called a peasant slut and a
whore for my pains. All I hope now is that whatever
happened wakes him from his lies and mad dreams so
he'll have to face the truth of himself in that mirror.
(*Sneeringly.*) But there's devil a chance he'll ever let
that happen. Instead, he'll come home as drunk as two
lords, boasting of his glorious victory over old Harford,
whatever the truth is! (*But* NORA *isn't listening. She has
heard the click of the latch on the street door at rear.*)

NORA (*Excitedly.*): Look, Sara! (*The door is opened slowly
and* JAMIE CREGAN *sticks his head in cautiously to peer
around the room. His face is battered, nose red and swollen, lips cut and puffed, and one eye so blackened it is
almost closed.* NORA'S *first reaction is a cry of relief.*)
Praise be to the Saints, you're back, Jamie!

CREGAN (*Puts a finger to his lips—cautioningly.*): Whist!

NORA (*Frightenedly.*): Jamie! Where's himself?

CREGAN (*Sharply.*): Whist, I'm telling you! (*In a whisper.*)
I've got him in a rig outside, but I had to make sure no
one was here. Lock the bar door, Sara, and I'll bring him
in. (*She goes and turns the key in the door, her expression contemptuous.* CREGAN *then disappears, leaving the
street door half open.*)

NORA: Did you see Jamie's face? They've been fightin'
terrible. Oh, I'm afraid, Sara.

SARA: Afraid of what? It's only what I told you to expect.
A crazy row—and now he's paralyzed drunk. (CREGAN
*appears in the doorway at rear. He is half leading, half
supporting* MELODY. *The latter moves haltingly and wood-
enly. But his movements do not seem those of drunkenness. It is more as if a sudden shock or stroke had
shattered his coordination and left him in a stupor. His
scarlet uniform is filthy and torn and pulled awry. The
pallor of his face is ghastly. He has a cut over his left*

eye, a blue swelling on his left cheekbone, and his lips are cut and bloody. From a big raw bruise on his forehead, near the temple, trickles of dried blood run down to his jaw. Both his hands are swollen, with skinned knuckles, as are CREGAN'S. *His eyes are empty and lifeless. He stares at his wife and daughter as if he did not recognize them.*)

NORA (*Rushes and puts her arm around him.*): Con, darlin'! Are you hurted bad? (*He pushes her away without looking at her. He walks dazedly to his chair at the head of the center table.* NORA *follows him, breaking into lamentation.*) Con, don't you know me? Oh, God help us, look at his head!

SARA: Be quiet, Mother. Do you want them in the bar to know he's come home—the way he is. (*She gives her father a look of disgust.*)

CREGAN: Ay, that's it, Sara. We've got to rouse him first. His pride'd nivir forgive us if we let thim see him dead bate like this. (*There is a pause. They stare at him and he stares sightlessly at the table top.* NORA *stands close by his side, behind the table, on his right,* SARA *behind her on her right,* CREGAN *at right of* SARA.)

SARA: He's drunk, isn't that all it is, Jamie?

CREGAN (*Sharply.*): He's not. He's not taken a drop since we left here. It's the clouts on the head he got, that's what ails him. A taste of whiskey would bring him back, if he'd only take it, but he won't.

SARA (*Gives her father a puzzled, uneasy glance.*): He won't?

NORA (*Gets the decanter and a glass and hands them to* CREGAN.): Here. Try and make him.

CREGAN (*Pours out a big drink and puts it before* MELODY— *coaxingly.*): Drink this now, Major, and you'll be right as rain! (MELODY *does not seem to notice. His expression remains blank and dead.* CREGAN *scratches his head puzzledly.*) He won't. That's the way he's been all the way back when I tried to persuade him. (*Then irritably.*) Well, if he won't, I will, be your leave. I'm needin' it bad. (*He downs the whiskey, and pours out another—to* NORA *and* SARA.) It's the divil's own rampage we've had.

SARA (*Quietly contemptuous, but still with the look of puzzled uneasiness at her father.*): From your looks it must have been.

CREGAN (*Indignantly.*): You're takin' it cool enough, and you seein' the marks av the batin' we got! (*He downs his second drink—boastfully.*) But if we're marked, there's others is marked worse and some av thim is police!

NORA: God be praised! The dirty cowards!

SARA: Be quiet, Mother. Tell us what happened, Jamie.

CREGAN: Faix, what didn't happen? Be the rock av Cashel, I've nivir engaged in a livelier shindy! We had no trouble findin' where Harford lived. It's a grand mansion, with a big walled garden behind it, and we wint to the front door. A flunky in livery answered wid two others behind. A big black naygur one was. That pig av a lawyer must have warned Harford to expect us. Con spoke wid the airs av a lord. "Kindly inform your master," he says, "that Major Cornelius Melody, late of His Majesty's Seventh Dragoons, respectfully requests a word with him." Well, the flunky put an insolent sneer on him. "Mr. Harford won't see you," he says. I could see Con's rage risin' but he kept polite. "Tell him," he says, "if he knows what's good for him he'll see me. For if he don't, I'll come in and see him." "Ye will, will ye?" says the flunky, "I'll have you know Mr. Harford don't allow drunken Micks to come here disturbing him. The police have been informed," he says, "and you'll be arrested if you make trouble." Then he started to shut the door. "Anyway, you've come to the wrong door," he says, "the place for the loiks av you is the servants' entrance."

NORA (*Angrily.*): Och, the impident divil!

SARA (*In spite of herself her temper has been rising. She looks at* MELODY *with angry scorn.*): You let Harford's servants insult you! (*Then quickly.*) But it serves you right! I knew what would happen! I warned you!

CREGAN: Let thim be damned! Kape your mouth shut, and lave me tell it, and you'll see if we let them! When he'd said that, the flunky tried to slam the door in our faces, but Con was too quick. He pushed it back on him and lept in the hall, roarin' mad, and hit the flunky a cut with his whip across his ugly mug that set him screaming like a stuck pig!

NORA (*Enthusiastically.*): Good for you, Con darlin'!

SARA (*Humiliatedly.*): Mother! Don't! (*To* MELODY *with biting scorn.*) The famous duelist—in a drunken brawl with butlers and coachmen! (*But he is staring sightlessly at the table top as if he didn't see her or know her.*)

CREGAN (*Angrily, pouring himself another drink.*): Shut your mouth, Sara, and don't be trying to plague him. You're wastin' breath anyway, the way he is. He doesn't know you or hear you. And don't put on lady's airs about fighting when you're the whole cause of it.

SARA (*Angrily.*): It's a lie! You know I tried to stop—

CREGAN (*Gulps down his drink, ignoring this, and turns to* NORA—*enthusiastically.*): Wait till you hear, Nora! (*He plunges into the midst of battle again.*) The naygur hit me a clout that had my head dizzy. He'd have had me down only Con broke the butt av the whip over his black skull and knocked him to his knees. Then the third man punched Con and I gave him a kick where it'd do him least good, and he rolled on the floor, grabbin' his guts. The naygur was in again and grabbed me, but Con came at him and knocked him down. Be the mortal, we had the three av thim licked, and we'd have dragged auld Harford from his burrow and tanned his Yankee hide if the police hadn't come!

NORA (*Furiously.*): Arrah, the dirthy cowards! Always takin' sides with the rich Yanks against the poor Irish!

SARA (*More and more humiliated and angry and torn by conflicting emotions—pleadingly.*): Mother! Can't you keep still?

CREGAN: Four av thim wid clubs came behind us. They grabbed us before we knew it and dragged us into the street. Con broke away and hit the one that held him, and I gave one a knee in his belly. And then, glory be, there was a fight! Oh, it'd done your heart good to see himself! He was worth two men, lettin' out right and left, roarin' wid rage and cursin' like a trooper—

MELODY (*Without looking up or any change in his dazed expression, suddenly speaks in a jeering mumble to himself.*): Bravely done, Major Melody! The Commander of the Forces honors your exceptional gallantry! Like the glorious field of Talavera! Like the charge on the French square! Cursing like a drunken, foul-mouthed son of a thieving shebeen keeper who sprang from the filth of a peasant hovel, with pigs on the floor—with that pale Yankee bitch watching from a window, sneering with disgust!

NORA (*Frightenedly.*): God preserve us, it's crazed he is!

SARA (*Stares at him startled and wondering. For a second there is angry pity in her eyes. She makes an impulsive move toward him.*): Father! (*Then her face hardening.*) He isn't crazed, Mother. He's come to his senses for once in his life! (*To* MELODY.) So she was sneering, was she? I don't blame her! I'm glad you've been taught a lesson! (*Then vindictively.*) But I've taught her one, too. She'll soon sneer from the wrong side of her mouth!

CREGAN (*Angrily.*): Will you shut your gab, Sara! Lave him be and don't heed him. It's the same crazy blather he's talked every once in a while since they brought him to —about the Harford woman—and speakin' av the pigs and his father one minute, and his pride and honor and his mare the next. (*He takes up the story again.*) Well, anyways, they was too much for us, the four av thim wid clubs. The last thing I saw before I was knocked senseless was three av thim clubbing Con. But, be the Powers, we wint down fightin' to the last for the glory av auld Ireland!

MELODY (*In a jeering mutter to himself.*): Like a rum-soaked trooper, brawling before a brothel on a Saturday night, puking in the gutter!

SARA (*Strickenly.*): Don't, Father!

CREGAN (*Indignantly to* MELODY.): We wasn't in condition. If we had been—but they knocked us senseless and rode us to the station and locked us up. And we'd be there yet if Harford hadn't made thim turn us loose, for he's rich and has influence. Small thanks to him! He was afraid the row would get in the paper and put shame on him. (MELODY *laughs crazily and springs to his feet. He sways dizzily, clutching his head—then goes toward the door at left front.*)

NORA: Con! Where are you goin'? (*She starts after him and grabs his arm. He shakes her hand off roughly as if he did not recognize her.*)

CREGAN: He don't know you. Don't cross him now, Nora. Sure, he's only goin' upstairs to bed. (*Wheedlingly.*) You know what's best for you, don't you, Major? (MELODY *feels his way gropingly through the door and disappears, leaving it open.*)

SARA (*Uneasy, but consoling her mother.*): Jamie's right, Mother. If he'll fall asleep, that's the best thing— (*Abruptly she is terrified.*) Oh God, maybe he'll take revenge on Simon— (*She rushes to the door and stands listening—with relief.*) No, he's gone to his room. (*She comes back—a bit ashamed.*) I'm a fool. He'd never harm a sick man, no matter— (*She takes her mother's arm—*

gently.) Don't stand there, Mother. Sit down. You're tired enough—

NORA (*Frightenedly.*): I've never heard him talk like that in all the years—with that crazy dead look in his eyes. Oh, I'm afeered, Sara. Lave go of me. I've got to make sure he's gone to bed. (*She goes quickly to the door and disappears.* SARA *makes a move to follow her.*)

CREGAN (*Roughly.*): Stay here, unless you're a fool, Sara. He might come to all av a sudden and give you a hell av a thrashin'. Troth, you deserve one. You're to blame for what's happened. Wasn't he fightin' to revenge the insults to you? (*He sprawls on a chair at rear of the table at center.*)

SARA (*Sitting down at rear of the small table at left front—angrily.*): I'll thank you to mind your own business, Jamie Cregan. Just because you're a relation—

CREGAN (*Harshly.*): Och, to hell with your airs! (*He pours out a drink and downs it. He is becoming drunk again.*)

SARA: I can revenge my own insults, and I have! I've beaten the Harfords—and he's only made a fool of himself for her to sneer at. But I've beaten her and I'll sneer last! (*She pauses, a hard, triumphant smile on her lips. It fades. She gives a little bewildered laugh.*) God forgive me, what a way to think of—I must be crazy, too.

CREGAN (*Drunkenly.*): Ah, don't be talkin'! Didn't the two of us lick them all! And Con's all right. He's all right, I'm sayin'! It's only the club on the head makes him quare a while. I've seen it often before. Ay, and felt it meself. I remember at a fair in the auld country I was clouted with the butt av a whip and I didn't remember a thing for hours, but they told me after I never stopped gabbin' but went around tellin' every stranger all my secrets. (*He pauses.* SARA *hasn't listened. He goes on uneasily.*) All the same, it's no fun listening to his mad blather about the pale bitch, as he calls her, like she was a ghost, haunting and scorning him. And his gab about his beautiful thoroughbred mare is madder still, raving what a grand, beautiful lady she is, with her slender ankles and dainty feet, sobbin' and beggin' her forgiveness and talkin' of dishonor and death— (*He shrinks superstitiously—then angrily, reaching for the decanter.*) Och, be damned to this night! (*Before he can pour a drink,* NORA *comes hurrying in from the door at left front.*)

NORA (*Breathless and frightened.*): He's come down! He pushed me away like he didn't see me. He's gone out to the barn. Go after him, Jamie.

CREGAN (*Drunkenly.*): I won't. He's all right. Lave him alone.

SARA (*Jeeringly.*): Sure, he's only gone to pay a call on his sweetheart, the mare, Mother, and hasn't he slept in her stall many a time when he was dead drunk, and she never even kicked him?

NORA (*Distractedly.*): Will you shut up, the two av you! I heard him openin' the closet in his room where he keeps his auld set of duelin' pistols, and he was carryin' the box when he came down—

CREGAN (*Scrambles hastily to his feet.*): Oh, the lunatic!

NORA: He'll ride the mare back to Harford's! He'll murther someone! For the love av God, stop him, Jamie!

CREGAN (*Drunkenly belligerent.*): Be Christ, I'll stop him for you, Nora, pistols or no pistols! (*He walks a bit unsteadily out the door at left front.*)

SARA (*Stands tensely—bursts out with a strange triumphant pride.*): Then he's not beaten! (*Suddenly she is overcome by a bitter, tortured revulsion of feeling.*) Merciful God, what am I thinking? As if he hadn't done enough to destroy— (*Distractedly.*) Oh, the mad fool! I wish he was— (*From the yard, off left front, there is the muffled crack of a pistol shot hardly perceptible above the noise in the barroom. But* SARA *and* NORA *both hear it and stand frozen with horror.* SARA *babbles hysterically.*) I didn't mean it, Mother! I didn't!

NORA (*Numb with fright—mumbles stupidly.*): A shot!

SARA: You know I didn't mean it, Mother!

NORA: A shot! God help us, he's kilt Jamie!

SARA (*Stammers.*): No—not Jamie— (*Wildly.*) Oh, I can't bear waiting! I've got to know— (*She rushes to the door at left front—then stops frightenedly.*) I'm afraid to know! I'm afraid—

NORA (*Mutters stupidly.*): Not Jamie? Then who else? (*She begins to tremble—in a horrified whisper.*) Sara! You think— Oh, God have mercy!

SARA: Will you hush, Mother! I'm trying to hear— (*She retreats quickly into the room and backs around the table at left front until she is beside her mother.*) Someone's at the yard door. It'll be Jamie coming to tell us—

NORA: It's a lie! He'd nivir. He'd nivir! (*They stand paralyzed by terror, clinging to each other, staring at the open door. There is a moment's pause in which the sound of drunken roistering in the bar seems louder. Then* MELODY *appears in the doorway with* CREGAN *behind him.* CREGAN *has him by the shoulder and pushes him roughly into the room, like a bouncer handling a drunk.* CREGAN *is shaken by the experience he has just been through and his reaction is to make him drunkenly angry at* MELODY. *In his free hand is a dueling pistol.* MELODY'S *face is like gray wax. His body is limp, his feet drag, his eyes seem to have no sight. He appears completely possessed by a paralyzing stupor.*)

SARA (*Impulsively.*): Father! Oh, thank God! (*She takes one step toward him—then her expression begins to harden.*)

NORA (*Sobs with relief.*): Oh, praise God you're alive! Sara and me was dead with fear— (*She goes toward them.*) Con! Con, darlin'!

CREGAN (*Dumps* MELODY *down on the nearest chair at left
of the small table—roughly, his voice trembling.*): Let
you sit still now, Con Melody, and behave like a gintleman! (*To* NORA.) Here he is for ye, Nora, and you're
welcome, bad luck to him! (*He moves back as* NORA
comes and puts her arms around MELODY *and hugs him
tenderly.*)

NORA: Oh, Con, Con, I was so afeered for you! (*He does
not seem to hear or see her, but she goes on crooning to
him comfortingly as if he were a sick child.*)

CREGAN: He was in the stable. He'd this pistol in his hand,
with the mate to it on the floor beside the mare. (*He
shudders and puts the pistol on the table shakenly.*) It's
mad he's grown entirely! Let you take care av him now,
his wife and daughter! I've had enough. I'm no damned
keeper av lunatics! (*He turns toward the barroom.*)

SARA: Wait, Jamie. We heard a shot. What was it?

CREGAN (*Angrily.*): Ask him, not me! (*Then with bewildered horror.*) He kilt the poor mare, the mad fool!
(SARA *stares at him in stunned amazement.*) I found him
on the floor with her head in his lap, and her dead. He
was sobbing like a soul in hell— (*He shudders.*) Let me
get away from the sight of him where there's men in their
right senses laughing and singing! (*He unlocks the barroom door.*) And don't be afraid, Sara, that I'll tell the
boys a word av this. I'll talk of our fight in the city only,
because it's all I want to remember. (*He jerks open the
door and goes in the bar, slamming the door quickly
behind him. A roar of welcome is heard as the crowd
greets his arrival.* SARA *locks the door again. She comes
back to the center table, staring at* MELODY, *an hysterical,
sneering grin making her lips quiver and twitch.*)

SARA: What a fool I was to be afraid! I might know you'd
never do it as long as a drink of whiskey was left in the
world! So it was the mare you shot? (*She bursts into*

uncontrollable, hysterical laugher. It penetrates MELODY's *stupor and he stiffens rigidly on his chair, but his eyes remain fixed on the table top.*)

NORA: Sara! Stop! For the love av God, how can you laugh—!

SARA: I can't—help it, Mother. Didn't you hear—Jamie? It was the mare he shot! (*She gives way to laughter again.*)

NORA (*Distractedly.*): Stop it, I'm sayin'! (SARA *puts her hand over her mouth to shut off the sound of her laughing, but her shoulders still shake.* NORA *sinks on the chair at rear of the table. She mutters dazedly.*) Kilt his beautiful mare? He must be mad entirely.

MELODY (*Suddenly speaks, without looking up, in the broadest brogue, his voice coarse and harsh.*): Lave Sara laugh. Sure, who could blame her? I'm roarin' meself inside me. It's the damnedest joke a man ivir played on himself since time began. (*They stare at him.* SARA's *laughter stops. She is startled and repelled by his brogue. Then she stares at him suspiciously, her face hardening.*)

SARA: What joke? Do you think murdering the poor mare a good joke? (MELODY *stiffens for a second, but that is all. He doesn't look up or reply.*)

NORA (*Frightened.*): Look at the dead face on him, Sara. He's like a corpse. (*She reaches out and touches one of his hands on the table top with a furtive tenderness—pleadingly.*) Con, darlin'. Don't!

MELODY (*Looks up at her. His expression changes so that his face loses all its remaining distinction and appears vulgar and common, with a loose, leering grin on his swollen lips.*): Let you not worry, Allanah. Sure, I'm no corpse, and with a few drinks in me, I'll soon be lively enough to suit you.

NORA (*Miserably confused.*): Will you listen to him, Sara— puttin' on the brogue to torment us.

SARA (*Growing more uneasy but sneering.*): Pay no heed to

him, Mother. He's play-acting to amuse himself. If he's that cruel and shameless after what he's done—

NORA (*Defensively.*): No, it's the blow on the head he got fightin' the police.

MELODY (*Vulgarly.*): The blow, me foot! That's Jamie Cregan's blather. Sure, it'd take more than a few clubs on the head to darken my wits long. Me brains, if I have any, is clear as a bell. And I'm not puttin' on brogue to tormint you, me darlint. Nor play-actin', Sara. That was the Major's game. It's quare, surely, for the two av ye to object when I talk in me natural tongue, and yours, and don't put on airs loike the late lamented auld liar and lunatic, Major Cornelius Melody, av His Majesty's Seventh Dragoons, used to do.

NORA: God save us, Sara, will you listen!

MELODY: But he's dead now, and his last bit av lyin' pride is murthered and stinkin'. (*He pats* NORA's *hand with what seems to be genuine comforting affection.*) So let you be aisy, darlint. He'll nivir again hurt you with his sneers, and his pretindin' he's a gintleman, blatherin' about pride and honor, and his boastin' av duels in the days that's gone, and his showin' off before the Yankees, and thim laughin' at him, prancing around drunk on his beautiful thoroughbred mare— (*He gulps as if he were choking back a sob.*) For she's dead, too, poor baste.

SARA (*This is becoming unbearable for her—tensely.*): Why —why did you kill her?

MELODY: Why did the Major, you mean! Be Christ, you're stupider than I thought you, if you can't see that. Wasn't she the livin' reminder, so to spake, av all his lyin' boasts and dreams? He meant to kill her first wid one pistol, and then himself wid the other. But faix, he saw the shot that killed her had finished him, too. There wasn't much pride left in the auld lunatic, anyway, and seeing her die made an end av him. So he didn't bother shooting him-

self, because it'd be a mad thing to waste a good bullet
on a corpse! (*He laughs coarsely.*)

SARA (*Tensely.*): Father! Stop it!

MELODY: Didn't I tell you there was a great joke in it? Well,
that's the joke. (*He begins to laugh again but he chokes
on a stifled sob. Suddenly his face loses the coarse, leering,
brutal expression and is full of anguished grief. He speaks
without brogue, not to them but aloud to himself.*)
Blessed Christ, the look in her eyes by the lantern light
with life ebbing out of them—wondering and sad, but
still trustful, not reproaching me—with no fear in them—
proud, understanding pride—loving me—she saw I was
dying with her. She understood! She forgave me! (*He
starts to sob but wrenches himself out of it and speaks in
broad, jeering brogue.*) Begorra, if that wasn't the mad
Major's ghost speakin'! But be damned to him, he won't
haunt me long, if I know it! I intind to live at my ease
from now on and not let the dead bother me, but enjoy
life in my proper station as auld Nick Melody's son. I'll
bury his Major's damned red livery av bloody England
deep in the ground and he can haunt its grave if he likes,
and boast to the lonely night av Talavera and the ladies
of Spain and fightin' the French! (*With a leer.*) Troth,
I think the boys is right when they say he stole the
uniform and he nivir fought under Wellington at all. He
was a terrible liar, as I remember him.

NORA: Con, darlin', don't be grievin' about the mare. Sure,
you can get another. I'll manage—

SARA: Mother! Hush! (*To* MELODY, *furiously.*) Father, will
you stop this mad game you're playing—?

MELODY (*Roughly.*): Game, is it? You'll find it's no game.
It was the Major played a game all his life, the crazy
auld loon, and cheated only himself. But I'll be content
to stay meself in the proper station I was born to, from
this day on. (*With a cunning leer at* SARA.) And it's

meself feels it me duty to give you a bit av fatherly advice, Sara darlint, while my mind is on it. I know you've great ambition, so remember it's to hell wid honor if ye want to rise in this world. Remember the blood in your veins and be your grandfather's true descendent. There was an able man for you! Be Jaysus, he nivir felt anything beneath him that could gain him something, and for lyin' tricks to swindle the bloody fools of gintry, there wasn't his match in Ireland, and he ended up wid a grand estate, and a castle, and a pile av gold in the bank.

SARA *(Distractedly.)*: Oh, I hate you!

NORA: Sara!

MELODY *(Goes on as if he hadn't heard.)*: I know he'd advise that to give you a first step up, darlint, you must make the young Yankee gintleman have you in his bed, and afther he's had you, weep great tears and appeal to his honor to marry you and save yours. Be God, he'll nivir resist that, if I know him, for he's a young fool, full av dacency and dreams, and looney, too, wid a touch av the poet in him. Oh, it'll be aisy for you—

SARA *(Goaded beyond bearing.)*: I'll make you stop your dirty brogue and your play-acting! *(She leans toward him and speaks with taunting vindictiveness, in broad brogue herself.)* Thank you kindly but I've already taken your wise advice, Father. I made him have me in his bed, while you was out drunk fightin' the police!

NORA *(Frightenedly.)*: Sara! Hault your brazen tongue!

MELODY *(His body stiffens on his chair and the coarse leer vanishes from his face. It becomes his old face. His eyes fix on her in a threatening stare. He speaks slowly, with difficulty keeping his words in brogue.)*: Did you now, God bless you! I might have known you'd not take any chance that the auld loon av a Major, going out to revenge an insult to you, would spoil your schemes. *(He forces a horrible grin.)* Be the living God, it's me should be proud this night that one av the Yankee gintry has stooped to be seduced by my slut av a daughter! (*Still keeping his eyes fixed on hers, he begins to rise from his chair, his right hand groping along the table top until it clutches the dueling pistol. He aims it at* SARA's *heart, like an automaton, his eyes as cold, deadly, and merciless as they must have been in his duels of long ago.* SARA *is terrified but she stands unflinchingly.*)

NORA (*Horror-stricken, lunges from her chair and grabs his arm.*): Con! For the love av God! Would you be murthering Sara? (*A dazed look comes over his face. He grows limp and sinks back on his chair and lets the pistol slide from his fingers on the table. He draws a shuddering breath—then laughs hoarsely.*)

MELODY (*With a coarse leer.*): Murtherin' Sara, is it? Are ye daft, Nora? Sure, all I want is to congratulate her!

SARA (*Hopelessly.*): Oh! (*She sinks down on her chair at rear of the center table and covers her face with her hands.*)

NORA (*With pitifully well-meant reassurance.*): It's all right, Con. The young lad wants to marry her as soon as can be, she told me, and he did before.

MELODY: Musha, but that's kind of him! Be God, we ought to be proud av our daughter, Nora. Lave it to her to get what she wants by hook or crook. And won't we be proud watchin' her rise in the world till she's a grand lady!

NORA (*Simply.*): We will, surely.

SARA: Mother!

MELODY: She'll have some trouble, rootin' out his dreams. He's set in his proud, noble ways, but she'll find the right trick! I'd lay a pound, if I had one, to a shilling she'll see the day when she'll wear fine silks and drive in a carriage wid a naygur coachman behind spankin' thoroughbreds, her nose in the air; and she'll live in a Yankee mansion, as big as a castle, on a grand estate av stately woodland and soft green meadows and a lake. (*With a leering chuckle.*) Be the Saints, I'll start her on her way by making her a wedding present av the Major's place where he let her young gintleman build his cabin—the land the Yankees swindled him into buyin' for his American estate, the mad fool! (*He glances at the dueling pistol—jeeringly.*) Speakin' av the departed, may his soul roast in hell, what am I doin' wid his pistol? Be God, I don't need pistols. Me fists, or a club if it's handy, is enough. Didn't me and Jamie lick a whole regiment av police this night?

NORA (*Stoutly.*): You did, and if there wasn't so many av thim—

MELODY (*Turns to her—grinningly.*): That's the talk, darlint! Sure, there's divil a more loyal wife in the whole world— (*He pauses, staring at her—then suddenly kisses her on the lips, roughly but with a strange real tenderness.*) and I love you.

NORA (*With amazed, unthinking joy.*): Oh, Con!

MELODY (*Grinning again.*): I've meant to tell you often, only the Major, damn him, had me under his proud thumb. (*He pulls her over and kisses her hair.*)

NORA: Is it kissin' my hair—!

MELODY: I am. Why wouldn't I? You have beautiful hair, God bless you! And don't remember what the Major used to tell you. The gintleman's sneers he put on is buried with him. I'll be a real husband to you, and help ye run this shebeen, instead of being a sponge. I'll fire Mickey and tend the bar myself, like my father's son ought to.

NORA: You'll not! I'll nivir let you!

MELODY (*Leering cunningly.*): Well, I offered, remember. It's you refused. Sure, I'm not in love with work, I'll confess, and maybe you're right not to trust me too near the whiskey. (*He licks his lips.*) Be Jaysus, that reminds me. I've not had a taste for hours. I'm dyin' av thirst.

NORA (*Starts to rise.*): I'll get you—

MELODY (*Pushes her back on her chair.*): Ye'll not. I want company and singin' and dancin' and great laughter. I'll join the boys in the bar and help Cousin Jamie celebrate our wonderful shindy wid the police. (*He gets up. His old soldierly bearing is gone. He slouches and his movements are shambling and clumsy, his big hairy hands dangling at his sides. In his torn, disheveled, dirt-stained uniform, he looks like a loutish, grinning clown.*)

NORA: You ought to go to bed, Con darlin', with your head hurted.

MELODY: Me head? Faix, it was nivir so clear while the Major lived to tormint me, makin' me tell mad lies to excuse his divilments. (*He grins.*) And I ain't tired a bit. I'm fresh as a man new born. So I'll say goodnight to you, darlint. (*He bends and kisses her.* SARA *has lifted her tear-stained face from her hands and is staring at him with a strange, anguished look of desperation. He leers at her.*) And you go to bed, too, Sara. Troth, you deserve a long, dreamless slape after all you've accomplished this day.

SARA: Please! Oh, Father, I can't bear— Won't you be yourself again?

MELODY (*Threatening her good-humoredly.*): Let you kape your mouth closed, ye slut, and not talk like you was ashamed of me, your father. I'm not the Major who was too much of a gintleman to lay hand on you. Faix, I'll give you a box on the ear that'll teach you respect, if ye kape on trying to raise the dead! (*She stares at him, sick and desperate. He starts toward the bar door.*)

SARA (*Springs to her feet.*): Father! Don't go in with those drunken scum! Don't let them hear and see you! You can drink all you like here. Jamie will come and keep you

company. He'll laugh and sing and help you celebrate
Talavera—

MELODY (*Roughly.*): To hell wid Talavera! (*His eyes are
fastened on the mirror. He leers into it.*) Be Jaysus, if
it ain't the mirror the auld loon was always admirin' his
mug in while he spouted Byron to pretend himself
was a lord wid a touch av the poet— (*He strikes a pose
which is a vulgar burlesque of his old before-the-mirror
one and recites in mocking brogue.*)

> "I have not loved the World, nor the World me;
> I have not flatthered uts rank breath, nor bowed
> To uts idolatries a pashunt knee,
> Nor coined me cheek to smiles,—nor cried aloud
> In worship av an echo: in the crowd
> They couldn't deem me one av such—I stood
> Among thim, but not av thim . . ."

(*He guffaws contemptuously.*) Be Christ, if he wasn't the
joke av the world, the Major. He should have been a
clown in a circus. God rest his soul in the flames av
tormint! (*Roughly.*) But to hell wid the dead. (*The
noise in the bar rises to an uproar of laughter as if* JAMIE
had just made some climactic point in his story. MELODY
looks away from the mirror to the bar door.) Be God,
I'm alive and in the crowd they *can* deem me one av
such! I'll be among thim and av thim, too—and make up
for the lonely dog's life the Major led me. (*He goes to the
bar door.*)

SARA (*Starts toward him—beseechingly.*): Father! Don't
put this final shame on yourself. You're not drunk now.
There's no excuse you can give yourself. You'll be as dead
to yourself after, as if you'd shot yourself along with the
mare!

MELODY (*Leering—with a wink at* NORA.): Listen to her,
Nora, reproachin' me because I'm not drunk. Troth,

that's a condition soon mended. (*He puts his hand on the knob of the door.*)

SARA: Father!

NORA (*Has given way to such complete physical exhaustion, she hardly hears, much less comprehends what is said —dully.*): Lave him alone, Sara. It's best.

MELODY (*As another roar is heard from the bar.*): I'm missin' a lot av fun. Be God, I've a bit of news to tell the boys that'll make them roar the house down. The Major's passin' to his eternal rest has set me free to jine the Democrats, and I'll vote for Andy Jackson, the friend av the common men like me, God bless him! (*He grins with anticipation.*) Wait till the boys hear that! (*He starts to turn the knob.*)

SARA (*Rushes to him and grabs his arm.*): No! I won't let you! It's my pride, too! (*She stammers.*) Listen! Forgive me, Father! I know it's my fault—always sneering and insulting you—but I only meant the lies in it. The truth—Talavera—the Duke praising your bravery— an officer in his army—even the ladies in Spain—deep down that's been my pride, too—that I was your daughter. So don't— I'll do anything you ask— I'll even tell Simon—that after his father's insult to you—I'm too proud to marry a Yankee coward's son!

MELODY (*Has been visibly crumbling as he listens until he appears to have no character left in which to hide and defend himself. He cries wildly and despairingly, as if he saw his last hope of escape suddenly cut off.*): Sara! For the love of God, stop—let me go—!

NORA (*Dully.*): Lave your poor father be. It's best. (*In a flash* MELODY *recovers and is the leering peasant again.*)

SARA (*With bitter hopelessness.*): Oh, Mother! Why couldn't you be still!

MELODY (*Roughly.*): Why can't you, ye mean. I warned ye what ye'd get if ye kept on interferin' and tryin' to raise the dead. (*He cuffs her on the side of the head. It is more of a playful push than a blow, but it knocks her off balance back to the end of the table at center.*)

NORA (*Aroused—bewilderedly.*): God forgive you, Con! (*Angrily.*) Don't you be hittin' Sara now. I've put up with a lot but I won't—

MELODY (*With rough good nature.*): Shut up, darlint. I won't have to again. (*He grins leeringly at* SARA.) That'll teach you, me proud Sara! I know you won't try raisin' the dead any more. And let me hear no more gab out of you about not marryin' the young lad upstairs. Be Jaysus, haven't ye any honor? Ye seduced him and ye'll make an honest gentleman av him if I have to march ye both by the scruff av the neck to the nearest church. (*He chuckles—then leeringly.*) And now with your permission, ladies both, I'll join me good friends in the bar. (*He opens the door and passes into the bar, closing the door behind him. There is a roar of welcoming drunken shouts, pounding of glasses on bar and tables, then quiet as if he had raised a hand for silence, followed by his voice greeting them and ordering drinks, and other roads of acclaim mingled with the music of* RILEY'S *pipes.* SARA *remains standing by the side of the center table, her shoulders bowed, her head hanging, staring at the floor.*)

NORA (*Overcome by physical exhaustion again, sighs.*): Don't mind his giving you a slap. He's still quare in his head. But he'll sing and laugh and drink a power av whiskey and slape sound after, and tomorrow he'll be himself again—maybe.

SARA (*Dully—aloud to herself rather than to her mother.*): No. He'll never be. He's beaten at last and he wants to stay beaten. Well, I did my best. Though why I did, I don't know. I must have his crazy pride in me. (*She lifts her head, her face hardening—bitterly.*) I mean, the late Major Melody's pride. I mean, I did have it. Now it's dead—thank God—and I'll make a better wife for Simon. (*There is a sudden lull in the noise from the bar, as if someone had called for silence—then* MELODY's *voice is plainly heard in the silence as he shouts a toast:* "Here's to our next President, Andy Jackson! Hurroo for Auld Hickory, God bless him!" *There is a drunken chorus of answering* "hurroos" *that shakes the walls.*)

NORA: Glory be to God, cheerin' for Andy Jackson! Did you hear him, Sara?

SARA (*Her face hard.*): I heard someone. But it wasn't any-one I ever knew or want to know.

NORA (*As if she hadn't heard.*): Ah well, that's good. They won't all be hatin' him now. (*She pauses—her tired, worn face becomes suddenly shy and tender.*) Did you hear him tellin' me he loved me, Sara? Did you see him kiss me on the mouth—and then kiss my hair? (*She gives a little, soft laugh.*) Sure, he must have gone mad altogether!

SARA (*Stares at her mother. Her face softens.*): No, Mother, I know he meant it. He'll keep on meaning it, too, Mother. He'll be free to, now. (*She smiles strangely.*) Maybe I deserved the slap for interfering.

NORA (*Preoccupied with her own thoughts.*): And if he wants to kape on makin' game of everyone, puttin' on the brogue and actin' like one av thim in there— (*She nods toward the bar.*) Well, why shouldn't he if it brings him peace and company in his loneliness? God pity him, he's had to live all his life alone in the hell av pride. (*Proudly.*) And I'll play any game he likes and give him love in it. Haven't I always? (*She smiles.*) Sure, I have no pride at all—except that.

SARA (*Stares at her—moved.*): You're a strange, noble woman, Mother. I'll try and be like you. (*She comes over and hugs her—then she smiles tenderly.*) I'll wager Simon never heard the shot or anything. He was sleeping like a baby when I left him. A cannon wouldn't wake him. (*In the bar,* RILEY *starts playing a reel on his pipes and there is the stamp of dancing feet. For a moment* SARA's *face becomes hard and bitter again. She tries to be mocking.*) Faith, Patch Riley don't know it but he's playing a requiem for the dead. (*Her voice trembles.*) May the hero of Talavera rest in peace! (*She breaks down and sobs, hiding her face on her mother's shoulder—bewilderedly.*) But why should I cry, Mother? Why do I mourn for him?

NORA (*At once forgetting her own exhaustion, is all tender, loving help and comfort.*): Don't, darlin', don't. You're destroyed with tiredness, that's all. Come on to bed, now, and I'll help you undress and tuck you in. (*Trying to rouse her—in a teasing tone.*) Shame on you to cry when you have love. What would the young lad think of you?

Curtain

Hughie

Characters

"ERIE" SMITH, *a teller of tales*

A NIGHT CLERK

SCENE—*The desk and a section of lobby of a small hotel on a West Side street in midtown New York. It is between 3 and 4 A.M. of a day in the summer of 1928.*

It is one of those hotels, built in the decade 1900–10 on side streets of the Great White Way sector, which began as respectable second class but soon were forced to deteriorate in order to survive. Following the First World War and Prohibition, it had given up all pretense of respectability, and now is anything a paying guest wants it to be, a third class dump, catering to the catch-as-catch-can trade. But still it does not prosper. It has not shared in the Great Hollow Boom of the twenties. The Everlasting Opulence of the New Economic Law has overlooked it. It manages to keep running by cutting the overhead for service, repairs, and cleanliness to a minimum.

The desk faces left along a section of seedy lobby with shabby chairs. The street entrance is off-stage, left. Behind the desk are a telephone switchboard and the operator's stool. At right, the usual numbered tiers of mailboxes, and above them a clock.

The NIGHT CLERK *sits on the stool, facing front, his back to the switchboard. There is nothing to do. He is not thinking. He is not sleepy. He simply droops and stares acquiescently at nothing. It would be discouraging to glance at the clock. He knows there are several hours to go before his shift is over. Anyway, he does not need to look at clocks. He has been a night clerk in New York hotels so long he can tell time by sounds in the street.*

He is in his early forties. Tall, thin, with a scrawny neck and jutting Adam's apple. His face is long and narrow, greasy with perspiration, sallow, studded with pimples from ingrowing hairs. His nose is large and without character. So is his mouth. So are his ears. So is his thinning brown hair, powdered with dandruff. Behind horn-rimmed spectacles, his blank brown eyes contain no discernible expression. One would say they had even forgotten how it feels to be bored. He wears an ill-fitting blue serge suit, white shirt and collar, a blue tie. The suit is old and shines at the elbows as if it had been waxed and polished.

Footsteps echo in the deserted lobby as someone comes in from the street. The NIGHT CLERK *rises wearily. His eyes remain empty but his gummy lips part automatically in a welcoming The-Patron-Is-Always-Right grimace, intended as a smile. His big uneven teeth are in bad condition.*

ERIE SMITH *enters and approaches the desk. He is about the same age as the* CLERK *and has the same pasty, perspiry, night-life complexion. There the resemblance ends.* ERIE *is around medium height but appears shorter because he is stout and his fat legs are too short for his body. So are his fat arms. His big head squats on a neck which seems part of his beefy shoulders. His face is round, his snub nose flattened at the tip. His blue eyes have drooping lids and puffy pouches under them. His sandy hair is falling out and the top of his head is bald. He walks to the desk with a breezy, familiar air, his gait a bit waddling because of his short legs. He carries a Panama hat and mops his face with a red and blue silk handkerchief. He wears a light grey suit cut in the extreme, tight-waisted, Broadway mode, the coat open to reveal an old and faded but expensive silk shirt in a shade of blue that sets teeth on edge, and a gay red and blue foulard tie, its knot stained by perspiration. His trousers are held up by a braided brown leather belt with a brass buckle. His shoes are tan and white, his socks white silk.*

In manner, he is consciously a Broadway sport and a Wise Guy—the type of small fry gambler and horse player, living hand to mouth on the fringe of the rackets. Infesting corners, doorways, cheap restaurants, the bars of minor speakeasies, he and his kind imagine they are in the Real Know, cynical oracles of the One True Grapevine.

ERIE *usually speaks in a low, guarded tone, his droop-lidded eyes suspiciously wary of nonexistent eavesdroppers. His face is set in the prescribed pattern of gambler's dead pan. His small, pursy mouth is always crooked in the cynical leer of one who possesses superior, inside information, and his shifty once-over glances never miss the price tags he detects on everything and everybody. Yet there is something phoney about his characterization of himself, some sentimental softness behind it which doesn't belong in the hard-boiled picture.*

ERIE *avoids looking at the* NIGHT CLERK, *as if he resented him.*

ERIE
    Peremptorily.
Key.
    Then as the NIGHT CLERK *gropes with his memory—grudgingly.*
Forgot you ain't seen me before. Erie Smith's the name. I'm an old timer in this fleabag. 492.
NIGHT CLERK
    In a tone of one who is wearily relieved when he does not have to remember anything—he plucks out the key.

492. Yes, sir.

ERIE

> *Taking the key, gives the* CLERK *the once-over. He appears not unfavorably impressed but his tone still holds resentment.*

How long you been on the job? Four, five days, huh? I been off on a drunk. Come to now, though. Tapering off. Well, I'm glad they fired that young squirt they took on when Hughie got sick. One of them fresh wise punks. Couldn't tell him nothing. Pleased to meet you, Pal. Hope you stick around.

> *He shoves out his hand. The* NIGHT CLERK *takes it obediently.*

NIGHT CLERK

> *With a compliant, uninterested smile.*

Glad to know you, Mr. Smith.

ERIE

What's your name?

NIGHT CLERK

> *As if he had half forgotten because what did it matter, anyway?*

Hughes. Charlie Hughes.

ERIE

> *Starts.*

Huh? Hughes? Say, is that on the level?

NIGHT CLERK

Charlie Hughes.

ERIE

Well, I be damned! What the hell d'you know about that!

> *Warming toward the* CLERK.

Say, now I notice, you don't look like Hughie, but you remind me of him somehow. You ain't by any chance related?

NIGHT CLERK

You mean to the Hughes who had this job so long
and died recently? No, sir. No relation.

ERIE

Gloomily.

No, that's right. Hughie told me he didn't have no relations left—except his wife and kids, of course.

He pauses—more gloomily.

Yeah. The poor guy croaked last week. His funeral
was what started me off on a bat.

Then boastfully, as if defending himself against gloom.

Some drunk! I don't go on one often. It's bum dope in
my book. A guy gets careless and gabs about things he
knows and when he comes to he's liable to find there's
guys who'd feel easier if he wasn't around no more.
That's the trouble with knowing things. Take my tip,
Pal. Don't never know nothin'. Be a sap and stay
healthy.

*His manner has become secretive, with sinister under-
tones. But the* NIGHT CLERK *doesn't notice this. Long
experience with guests who stop at his desk in the
small hours to talk about themselves has given him
a foolproof technique of self-defense. He appears to
listen with agreeable submissiveness and be impressed,
but his mind is blank and he doesn't hear unless a
direct question is put to him, and sometimes not even
then.* ERIE *thinks he is impressed.*

But hell, I always keep my noggin working, booze or
no booze. I'm no sucker. What was I sayin'? Oh, some
drunk. I sure hit the high spots. You shoulda seen the
doll I made night before last. And did she take me to
the cleaners! I'm a sucker for blondes.

He pauses—giving the NIGHT CLERK *a cynical, contemptuous glance.*

You're married, ain't you?

NIGHT CLERK

*Long ago he gave up caring whether questions were
personal or not.*

Yes, sir.

ERIE

Yeah, I'd'a laid ten to one on it. You got that old look.
Like Hughie had. Maybe that's the resemblance.

He chuckles contemptuously.

Kids, too, I bet?

NIGHT CLERK

Yes, sir. Three.

ERIE

You're worse off than Hughie was. He only had
two. Three, huh? Well that's what comes of being careless!

He laughs. The NIGHT CLERK *smiles at a guest. He had
been a little offended when a guest first made that
crack—must have been ten years ago—yes, Eddie, the
oldest, is eleven now—or is it twelve?* ERIE *goes on
with good-natured tolerance.*

Well, I suppose marriage ain't such a bum racket, if
you're made for it. Hughie didn't seem to mind it much,
although if you want my low-down, his wife is a bum
—in spades! Oh, I don't mean cheatin'. With her puss
and figure, she'd never make no one except she raided
a blind asylum.

The NIGHT CLERK *feels that he has been standing a long
time and his feet are beginning to ache and he wishes
492 would stop talking and go to bed so he can sit
down again and listen to the noises in the street and
think about nothing.* ERIE *gives him an amused, condescending glance.*

How old are you? Wait! Let me guess. You look fifty
or over but I'll lay ten to one you're forty-three or maybe
forty-four.

NIGHT CLERK

I'm forty-three.

He adds vaguely.

Or maybe it is forty-four.

ERIE

Elated.

I win, huh? I sure can call the turn on ages, Buddy. You ought to see the dolls get sored up when I work it on them! You're like Hughie. He looked like he'd never see fifty again and he was only forty-three. Me, I'm forty-five. Never think it, would you? Most of the dames don't think I've hit forty yet.

The NIGHT CLERK shifts his position so he can lean more on the desk. Maybe those shoes he sees advertised for fallen arches— But they cost eight dollars, so that's out— Get a pair when he goes to heaven. ERIE is sizing him up with another cynical, friendly glance.

I make another bet about you. Born and raised in the sticks, wasn't you?

NIGHT CLERK

Faintly aroused and defensive.

I come originally from Saginaw, Michigan, but I've lived here in the Big Town so long I consider myself a New Yorker now.

This is a long speech for him and he wonders sadly why he took the trouble to make it.

ERIE

I don't deserve no medal for picking that one. Nearly every guy I know on the Big Stem—and I know most of 'em—hails from the sticks. Take me. You'd never guess it but I was dragged up in Erie, P-a. Ain't that a knockout! Erie, P-a! That's how I got my moniker. No one calls me nothing but Erie. You better call me Erie, too, Pal, or I won't know when you're talkin' to me.

NIGHT CLERK

All right, Erie.

ERIE

Atta Boy.

He chuckles.

Here's another knockout. Smith is my real name. A Broadway guy like me named Smith and it's my real name! Ain't that a knockout!

He explains carefully so there will be no misunderstanding.

I don't remember nothing much about Erie, P-a, you understand—or want to. Some punk burg! After grammar school, my Old Man put me to work in his store, dealing out groceries. Some punk job! I stuck it till I was eighteen before I took a run-out powder.

The NIGHT CLERK seems turned into a drooping waxwork, draped along the desk. This is what he used to dread before he perfected his technique of not listening: The Guest's Story of His Life. He fixes his mind on his aching feet. ERIE chuckles.

Speaking of marriage, that was the big reason I ducked. A doll nearly had me hooked for the old shotgun ceremony. Closest I ever come to being played for a sucker. This doll in Erie—Daisy's her name—was one of them dumb wide-open dolls. All the guys give her a play. Then one day she wakes up and finds she's going to have a kid. I never figured she meant to frame me in particular. Way I always figured, she didn't have no idea who, so she holds a lottery all by herself. Put about a thousand guys' names in a hat—all she could remember—and drew one out and I was it. Then she told her Ma, and her Ma told her Pa, and her Pa come round looking for me. But I was no fall guy even in them days. I took it on the lam. For Saratoga, to look the bangtails over. I'd started to be a horse player in Erie, though I'd never seen a track. I been one ever since.

With a touch of bravado.

And I ain't done so bad, Pal. I've made some killings
in my time the gang still gab about. I've been in the
big bucks. More'n once, and I will be again. I've had
tough breaks too, but what the hell, I always get by.
When the horses won't run for me, there's draw or
stud. When they're bad, there's a crap game. And when
they're all bad, there's always bucks to pick up for
little errands I ain't talkin' about, which they give a guy
who can keep his clam shut. Oh, I get along, Buddy. I
get along fine.

He waits for approving assent from the NIGHT CLERK,
*but the latter is not hearing so intently he misses his
cue until the expectant silence crashes his ears.*

NIGHT CLERK

Hastily, gambling on "yes."

Yes, sir.

ERIE

Bitingly.

Sorry if I'm keeping you up, Sport.

With an aggrieved air.

Hughie was a wide-awake guy. He was always waiting
for me to roll in. He'd say, "Hello, Erie, how'd the
bangtails treat you?" Or, "How's luck?" Or, "Did you
make the old bones behave?" Then I'd tell him how
I'd done. He'd ask, "What's new along the Big Stem?"
and I'd tell him the latest off the grapevine.

He grins with affectionate condescension.

It used to hand me a laugh to hear old Hughie crackin'
like a sport. In all the years I knew him, he never bet
a buck on nothin'.

Excusingly.

But it ain't his fault. He'd have took a chance, but how

could he with his wife keepin' cases on every nickel of
his salary? I showed him lots of ways he could cross
her up, but he was too scared.

He chuckles.

The biggest knockout was when he'd kid me about
dames. He'd crack, "What? No blonde to-night, Erie?
You must be slippin'." Jeez, you never see a guy more
bashful with a doll around than Hughie was. I used to
introduce him to the tramps I'd drag home with me.
I'd wise them up to kid him along and pretend they'd
fell for him. In two minutes, they'd have him hanging
on the ropes. His face'd be red and he'd look like he
wanted to crawl under the desk and hide. Some of
them dolls was raw babies. They'd make him pretty
raw propositions. He'd stutter like he was paralyzed.
But he ate it up, just the same. He was tickled pink.
I used to hope maybe I could nerve him up to do a
little cheatin'. I'd offer to fix it for him with one of my
dolls. Hell, I got plenty, I wouldn't have minded. I'd
tell him, "Just let that wife of yours know you're
cheatin', and she'll have some respect for you." But he
was too scared.

He pauses—boastfully.

Some queens I've brought here in my time, Brother—
frails from the Follies, or the Scandals, or the Frolics,
that'd knock your eye out! And I still can make 'em.
You watch. I ain't slippin'.

He looks at the NIGHT CLERK *expecting reassurance,
but the* CLERK's *mind has slipped away to the clanging
bounce of garbage cans in the outer night. He is
thinking: "A job I'd like. I'd bang those cans louder
than they do! I'd wake up the whole damned city!"*
ERIE *mutters disgustedly to himself.*

Jesus, what a dummy!

He makes a move in the direction of the elevator, off right front—gloomily.

Might as well hit the hay, I guess.

NIGHT CLERK

Comes to—with the nearest approach to feeling he has shown in many a long night—approvingly.

Good night, Mr. Smith. I hope you have a good rest.

But ERIE *stops, glancing around the deserted lobby with forlorn distaste, jiggling the room key in his hand.*

ERIE

What a crummy dump! What did I come back for? I shoulda stayed on a drunk. You'd never guess it, Buddy, but when I first come here this was a classy hotel—and clean, can you believe it?

He scowls.

I've been campin' here, off and on, fifteen years, but I've got a good notion to move out. It ain't the same place since Hughie was took to the hospital.

Gloomily.

Hell with going to bed! I'll just lie there worrying—

He turns back to the desk. The CLERK's *face would express despair, but the last time he was able to feel despair was back around World War days when the cost of living got so high and he was out of a job for three months.* ERIE *leans on the desk—in a dejected, confidential tone.*

Believe me, Brother, I never been a guy to worry, but this time I'm on a spot where I got to, if I ain't a sap.

NIGHT CLERK

In the vague tone of a corpse which admits it once overheard a favorable rumor about life.

That's too bad, Mr. Smith. But they say most of the things we worry about never happen.

His mind escapes to the street again to play bouncing cans with the garbage men.

ERIE

Grimly.

This thing happens, Pal. I ain't won a bet at nothin' since Hughie was took to the hospital. I'm jinxed. And that ain't all— But to hell with it! You're right, at that. Something always turns up for me. I was born lucky. I ain't worried. Just moaning low. Hell, who don't when they're getting over a drunk? You know how it is. The Brooklyn Boys march over the bridge with bloodhounds to hunt you down. And I'm still carrying the torch for Hughie. His checking out was a real K.O. for me. Damn if I know why. Lots of guys I've been pals with, in a way, croaked from booze or something, or got rubbed out, but I always took it as part of the game. Hell, we all gotta croak. Here today, gone tomorrow, so what's the good of beefin'? When a guy's dead, he's dead. He don't give a damn, so why should anybody else?

But this fatalistic philosophy is no comfort and ERIE *sighs.*

I miss Hughie, I guess. I guess I'd got to like him a lot.

Again he explains carefully so there will be no misunderstanding.

Not that I was ever real pals with him, you understand. He didn't run in my class. He didn't know none of the answers. He was just a sucker.

He sighs again.

But I sure am sorry he's gone. You missed a lot not knowing Hughie, Pal. He sure was one grand little guy.

He stares at the lobby floor. The NIGHT CLERK *regards him with vacant, bulging eyes full of a vague envy for the blind. The garbage men have gone their predestined way. Time is that much older. The* CLERK's *mind remains in the street to greet the noise of a far-off El train. Its approach is pleasantly like a memory of hope; then it roars and rocks and rattles past*

*the nearby corner, and the noise pleasantly deafens
memory; then it recedes and dies, and there is something melancholy about that. But there is hope. Only
so many El trains pass in one night, and each one
passing leaves one less to pass, so the night recedes,
too, until at last it must die and join all the other long
nights in Nirvana, the Big Night of Nights. And
that's life. "What I always tell Jess when she nags me
to worry about something: 'That's life, isn't it? What
can you do about it?'"* ERIE *sighs again—then turns
to the* CLERK, *his foolishly wary, wise-guy eyes defense-
less, his poker face as self-betraying as a hurt dog's—
appealingly.*

Say, you do remind me of Hughie somehow, Pal. You
got the same look on your map.

But the CLERK'S *mind is far away attending the ob-
sequies of night, and it takes it some time to get back.*
ERIE *is hurt—contemptuously.*

But I guess it's only that old night clerk look! There's
one of 'em born every minute!

NIGHT CLERK

*His mind arrives just in time to catch this last—with
a bright grimace.*

Yes, Mr. Smith. That's what Barnum said, and it's
certainly true, isn't it?

ERIE

Grateful even for this sign of companionship, growls.
Nix on the Mr. Smith stuff, Charlie. There's ten of *them*
born every minute. Call me Erie, like I told you.

NIGHT CLERK

Automatically, as his mind tiptoes into the night again.
All right, Erie.

ERIE

*Encouraged, leans on the desk, clacking his room key
like a castanet.*

Yeah. Hughie was one grand little guy. All the same, like I said, he wasn't the kind of guy you'd ever figger a guy like me would take to. Because he was a sucker, see—the kind of sap you'd take to the cleaners a million times and he'd never wise up he was took. Why, night after night, just for a gag, I'd get him to shoot crap with me here on the desk. With *my* dice. And he'd never ask to give 'em the once-over. Can you beat that!

He chuckles—then earnestly.

Not that I'd ever ring in no phoneys on a pal. I'm no heel.

He chuckles again.

And anyway, I didn't need none to take Hughie because he never even made me knock 'em against nothing. Just a roll on the desk here. Boy, if they'd ever let me throw 'em that way in a real game, I'd be worth ten million dollars.

He laughs.

You'da thought Hughie woulda got wise something was out of order when, no matter how much he'd win on a run of luck like suckers have sometimes, I'd always take him to the cleaners in the end. But he never suspicioned nothing. All he'd say was "Gosh, Erie, no wonder you took up gambling. You sure were born lucky."

He chuckles.

Can you beat that?

He hastens to explain earnestly.

Of course, like I said, it was only a gag. We'd play with real jack, just to make it look real, but it was all my jack. He never had no jack. His wife dealt him four bits a day for spending money. So I'd stake him at the start to half of what I got—in chicken feed, I mean. We'd pretend a cent was a buck, and a nickel was a fin and so on. Some big game! He got a big kick out of it. He'd get all het up. It give me a kick, too—especially when

he'd say, "Gosh, Erie, I don't wonder you never worry
about money, with your luck."

He laughs.

That guy would believe anything! Of course, I'd stall
him off when he'd want to shoot nights when I didn't
have a goddamned nickel.

He chuckles.

What laughs he used to hand me! He'd always call
horses "the bangtails," like he'd known 'em all his life
—and he'd never seen a race horse, not till I kidnaped
him one day and took him down to Belmont. What a
kick he got out of that! I got scared he'd pass out with
excitement. And he wasn't doing no betting either. All he
had was four bits. It was just the track, and the crowd,
and the horses got him. Mostly the horses.

With a surprised, reflective air.

Y'know, it's funny how a dumb, simple guy like Hughie
will all of a sudden get something right. He says,
"They're the most beautiful things in the world, I think."
And he wins! I tell you, Pal, I'd rather sleep in the
same stall with old Man o' War than make the whole
damn Follies. What do you think?

NIGHT CLERK

*His mind darts back from a cruising taxi and blinks
bewilderedly in the light: "Say yes."*

Yes, I agree with you, Mr.—I mean, Erie.

ERIE

With good-natured contempt.

Yeah? I bet you never seen one, except back at the old
Fair Grounds in the sticks. I don't mean them kind of
turtles. I mean a real horse.

The CLERK *wonders what horses have to do with anything—or for that matter, what anything has to do
with anything—then gives it up.* ERIE *takes up his tale.*

And what d'you think happened the next night? Damned

if Hughie didn't dig two bucks out of his pants and try to slip 'em to me. "Let this ride on the nose of whatever horse you're betting on tomorrow," he told me. I got sore. "Nix," I told him, "if you're going to start playin' sucker and bettin' on horse races, you don't get no assist from me."

He grins wryly.

Was that a laugh! Me advising a sucker not to bet when I've spent a lot of my life tellin' saps a story to make 'em bet! I said, "Where'd you grab this dough? Outa the Little Woman's purse, huh? What tale you going to give her when you lose it? She'll start breaking up the furniture with you!" "No," he says, "she'll just cry." "That's worse," I said, "no guy can beat that racket. I had a doll cry on me once in a restaurant full of people till I had to promise her a diamond engagement ring to sober her up." Well, anyway, Hughie sneaked the two bucks back in the Little Woman's purse when he went home that morning, and that was the end of that.

Cynically.

Boy Scouts got nothin' on me, Pal, when it comes to good deeds. That was one I done. It's too bad I can't remember no others.

He is well wound up now and goes on without noticing that the NIGHT CLERK's *mind has left the premises in his sole custody.*

Y'know I had Hughie sized up for a sap the first time I see him. I'd just rolled in from Tia Juana. I'd made a big killing down there and I was lousy with jack. Came all the way in a drawing room, and I wasn't lonely in it neither. There was a blonde movie doll on the train— and I was lucky in them days. Used to follow the horses South every winter. I don't no more. Sick of traveling. And I ain't as lucky as I was—

Hastily.

Anyway, this time I'm talkin' about, soon as I hit this lobby I see there's a new night clerk, and while I'm signing up for the bridal suite I make a bet with myself he's never been nothin' but a night clerk. And I win. At first, he wouldn't open up. Not that he was cagey about gabbin' too much. But like he couldn't think of nothin' about himself worth saying. But after he'd seen me roll in here the last one every night, and I'd stop to kid him along and tell him the tale of what I'd win that day, he got friendly and talked. He'd come from a hick burg upstate. Graduated from high school, and had a shot at different jobs in the old home town but couldn't make the grade until he was took on as night clerk in the hotel there. Then he made good. But he wasn't satisfied. Didn't like being only a night clerk where everybody knew him. He'd read somewhere— in the Suckers' Almanac, I guess—that all a guy had to do was come to the Big Town and Old Man Success would be waitin' at the Grand Central to give him the key to the city. What a gag that is! Even I believed that once, and no one could ever call me a sap. Well, anyway, he made the break and come here and the only job he could get was night clerk. Then he fell in love—or kidded himself he was—and got married. Met her on a subway train. It stopped sudden and she was jerked into him, and he puts his arms around her, and they started talking, and the poor boob never stood a chance. She was a sales girl in some punk department store, and she was sick of standing on her dogs all day, and all the way home to Brooklyn, too. So, the way I figger it, knowing Hughie and dames, she proposed and said "yes" for him, and married him, and after that, of course, he never dared stop being a night clerk, even if he could.

He pauses.

Maybe you think I ain't giving her a square shake. Well, maybe I ain't. She never give me one. She put me down as a bad influence, and let her chips ride. And maybe Hughie couldn't have done no better. Dolls didn't call him no riot. Hughie and her seemed happy enough the time he had me out to dinner in their flat. Well, not happy. Maybe contented. No, that's boosting it, too. Resigned comes nearer, as if each was givin' the other a break by thinking, "Well, what more could I expect?"

Abruptly he addresses the NIGHT CLERK *with contemptuous good nature.*

How d'you and your Little Woman hit it off, Brother?

NIGHT CLERK

His mind has been counting the footfalls of the cop on the beat as they recede, sauntering longingly toward the dawn's release. "If he'd only shoot it out with a gunman some night! Nothing exciting has happened in any night I've ever lived through!" He stammers gropingly among the echoes of ERIE's *last words.*

Oh—you mean *my* wife? Why, we get along all right, I guess.

ERIE

Disgustedly.

Better lay off them headache pills, Pal. First thing you know, some guy is going to call you a dope.

But the NIGHT CLERK *cannot take this seriously. It is years since he cared what anyone called him. So many guests have called him so many things. The Little Woman has, too. And, of course, he has, himself. But that's all past. Is daybreak coming now? No, too early yet. He can tell by the sound of that surface car. It is still lost in the night. Flat wheeled and tired. Distant the carbarn, and far away the sleep.* ERIE, *having soothed resentment with his wisecrack, goes on with a friendly grin.*

Well, keep hoping, Pal. Hughie was as big a dope as you until I give him some interest in life.

Slipping back into narrative.

That time he took me home to dinner. Was that a knockout! It took him a hell of a while to get up nerve to ask me. "Sure, Hughie," I told him, "I'll be tickled to death." I was thinking, I'd rather be shot. For one thing, he lived in Brooklyn, and I'd sooner take a trip to China. Another thing, I'm a guy that likes to eat what I order and not what somebody deals me. And he had kids and a wife, and the family racket is out of my line. But Hughie looked so tickled I couldn't welsh on him. And it didn't work out so bad. Of course, what he called home was only a dump of a cheap flat. Still, it wasn't so bad for a change. His wife had done a lot of stuff to doll it up. Nothin' with no class, you understand. Just cheap stuff to make it comfortable. And his kids wasn't the gorillas I'd expected, neither. No throwin' spitballs in my soup or them kind of gags. They was quiet like Hughie. I kinda liked 'em. After dinner I started tellin' 'em a story about a race horse a guy I know owned once. I thought it was up to me to put out something, and kids like animal stories, and this one was true, at that. This old turtle never wins a race, but he was as foxy as ten guys, a natural born crook, the goddamnedest thief, he'd steal anything in reach that wasn't nailed down— Well, I didn't get far. Hughie's wife butt in and stopped me cold. Told the kids it was bedtime and hustled 'em off like I was giving 'em measles. It got my goat, kinda. I coulda liked her—a little—if she'd give me a chance. Not that she was nothin' Ziegfeld would want to glorify. When you call her plain, you give her all the breaks.

Resentfully.

Well, to hell with it. She had me tagged for a bum, and

seein' me made her sure she was right. You can bet she
told Hughie never invite me again, and he never did.
He tried to apologize, but I shut him up quick. He
says, "Irma was brought up strict. She can't help being
narrow-minded about gamblers." I said, "What's it to
me? I don't want to hear your dame troubles. I got
plenty of my own. Remember that doll I brung home
night before last? She gives me an argument I promised
her ten bucks. I told her, 'Listen, Baby, I got an im-
pediment in my speech. Maybe it sounded like ten, but
it was two, and that's all you get. Hell, I don't want to
buy your soul! What would I do with it?' Now she's
peddling the news along Broadway I'm a rat and a
chiseler, and of course all the rats and chiselers believe
her. Before she's through, I won't have a friend left."

He pauses—confidentially.

I switched the subject on Hughie, see, on purpose. He
never did beef to me about his wife again.

He gives a forced chuckle.

Believe me, Pal, I can stop guys that start telling me their
family troubles!

NIGHT CLERK

*His mind has hopped an ambulance clanging down
Sixth, and is asking without curiosity: "Will he die,
Doctor, or isn't he lucky?" "I'm afraid not, but he'll
have to be absolutely quiet for months and months."
"With a pretty nurse taking care of him?" "Probably
not pretty." "Well, anyway, I claim he's lucky. And now
I must get back to the hotel. 492 won't go to bed and
insists on telling me jokes. It must have been a joke
because he's chuckling." He laughs with a heartiness
which has forgotten that heart is more than a word
used in "Have a heart," an old slang expression.*

Ha— Ha! That's a good one, Erie. That's the best I've
heard in a long time!

ERIE

> *For a moment is so hurt and depressed he hasn't the
> spirit to make a sarcastic crack. He stares at the floor,
> twirling his room key—to himself.*

Jesus, this sure is a dead dump. About as homey as the
Morgue.

> *He glances up at the clock.*

Gettin' late. Better beat it up to my cell and grab some
shut eye.

> *He makes a move to detach himself from the desk but
> fails and remains wearily glued to it. His eyes prowl
> the lobby and finally come to rest on the* CLERK's
> *glistening, sallow face. He summons up strength for a
> withering crack.*

Why didn't you tell me you was deaf, Buddy? I know
guys is sensitive about them little afflictions, but I'll keep
it confidential.

> *But the* CLERK's *mind has rushed out to follow the siren
> wail of a fire engine. "A fireman's life must be ex-
> citing." His mind rides the engine, and asks a fireman
> with disinterested eagerness: "Where's the fire? Is it
> a real good one this time? Has it a good start? Will
> it be big enough, do you think?"* ERIE *examines his
> face—bitingly.*

Take my tip, Pal, and don't never try to buy from a dope
peddler. He'll tell you you had enough already.

> *The* CLERK's *mind continues its dialogue with the
> fireman: "I mean, big enough to burn down the whole
> damn city?" "Sorry, Brother, but there's no chance.
> There's too much stone and steel. There'd always be
> something left." "Yes, I guess you're right. There's
> too much stone and steel. I wasn't really hoping, any-
> way. It really doesn't matter to me."* ERIE *gives him up
> and again attempts to pry himself from the desk,*

twirling his key frantically as if it were a fetish which might set him free.

Well, me for the hay.

But he can't dislodge himself—dully.

Christ, it's lonely. I wish Hughie was here. By God, if he was, I'd tell him a tale that'd make his eyes pop! The bigger the story the harder he'd fall. He was that kind of sap. He thought gambling was romantic. I guess I saw me like a sort of dream guy, the sort of guy he'd like to be if he could take a chance. I guess he lived a sort of double life listening to me gabbin' about hittin' the high spots. Come to figger it, I'll bet he even cheated on his wife that way, using me and my dolls.

He chuckles.

No wonder he liked me, huh? And the bigger I made myself the more he lapped it up. I went easy on him at first. I didn't lie—not any more'n a guy naturally does when he gabs about the bets he wins and the dolls he's made. But I soon see he was cryin' for more, and when a sucker cries for more, you're a dope if you don't let him have it. Every tramp I made got to be a Follies' doll. Hughie liked 'em to be Follies' dolls. Or in the Scandals or Frolics. He wanted me to be the Sheik of Araby, or something that any blonde'd go round-heeled about. Well, I give him plenty of that. And I give him plenty of gambling tales. I explained my campin' in this dump was because I don't want to waste jack on nothin' but gambling. It was like dope to me, I told him. I couldn't quit. He lapped that up. He liked to kid himself I'm mixed up in the racket. He thought gangsters was romantic. So I fed him some baloney about high-jacking I'd done once. I told him I knew all the Big Shots. Well, so I do, most of 'em, to say hello, and sometimes they hello back. Who wouldn't know 'em that

hangs around Broadway and the joints? I run errands
for 'em sometimes, because there's dough in it, but I'm
cagey about gettin' in where it ain't healthy. Hughie
wanted to think me and Legs Diamond was old pals. So
I give him that too. I give him anything he cried for.

Earnestly.

Don't get the wrong idea, Pal. What I fed Hughie wasn't
all lies. The tales about gambling wasn't. They was
stories of big games and killings that really happened
since I've been hangin' round. Only I wasn't in on 'em
like I made out—except one or two from way back when
I had a run of big luck and was in the bucks for a while
until I was took to the cleaners.

*He stops to pay tribute of a sigh to the memory of
brave days that were and that never were—then medita-
tively.*

Yeah, Hughie lapped up my stories like they was duck
soup, or a beakful of heroin. I sure took him around
with me in tales and showed him one hell of a time.

He chuckles—then seriously.

And, d'you know, it done me good, too, in a way. Sure.
I'd get to seein' myself like he seen me. Some nights I'd
come back here without a buck, feeling lower than a
snake's belly, and first thing you know I'd be lousy with
jack, bettin' a grand a race. Oh, I was wise I was kiddin'
myself. I ain't a sap. But what the hell, Hughie loved it,
and it didn't cost nobody nothin', and if every guy along
Broadway who kids himself was to drop dead there
wouldn't be nobody left. Ain't it the truth, Charlie?

He again stares at the NIGHT CLERK *appealingly, forgetting past rebuffs. The* CLERK's *face is taut with
vacancy. His mind has been trying to fasten itself to
some noise in the night, but a rare and threatening
pause of silence has fallen on the city, and here he is,
chained behind a hotel desk forever, awake when*

everyone else in the world is asleep, except Room 492, and he won't go to bed, he's still talking, and there is no escape.

NIGHT CLERK

His glassy eyes stare through ERIE's *face. He stammers deferentially.*

Truth? I'm afraid I didn't get— What's the truth?

ERIE

Hopelessly.

Nothing, Pal. Not a thing.

His eyes fall to the floor. For a while he is too defeated even to twirl his room key. The CLERK's *mind still cannot make a getaway because the city remains silent, and the night vaguely reminds him of death, and he is vaguely frightened, and now that he remembers, his feet are giving him hell, but that's no excuse not to act as if the Guest is always right: "I should have paid 492 more attention. After all, he is company. He is awake and alive. I should use him to help me live through the night. What's he been talking about? I must have caught some of it without meaning to." The* NIGHT CLERK's *forehead puckers perspiringly as he tries to remember.* ERIE *begins talking again but this time it is obviously aloud to himself, without hope of a listener.*

I could tell by Hughie's face before he went to the hospital, he was through. I've seen the same look on guys' faces when they knew they was on the spot, just before guys caught up with them. I went to see him twice in the hospital. The first time, his wife was there and give me a dirty look, but he cooked up a smile and said, "Hello, Erie, how're the bangtails treating you?" I see he wants a big story to cheer him, but his wife butts in and says he's weak and he mustn't get excited. I felt like crackin', "Well, the Docs in this dump got the right

dope. Just leave you with him and he'll never get excited." The second time I went, they wouldn't let me see
him. That was near the end. I went to his funeral, too.
There wasn't nobody but a coupla his wife's relations. I
had to feel sorry for her. She looked like she ought to be
parked in a coffin, too. The kids was bawlin'. There
wasn't no flowers but a coupla lousy wreaths. It woulda
been a punk showing for poor old Hughie, if it hadn't
been for my flower piece.

He swells with pride.

That was some display, Pal. It'd knock your eye out! Set
me back a hundred bucks, and no kiddin'! A big horseshoe of red roses! I knew Hughie'd want a horseshoe because that made it look like he'd been a horse player.
And around the top printed in forget-me-nots was
"Good-by, Old Pal." Hughie liked to kid himself he was
my pal.

He adds sadly.

And so he was, at that—even if he was a sucker.

*He pauses, his false poker face as nakedly forlorn as an
organ grinder's monkey's. Outside, the spell of ab-
normal quiet presses suffocatingly upon the street,
enters the deserted, dirty lobby. The* NIGHT CLERK's *mind
cowers away from it. He cringes behind the desk, his
feet aching like hell. There is only one possible escape.
If his mind could only fasten onto something 492 has
said.* "What's he been talking about? A clerk should
always be attentive. You even are duty bound to laugh
at a guest's smutty jokes, no matter how often you've
heard them. That's the policy of the hotel. 492 has been
gassing for hours. What's he been telling me? I must
be slipping. Always before this I've been able to hear
without bothering to listen, but now when I need company— Ah! I've got it! Gambling! He said a lot about
gambling. That's something I've always wanted to

*know more about, too. Maybe he's a professional
gambler. Like Arnold Rothstein."*

NIGHT CLERK

Blurts out with an uncanny, almost lifelike eagerness.
I beg your pardon, Mr.—Erie—but did I understand you
to say you are a gambler by profession? Do you, by any
chance, know the Big Shot, Arnold Rothstein?

But this time it is ERIE *who doesn't hear him. And the*
CLERK's *mind is now suddenly impervious to the threat
of Night and Silence as it pursues an ideal of fame and
glory within itself called Arnold Rothstein.*

ERIE

Christ, I wish Hughie was alive and kickin'. I'd tell him
I win ten grand from the bookies, and ten grand at stud,
and ten grand in a crap game! I'd tell him I bought one
of those Mercedes sport roadsters with nickel pipes sticking out of the hood! I'd tell him I lay three babes from
the Follies—two blondes and one brunette!

The NIGHT CLERK *dreams, a rapt hero worship trans-
figuring his pimply face:* "Arnold Rothstein! He must
be some guy! I read a story about him. He'll gamble
for any limit on anything, and always wins. The story
said he wouldn't bother playing in a poker game unless
the smallest bet you could make—one white chip!—
was a hundred dollars. Christ, that's going some! I'd
like to have the dough to get in a game with him once!
The last pot everyone would drop out but him and me.
I'd say, 'Okay, Arnold, the sky's the limit,' and I'd
raise him five grand, and he'd call, and I'd have a royal
flush to his four aces. Then I'd say, 'Okay, Arnold,
I'm a good sport, I'll give you a break. I'll cut you
double or nothing. Just one cut. I want quick action
for my dough.' And I'd cut the ace of spades and win
again." Beatific vision swoons on the empty pools of
the* NIGHT CLERK's *eyes. He resembles a holy saint, re-*

cently elected to Paradise. ERIE *breaks the silence—
bitterly resigned.*

But Hughie's better off, at that, being dead. He's got
all the luck. He needn't do no worryin' now. He's out of
the racket. I mean, the whole goddamned racket. I mean
life.

NIGHT CLERK

*Kicked out of his dream—with detached, pleasant ac-
quiescence.*

Yes, it is a goddamned racket when you stop to think,
isn't it, 492? But we might as well make the best of it,
because— Well, you can't burn it all down, can you?
There's too much steel and stone. There'd always be
something left to start it going again.

ERIE

Scowls bewilderedly.

Say, what is this? What the hell you talkin' about?

NIGHT CLERK

At a loss—in much confusion.

Why, to be frank, I really don't— Just something that
came into my head.

ERIE

*Bitingly, but showing he is comforted at having made
some sort of contact.*

Get it out of your head quick, Charlie, or some guys in
uniform will walk in here with a butterfly net and catch
you.

He changes the subject—earnestly.

Listen, Pal, maybe you guess I was kiddin' about that
flower piece for Hughie costing a hundred bucks? Well,
I ain't! I didn't give a damn what it cost. It was up to me
to give Hughie a big-time send-off, because I knew nobody else would.

NIGHT CLERK

Oh, I'm not doubting your word, Erie. You won the

money gambling, I suppose— I mean, I beg your pardon
if I'm mistaken, but you are a gambler, aren't you?

ERIE

Preoccupied.

Yeah, sure, when I got scratch to put up. What of it? But
I don't win that hundred bucks. I don't win a bet since
Hughie was took to the hospital. I had to get down on
my knees and beg every guy I know for a sawbuck here
and a sawbuck there until I raised it.

NIGHT CLERK

*His mind concentrated on the Big Ideal—insist-
ently.*

Do you by any chance know—Arnold Rothstein?

ERIE

His train of thought interrupted—irritably.

Arnold? What's he got to do with it? He wouldn't loan
a guy like me a nickel to save my grandmother from
streetwalking.

NIGHT CLERK

With humble awe.

Then you do know him!

ERIE

Sure I know the bastard. Who don't on Broadway? And
he knows me—when he wants to. He uses me to run
errands when there ain't no one else handy. But he ain't
my trouble, Pal. My trouble is, some of these guys I put
the bite on is dead wrong G's, and they expect to be paid
back next Tuesday, or else I'm outa luck and have to
take it on the lam, or I'll get beat up and maybe sent
to a hospital.

*He suddenly rouses himself and there is something pa-
thetically but genuinely gallant about him.*

But what the hell. I was wise I was takin' a chance. I've
always took a chance, and if I lose I pay, and no welshing!
It sure was worth it to give Hughie the big send-off.

He pauses. The NIGHT CLERK *hasn't paid any attention except to his own dream. A question is trembling on his parted lips, but before he can get it out* ERIE *goes on gloomily.*

But even that ain't my big worry, Charlie. My big worry is the run of bad luck I've had since Hughie got took to the hospital. Not a win. That ain't natural. I've always been a lucky guy—lucky enough to get by and pay up, I mean. I wouldn't never worry about owing guys, like I owe them guys. I'd always know I'd make a win that'd fix it. But now I got a lousy hunch when I lost Hughie I lost my luck—I mean, I've lost the old confidence. He used to give me confidence.

He turns away from the desk.

No use gabbin' here all night. You can't do me no good.

He starts toward the elevator.

NIGHT CLERK

   Pleadingly.

Just a minute, Erie, if you don't mind.

   With awe.

So you're an old friend of Arnold Rothstein! Would you mind telling me if it's really true when Arnold Rothstein plays poker, one white chip is—a hundred dollars?

ERIE

   Dully exasperated.

Say, for Christ's sake, what's it to you—?

He stops abruptly, staring probingly at the CLERK. *There is a pause. Suddenly his face lights up with a saving revelation. He grins warmly and saunters confidently back to the desk.*

Say, Charlie, why didn't you put me wise before, you was interested in gambling? Hell, I got you all wrong, Pal. I been tellin' myself, this guy ain't like old Hughie. He ain't got no sportin' blood. He's just a dope.

   Generously.

Now I see you're a right guy. Shake.

He shoves out his hand which the CLERK *clasps with a limp pleasure.* ERIE *goes on with gathering warmth and self-assurance.*

That's the stuff. You and me'll get along. I'll give you all the breaks, like I give Hughie.

NIGHT CLERK

Gratefully.

Thank you, Erie.

Then insistently.

Is it true when Arnold Rothstein plays poker, one white chip—

ERIE

With magnificent carelessness.

Sets you back a hundred bucks? Sure. Why not? Arnold's in the bucks, ain't he? And when you're in the bucks, a C note is chicken feed. I ought to know, Pal. I was in the bucks when Arnold was a piker. Why, one time down in New Orleans I lit a cigar with a C note, just for a gag, y'understand. I was with a bunch of high class dolls and I wanted to see their eyes pop out—and believe me, they sure popped! After that, I coulda made 'em one at a time or all together! Hell, I once win twenty grand on a single race. That's action! A good crap game is action, too. Hell, I've been in games where there was a hundred grand in real folding money lying around the floor. That's travelin'!

He darts a quick glance at the CLERK's *face and begins to hedge warily. But he needn't. The* CLERK *sees him now as the Gambler in 492, the Friend of Arnold Rothstein—and nothing is incredible.* ERIE *goes on.*

Of course, I wouldn't kid you. I'm not in the bucks now —not right this moment. You know how it is, Charlie. Down today and up tomorrow. I got some dough ridin' on the nose of a turtle in the 4th at Saratoga. I hear a story he'll be so full of hop, if the joc can keep him from jumpin' over the grandstand, he'll win by a mile. So if I roll in here with a blonde that'll knock your eyes out, don't be surprised.

He winks and chuckles.

NIGHT CLERK

Ingratiatingly pally, smiling.

Oh, you can't surprise me that way. I've been a night clerk in New York all my life, almost.

He tries out a wink himself.

I'll forget the house rules, Erie.

ERIE

Dryly.

Yeah. The manager wouldn't like you to remember something he ain't heard of yet.

Then slyly feeling his way.

How about shootin' a little crap, Charlie? I mean just in fun, like I used to with Hughie. I know you can't afford takin' no chances. I'll stake you, see? I got a coupla bucks. We gotta use real jack or it don't look real. It's all my jack, get it? You can't lose. I just want to show you how I'll take you to the cleaners. It'll give me confidence.

He has taken two one-dollar bills and some change from his pocket. He pushes most of it across to the
CLERK.

Here y'are.

He produces a pair of dice—carelessly.

Want to give these dice the once-over before we start?

NIGHT CLERK

Earnestly.

What do you think I am? I know I can trust you.

ERIE

Smiles.

You remind me a lot of Hughie, Pal. He always trusted me. Well, don't blame me if I'm lucky.

He clicks the dice in his hand—thoughtfully.

Y'know, it's time I quit carryin' the torch for Hughie. Hell, what's the use? It don't do him no good. He's gone. Like we all gotta go. Him yesterday, me or you tomorrow, and who cares, and what's the difference? It's all in the racket, huh?

His soul is purged of grief, his confidence restored.

I shoot two bits.

NIGHT CLERK

Manfully, with an excited dead-pan expression he hopes resembles Arnold Rothstein's.

I fade you.

ERIE

Throws the dice.

Four's my point.

Gathers them up swiftly and throws them again.

Four it is.

He takes the money.

Easy when you got my luck—and know how. Huh, Charlie?

He chuckles, giving the NIGHT CLERK *the slyly amused, contemptuous, affectionate wink with which a Wise Guy regales a Sucker.*

Curtain

A Moon for the Misbegotten

A PLAY IN FOUR ACTS

A Moon for the Misbegotten is published herewith with no revisions or deletions. It is an exact reproduction of the original manuscript which I delivered to Random House, Inc., on completing the play in 1943.

It has never been presented on the New York stage nor are there outstanding rights or plans for its production. Since I cannot presently give it the attention required for appropriate presentation, I have decided to make it available in book form.

April, 1952

E. O'N.

Characters

JOSIE HOGAN

PHIL HOGAN, *her father*

MIKE HOGAN, *her brother*

JAMES TYRONE, JR.

T. STEDMAN HARDER

Scenes

Scene of the Play

The play takes place in Connecticut at the home of tenant farmer, PHIL HOGAN, *between the hours of noon on a day in early September, 1923, and sunrise of the following day.*

The house is not, to speak mildly, a fine example of New England architecture, placed so perfectly in its setting that it appears a harmonious part of the landscape, rooted in the earth. It has been moved to its present site, and looks it. An old boxlike, clapboarded affair, with a shingled roof and brick chimney, it is propped up about two feet above ground by layers of timber blocks. There are two windows on the lower floor of this side of the house which faces front, and one window on the floor above. These windows have no shutters, curtains or shades. Each has at least one pane missing, a square of cardboard taking its place. The house had once been painted a repulsive yellow with brown trim, but the walls now are a blackened and weathered gray, flaked with streaks and splotches of dim lemon. Just around the left corner of the house, a flight of steps leads to the front door.

To make matters worse, a one-story, one-room addition has been tacked on at right. About twelve feet long by six high, this room, which is JOSIE HOGAN'S *bedroom, is evidently homemade. Its walls and sloping roof are covered with tar paper, faded to dark gray. Close to where it joins the house, there is a door with a flight of three unpainted steps leading to the ground. At right of door is a small window.*

From these steps there is a footpath going around an old pear tree, at right-rear, through a field of hay stubble to a patch of woods. The same path also extends left to join a dirt road which leads up from the county highway (about a hundred yards off left) to the front door of the house, and thence back through a scraggly orchard of apple trees to the barn. Close to the house, under the window next to JOSIE's bedroom, there is a big boulder with a flat top.

Act One

SCENE—*As described. It is just before noon. The day is clear and hot.*

The door of JOSIE'S *bedroom opens and she comes out on the steps, bending to avoid bumping her head.*

JOSIE *is twenty-eight. She is so oversize for a woman that she is almost a freak—five feet eleven in her stockings and weighs around one hundred and eighty. Her sloping shoulders are broad, her chest deep with large, firm breasts, her waist wide but slender by contrast with her hips and thighs. She has long smooth arms, immensely strong, although no muscles show. The same is true of her legs.*

She is more powerful than any but an exceptionally strong man, able to do the manual labor of two ordinary men. But there is no mannish quality about her. She is all woman.

The map of Ireland is stamped on her face, with its long upper lip and small nose, thick black eyebrows, black hair as coarse as a horse's mane, freckled, sunburned fair skin, high cheekbones and heavy jaw. It is not a pretty face, but her large dark-blue eyes give it a note of beauty, and her smile, revealing even white teeth, gives it charm.

She wears a cheap, sleeveless, blue cotton dress. Her feet are bare, the soles earth-stained and tough as leather.

She comes down the steps and goes left to the corner of the house and peers around it toward the barn. Then she moves swiftly to the right of the house and looks back.

JOSIE: Ah, thank God. (*She goes back toward the steps as her brother,* MIKE, *appears hurrying up from right-rear.*)

(MIKE HOGAN *is twenty, about four inches shorter than his sister. He is sturdily built, but seems almost puny compared to her. He has a common Irish face, its expression sullen, or slyly cunning, or primly self-righteous. He never forgets that he is a good Catholic, faithful to all the observances, and so is one of the élite of Almighty God in a world of damned sinners composed of Protestants and bad Catholics. In brief,* MIKE *is a New England Irish Catholic Puritan, Grade B, and an extremely irritating youth to have around.*)

(MIKE *wears dirty overalls, a sweat-stained brown shirt. He carries a pitchfork.*)

JOSIE: Bad luck to you for a slowpoke. Didn't I tell you half-past eleven?

MIKE: How could I sneak here sooner with him peeking round the corner of the barn to catch me if I took a minute's rest, the way he always does? I had to wait till he went to the pig pen. (*He adds viciously*) Where he belongs, the old hog! (JOSIE's *right arm strikes with surprising swiftness and her big hand lands on the side of his jaw. She means it to be only a slap, but his head jerks back and he stumbles, dropping the pitchfork, and pleads cringingly*) Don't hit me, Josie! Don't, now!

JOSIE (*Quietly*): Then keep your tongue off him. He's my father, too, and I like him, if you don't.

MIKE (*Out of her reach—sullenly*): You're two of a kind, and a bad kind.

JOSIE (*Good-naturedly*): I'm proud of it. And I didn't hit you, or you'd be flat on the ground. It was only a love tap to waken your wits, so you'll use them. If he catches you running away, he'll beat you half to death. Get your bag now. I've packed it. It's inside the door of my room with your coat laid over it. Hurry now, while I see what he's doing. (*She moves quickly to peer around the corner of the house at left. He goes up the steps into her room and returns carrying an old coat and a cheap bulging satchel. She comes back*) There's no sight of him. (MIKE *drops the satchel on the ground while he puts on the coat*) I put everything in the bag. You can change to your Sunday suit in the can at the station or in the train, and don't forget to wash your face. I know you want to look your best when our brother, Thomas, sees you on his doorstep. (*Her tone becomes derisively amused*) And him way up in the world, a noble sergeant of the Bridgeport police. Maybe he'll get you on the force. It'd suit you. I can see you leading drunks to the lockup while you give them a lecture on temperance. Or if Thomas can't get you a job, he'll pass you along to our brother, John, the noble barkeep in Meriden. He'll teach you the trade. You'll make a nice one, who'll never steal from the till, or drink, and who'll tell customers they've had enough and better go home just when they're beginning to feel happy. (*She sighs regretfully*) Ah, well, Mike, you was born a priest's pet, and there's no help for it.

MIKE: That's right! Make fun of me again, because I want to be decent.

JOSIE: You're worse than decent. You're virtuous.

MIKE: Well, that's a thing nobody can say about— (*He stops, a bit ashamed, but mostly afraid to finish.*)

JOSIE (*Amused*): About me? No, and what's more, they don't. (*She smiles mockingly*) I know what a trial it's been to you, Mike, having a sister who's the scandal of the neighborhood.

MIKE: It's you that's saying it, not me. I don't want to part with hard feelings. And I'll keep on praying for you.

JOSIE (*Roughly*): Och! To hell with your prayers!

MIKE (*Stiffly*): I'm going. (*He picks up his bag.*)

JOSIE (*Her manner softening*): Wait. (*She comes to him*) Don't mind my rough tongue, Mike. I'm sorry to see you go, but it's the best thing for you. That's why I'm helping you, the same as I helped Thomas and John. You can't stand up to the Old Man any more than Thomas or John could, and the old divil would always keep you a slave. I wish you all the luck in the world, Mike. I know you'll get on—and God bless you. (*Her voice has softened, and she blinks back tears. She kisses him—then fumbling in the pocket of her dress, pulls out a little roll of one-dollar bills and presses it in his hand*) Here's a little present over your fare. I took it from his little green bag, and won't he be wild when he finds out! But I can handle him.

MIKE (*Enviously*): You can. You're the only one. (*Gratefully moved for a second*) Thank you, Josie. You've a kind heart. (*Then virtuously*) But I don't like taking stolen money.

JOSIE: Don't be a bigger jackass than you are already. Tell your conscience it's a bit of the wages he's never given you.

MIKE: That's true, Josie. It's rightfully mine. (*He shoves the money into his pocket.*)

JOSIE: Get along now, so you won't miss the trolley. And don't forget to get off the train at Bridgeport. Give my love to Thomas and John. No, never mind. They've not written me in years. Give them a boot in the tail for me.

MIKE: That's nice talk for a woman. You've a tongue as dirty as the Old Man's.

JOSIE (*Impatiently*): Don't start preaching, like you love to, or you'll never go.

MIKE: You're as bad as he is, almost. It's his influence made you what you are, and him always scheming how he'll cheat people, selling them a broken-down nag or a sick cow or pig that he's doctored up to look good for a day or two. It's no better than stealing, and you help him.

JOSIE: I do. Sure, it's grand fun.

MIKE: You ought to marry and have a home of your own away from this shanty and stop your shameless ways with men. (*He adds, not without moral satisfaction*) Though it'd be hard to find a decent man who'd have you now.

JOSIE: I don't want a decent man, thank you. They're no fun. They're all sticks like you. And I wouldn't marry the best man on earth and be tied down to him alone.

MIKE (*With a cunning leer*): Not even Jim Tyrone, I suppose? (*She stares at him*) You'd like being tied to money, I know that, and he'll be rich when his mother's estate is settled. (*Sarcastically*) I suppose you've never thought of that? Don't tell me! I've watched you making sheep's eyes at him.

JOSIE (*Contemptuously*): So I'm leading Jim on to propose, am I?

MIKE: I know it's crazy, but maybe you're hoping if you got hold of him alone when he's mad drunk— Anyway, talk all you please to put me off, I'll bet my last penny you've cooked up some scheme to hook him, and the Old Man put you up to it. Maybe he thinks if he caught you with Jim and had witnesses to prove it, and his shotgun to scare him—

JOSIE (*Controlling her anger*): You're full of bright thoughts. I wouldn't strain my brains any more, if I was you.

MIKE: Well, I wouldn't put it past the Old Man to try any trick. And I wouldn't put it past you, God forgive you. You've never cared about your virtue, or what man you went out with. You've always been brazen as brass and proud of your disgrace. You can't deny that, Josie.

JOSIE: I don't. (*Then ominously*) You'd better shut up

now. I've been holding my temper, because we're saying
good-bye. (*She stands up*) But I'm losing patience.

MIKE (*Hastily*): Wait till I finish and you won't be mad
at me. I was going to say I wish you luck with your
scheming, for once. I hate Jim Tyrone's guts, with his
quotin' Latin and his high-toned Jesuit College education,
putting on airs as if he was too good to wipe his shoes
on me, when he's nothing but a drunken bum who never
done a tap of work in his life, except acting on the stage
while his father was alive to get him the jobs. (*Vindictively*) I'll pray you'll find a way to nab him, Josie, and
skin him out of his last nickel!

JOSIE (*Makes a threatening move toward him*): One more
word out of you— (*Then contemptuously*) You're a
dirty tick and it'd serve you right if I let you stay gabbing until Father came and beat you to a jelly, but I
won't. I'm too anxious to be rid of you. (*Roughly*) Get
out of here, now! Do you think he'll stay all day with
the pigs, you gabbing fool? (*She goes left to peer around
the corner of the house—with real alarm*) There he is,
coming up to the barn. (MIKE *grabs the satchel, terrified.
He slinks swiftly around the corner and disappears along
the path to the woods, right-rear. She keeps watching her
father and does not notice* MIKE's *departure*) He's looking toward the meadow. He sees you're not working.
He's running down there. He'll come here next. You'd
better run for your life! (*She turns and sees he's gone—
contemptuously*) I might have known. I'll bet you're a
mile away by now, you rabbit! (*She peeks around the
corner again—with amused admiration*) Look at my
poor old father pelt. He's as spry on his stumpy legs as
a yearling—and as full of rage as a nest of wasps! (*She
laughs and comes back to look along the path to the
woods*) Well, that's the last of you, Mike, and good riddance. It was the little boy you used to be that I had to

mother, and not you, I stole the money for. (*This dismisses him. She sighs*) Well, himself will be here in a minute. I'd better be ready. (*She reaches in her bedroom corner by the door and takes out a sawed-off broom handle*) Not that I need it, but it saves his pride. (*She sits on the steps with the broom handle propped against the steps near her right hand. A moment later, her father,* PHIL HOGAN, *comes running up from left-rear and charges around the corner of the house, his arms pumping up and down, his fists clenched, his face full of fighting fury.*)

(HOGAN *is fifty-five, about five feet six. He has a thick neck, lumpy, sloping shoulders, a barrel-like trunk, stumpy legs, and big feet. His arms are short and muscular, with large hairy hands. His head is round with thinning sandy hair. His face is fat with a snub nose, long upper lip, big mouth, and little blue eyes with bleached lashes and eyebrows that remind one of a white pig's. He wears heavy brogans, filthy overalls, and a dirty short-sleeved undershirt. Arms and face are sunburned and freckled. On his head is an old wide-brimmed hat of coarse straw that would look more becoming on a horse. His voice is high-pitched with a pronounced brogue.*)

HOGAN (*Stops as he turns the corner and sees her—furiously*): Where is he? Is he hiding in the house? I'll wipe the floors with him, the lazy bastard! (*Turning his anger against her*) Haven't you a tongue in your head, you great slut you?

JOSIE (*With provoking calm*): Don't be calling me names, you bad-tempered old hornet, or maybe I'll lose my temper, too.

HOGAN: To hell with your temper, you overgrown cow!

JOSIE: I'd rather be a cow than an ugly little buck goat. You'd better sit down and cool off. Old men shouldn't run around raging in the noon sun. You'll get sunstroke.

HOGAN: To hell with sunstroke! Have you seen him?

JOSIE: Have I seen who?

HOGAN: Mike! Who else would I be after, the Pope? He was in the meadow, but the minute I turned my back he sneaked off. (*He sees the pitchfork*) There's his pitchfork! Will you stop your lying!

JOSIE: I haven't said I didn't see him.

HOGAN: Then don't try to help him hide from me, or— Where is he?

JOSIE: Where you'll never find him.

HOGAN: We'll soon see! I'll bet he's in your room under the bed, the cowardly lump! (*He moves toward the steps.*)

JOSIE: He's not. He's gone like Thomas and John before him to escape your slave-driving.

HOGAN (*Stares at her incredulously*): You mean he's run off to make his own way in the world?

JOSIE: He has. So make up your mind to it, and sit down.

HOGAN (*Baffled, sits on the boulder and takes off his hat to scratch his head—with a faint trace of grudging respect*): I'd never dream he had that much spunk. (*His temper rising again*) And I know damned well he hadn't, not without you to give him the guts and help him, like the great soft fool you are!

JOSIE: Now don't start raging again, Father.

HOGAN (*Seething*): You've stolen my satchel to give him, I suppose, like you did before for Thomas and John?

JOSIE: It was my satchel, too. Didn't I help you in the trade for the horse, when you got the Crowleys to throw in the satchel for good measure? I was up all night fixing that nag's forelegs so his knees wouldn't buckle together till after the Crowleys had him a day or two.

HOGAN (*Forgets his anger to grin reminiscently*): You've a wonderful way with animals, God bless you. And do you remember the two Crowleys came back to give me a beating, and I licked them both?

JOSIE (*With calculating flattery*): You did. You're a wonderful fighter. Sure, you could give Jack Dempsey himself a run for his money.

HOGAN (*With sharp suspicion*): I could, but don't try to change the subject and fill me with blarney.

JOSIE: All right. I'll tell the truth then. They were getting the best of you till I ran out and knocked one of them tail over tin cup against the pigpen.

HOGAN (*Outraged*): You're a liar! They was begging for mercy before you came. (*Furiously*) You thief, you! You stole my fine satchel for that lump! And I'll bet that's not all. I'll bet, like when Thomas and John sneaked off, you— (*He rises from the boulder threateningly*) Listen, Josie, if you found where I hid my little green bag, and stole my money to give to that lousy altar boy, I'll—

JOSIE (*Rises from the steps with the broom handle in her right hand*): Well, I did. So now what'll you do? Don't be threatening me. You know I'll beat better sense in your skull if you lay a finger on me.

HOGAN: I never yet laid hands on a woman—not when I was sober—but if it wasn't for that club— (*Bitterly*) A fine curse God put on me when he gave me a daughter as big and strong as a bull, and as vicious and disrespectful. (*Suddenly his eyes twinkle and he grins admiringly*) Be God, look at you standing there with the club! If you ain't the damnedest daughter in Connecticut, who is? (*He chuckles and sits on the boulder again.*)

JOSIE (*Laughs and sits on the steps, putting the club away*): And if you ain't the damnedest father in Connecticut, who is?

HOGAN (*Takes a clay pipe and plug of tobacco and knife from his pocket. He cuts the plug and stuffs his pipe— without rancor*): How much did you steal, Josie?

JOSIE: Six dollars only.

HOGAN: *Only!* Well, God grant someone with wits will see

that dopey gander at the depot and sell him the railroad for the six. (*Grumbling*) It isn't the money I mind, Josie—

JOSIE: I know. Sure, what do you care for money? You'd give your last penny to the first beggar you met—if he had a shotgun pointed at your heart!

HOGAN: Don't be teasing. You know what I mean. It's the thought of that pious lump having my money that maddens me. I wouldn't put it past him to drop it in the collection plate next Sunday, he's that big a jackass.

JOSIE: I knew when you'd calmed down you'd think it worth six dollars to see the last of him.

HOGAN (*Finishes filling his pipe*): Well, maybe I do. To tell the truth, I never liked him. (*He strikes a match on the seat of his overalls and lights his pipe*) And I never liked Thomas and John, either.

JOSIE (*Amused*): You've the same bad luck in sons I have in brothers.

HOGAN (*Puffs ruminatively*): They all take after your mother's family. She was the only one in it had spirit, God rest her soul. The rest of them was a pious lousy lot. They wouldn't dare put food in their mouths before they said grace for it. They was too busy preaching temperance to have time for a drink. They spent so much time confessing their sins, they had no chance to do any sinning. (*He spits disgustedly*) The scum of the earth! Thank God, you're like me and your mother.

JOSIE: I don't know if I should thank God for being like you. Sure, everyone says you're a wicked old tick, as crooked as a corkscrew.

HOGAN: I know. They're an envious lot, God forgive them. (*They both chuckle. He pulls on his pipe reflectively*) You didn't get much thanks from Mike, I'll wager, for your help.

JOSIE: Oh, he thanked me kindly. And then he started to preach about my sins—and yours.

HOGAN: Oho, did he? (*Exploding*) For the love of God, why didn't you hold him till I could give him one good kick for a father's parting blessing!

JOSIE: I near gave him one myself.

HOGAN: When I think your poor mother was killed bringing that crummy calf into life! (*Vindictively*) I've never set foot in a church since, and never will. (*A pause. He speaks with a surprising sad gentleness*) A sweet woman. Do you remember her, Josie? You were only a little thing when she died.

JOSIE: I remember her well. (*With a teasing smile which is half sad*) She was the one could put you in your place when you'd come home drunk and want to tear down the house for the fun of it.

HOGAN (*With admiring appreciation*): Yes, she could do it, God bless her. I only raised my hand to her once— just a slap because she told me to stop singing, it was after daylight. The next moment I was on the floor thinking a mule had kicked me. (*He chuckles*) Since you've grown up, I've had the same trouble. There's no liberty in my own home.

JOSIE: That's lucky—or there wouldn't be any home.

HOGAN (*After a pause of puffing on his pipe*): What did that donkey, Mike, preach to you about?

JOSIE: Oh, the same as ever—that I'm the scandal of the countryside, carrying on with men without a marriage license.

HOGAN (*Gives her a strange, embarrassed glance and then looks away. He does not look at her during the following dialogue. His manner is casual*): Hell roast his soul for saying it. But it's true enough.

JOSIE (*Defiantly*): It is, and what of it? I don't care a damn for the scandal.

HOGAN: No. You do as you please and to hell with everyone.

JOSIE: Yes, and that goes for you, too, if you are my father. So don't you start preaching too.

HOGAN: Me, preach? Sure, the divil would die laughing. Don't bring me into it. I learned long since to let you go your own way because there's no controlling you.

JOSIE: I do my work and I earn my keep and I've a right to be free.

HOGAN: You have. I've never denied it.

JOSIE: No. You've never. I've often wondered why a man that likes fights as much as you didn't grab at the excuse of my disgrace to beat the lights out of the men.

HOGAN: Wouldn't I look a great fool, when everyone knows any man who tried to make free with you, and you not willing, would be carried off to the hospital? Anyway, I wouldn't want to fight an army. You've had too many sweethearts.

JOSIE (*With a proud toss of her head—boastfully*): That's because I soon get tired of any man and give him his walking papers.

HOGAN: I'm afraid you were born to be a terrible wanton woman. But to tell the truth, I'm well satisfied you're what you are, though I shouldn't say it, because if you was the decent kind, you'd have married some fool long ago, and I'd have lost your company and your help on the farm.

JOSIE (*With a trace of bitterness*): Leave it to you to think of your own interest.

HOGAN (*Puffs on his pipe*): What else did my beautiful son, Mike, say to you?

JOSIE: Oh, he was full of stupid gab, as usual. He gave me good advice—

HOGAN (*Grimly*): That was kind of him. It must have been good—

JOSIE: I ought to marry and settle down—if I could find a

decent man who'd have me, which he was sure I couldn't.

HOGAN (*Beginning to boil*): I tell you, Josie, it's going to be the saddest memory of my life I didn't get one last swipe at him!

JOSIE: So the only hope, he thought, was for me to catch some indecent man, who'd have money coming to him I could steal.

HOGAN (*Gives her a quick, probing side glance—casually*): He meant Jim Tyrone?

JOSIE: He did. And the dirty tick accused you and me of making up a foxy scheme to trap Jim. I'm to get him alone when he's crazy drunk and lead him on to marry me. (*She adds in a hard, scornful tone*) As if that would ever work. Sure, all the pretty little tarts on Broadway, New York, must have had a try at that, and much good it did them.

HOGAN (*Again with a quick side glance—casually*): They must have, surely. But that's in the city where he's suspicious. You never can tell what he mightn't do here in the country, where he's innocent, with a moon in the sky to fill him with poetry and a quart of bad hootch inside of him.

JOSIE (*Turns on him angrily*): Are you taking Mike's scheme seriously, you old goat?

HOGAN: I'm not. I only thought you wanted my opinion. (*She regards him suspiciously, but his face is blank, as if he hadn't a thought beyond enjoying his pipe.*)

JOSIE (*Turning away*): And if that didn't work, Mike said maybe we had a scheme that I'd get Jim in bed with me and you'd come with witnesses and a shotgun, and catch him there.

HOGAN: Faith, me darlin' son never learnt that from his prayer book! He must have improved his mind on the sly.

JOSIE: The dirty tick!

HOGAN: Don't call him a tick. I don't like ticks but I'll say this for them, I never picked one off me yet was a hypocrite.

JOSIE: Him daring to accuse us of planning a rotten trick like that on Jim!

HOGAN (*As if he misunderstood her meaning*): Yes, it's as old as the hills. Everyone's heard of it. But it still works now and again, I'm told, and sometimes an old trick is best because it's so ancient no one would suspect you'd try it.

JOSIE (*Staring at him resentfully*): That's enough out of you, Father. I never can tell to this day, when you put that dead mug on you, whether you're joking or not, but I don't want to hear any more—

HOGAN (*Mildly*): I thought you wanted my honest opinion on the merits of Mike's suggestion.

JOSIE: Och, shut up, will you? I know you're only trying to make game of me. You like Jim and you'd never play a dirty trick on him, not even if I was willing.

HOGAN: No—not unless I found he was playing one on me.

JOSIE: Which he'd never.

HOGAN: No, I wouldn't think it, but my motto in life is never trust anyone too far, not even myself.

JOSIE: You've reason for the last. I've often suspected you sneak out of bed in the night to pick your own pockets.

HOGAN: I wouldn't call it a dirty trick on him to get you for a wife.

JOSIE (*Exasperatedly*): God save us, are you off on that again?

HOGAN: Well, you've put marriage in my head and I can't help considering the merits of the case, as they say. Sure, you're two of a kind, both great disgraces. That would help make a happy marriage because neither of you could look down on the other.

JOSIE: Jim mightn't think so.

HOGAN: You mean he'd think he was marrying beneath his station? He'd be a damned fool if he had that notion, for his Old Man who'd worked up from nothing to be rich and famous didn't give a damn about station. Didn't I often see him working on his grounds in clothes I wouldn't put on a scarecrow, not caring who saw him? (*With admiring affection*) God rest him, he was a true Irish gentleman.

JOSIE: He was, and didn't you swindle him, and make me help you at it? I remember when I was a slip of a girl, and you'd get a letter saying his agent told him you were a year behind in the rent, and he'd be damned if he'd stand for it, and he was coming here to settle the matter. You'd make me dress up, with my hair brushed and a ribbon in it, and leave me to soften his heart before he saw you. So I'd skip down the path to meet him, and make him a courtesy, and hold on to his hand, and bat my eyes at him and lead him in the house, and offer him a drink of the good whiskey you didn't keep for company, and gape at him and tell him he was the handsomest man in the world, and the fierce expression he'd put on for you would go away.

HOGAN (*Chuckles*): You did it wonderful. You should have gone on the stage.

JOSIE (*Dryly*): Yes, that's what he'd tell me, and he'd reach in his pocket and take out a half dollar, and ask me if you hadn't put me up to it. So I'd say yes, you had.

HOGAN (*Sadly*): I never knew you were such a black traitor, and you only a child.

JOSIE: And then you'd come and before he could get a word out of him, you'd tell him you'd vacate the premises unless he lowered the rent and painted the house.

HOGAN: Be God, that used to stop him in his tracks.

JOSIE: It didn't stop him from saying you were the damnedest crook ever came out of Ireland.

HOGAN: He said it with admiration. And we'd start drinking and telling stories, and singing songs, and by the time he left we were both too busy cursing England to worry over the rent. (*He grins affectionately*) Oh, he was a great man entirely.

JOSIE: He was. He always saw through your tricks.

HOGAN: Didn't I know he would? Sure, all I wanted was to give him the fun of seeing through them so he couldn't be hard-hearted. That was the real trick.

JOSIE (*Stares at him*): You old divil, you've always a trick hidden behind your tricks, so no one can tell at times what you're after.

HOGAN: Don't be so suspicious. Sure, I'd never try to fool you. You know me too well. But we've gone off the track. It's Jim we're discussing, not his father. I was telling you I could see the merit in your marrying him.

JOSIE (*Exasperatedly*): Och, a cow must have kicked you in the head this morning.

HOGAN: I'd never give it a thought if I didn't know you had a soft spot in your heart for him.

JOSIE (*Resentfully*): Well, I haven't! I like him, if that's what you mean, but it's only to talk to, because he's educated and quiet-spoken and has politeness even when he's drunkest, and doesn't roar around cursing and singing, like some I could name.

HOGAN: If you could see the light in your eyes when he blarneys you—

JOSIE (*Roughly*): The light in me foot! (*Scornfully*) I'm in love with him, you'll be saying next!

HOGAN (*Ignores this*): And another merit of the case is, he likes you.

JOSIE: Because he keeps dropping in here lately? Sure, it's only when he gets sick of the drunks at the Inn, and it's more to joke with you than see me.

HOGAN: It's your happiness I'm considering when I recommend your using your wits to catch him, if you can.

JOSIE (*Jeeringly*): If!

HOGAN: Who knows? With all the sweethearts you've had, you must have a catching way with men.

JOSIE (*Boastfully*): Maybe I have. But that doesn't mean—

HOGAN: If you got him alone tonight—there'll be a beautiful moon to fill him with poetry and loneliness, and—

JOSIE: That's one of Mike's dirty schemes.

HOGAN: Mike be damned! Sure, that's every woman's scheme since the world was created. Without it there'd be no population. (*Persuasively*) There'd be no harm trying it, anyway.

JOSIE: And no use, either. (*Bitterly*) Och, Father, don't play the jackass with me. You know, and I know, I'm an ugly overgrown lump of a woman, and the men that want me are no better than stupid bulls. Jim can have all the pretty, painted little Broadway girls he wants— and dancers on the stage, too—when he comes into his estate. That's the kind he likes.

HOGAN: I notice he's never married one. Maybe he'd like a fine strong handsome figure of a woman for a change, with beautiful eyes and hair and teeth and a smile.

JOSIE (*Pleased, but jeering*): Thank you kindly for your compliments. Now I know a cow kicked you in the head.

HOGAN: If you think Jim hasn't been taking in your fine points, you're a fool.

JOSIE: You mean you've noticed him? (*Suddenly furious*) Stop your lying!

HOGAN: Don't fly in a temper. All I'm saying is, there may be a chance in it to better yourself.

JOSIE (*Scornfully*): Better myself by being tied down to a man who's drunk every night of his life? No, thank you!

HOGAN: Sure, you're strong enough to reform him. A taste

of that club you've got, when he came home to you paralyzed, and in a few weeks you'd have him a dirty prohibitionist.

JOSIE (*Seriously*): It's true, if I was his wife, I'd cure him of drinking himself to death, if I had to kill him. (*Then angrily*) Och, I'm sick of your crazy gab, Father! Leave me alone!

HOGAN: Well, let's put it another way. Don't tell me you couldn't learn to love the estate he'll come into.

JOSIE (*Resentfully*): Ah, I've been waiting for that. That's what Mike said, again. Now we've come to the truth behind all your blather of my liking him or him liking me. (*Her manner changing—defiantly*) All right, then. Of course I'd love the money. Who wouldn't? And why shouldn't I get my hands on it, if I could? He's bound to be swindled out of it, anyway. He'll go back to the Broadway he thinks is heaven, and by the time the pretty little tarts, and the barroom sponges and race-track touts and gamblers are through with him he'll be picked clean. I'm no saint, God knows, but I'm decent and deserving compared to those scum.

HOGAN (*Eagerly*): Be God, now you're using your wits. And where there's a will there's a way. You and me have never been beat when we put our brains together. I'll keep thinking it over, and you do the same.

JOSIE (*With illogical anger*): Well, I won't! And you keep your mad scheming to yourself. I won't listen to it.

HOGAN (*As if he were angry, too*): All right. The divil take you. It's all you'll hear from me. (*He pauses—then with great seriousness, turning toward her*) Except one thing— (*As she starts to shut him up—sharply*) I'm serious, and you'd better listen, because it's about this farm, which is home to us.

JOSIE (*Surprised, stares at him*): What about the farm?

HOGAN: Don't forget, if we have lived on it twenty years,

we're only tenants and we could be thrown out on our necks any time. (*Quickly*) Mind you, I don't say Jim would ever do it, rent or no rent, or let the executors do it, even if they wanted, which they don't, knowing they'd never find another tenant.

JOSIE: What's worrying you, then?

HOGAN: This. I've been afraid lately the minute the estate is out of probate, Jim will sell the farm.

JOSIE (*Exasperatedly*): Of course he will! Hasn't he told us and promised you can buy it on easy time payments at the small price you offered?

HOGAN: Jim promises whatever you like when he's full of whiskey. He might forget a promise as easy when he's drunk enough.

JOSIE (*Indignantly*): He'd never! And who'd want it except us? No one ever has in all the years—

HOGAN: Someone has lately. The agent got an offer last month, Jim told me, bigger than mine.

JOSIE: Och, Jim loves to try and get your goat. He was kidding you.

HOGAN: He wasn't. I can tell. He said he told the agent to tell whoever it was the place wasn't for sale.

JOSIE: Of course he did. Did he say who'd made the offer?

HOGAN: He didn't know. It came through a real-estate man who wouldn't tell who his client was. I've been trying to guess, but I can't think of anyone crazy enough unless it'd be some damn fool of a millionaire buying up land to make a great estate for himself, like our beautiful neighbor, Harder, the Standard Oil thief, did years ago. (*He adds with bitter fervency*) May he roast in hell and his Limey superintendent with him!

JOSIE: Amen to that. (*Then scornfully*) This land for an estate? And if there was an offer, Jim's refused it, and that ends it. He wouldn't listen to any offer, after he's given his word to us.

HOGAN: Did I say he would—when he's in his right mind? What I'm afraid of is, he might be led into it sometime when he has one of his sneering bitter drunks on and talks like a Broadway crook himself, saying money is the only thing in the world, and everything and anyone can be bought if the price is big enough. You've heard him.

JOSIE: I have. But he doesn't fool me at all. He only acts like he's hard and shameless to get back at life when it's tormenting him—and who doesn't? (*He gives her a quick, curious side glance which she doesn't notice.*)

HOGAN: Or take the other kind of queer drunk he gets on sometimes when, without any reason you can see, he'll suddenly turn strange, and look sad, and stare at nothing as if he was mourning over some ghost inside him, and—

JOSIE: I think I know what comes over him when he's like that. It's the memory of his mother comes back and his grief for her death. (*Pityingly*) Poor Jim.

HOGAN (*Ignoring this*): And whiskey seems to have no effect on him, like water off a duck's back. He'll keep acting natural enough, and you'd swear he wasn't bad at all, but the next day you find his brain was so paralyzed he don't remember a thing until you remind him. He's done a lot of mad things, when he was that way, he was sorry for after.

JOSIE (*Scornfully*): What drunk hasn't? But he'd never— (*Resentfully*) I won't have you suspecting Jim without any cause, d'you hear me!

HOGAN: I don't suspect him. All I've said is, when a man gets as queer drunk as Jim, he doesn't know himself what he mightn't do, and we'd be damned fools if we didn't fear the possibility, however small it is, and do all we can to guard against it.

JOSIE: There's no possibility! And how could we guard against it, if there was?

HOGAN: Well, you can put yourself out to be extra nice to him, for one thing.

JOSIE: How nice is extra nice?

HOGAN: You ought to know. But here's one tip. I've noticed when you talk rough and brazen like you do to other men, he may grin like they do, as if he enjoyed it, but he don't. So watch your tongue.

JOSIE (*With a defiant toss of her head*): I'll talk as I please, and if he don't like it he can lump it! (*Scornfully*) I'm to pretend I'm a pure virgin, I suppose? That would fool him, wouldn't it, and him hearing all about me from the men at the Inn? (*She gets to her feet, abruptly changing the subject*) We're wasting the day, blathering. (*Then her face hardening*) If he ever went back on his word, no matter how drunk he was, I'd be with you in any scheme you made against him, no matter how dirty. (*Hastily*) But it's all your nonsense. I'd never believe it. (*She comes and picks up the pitchfork*) I'll go to the meadow and finish Mike's work. You needn't fear you'll miss his help on the farm.

HOGAN: A hell of a help! A weak lazy back and the appetite of a drove of starving pigs! (*As she turns to go—suddenly bellicose*) Leaving me, are you? When it's dinner time? Where's my dinner, you lazy cow?

JOSIE: There's stew on the stove, you bad-tempered runt. Go in and help yourself. I'm not hungry. Your gab has bothered my mind. I need hard work in the sun to clear it. (*She starts to go off toward rear-right.*)

HOGAN (*Glancing down the road, off left-front*): You'd better wait. There's a caller coming to the gate—and if I'm not mistaken, it's the light of your eyes himself.

JOSIE (*Angrily*): Shut up! (*She stares off—her face softens and grows pitying*) Look at him when he thinks no one is watching, with his eyes on the ground. Like a

dead man walking slow behind his own coffin. (*Then
roughly*) Faith, he must have a hangover. He sees u
now. Look at the bluff he puts up, straightening him
self and grinning. (*Resentfully*) I don't want to mee
him. Let him make jokes with you and play the ol
game about a drink you both think is such fun. That'
all he comes for, anyway. (*She starts off again.*)

HOGAN: Are you running away from him? Sure, you mus
be afraid you're in love. (JOSIE *halts instantly and turn.
back defiantly. He goes on*) Go in the house now, an
wash your face, and tidy your dress, and give a touch t
your hair. You want to look decent for him.

JOSIE (*Angrily*): I'll go in the house, but only to see the
stew ain't burned, for I suppose you'll have the foxines
to ask him to have a bite to eat to keep in his good graces

HOGAN: Why shouldn't I ask him? I know damned wel
he has no appetite this early in the day, but only a thirst

JOSIE: Och, you make me sick, you sly miser! (*She goe:
in through her bedroom, slamming the door behind her
HOGAN refills his pipe, pretending he doesn't notice TYRONE
approaching, his eyes bright with droll expectation. JIM
TYRONE enters along the road from the highway, left.*)

(TYRONE *is in his early forties, around five feet nine
broad-shouldered and deep-chested. His naturally fine
physique has become soft and soggy from dissipation
but his face is still good-looking despite its unhealthy
puffiness and the bags under the eyes. He has thinning
dark hair, parted and brushed back to cover a bald spot.
His eyes are brown, the whites congested and yellowish.
His nose, big and aquiline, gives his face a certain
Mephistophelian quality which is accentuated by his ha-
bitually cynical expression. But when he smiles without sneering, he still has the ghost of a former youthful, irresponsible Irish charm—that of the beguiling*

ne'er-do-well, sentimental and romantic. It is his humor and charm which have kept him attractive to women, and popular with men as a drinking companion. He is dressed in an expensive dark-brown suit, tight-fitting and drawn in at the waist, dark-brown made-to-order shoes and silk socks, a white silk shirt, silk handkerchief in breast pocket, a dark tie. This get-up suggests that he follows a style set by well-groomed Broadway gamblers who would like to be mistaken for Wall Street brokers.)

(He has had enough pick-me-ups to recover from morning-after nausea and steady his nerves. During the following dialogue, he and HOGAN *are like players at an old familiar game where each knows the other's moves, but which still amuses them.)*

TYRONE *(Approaches and stands regarding* HOGAN *with sardonic relish.* HOGAN *scratches a match on the seat of his overalls and lights his pipe, pretending not to see him.* TYRONE *recites with feeling)*:

"Fortunate senex, ergo tua rura manebunt,
et tibi magna satis, quamvis lapis omnia nudus."

HOGAN *(Mutters)*: It's the landlord again, and my shotgun not handy. *(He looks up at* TYRONE*)* Is it Mass you're saying, Jim? That was Latin. I know it by ear. What the hell—insult does it mean?

TYRONE: Translated very freely into Irish English, something like this. *(He imitates* HOGAN's *brogue)* "Ain't you the lucky old bastard to have this beautiful farm, if it is full of nude rocks."

HOGAN: I like that part about the rocks. If cows could eat them this place would make a grand dairy farm. *(He spits)* It's easy to see you've a fine college education. It must be a big help to you, conversing with whores and barkeeps.

TYRONE: Yes, a very valuable worldly asset. I was once offered a job as office boy—until they discovered I wasn't qualified because I had no Bachelor of Arts diploma. There had been a slight misunderstanding just before I was to graduate.

HOGAN: Between you and the Fathers? I'll wager!

TYRONE: I made a bet with another Senior I could get a tart from the Haymarket to visit me, introduce her to the Jebs as my sister—and get away with it.

HOGAN: But you didn't?

TYRONE: Almost. It was a memorable day in the halls of learning. All the students were wise and I had them rolling in the aisles as I showed Sister around the grounds, accompanied by one of the Jebs. He was a bit suspicious at first, but Dutch Maisie—her professional name—had no make-up on, and was dressed in black, and had eaten a pound of Sen-Sen to kill the gin on her breath, and seemed such a devout girl that he forgot his suspicions. (*He pauses*) Yes, all would have been well, but she was a mischievous minx, and had her own ideas of improving on my joke. When she was saying good-bye to Father Fuller, she added innocently: "Christ, Father, it's nice and quiet out here away from the damned Sixth Avenue El. I wish to hell I could stay here!" (*Dryly*) But she didn't, and neither did I.

HOGAN (*Chuckles delightedly*): I'll bet you didn't! God bless Dutch Maisie! I'd like to have known her.

TYRONE (*Sits down on the steps—with a change of manner*): Well, how's the Duke of Donegal this fine day?

HOGAN: Never better.

TYRONE: Slaving and toiling as usual, I see.

HOGAN: Hasn't a poor man a right to his noon rest without being sneered at by his rich landlord?

TYRONE: "Rich" is good. I would be, if you'd pay up your back rent.

HOGAN: You ought to pay me, instead, for occupying this rockpile, miscalled a farm. (*His eyes twinkling*) But I have fine reports to give you of a promising harvest. The milkweed and the thistles is in thriving condition, and I never saw the poison ivy so bounteous and beautiful. (TYRONE *laughs. Without their noticing,* JOSIE *appears in the doorway behind* TYRONE. *She has tidied up and arranged her hair. She smiles down at* JIM, *her face softening, pleased to hear him laugh.*)

TYRONE: You win. Where did Josie go, Phil? I saw her here—

HOGAN: She ran in the house to make herself beautiful for you.

JOSIE (*Breaks in roughly*): You're a liar. (*To* TYRONE, *her manner one of bold, free-and-easy familiarity*) Hello, Jim.

TYRONE (*Starts to stand up*): Hello, Josie.

JOSIE (*Puts a hand on his shoulder and pushes him down*): Don't get up. Sure, you know I'm no lady. (*She sits on the top step—banteringly*) How's my fine Jim this beautiful day? You don't look so bad. You must have stopped at the Inn for an eye-opener—or ten of them.

TYRONE: I've felt worse. (*He looks up at her sardonically*) And how's my Virgin Queen of Ireland?

JOSIE: Yours, is it? Since when? And don't be miscalling me a virgin. You'll ruin my reputation, if you spread that lie about me. (*She laughs.* TYRONE *is staring at her. She goes on quickly*) How is it you're around so early? I thought you never got up till afternoon.

TYRONE: Couldn't sleep. One of those heebie-jeebie nights when the booze keeps you awake instead of— (*He catches her giving him a pitying look—irritably*) But what of it!

JOSIE: Maybe you had no woman in bed with you, for a change. It's a terrible thing to break the habit of years.

TYRONE (*Shrugs his shoulders*): Maybe.

JOSIE: What's the matter with the tarts in town, they let you do it? I'll bet the ones you know on Broadway, New York, wouldn't neglect their business.

TYRONE (*Pretends to yawn boredly*): Maybe not. (*Then irritably*) Cut out the kidding, Josie. It's too early.

HOGAN (*Who has been taking everything in without seeming to*): I told you not to annoy the gentleman with your rough tongue.

JOSIE: Sure I thought I was doing my duty as hostess making him feel at home.

TYRONE (*Stares at her again*): Why all the interest lately in the ladies of the profession, Josie?

JOSIE: Oh, I've been considering joining their union. It's easier living than farming, I'm sure. (*Then resentfully*) You think I'd starve at it, don't you, because your fancy is for dainty dolls of women? But other men like—

TYRONE (*With sudden revulsion*): For God's sake, cut out that kind of talk, Josie! It sounds like hell.

JOSIE (*Stares at him startledly—then resentfully*): Oh, it does, does it? (*Forcing a scornful smile*) I'm shocking you, I suppose? (HOGAN *is watching them both, not missing anything in their faces, while he seems intent on his pipe.*)

TYRONE (*Looking a bit sheepish and annoyed at himself for his interest—shrugs his shoulders*): No. Hardly. Forget it. (*He smiles kiddingly*) Anyway, who told you I fall for the dainty dolls? That's all a thing of the past. I like them tall and strong and voluptuous, now, with beautiful big breasts. (*She blushes and looks confused and is furious with herself for doing so.*)

HOGAN: There you are, Josie, darlin'. Sure he couldn't speak fairer than that.

JOSIE (*Recovers herself*): He couldn't, indeed. (*She pats* TYRONE's *head—playfully*) You're a terrible blarneying liar, Jim, but thank you just the same. (TYRONE *turns his attention to* HOGAN. *He winks at* JOSIE *and begins in an exaggeratedly casual manner.*)

TYRONE: I don't blame you, Mr. Hogan, for taking it easy on such a blazing hot day.

HOGAN (*Doesn't look at him. His eyes twinkle*): Hot, did you say? I find it cool, meself. Take off your coat if you're hot, Mister Tyrone.

TYRONE: One of the most stifling days I've ever known. Isn't it, Josie?

JOSIE (*Smiling*): Terrible. I know you must be perishing.

HOGAN: I wouldn't call it a damned bit stifling.

TYRONE: It parches the membranes in your throat.

HOGAN: The what? Never mind. I can't have them, for my throat isn't parched at all. If yours is, Mister Tyrone, there's a well full of water at the back.

TYRONE: Water? That's something people wash with, isn't it? I mean, some people.

HOGAN: So I've heard. But, like you, I find it hard to believe. It's a dirty habit. They must be foreigners.

TYRONE: As I was saying, my throat is parched after the long dusty walk I took just for the pleasure of being your guest.

HOGAN: I don't remember inviting you, and the road is hard macadam with divil a spec of dust, and it's less than a quarter mile from the Inn here.

TYRONE: I didn't have a drink at the Inn. I was waiting until I arrived here, knowing that you—

HOGAN: Knowing I'd what?

TYRONE: Your reputation as a generous host—

HOGAN: The world must be full of liars. So you didn't have a drink at the Inn? Then it must be the air itself smells of whiskey today, although I didn't notice it before you came. You've gone on the water-wagon, I suppose? Well, that's fine, and I ask pardon for misjudging you.

TYRONE: I've wanted to go on the wagon for the past

twenty-five years, but the doctors have strictly forbidden it. It would be fatal—with my weak heart.

HOGAN: So you've a weak heart? Well, well, and me thinking all along it was your head. I'm glad you told me. I was just going to offer you a drink, but whiskey is the worst thing—

TYRONE: The Docs say it's a matter of life and death. I must have a stimulant—one big drink, at least, whenever I strain my heart walking in the hot sun.

HOGAN: Walk back to the Inn, then, and give it a good strain, so you can buy yourself two big drinks.

JOSIE (*Laughing*): Ain't you the fools, playing that old game between you, and both of you pleased as punch!

TYRONE (*Gives up with a laugh*): Hasn't he ever been known to loosen up, Josie?

JOSIE: You ought to know. If you need a drink you'll have to buy it from him or die of thirst.

TYRONE: Well, I'll bet this is one time he's going to treat.

HOGAN: Be God, I'll take that bet!

TYRONE: After you've heard the news I've got for you, you'll be so delighted you won't be able to drag out the old bottle quick enough.

HOGAN: I'll have to be insanely delighted.

JOSIE (*Full of curiosity*): Shut up, Father. What news, Jim?

TYRONE: I have it off the grapevine that a certain exalted personage will drop in on you before long.

HOGAN: It's the sheriff again. I know by the pleased look on your mug.

TYRONE: Not this time (*He pauses tantalizingly.*)

JOSIE: Bad luck to you, can't you tell us who?

TYRONE: A more eminent grafter than the sheriff— (*Sneeringly*) A leading aristocrat in our Land of the Free and Get-Rich-Quick, whose boots are licked by one and all— one of the Kings of our Republic by Divine Right of

Inherited Swag. In short, I refer to your good neighbor,
T. Stedman Harder, Standard Oil's sappiest child, whom
I know you both love so dearly. (*There is a pause after
this announcement.* HOGAN *and* JOSIE *stiffen, and their
eyes begin to glitter. But they can't believe their luck at
first.*)

HOGAN (*In an ominous whisper*): Did you say Harder is
coming to call on us, Jim?

JOSIE: It's too good to be true.

TYRONE (*Watching them with amusement*): No kidding.
The great Mr. Harder intends to stop here on his way
back to lunch from a horseback ride.

JOSIE: How do you know?

TYRONE: Simpson told me. I ran into him at the Inn.

HOGAN: That English scum of a superintendent!

TYRONE: He was laughing himself sick. He said he suggested the idea to Harder—told him you'd be overwhelmed with awe if he deigned to interview you in
person.

HOGAN: Overwhelmed isn't the word. Is it, Josie?

JOSIE: It isn't indeed, Father.

TYRONE: For once in his life, Simpson is cheering for you.
He doesn't like his boss. In fact, he asked me to tell you
he hopes you kill him.

HOGAN (*Disdainfully*): To hell with the Limey's good
wishes. I'd like both of them to call together.

JOSIE: Ah, well, we can't have everything. (*To* TYRONE)
What's the reason Mr. Harder decided to notice poor,
humble scum the like of us?

TYRONE (*Grinning*): That's right, Josie. Be humble. He'll
expect you to know your place.

HOGAN: Will he now? Well, well. (*With a great happy
sigh*) This is going to be a beautiful day entirely.

JOSIE: But what's Harder's reason, Jim?

TYRONE: Well, it seems he has an ice pond on his estate.

HOGAN: Oho! So that's it!

TYRONE: Yes. That's it. Harder likes to keep up the good old manorial customs. He clings to his ice pond. And your pigpen isn't far from his ice pond.

HOGAN: A nice little stroll for the pigs, that's all.

TYRONE: And somehow Harder's fence in that vicinity has a habit of breaking down.

HOGAN: Fences are queer things. You can't depend on them.

TYRONE: Simpson says he's had it repaired a dozen times, but each time on the following night it gets broken down again.

JOSIE: What a strange thing! It must be the bad fairies. I can't imagine who else could have done it. Can you, Father?

HOGAN: I can't, surely.

TYRONE: Well, Simpson can. He knows you did it and he told his master so.

HOGAN (*Disdainfully*): Master is the word. Sure, the English can't live unless they have a lord's backside to kiss, the dirty slaves.

TYRONE: The result of those breaks in the fence is that your pigs stroll—as you so gracefully put it—stroll through to wallow happily along the shores of the ice pond.

HOGAN: Well, why not? Sure, they're fine ambitious American-born pigs and they don't miss any opportunities. They're like Harder's father who made the money for him.

TYRONE: I agree, but for some strange reason Harder doesn't look forward to the taste of pig in next summer's ice water.

HOGAN: He must be delicate. Remember he's delicate, Josie, and leave your club in the house. (*He bursts into joyful menacing laughter*) Oh, be God and be Christ in the mountains! I've pined to have a quiet word with Mr. Harder for years, watching him ride past in his big shiny automobile with his snoot in the air, and being tormented always by the complaints of his Limey superintendent. Oh, won't I welcome him!

JOSIE: Won't *we,* you mean. Sure, I love him as much as you.

HOGAN: I'd kiss you, Jim, for this beautiful news, if you wasn't so damned ugly. Maybe Josie'll do it for me. She has a stronger stomach.

JOSIE: I will! He's earned it. (*She pulls* TYRONE's *head back and laughingly kisses him on the lips. Her expression changes. She looks startled and confused, stirred and at the same time frightened. She forces a scornful laugh*) Och, there's no spirit in you! It's like kissing a corpse.

TYRONE (*Gives her a strange surprised look—mockingly*): Yes? (*Turning to* HOGAN) Well, how about that drink, Phil? I'll leave it to Josie if drinks aren't on the house.

HOGAN: *I* won't leave it to Josie. She's prejudiced, being in love.

JOSIE (*Angrily*): Shut up, you old liar! (*Then guiltily, forcing a laugh*) Don't talk nonsense to sneak out of treating Jim.

HOGAN (*Sighing*): All right, Josie. Go get the bottle and one small glass, or he'll never stop nagging me. I can turn my back, so the sight of him drinking free won't break my heart (JOSIE *gets up, laughing, and goes in the house.* HOGAN *peers at the road off left*) On his way back to lunch, you said? Then it's time— (*Fervently*) O Holy Joseph, don't let the bastard change his mind!

TYRONE (*Beginning to have qualms*): Listen, Phil. Don't get too enthusiastic. He has a big drag around here, and he'll have you pinched, sure as hell, if you beat him up.

HOGAN: Och, I'm no fool. (JOSIE *comes out with a bottle and a tumbler*) Will you listen to this, Josie. He's warning me not to give Harder a beating—as if I'd dirty my hands on the scum.

JOSIE: As if we'd need to. Sure, all we want is a quiet chat with him.

HOGAN: That's all. As neighbor to neighbor.

JOSIE (*Hands* TYRONE *the bottle and tumbler*): Here you are, Jim. Don't stint yourself.

HOGAN (*Mournfully*): A fine daughter! I tell you a small glass and you give him a bucket! (*As* TYRONE *pours a big drink, grinning at him, he turns away with a comic shudder*) That's a fifty-dollar drink, at least.

TYRONE: Here's luck, Phil.

HOGAN: I hope you drown. (TYRONE *drinks and makes a wry face.*)

TYRONE: The best chicken medicine I've ever tasted.

HOGAN: That's gratitude for you! Here, pass me the bottle. A drink will warm up my welcome for His Majesty. (*He takes an enormous swig from the bottle.*)

JOSIE (*Looking off left*): There's two horseback riders on the county road now.

HOGAN: Praise be to God! It's him and a groom. (*He sets the bottle on top of the boulder.*)

JOSIE: That's McCabe. An old sweetheart of mine. (*She glances at* TYRONE *provokingly—then suddenly worried and protective*) You get in the house, Jim. If Harder sees you here, he'll lay the whole blame on you.

TYRONE: Nix, Josie. You don't think I'm going to miss this, do you?

JOSIE: You can sit inside by my window and take in everything. Come on, now, don't be stubborn with me. (*She puts her hands under his arms and lifts him to his feet as easily as if he was a child—banteringly*) Go into my beautiful bedroom. It's a nice place for you.

TYRONE (*Kiddingly*): Just what I've been thinking for some time, Josie.

JOSIE (*Boldly*): Sure, you've never given me a sign of it.

Come up tonight and we'll spoon in the moonlight and
you can tell me your thoughts.

TYRONE: That's a date. Remember, now.

JOSIE: It's you who'll forget. Get inside now, before it's
too late. (*She gives him a shove inside and closes the
door.*)

HOGAN (*Has been watching the visitor approach*): He's
dismounting—as graceful as a scarecrow, and his poor
horse longing to give him a kick. Look at Mac grinning
at us. Sit down, Josie. (*She sits on the steps, he on the
boulder*) Pretend you don't notice him. (T. STEDMAN
HARDER *appears at left. They act as if they didn't see him.*
HOGAN *knocks out his pipe on the palm of his hand.*)

(HARDER *is in his late thirties but looks younger because
his face is unmarked by worry, ambition, or any of the
common hazards of life. No matter how long he lives,
his four undergraduate years will always be for him the
most significant in his life, and the moment of his
highest achievement the time he was tapped for an ex-
clusive Senior Society at the Ivy university to which his
father had given millions. Since that day he has felt no
need for further aspiring, no urge to do anything except settle down on his estate and live the life of a
country gentleman, mildly interested in saddle horses
and sport models of foreign automobiles. He is not the
blatantly silly, playboy heir to millions whose antics
make newspaper headlines. He doesn't drink much
except when he attends his class reunion every spring—
the most exciting episode of each year for him. He
doesn't give wild parties, doesn't chase after musical-
comedy cuties, is a mildly contented husband and father
of three children. A not unpleasant man, affable, good-
looking in an ordinary way, sunburnt and healthy,*)

beginning to take on fat, he is simply immature, naturally lethargic, a bit stupid. Coddled from birth, everything arranged and made easy for him, deferred to because of his wealth, he usually has the self-confident attitude of acknowledged superiority, but assumes a supercilious, insecure air when dealing with people beyond his ken. He is dressed in a beautifully tailored English tweed coat and whipcord riding breeches, immaculately polished English riding boots with spurs, and carries a riding crop in his hand.

(*It would be hard to find anyone more ill-equipped for combat with the* HOGANS. *He has never come in contact with anyone like them. To make matters easier for them he is deliberate in his speech, slow on the uptake, and has no sense of humor. The experienced strategy of the* HOGANS *in verbal battle is to take the offensive at once and never let an opponent get set to hit back. Also, they use a beautifully co-ordinated, bewildering change of pace, switching suddenly from jarring shouts to low, confidential vituperation. And they exaggerate their Irish brogues to confuse an enemy still further.*)

HARDER (*Walks toward* HOGAN—*stiffly*): Good morning. I want to see the man who runs this farm.

HOGAN (*Surveys him deliberately, his little pig eyes gleaming with malice*): You do, do you? Well, you've seen him. So run along now and play with your horse, and don't bother me. (*He turns to* JOSIE, *who is staring at* HARDER, *much to his discomfiture, as if she had discovered a cockroach in her soup*) D'you see what I see, Josie? Be God, you'll have to give that damned cat of yours a spanking for bringing it to our doorstep.

HARDER (*Determined to be authoritative and command respect—curtly*): Are you Hogan?

HOGAN (*Insultingly*): I am *Mister* Philip Hogan—to a gentleman.

JOSIE (*Glares at* HARDER): Where's your manners, you spindle-shanked jockey? Were you brought up in a stable?

HARDER (*Does not fight with ladies, and especially not with this lady—ignoring her*): My name is Harder. (*He obviously expects them to be immediately impressed and apologetic.*)

HOGAN (*Contemptuously*): Who asked you your name, me little man?

JOSIE: Sure, who in the world cares who the hell you are?

HOGAN: But if you want to play politeness, we'll play with you. Let me introduce you to my daughter, Harder—Miss Josephine Hogan.

JOSIE (*Petulantly*): I don't want to meet him, Father. I don't like his silly sheep's face, and I've no use for jockeys, anyway. I'll wager he's no damned good to a woman. (*From inside her bedroom comes a burst of laughter. This revelation of an unseen audience startles* HARDER. *He begins to look extremely unsure of himself.*)

HOGAN: I don't think he's a jockey. It's only the funny pants he's wearing. I'll bet if you asked his horse, you'd find he's no cowboy either. (*To* HARDER, *jeeringly*) Come, tell us the truth, me honey. Don't you kiss your horse each time you mount and beg him, please don't throw me today, darlin', and I'll give you an extra bucket of oats. (*He bursts into an extravagant roar of laughter, slapping his thigh, and* JOSIE *guffaws with him, while they watch the disconcerting effect of this theatrical mirth on* HARDER.)

HARDER (*Beginning to lose his temper*): Listen to me, Hogan! I didn't come here— (*He is going to add "to listen to your damned jokes" or something like that, but* HOGAN *silences him.*)

HOGAN (*Shouts*): What? What's that you said? (*He stares at the dumbfounded* HARDER *with droll amazement, as if he couldn't believe his ears*) You didn't come here? (*He turns to* JOSIE—*in a whisper*) Did you hear that, Josie? (*He takes off his hat and scratches his head in comic bewilderment*) Well, that's a puzzle, surely. How d'you suppose he got here?

JOSIE: Maybe the stork brought him, bad luck to it for a dirty bird. (*Again* TYRONE's *laughter is heard from the bedroom.*)

HARDER (*So off balance now he can only repeat angrily*): I said I didn't come here—

HOGAN (*Shouts*): Wait! Wait, now! (*Threateningly*) We've had enough of that. Say it a third time and I'll send my daughter to telephone the asylum.

HARDER (*Forgetting he's a gentleman*): Damn you, I'm the one who's had enough—!

JOSIE (*Shouts*): Hold your dirty tongue! I'll have no foul language in my presence.

HOGAN: Och, don't mind him, Josie. He's said he isn't here, anyway, so we won't talk to him behind his back. (*He regards* HARDER *with pitying contempt*) Sure, ain't you the poor crazy creature? Do you want us to believe you're your own ghost?

HARDER (*Notices the bottle on the boulder for the first time —tries to be contemptuously tolerant and even to smile with condescending disdain*): Ah! I understand now. You're drunk. I'll come back sometime when you're sober —or send Simpson— (*He turns away, glad of an excuse to escape.*)

JOSIE (*Jumps up and advances on him menacingly*): No, you don't! You'll apologize first for insulting a lady— insinuating I'm drunk this early in the day—or I'll knock some good breeding in you!

HARDER (*Actually frightened now*): I—I said nothing about you—

HOGAN (*Gets up to come between them*): Aisy now, Josie.

He didn't mean it. He don't know what he means, the poor loon. (*To* HARDER—*pityingly*) Run home, that's a good lad, before your keeper misses you.

HARDER (*Hastily*): Good day. (*He turns eagerly toward left but suddenly* HOGAN *grabs his shoulder and spins him around—then shifts his grip to the lapel of* HARDER's *coat*.)

HOGAN (*Grimly*): Wait now, me Honey Boy. I'll have a word with you, if you plaze. I'm beginning to read some sense into this. You mentioned that English bastard, Simpson. I know who you are now.

HARDER (*Outraged*): Take your hands off me, you drunken fool. (*He raises his riding crop.*)

JOSIE (*Grabs it and tears it from his hand with one powerful twist—fiercely*): Would you strike my poor infirm old father, you coward, you!

HARDER (*Calling for help*): McCabe!

HOGAN: Don't think McCabe will hear you, if you blew Gabriel's horn. He knows I or Josie can lick him with one hand. (*Sharply*) Josie! Stand between us and the gate. (JOSIE *takes her stand where the path meets the road. She turns her back for a moment, shaking with suppressed laughter, and waves her hand at* MC CABE *and turns back.* HOGAN *releases his hold on* HARDER's *coat*) There now. Don't try running away or my daughter will knock you senseless. (*He goes on grimly before* HARDER *can speak*) You're the blackguard of a millionaire that owns the estate next to ours, ain't you? I've been meaning to call on you, for I've a bone to pick with you, you bloody tyrant! But I couldn't bring myself to set foot on land bought with Standard Oil money that was stolen from the poor it ground in the dust beneath its dirty heel—land that's watered with the tears of starving widows and orphans— (*He abruptly switches from this eloquence to a matter-of-fact tone*) But never mind that, now. I won't waste words trying to reform a born crook. (*Fiercely,*

shoving his dirty unshaven face almost into HARDER's)
What I want to know is, what the hell d'you mean by
your contemptible trick of breaking down your fence to
entice my poor pigs to take their death in your ice pond?
(*There is a shout of laughter from* JOSIE's *bedroom, and*
JOSIE *doubles up and holds her sides.* HARDER *is so flabbergasted by this mad accusation he cannot even sputter. But*
HOGAN *acts as if he'd denied it—savagely*) Don't lie, now!
None of your damned Standard Oil excuses, or be Jaysus,
I'll break you in half! Haven't I mended that fence morning after morning, and seen the footprints where you had
sneaked up in the night to pull it down again. How many
times have I mended that fence, Josie?

JOSIE: If it's once, it's a hundred, Father.

HOGAN: Listen, me little millionaire! I'm a peaceful, mild
man that believes in live and let live, and as long as the
neighboring scum leave me alone, I'll let them alone, but
when it comes to standing by and seeing my poor pigs
murthered one by one—! Josie! How many pigs is it
caught their death of cold in his damned ice pond and
died of pneumonia?

JOSIE: Ten of them, Father. And ten more died of cholera
after drinking the dirty water in it.

HOGAN: All prize pigs, too! I was offered two hundred
dollars apiece for them. Twenty pigs at two hundred,
that's four thousand. And a thousand to cure the sick and
cover funeral expenses for the dead. Call it four thousand
you owe me. (*Furiously*) And you'll pay it, or I'll sue
you, so help me Christ! I'll drag you in every court in
the land! I'll paste your ugly mug on the front page of
every newspaper as a pig-murdering tyrant! Before I'm
through with you, you'll think you're the King of England at an Irish wake! (*With a quick change of pace to
a wheedling confidential tone*) Tell me now, if it isn't a
secret, whatever made you take such a savage grudge

against pigs? Sure, it isn't reasonable for a Standard Oil man to hate hogs.

HARDER (*Manages to get in three sputtering words*): I've had enough—!

HOGAN (*With a grin*): Be God, I believe you! (*Switching to fierceness and grabbing his lapel again*) Look out, now! Keep your place and be soft-spoken to your betters! You're not in your shiny automobile now with your funny nose cocked so you won't smell the poor people. (*He gives him a shake*) And let me warn you! I have to put up with a lot of pests on this heap of boulders some joker once called a farm. There's a cruel skinflint of a land-lord who swindles me out of my last drop of whiskey, and there's poison ivy, and ticks and potato bugs, and there's snakes and skunks! But, be God, I draw the line somewhere, and I'll be damned if I'll stand for a Standard Oil man trespassing! So will you kindly get the hell out of here before I plant a kick on your backside that'll land you in the Atlantic Ocean! (*He gives* HARDER *a shove*) Beat it now! (HARDER *tries to make some sort of disdainfully dignified exit. But he has to get by* JOSIE.)

JOSIE (*Leers at him idiotically*): Sure, you wouldn't go without a word of good-bye to me, would you, darlin'? Don't scorn me just because you have on your jockey's pants. (*In a hoarse whisper*) Meet me tonight, as usual, down by the pigpen. (HARDER's *retreat becomes a rout. He disappears on left, but a second later his voice, trembling with anger, is heard calling back threateningly.*)

HARDER: If you dare touch that fence again, I'll put this matter in the hands of the police!

HOGAN (*Shouts derisively*): And I'll put it in my lawyer's hands and in the newspapers! (*He doubles up with glee*) Look at him fling himself on his nag and spur the poor beast! And look at McCabe behind him! He can hardly stay in the saddle for laughing! (*He slaps his thigh*)

O Jaysus, this is a great day for the poor and oppressed! I'll do no more work! I'll go down to the Inn and spend money and get drunk as Moses!

JOSIE: Small blame to you. You deserve it. But you'll have your dinner first, to give you a foundation. Come on, now. (*They turn back toward the house. From inside another burst of laughter from* TYRONE *is heard.* JOSIE *smiles*) Listen to Jim still in stitches. It's good to hear him laugh as if he meant it. (TYRONE *appears in the doorway of her bedroom.*)

TYRONE: O God, my sides are sore. (*They all laugh together. He joins them at the left corner of the house.*)

JOSIE: It's dinner time. Will you have a bite to eat with us, Jim? I'll boil you some eggs.

HOGAN: Och, why do you have to mention eggs? Don't you know it's the one thing he might eat? Well, no matter. Anything goes today. (*He gets the bottle of whiskey*) Come in, Jim. We'll have a drink while Josie's fixing the grub. (*They start to go in the front door,* HOGAN *in the lead.*)

TYRONE (*Suddenly—with sardonic amusement*): Wait a minute. Let us pause to take a look at this very valuable property. Don't you notice the change, Phil? Every boulder on the place has turned to solid gold.

HOGAN: What the hell—? You didn't get the D.T.'s from my whiskey, I know that.

TYRONE: No D.T.'s about it. This farm has suddenly become a gold mine. You know that offer I told you about? Well, the agent did a little detective work and he discovered it came from Harder. He doesn't want the damned place but he dislikes you as a neighbor and he thinks the best way to get rid of you would be to become your landlord.

HOGAN: The sneaking skunk! I'm sorry I didn't give him that kick.

TYRONE: Yes. So am I. That would have made the place even more valuable. But as it is, you did nobly. I expect him to double or triple his first offer. In fact, I'll bet the sky is the limit now.

HOGAN (*Gives* JOSIE *a meaningful look*): I see your point! But we're not worrying you'd ever forget your promise to us for any price.

TYRONE: Promise? What promise? You know what Kipling wrote: (*Paraphrasing the "Rhyme of the Three Sealers"*) There's never a promise of God or man goes north of ten thousand bucks.

HOGAN: D'you hear him, Josie? We can't trust him.

JOSIE: Och, you know he's kidding.

HOGAN: I don't! I'm becoming suspicious.

TYRONE (*A trace of bitterness beneath his amused tone*): That's wise dope, Phil. Trust and be a sucker. If I were you, I'd be seriously worried. I've always wanted to own a gold mine—so I could sell it.

JOSIE (*Bursts out*): Will you shut up your rotten Broadway blather!

TYRONE (*Stares at her in surprise*): Why so serious and indignant, Josie? You just told your unworthy Old Man I was kidding. (*To* HOGAN) At last, I've got you by the ears, Phil. We must have a serious chat about when you're going to pay that back rent.

HOGAN (*Groans*): A landlord who's a blackmailer! Holy God, what next! (JOSIE *is smiling with relief now.*)

TYRONE: And you, Josie, please remember when I keep that moonlight date tonight I expect you to be very sweet to me.

JOSIE (*With a bold air*): Sure, you don't have to blackmail me. I'd be that to you, anyway.

HOGAN: Are you laying plots in my presence to seduce my only daughter? (*Then philosophically*) Well, what can I do? I'll be drunk at the Inn, so how could I prevent it?

(*He goes up the steps*) Let's eat, for the love of God. I'm starving. (*He disappears inside the house.*)

JOSIE (*With an awkward playful gesture, takes* TYRONE *by the hand*): Come along, Jim.

TYRONE (*Smiles kiddingly*): Afraid you'll lose me? Swell chance! (*His eyes fix on her breasts—with genuine feeling*) You have the most beautiful breasts in the world, do you know it, Josie?

JOSIE (*Pleased—shyly*): I don't—but I'm happy if you think— (*Then quickly*) But I've no time now to listen to your kidding, with my mad old father waiting for his dinner. So come on. (*She tugs at his hand and he follows her up the steps. Her manner changes to worried solicitude*) Promise me you'll eat something, Jim. You've got to eat. You can't go on the way you are, drinking and never eating, hardly. You're killing yourself.

TYRONE (*Sardonically*): That's right. Mother me, Josie, I love it.

JOSIE (*Bullyingly*): I will, then. You need one to take care of you. (*They disappear inside the house.*)

Curtain

Act Two

SCENE—*The same, with the wall of the living room removed. It is a clear warm moonlight night, around eleven o'clock.*

JOSIE *is sitting on the steps before the front door. She has changed to her Sunday best, a cheap dark-blue dress, black stockings and shoes. Her hair is carefully arranged, and by way of adornment a white flower is pinned on her bosom. She is hunched up, elbows on knees, her chin in her hands. There is an expression on her face we have not seen before, a look of sadness and loneliness and humiliation.*

She sighs and gets slowly to her feet, her body stiff from sitting long in the same position. She goes into the living room, fumbles around for a box of matches, and lights a kerosene lamp on the table.

The living room is small, low-ceilinged, with faded, fly-specked wallpaper, a floor of bare boards. It is cluttered up with furniture that looks as if it had been picked up at a fire sale. There is a table at center, a disreputable old Morris chair beside it; two ugly sideboards, one at left, the other at right-rear; a porch rocking-chair, painted green, with a hole in its cane bottom; a bureau against the rear wall, with two chairs on either side of a door to the kitchen. On the bureau is an alarm clock which shows the time to be five past eleven. At right-front is the door to JOSIE'S *bedroom.*

JOSIE (*Looks at the clock—dully*): Five past eleven, and he said he'd be here around nine. (*Suddenly in a burst of humiliated anger, she tears off the flower pinned to her bosom and throws it in the corner*) To hell with you, Jim Tyrone! (*From down the road, the quiet of the night is shattered by a burst of melancholy song. It is unmistakably* HOGAN's *voice wailing an old Irish lament at the top of his lungs.* JOSIE *starts—then frowns irritably*) What's bringing him home an hour before the Inn closes? He must be more paralyzed than ever I've known him. (*She listens to the singing—grimly*) Ah, here you come, do you, full as a tick! I'll give you a welcome, if you start cutting up! I'm in no mood to put up with you. (*She goes into her bedroom and returns with her broomstick club. Outside the singing grows louder as* HOGAN *approaches the house. He only remembers one verse of the song and he has been repeating it.*)

HOGAN:

> "Oh the praties they grow small
> Over here, over here,
> Oh, the praties they grow small
> Over here.
> Oh the praties they grow small
> And we dig them in the fall
> And we eat them skins and all
> Over here, over here."

(*He enters left-front, weaving and lurching a bit. But he is not as drunk as he appears. Or rather, he is one of those people who can drink an enormous amount and be absolutely plastered when they want to be for their own pleasure, but at the same time are able to pull themselves together when they wish and be cunningly clear-headed. Just now, he is letting himself go and getting great satis-*

faction from it. He pauses and bellows belligerently at the house) Hurroo! Down with all tyrants, male and female! To hell with England, and God damn Standard Oil!

JOSIE *(Shouts back)*: Shut up your noise, you crazy old billy goat!

HOGAN *(Hurt and mournful)*: A sweet daughter and a sweet welcome home in the dead of night. *(Beginning to boil)* Old goat! There's respect for you! *(Angrily—starting for the front door)* Crazy billy goat, is it? Be God, I'll learn you manners! *(He pounds on the door with his fist)* Open the door! Open this door, I'm saying, before I drive a fist through it, or kick it into flinders! *(He gives it a kick.)*

JOSIE: It's not locked, you drunken old loon! Open it yourself!

HOGAN *(Turns the knob and stamps in)*: Drunken old loon, am I? Is that the way to address your father?

JOSIE: No. It's too damned good for him.

HOGAN: It's time I taught you a lesson. Be Jaysus, I'll take you over my knee and spank your tail, if you are as big as a cow! *(He makes a lunge to grab her.)*

JOSIE: Would you, though! Take that, then! *(She raps him smartly, but lightly, on his bald spot with the end of her broom handle.)*

HOGAN *(With an exaggerated howl of pain)*: Ow! *(His anger evaporates and he rubs the top of his head ruefully—with bitter complaint)* God forgive you, it's a great shame to me I've raised a daughter so cowardly she has to use a club.

JOSIE *(Puts her club on the table—grimly)*: Now I've no club.

HOGAN *(Evades the challenge)*: I never thought I'd see the day when a daughter of mine would be such a coward as to threaten her old father when he's helpless drunk and can't hit back. (*He slumps down on the Morris chair.*)

JOSIE: Ah, that's better. Now that little game is over. (*Then angrily*) Listen to me, Father. I have no patience left, so get up from that chair, and go in your room, and go to bed, or I'll take you by the scruff of your neck and the seat of your pants and throw you in and lock the door on you! I mean it, now! (*On the verge of angry tears*) I've had all I can bear this night, and I want some peace and sleep, and not to listen to an old lush!

HOGAN (*Appears drunker, his head wagging, his voice thick, his talk rambling*): That's right. Fight with me. My own daughter has no feelings or sympathy. As if I hadn't enough after what's happened tonight.

JOSIE (*With angry disgust*): Och, don't try— (*Then curiously*) What's happened? I thought something must be queer, you coming home before the Inn closed, but then I thought maybe for once you'd drunk all you could hold. (*Scathingly*) And, God pity you, if you ain't that full, you're damned close to it.

HOGAN: Go on. Make fun of me. Old lush! You wouldn't feel so comical, if— (*He stops, mumbling to himself.*)

JOSIE: If what?

HOGAN: Never mind. Never mind. I didn't come home to fight, but seek comfort in your company. And if I was singing coming along the road, it was only because there's times you have to sing to keep from crying.

JOSIE: I can see you crying!

HOGAN: You will. And you'll see yourself crying, too, when— (*He stops again and mumbles to himself.*)

JOSIE: When what? (*Exasperatedly*) Will you stop your whiskey drooling and talk plain?

HOGAN (*Thickly*): No matter. No matter. Leave me alone.

JOSIE (*Angrily*): That's good advice. To hell with you! I know your game. Nothing at all has happened. All you want is to keep me up listening to your guff. Go to your room, I'm saying, before—

HOGAN: I won't. I couldn't sleep with my thoughts tormented the way they are. I'll stay here in this chair, and you go to your room and let me be.

JOSIE (*Snorts*): And have you singing again in a minute and smashing the furniture—

HOGAN: Sing, is it? Are you making fun again? I'd give a keen of sorrow or howl at the moon like an old mangy hound in his sadness if I knew how, but I don't. So rest aisy. You won't hear a sound from me. Go on and snore like a pig to your heart's content. (*He mourns drunkenly*) A fine daughter! I'd get more comfort from strangers.

JOSIE: Och, for God's sake, dry up! You'll sit in the dark then. I won't leave the lamp lit for you to tip over and burn down the house. (*She reaches out to turn down the lamp.*)

HOGAN (*Thickly*): Let it burn to the ground. A hell of a lot I care if it burns.

JOSIE (*In the act of turning down the lamp, stops and stares at him, puzzled and uneasy*): I never heard you talk that way before, no matter how drunk you were. (*He mumbles. Her tone becomes persuasive*) What's happened to you, Father?

HOGAN (*Bitterly*): Ah it's "Father" now, is it, not old billy goat? Well, thank God for small favors. (*With heavy sarcasm*) Oh, nothing's happened to me at all, at all. A trifle, only. I wouldn't waste your time mentioning it, or keep you up when you want sleep so bad.

JOSIE (*Angrily*): Och, you old loon, I'm sick of you. Sleep it off till you get some sense. (*She reaches for the lamp again.*)

HOGAN: Sleep it off? We'll see if you'll sleep it off when you know— (*He lapses into drunken mumbling.*)

JOSIE (*Again stares at him*): Know what, Father?

HOGAN (*Mumbles*): The son of a bitch!

JOSIE (*Trying a light tone*): Sure, there's a lot of those in the neighborhood. Which one do you mean? Is Harder on your mind again?

HOGAN (*Thickly*): He's one and a prize one, but I don't mean him. I'll say this for Harder, you know what to expect from him. He's no wolf in sheep's clothing, nor a treacherous snake in the grass who stabs you in the back with a knife—

JOSIE (*Apprehensive now—forces a joke*): Sure, if you've found a snake who can stab you with a knife, you'd better join the circus with him and make a pile of money.

HOGAN (*Bitterly*): Make jokes, God forgive you! You'll soon laugh from the wrong end of your mouth! (*He mumbles*) Pretending he's our friend! The lying bastard!

JOSIE (*Bristles resentfully*): Is it Jim Tyrone you're calling hard names?

HOGAN: That's right. Defend him, you big soft fool! Faith, you're a prize dunce! You've had a good taste of believing his word, waiting hours for him dressed up in your best like a poor sheep without pride or spirit—

JOSIE (*Stung*): Shut up! I was calling him a lying bastard myself before you came, and saying I'd never speak to him again. And I knew all along he'd never remember to keep his date after he got drunk.

HOGAN: He's not so drunk he forgot to attend to business.

JOSIE (*As if she hadn't heard—defiantly*): I'd have stayed up anyway a beautiful night like this to enjoy the moonlight, if there wasn't a Jim Tyrone in the world.

HOGAN (*With heavy sarcasm*): In your best shoes and stockings? Well, well. Sure, the moon must feel flattered by your attentions.

JOSIE (*Furiously*): You won't feel flattered if I knock you tail over tin cup out of that chair! And stop your whiskey gabble about Jim. I see what you're driving at with your dark hints and curses, and if you think I'll believe— (*With forced assurance*) Sure, I know what's happened as well as if I'd been there. Jim saw you'd got drunker than usual and you were an easy mark for a joke, and he's made a goat of you!

HOGAN (*Bitterly*): Goat, again! (*He struggles from his chair and stands swaying unsteadily—with offended dignity*) All right, I won't say another word. There's no use telling the truth to a bad-tempered woman in love.

JOSIE: Love be damned! I hate him now!

HOGAN: Be Christ, you have me stumped. A great proud slut who's played games with half the men around here, and now you act like a numbskull virgin that can't believe a man would tell her a lie!

JOSIE (*Threateningly*): If you're going to your room, you'd better go quick!

HOGAN (*Fixes his eyes on the door at rear—with dignity*): That's where I'm going, yes—to talk to meself so I'll know someone with brains is listening. Good night to you, Miss Hogan. (*He starts—swerves left—tries to correct this and lurches right and bumps against her, clutching the supporting arm she stretches out.*)

JOSIE: God help you, if you try to go upstairs now, you'll end up in the cellar.

HOGAN (*Hanging on to her arm and shoulder—maudlinly affectionate now*): You're right. Don't listen to me. I'm wrong to bother you. You've had sorrow enough this night. Have a good sleep, while you can, Josie, darlin'— and good night and God bless you. (*He tries to kiss her, but she wards him off and steers him back to the chair.*)

JOSIE: Sit down before you split in pieces on the floor and

I have to get the wheelbarrow to collect you. (*She dumps him in the chair where he sprawls limply, his chin on his chest.*)

HOGAN (*Mumbles dully*): It's too late. It's all settled. We're helpless, entirely.

JOSIE (*Really worried now*): How is it all settled? If you're helpless, I'm not. (*Then as he doesn't reply— scornfully*) It's the first time I ever heard you admit you were licked. And it's the first time I ever saw you so paralyzed you couldn't shake the whiskey from your brains and get your head clear when you wanted. Sure, that's always been your pride—and now look at you, the stupid object you are, mumbling and drooling!

HOGAN (*Struggles up in his chair—angrily*): Shut up your insults! Be God, I can get my head clear if I like! (*He shakes his head violently*) There! It's clear. I can tell you each thing that happened tonight as clear as if I'd not taken a drop, if you'll listen and not keep calling me a liar.

JOSIE: I'll listen, now I see you have hold of your wits.

HOGAN: All right, then. I'll begin at the beginning when him and me left here, and you gave him a sweet smile, and rolled your big beautiful cow's eyes at him, and wiggled your backside, and stuck out your beautiful breasts you know he admires, and said in a sick sheep's voice: "Don't forget our moonlight date, Jim."

JOSIE (*With suppressed fury*): You're a—! I never—! You old—!

HOGAN: And he said: "You bet I won't forget, Josie."

JOSIE: The lying crook!

HOGAN (*His voice begins to sink into a dejected monotone*): We went to the Inn and started drinking whiskey. And I got drunk.

JOSIE (*Exasperatedly*): I guessed that! And Jim got drunk, too. And then what?

HOGAN (*Dully*): Who knows how drunk he got? He had one of his queer fits when you can't tell. He's the way I told you about this morning, when he talks like a Broadway crook, who'd sell his soul for a price, and there's a sneering divil in him, and he loves to pick out the weakness in people and say cruel, funny things that flay the hide off them, or play cruel jokes on them. (*With sudden rage*) God's curse on him, I'll wager he's laughing to himself this minute, thinking it's the cutest joke in the world, the fools he's made of us. You in particular. Be God, I had my suspicions, at least, but your head was stuffed with mush and love, and you wouldn't—

JOSIE (*Furiously*): You'll tell that lie about my love once too often! And I'll play a joke on him yet that'll make him sorry he—

HOGAN (*Sunk in drunken defeatism again*): It's too late. You shouldn't have let him get away from you to the Inn. You should have kept him here. Then maybe, if you'd got him drunk enough you could have— (*His head nodding, his eyes blinking—thickly*) But it's no good talking now—no good at all—no good—

JOSIE (*Gives him a shake*): Keep hold of your wits or I'll give you a cuff on both ears! Will you stop blathering like an old woman and tell me plainly what he's done!

HOGAN: He's agreed to sell the farm, that's what! Simpson came to the Inn to see him with a new offer from Harder. Ten thousand, cash.

JOSIE (*Overwhelmed*): Ten thousand! Sure, three is all it's worth at most. And two was what you offered that Jim promised—

HOGAN: What's money to Harder? After what we did to him, all he wants is revenge. And here's where he's foxy. Simpson must have put him up to it knowing how Jim hates it here living on a small allowance, and he longs to go back to Broadway and his whores. Jim won't have to wait for his half of the cash till the estate's settled. Harder offers to give him five thousand cash as a loan against the estate the second the sale is made. Jim can take the next train to New York.

JOSIE (*Tensely, on the verge of tears*): And Jim accepted? I don't believe it!

HOGAN: Don't then. Be God, you'll believe it tomorrow! Harder proposed that he meet with Jim and the executors in the morning and settle it, and Jim promised Simpson he would.

JOSIE (*Desperately*): Maybe he'll get so drunk he'll never remember—

HOGAN: He won't. Harder's coming in his automobile to pick him up and make sure of him. Anyway don't think because he forgot you were waiting—in the moonlight, eating your heart out, that he'd ever miss a date with five thousand dollars, and all the pretty whores of Broadway he can buy with it.

JOSIE (*Distractedly*): Will you shut up! (*Angrily*) And where were you when all this happened? Couldn't you do anything to stop it, you old loon?

HOGAN: I couldn't. Simpson came and sat at the table with us—

JOSIE: And you let him!

HOGAN: Jim invited him. Anyway, I wanted to find out what trick he had up his sleeve, and what Jim would do. When it was all over, I got up and took a swipe at Simpson, but I missed him. (*With drunken sadness*) I was too drunk—too drunk—too drunk— I missed him, God forgive me! (*His chin sinks on his chest and his eyes shut.*)

JOSIE (*Shakes him*): If you don't keep awake, be God, I won't miss you!

HOGAN: I was going to take a swipe at Jim, too, but I couldn't do it. My heart was too broken with sorrow. I'd

come to love him like a son—a real son of my heart!—
to take the place of that jackass, Mike, and me two other
jackasses.

JOSIE (*Her face hard and bitter*): I think now Mike was
the only one in this house with sense.

HOGAN: I was too drowned in sorrow by his betraying me
—and you he'd pretended to like so much. So I only
called him a dirty lying skunk of a treacherous bastard,
and I turned my back on him and left the Inn, and I
made myself sing on the road so he'd hear, and they'd
all hear in the Inn, to show them I didn't care a damn.

JOSIE (*Scathingly*): Sure, wasn't you the hero! A hell of a
lot of good—

HOGAN: Ah, well, I suppose the temptation was too great.
He's weak, with one foot in the grave from whiskey.
Maybe we shouldn't blame him.

JOSIE (*Her eyes flashing*): Not blame him? Well, I blame
him, God damn him! Are you making excuses for him,
you old fool!

HOGAN: I'm not. He's a dirty snake! But I was thinking
how do I know what I wouldn't do for five thousand
cash, and how do you know what you wouldn't do?

JOSIE: Nothing could make me betray him! (*Her face
grows hard and bitter*) Or it couldn't before. There's
nothing I wouldn't do now. (HOGAN *suddenly begins to
chuckle*) Do you think I'm lying? Just give me a
chance—

HOGAN: I remembered something. (*He laughs drunkenly*)
Be Christ, Josie, for all his Broadway wisdom about
women, you've made a prize damned fool of him and
that's some satisfaction!

JOSIE (*Bewildered*): How'd you mean?

HOGAN: You'll never believe it. Neither did I, but he kept
on until, be God, I saw he really meant it.

JOSIE: Meant what?

HOGAN: It was after he'd turned queer—early in the night before Simpson came. He started talking about you, as if you was on his mind, worrying him—and before he finished I take my oath I began to hope you could really work Mike's first scheme on him, if you got him alone in the moonlight, because all his gab was about his great admiration for you.

JOSIE: Och! The liar!

HOGAN: He said you had great beauty in you that no one appreciated but him.

JOSIE (*Shakenly*): You're lying.

HOGAN: Great strength you had, and great pride, he said —and great goodness, no less! But here's where you've made a prize jackass of him, like I said. (*With a drunken leer*) Listen now, darlin', and don't drop dead with amazement. (*He leans toward her and whispers*) He believes you're a virgin! (JOSIE *stiffens as if she'd been insulted*. HOGAN *goes on*) He does, so help me! He means it, the poor dunce! He thinks you're a poor innocent virgin! He thinks it's all boasting and pretending you've done about being a slut. (*He chuckles*) A virgin, no less! You!

JOSIE (*Furiously*): Stop saying it! Boasting and pretending, am I? The dirty liar!

HOGAN: Faith, you don't have to tell me. (*Then he looks at her in drunken surprise—thickly*) Are you taking it as an insult? Why the hell don't you laugh? Be God, you ought to see what a stupid sheep that makes him.

JOSIE (*Forces a laugh*): I do see it.

HOGAN (*Chuckling drunkenly*): Oh, be God, I've just re-membered another thing, Josie. I know why he didn't keep his date with you. It wasn't that he'd forgot. He remembered well enough, for he talked about it—

JOSIE: You mean he deliberately, knowing I'd be waiting—(*Fiercely*) God damn him!

HOGAN: He as much as told me his reason, though he wouldn't come out with it plain, me being your father. His conscience was tormenting him. He's going to leave you alone and not see you again—for your sake, because he loves you! (*He chuckles.*)

JOSIE (*Looks stricken and bewildered—her voice trembling*): Loves me? You're making it up.

HOGAN: I'm not. I know it sounds crazy but—

JOSIE: What did he mean, for my sake?

HOGAN: Can't you see? You're a pure virgin to him, but all the same there's things besides your beautiful soul he feels drawn to, like your beautiful hair and eyes, and—

JOSIE (*Strickenly*): Och, don't, Father! You know I'm only a big—

HOGAN (*As if she hadn't spoken*): So he'll keep away from temptation because he can't trust himself, and it'd be a sin on his conscience if he was to seduce you. (*He laughs drunkenly*) Oh, be God! If that ain't rich!

JOSIE (*Her voice trembles*): So that was his reason— (*Then angrily*) So he thinks all he has to do is crook a finger and I'll fall for him, does he, the vain Broadway crook!

HOGAN (*Chuckling*): Be Jaysus, it was the maddest thing in the world, him gabbing like a soft loon about you—and there at the bar in plain sight was two of the men you've been out with, the gardener at Smith's and Regan, the chauffeur for Driggs, having a drink together!

JOSIE (*With a twitching smile*): It must have been mad, surely. I wish I'd been there to laugh up my sleeve. (*Angry*) But what's all his crazy lying blather got to do with him betraying us and selling the place?

HOGAN (*At once hopelessly dejected again*): Nothing at all. I only thought you'd like to know you'd had that much revenge.

JOSIE: A hell of a revenge! I'll have a better one than that on him— or I'll try to! I'm not like you, owning up I'm beaten and crying wurra-wurra like a coward and getting hopeless drunk! (*She gives him a shake*) Get your wits about you and answer me this: Did Simpson get him to sign a paper?

HOGAN: No, but what good is that? In the morning he'll sign all they shove in front of him.

JOSIE: It's this good. It means we still have a chance. Or I have.

HOGAN: What chance? Are you going to beg him to take pity on us?

JOSIE: I'll see him in hell first! There's another chance, and a good one. But I'll need your help— (*Angrily*) And look at you, your brains drowned in whiskey, so I can't depend on you!

HOGAN (*Rousing himself*): You can, if there's any chance. Be God, I'll make myself as sober as a judge for you in the wink of an eye! (*Then dejectedly*) But what can you do now, darlin'? You haven't even got him here. He's down at the Inn sitting alone, drinking and dreaming of the little whores he'll be with tomorrow night on Broadway.

JOSIE: I'll get him here! I'll humble my pride and go down to the Inn for him! And if he doesn't want to come I've a way to make him. I'll raise a scene and pretend I'm in a rage because he forgot his date. I'll disgrace him till he'll be glad to come with me to shut me up. I know his weakness, and it's his vanity about his women. If I was a dainty, pretty tart he'd be proud I'd raise a rumpus about him. But when it's a big, ugly hulk like me— (*She falters and forces herself to go on*) If he ever was tempted to want me, he'd be ashamed of it. That's the truth behind the lies he told you of his conscience and his fear he might ruin me, God damn him!

HOGAN: No, he meant it, Josie. But never mind that now. Let's say you've got him here. Then what will you do?

JOSIE: I told you this morning if he ever broke his promise to us I'd do anything and not mind how crooked it was. And I will! Your part in it is to come at sunrise with witnesses and catch us in— (*She falters.*)

HOGAN: In bed, is it? Then it's Mike's second scheme you're thinking about?

JOSIE: I told you I didn't care how dirty a trick— (*With a hard bitter laugh*) The dirtier the better now!

HOGAN: But how'll you get him in bed, with all his honorable scruples, thinking you're a virgin? But I'm forgetting he stayed away because he was afraid he'd be tempted. So maybe—

JOSIE (*Tensely*): For the love of God, don't harp on his lies. He won't be tempted at all. But I'll get him so drunk he'll fall asleep and I'll carry him in and put him in bed—

HOGAN: Be God, that's the way! But you'll have to get a pile of whiskey down him. You'll never do it unless you're more sociable and stop looking at him, the way you do, whenever he takes a drink, as if you was praying Almighty God to forgive a poor drunkard. You've got to encourage him. The best way would be for you to drink with him. It would put him at his ease and unsuspecting, and it'd give you courage, too, so you'd act bold for a change instead of giving him brazen talk he's tired of hearing, while you act shy as a mouse.

JOSIE (*Gives her father a bitter, resentful look*): You're full of sly advice all of a sudden, ain't you? You dirty little tick!

HOGAN (*Angrily*): Didn't you tell me to get hold of my wits? Be God, if you want me drunk, I've only to let go. That'd suit me. I want to forget my sorrow, and I've no faith in your scheme because you'll be too full of scruples. Like the drinking. You're such a virtuous teetotaller—

JOSIE: I've told you I'd do anything now! (*Then con-fusedly*) All I meant was, it's not right, a father to tell his daughter how to— (*Then angrily*) I don't need your advice. Haven't I had every man I want around here?

HOGAN: Ah, thank God, that sounds natural! Be God, I thought you'd started playing virgin with me just because that Broadway sucker thinks you're one.

JOSIE (*Furiously*): Shut up! I'm not playing anything. And don't worry I can't do my part of the trick.

HOGAN: That's the talk! But let me get it all clear. I come at sunrise with my witnesses, and you've forgot to lock your door, and we walk in, and there's the two of you in bed, and I raise the roof and threaten him if he don't marry you—

JOSIE: Marry him? After what he's done to us? I wouldn't marry him now if he was the last man on earth! All we want is a paper signed by him with witnesses that he'll sell the farm to you for the price you offered, and not to Harder.

HOGAN: Well, that's justice, but that's all it is. I thought you wanted to make him pay for his black treachery against us, the dirty bastard!

JOSIE: I do want! (*She again gives him a bitter resentful glance*) It's the estate money you're thinking of, isn't it? Leave it to you! (*Hastily*) Well, so am I! I'd like to get my hooks on it! (*With a hard, brazen air*) Be God, if I'm to play whore, I deserve my pay! We'll make him sign a paper he owes me ten thousand dollars the minute the estate is settled. (*She laughs*) How's that? I'll bet none of his tarts on Broadway ever got a thousandth part of that out of him, no matter how dainty and pretty! (*Laughing again*) And here's what'll be the greatest joke to teach him a lesson. He'll pay it for nothing! I'll get him in bed but I'll never let him—

HOGAN (*With delighted admiration*): Och, by Jaysus, Josie, that's the best yet! (*He slaps his thigh enthusiastically*) Oh, that'll teach him to double-cross his friends! That'll show him two can play at tricks! And him believing you so innocent! Be God, you'll make him the prize sucker of the world! Won't I roar inside me when I see his face in the morning! (*He bursts into coarse laughter.*)

JOSIE (*Again with illogical resentment*): Stop laughing! You're letting yourself be drunk again. (*Then with a hard, business-like air*) We've done enough talking. Let's start—

HOGAN: Wait, now. There's another thing. Just what do you want me to threaten him with when I catch you? That we'll sue him for outraging your virtue? Sure, his lawyer would have all your old flames in the witness box, till the jury would think you'd been faithful to the male inhabitants of America. So what threat—I can't think of any he wouldn't laugh at.

JOSIE (*Tensely*): Well, I can! Do I have to tell you his weakness again? It's his vanity about women, and his Broadway pride he's so wise no woman could fool him. It's the disgrace to his vanity—being caught with the likes of me— (*Falteringly, but forcing herself to go on*) My mug beside his in all the newspapers—the New York papers, too—he'll see the whole of Broadway splitting their sides laughing at him—and he'll give anything to keep us quiet, I tell you. He will! I know him! So don't worry— (*She ends up on the verge of bitter humiliated tears.*)

HOGAN (*Without looking at her—enthusiastic again*): Be God, you're right!

JOSIE (*Gives him a bitter glance—fiercely*): Then get the hell out of that chair and let's start it! (*He gets up. She surveys him resentfully*) You're steady on your pins, ain't you, you scheming old thief, now there's the smell of money around! (*Quickly*) Well, I'm glad. I know I can depend on you now. You'll walk down to the Inn with me and hide outside until you see me come out with him. Then you can sneak in the Inn yourself and pick the witnesses to stay up with you. But mind you don't get drunk again, and let them get too drunk.

HOGAN: I won't, I take my oath! (*He pats her on the shoulder approvingly*) Be God, you've got the proud, fighting spirit in you that never says die, and you make me ashamed of my weakness. You're that eager now, be damned if I don't almost think you're glad of the excuse!

JOSIE (*Stiffens*): Excuse for what, you old—

HOGAN: To show him no man can get the best of you— what else?—like you showed all the others.

JOSIE: I'll show him to his sorrow! (*Then abruptly, starting for the screen door at left*) Come on. We've no time to waste. (*But when she gets to the door, she appears suddenly hesitant and timid—hurriedly*) Wait. I'd better give a look at myself in the mirror. (*In a brazen tone*) Sure, those in my trade have to look their best! (*She hurries back across the room into her bedroom and closes the door.* HOGAN *stares after her. Abruptly he ceases to look like a drunk who, by an effort, is keeping himself half-sober. He is a man who has been drinking a lot but is still clear-headed and has complete control of himself.*)

HOGAN (*Watches the crack under* JOSIE's *door and speaks half-aloud to himself, shaking his head pityingly*): A look in the mirror and she's forgot to light her lamp! (*Remorsefully*) God forgive me, it's bitter medicine. But it's the only way I can see that has a chance now. (*JOSIE's door opens. At once, he is as he was. She comes out, a fixed smile on her lips, her head high, her face set defiantly. But she has evidently been crying.*)

JOSIE (*Brazenly*): There, now. Don't I look ten thousand dollars' worth to any drunk?

HOGAN: You look a million, darlin'!

JOSIE (*Goes to the screen door and pushes it open with the manner of one who has burned all bridges*): Come along, then. (*She goes out. He follows close on her heels. She stops abruptly on the first step—startledly*) Look! There's someone on the road—

HOGAN (*Pushes past her down the steps—peering off left-front—as if aloud to himself, in dismay*): Be God, it's him! I never thought—

JOSIE (*As if aloud to herself*): So he didn't forget—

HOGAN (*Quickly*): Well, it proves he can't keep away from you, and that'll make it easier for you— (*Then furiously*) Oh, the dirty, double-crossing bastard! The nerve of him! Coming to call on you, after making you wait for hours, thinking you don't know what he's done to us this night, and it'll be a fine cruel joke to blarney you in the moonlight, and you trusting him like a poor sheep, and never suspecting—

JOSIE (*Stung*): Shut up! I'll teach him who's the joker! I'll let him go on as if you hadn't told me what he's done—

HOGAN: Yes, don't let him suspect it, or you wouldn't fool him. He'd know you were after revenge. But he can see me here now. I can't sneak away or he'd be suspicious. We've got to think of a new scheme quick to get me away—

JOSIE (*Quickly*): I know how. Pretend you're as drunk as when you came. Make him believe you're so drunk you don't remember what he's done so he can't suspect you told me.

HOGAN: I will. Be God, Josie, damned if I don't think he's so queer drunk himself he don't remember, or he'd never come here.

JOSIE: The drunker he is the better! (*Lowering her voice—quickly*) He's turned in the gate where he can hear us. Pretend we're fighting and I'm driving you off till you're sober. Say you won't be back tonight. It'll make him sure he'll have the night alone with me. You start the fight.

HOGAN (*Becomes at once very drunk. He shouts*): Put me out of my own home, will you, you undutiful slut!

JOSIE: Celebration or not, I'll have no drunks cursing and singing all night. Go back to the Inn.

HOGAN: I will! I'll get a room and two bottles and stay drunk as long as I please!

JOSIE: Don't come back till you've slept it off, or I'll wipe the floor with you! (*TYRONE enters, left-front. He does not appear to be drunk—that is, he shows none of the usual symptoms. He seems much the same as in Act One. The only perceptible change is that his eyes have a peculiar fixed, glazed look, and there is a certain vague quality in his manner and speech, as if he were a bit hazy and absent-minded.*)

TYRONE (*Dryly*): Just in time for the Big Bout. Or is this the final round?

HOGAN (*Whirls on him unsteadily*): Who the hell— (*Peering at him*) Oh, it's you, is it?

TYRONE: What was the big idea, Phil, leaving me flat?

HOGAN: Leave you flat? Be Jaysus, that reminds me I owe you a swipe on the jaw for something. What was it? Be God, I'm too drunk to remember. But here it is, anyway. (*He turns loose a round-house swing that misses TYRONE by a couple of feet, and reels away. TYRONE regards him with vague surprise.*)

JOSIE: Stop it, you damned old fool, and get out of here!

HOGAN: Taking his side against your poor old father, are you? A hell of a daughter! (*He draws himself up with drunken dignity*) Don't expect me home tonight, Miss Hogan, or tomorrow either, maybe. You can take your bad temper out on your sweetheart here. (*He starts off down the road, left-front, with a last word over his shoulder*) Bad luck to you both. (*He disappears. A moment later he begins to bawl his mournful Irish song*) "Oh, the praties they grow small, Over here, over here," etc. (*During a part of the following scene the song continues to be heard at intervals, receding as he gets farther off on his way to the Inn.*)

JOSIE: Well, thank God. That's good riddance. (*She comes to* TYRONE, *who stands staring after* HOGAN *with a puzzled look.*)

TYRONE: I've never seen him that stinko before. Must have got him all of a sudden. He didn't seem so lit up at the Inn, but I guess I wasn't paying much attention.

JOSIE (*Forcing a playful air*): I should think, if you were a real gentleman, you'd be apologizing to me, not thinking of him. Don't you know you're two hours and a half late? I oughtn't to speak to you, if I had any pride.

TYRONE (*Stares at her curiously*): You've got too damn much pride, Josie. That's the trouble.

JOSIE: And just what do you mean by that, Jim?

TYRONE (*Shrugs his shoulders*): Nothing. Forget it. I do apologize, Josie. I'm damned sorry. Haven't any excuse. Can't think up a lie. (*Staring at her curiously again*) Or, now I think of it, I had a damned good honorable excuse, but— (*He shrugs*) Nuts. Forget it.

JOSIE: Holy Joseph, you're full of riddles tonight. Well, I don't need excuses. I forgive you, anyway, now you're here. (*She takes his hand—playfully*) Come on now and we'll sit on my bedroom steps and be romantic in the moonlight, like we planned to. (*She leads him there. He goes along in an automatic way, as if only half-con-*

*scious of what he is doing. She sits on the top step and
pulls him down on the step beneath her. A pause. He
stares vaguely at nothing. She bends to give him an uneasy appraising glance.*)

TYRONE (*Suddenly, begins to talk mechanically*): Had to
get out of the damned Inn. I was going batty alone
there. The old heebie-jeebies. So I came to you. (*He
pauses—then adds with strange, wondering sincerity*)
I've really begun to love you a lot, Josie.

JOSIE (*Blurts out bitterly*): Yes, you've proved that tonight, haven't you? (*Hurriedly regaining her playful
tone*) But never mind. I said I'd forgive you for being
so late. So go on about love. I'm all ears.

TYRONE (*As if he hadn't listened*): I thought you'd have
given me up and gone to bed. I remember I had some
nutty idea I'd get in bed with you—just to lie with my
head on your breast.

JOSIE (*Moved in spite of herself—but keeps her bold, playful tone*): Well, maybe I'll let you— (*Hurriedly*) Later
on, I mean. The night's young yet, and we'll have it all
to ourselves. (*Boldly again*) But here's for a starter. (*She
puts her arms around him and draws him back till his
head is on her breast*) There, now.

TYRONE (*Relaxes—simply and gratefully*): Thanks, Josie.
(*He closes his eyes. For a moment, she forgets everything and stares down at his face with a passionate, possessive tenderness. A pause. From far-off on the road to the
Inn,* HOGAN's *mournful song drifts back through the
moonlight quiet: "Oh, the praties they grow small, Over
here, over here."* TYRONE *rouses himself and straightens
up. He acts embarrassed, as if he felt he'd been making
a fool of himself—mockingly*) Hark, Hark, the Donegal
lark! "Thou wast not born for death, immortal bird."
Can't Phil sing anything but that damned dirge, Josie?
(*She doesn't reply. He goes on hazily*) Still, it seems to

belong tonight—in the moonlight—or in my mind— (*He quotes*)

> "Now more than ever seems it rich to die,
> To cease upon the midnight with no pain,
> In such an ecstasy!"

(*He has recited this with deep feeling. Now he sneers*) Good God! Ode to Phil the Irish Nightingale! I must have the D.T.'s.

JOSIE (*Her face grown bitter*): Maybe it's only your bad conscience.

TYRONE (*Starts guiltily and turns to stare into her face—suspiciously*): What put that in your head? Conscience about what?

JOSIE (*Quickly*): How would I know, if you don't? (*Forcing a playful tone*) For the sin of wanting to be in bed with me. Maybe that's it.

TYRONE (*With strange relief*): Oh. (*A bit shamefacedly*) Forget that stuff, Josie. I was half nutty.

JOSIE (*Bitterly*): Och, for the love of God, don't apologize as if you was ashamed of— (*She catches herself.*)

TYRONE (*With a quick glance at her face*): All right. I certainly won't apologize—if you're not kicking. I was afraid I might have shocked your modesty.

JOSIE (*Roughly*): *My* modesty? Be God, I didn't know I had any left.

TYRONE (*Draws away from her—irritably*): Nix, Josie. Lay off that line, for tonight at least. (*He adds slowly*) I'd like tonight to be different.

JOSIE: Different from what? (*He doesn't answer. She forces a light tone*) All right. I'll be as different as you please.

TYRONE (*Simply*): Thanks, Josie. Just be yourself. (*Again as if he were ashamed, or afraid he had revealed some weakness—off-handedly*) This being out in the moonlight instead of the lousy Inn isn't a bad bet, at that. I don't know why I hang out in that dump, except I'm even more bored in the so-called good hotels in this hick town.

JOSIE (*Trying to examine his face without his knowing*): Well, you'll be back on Broadway soon now, won't you?

TYRONE: I hope so.

JOSIE: Then you'll have all the pretty little tarts to comfort you when you get your sorrowful spell on.

TYRONE: Oh, to hell with the rough stuff, Josie! You promised you'd can it tonight.

JOSIE (*Tensely*): You're a fine one to talk of promises!

TYRONE (*Vaguely surprised by her tone*): What's the matter? Still sore at me for being late?

JOSIE (*Quickly*): I'm not. I was teasing you. To prove there's no hard feelings, how would you like a drink? But I needn't ask. (*She gets up*) I'll get a bottle of his best.

TYRONE (*Mechanically*): Fine. Maybe that will have some kick. The booze at the Inn didn't work tonight.

JOSIE: Well, this'll work. (*She starts to go into her bedroom. He sits hunched up on the step, staring at nothing. She pauses in the doorway to glance back. The hard, calculating expression on her face softens. For a second she stares at him, bewildered by her conflicting feelings. Then she goes inside, leaving the door open. She opens the door from her room to the lighted living room, and is seen going to the kitchen on the way to the cellar. She has left the door from the living room to her bedroom open and the light reveals a section of the bedroom framed in the doorway behind* TYRONE. *The foot of the bed which occupies most of the room can be seen, and that is all except that the walls are unpainted pine boards.* TYRONE *continues to stare at nothing, but becomes restless. His hands and mouth twitch.*)

TYRONE (*Suddenly, with intense hatred*): You rotten bastard! (*He springs to his feet—fumbles in his pockets for cigarettes—strikes a match which lights up his face, on which there is now an expression of miserable guilt. His hand is trembling so violently he cannot light the cigarette.*)

Curtain

Act Three

SCENE—*The living-room wall has been replaced and all we see now of its lighted interior is through the two windows. Otherwise, everything is the same, and this Act follows the preceding without any lapse of time.* TYRONE *is still trying with shaking hands to get his cigarette lighted. Finally he succeeds, and takes a deep inhale, and starts pacing back and forth a few steps, as if in a cell of his own thought. He swears defensively*) God damn it. You'll be crying in your beer in a minute. (*He begins to sing sneeringly half under his breath a snatch from an old sob song, popular in the Nineties*)

> *"And baby's cries can't waken her*
> *In the baggage coach ahead."*

(*His sneer changes to a look of stricken guilt and grief*) Christ! (*He seems about to break down and sob but he fights this back*) Cut it out, you drunken fool! (JOSIE *can be seen through the windows, returning from the kitchen. He turns with a look of relief and escape*) Thank God! (*He sits on the boulder and waits.* JOSIE *stops by the table in the living room to turn down the lamp until only a dim light remains. She has a quart of whiskey under her arm, two tumblers, and a pitcher of water. She goes through her bedroom and appears in the outer doorway.* TYRONE *gets up*) Ah! At last the old booze! (*He relieves her of the pitcher and tumblers as she comes down the steps.*)

JOSIE (*With a fixed smile*): You'd think I'd been gone years. You didn't seem so perishing for a drink.

TYRONE (*In his usual, easy, kidding way*): It's you I was perishing for. I've been dying of loneliness—

JOSIE: You'll die of lying some day. But I'm glad you're alive again. I thought when I left you really were dying on me.

TYRONE: No such luck.

JOSIE: Och, don't talk like that. Come have a drink. We'll use the boulder for a table and I'll be barkeep. (*He puts the pitcher and tumblers on the boulder and she uncorks the bottle. She takes a quick glance at his face —startledly*) What's come over you, Jim? You look as if you've seen a ghost.

TYRONE (*Looks away—dryly*): I have. My own. He's punk company.

JOSIE: Yes, it's the worst ghost of all, your own. Don't I know? But this will keep it in its place. (*She pours a tumbler half full of whiskey and hands it to him*) Here. But wait till I join you. (*She pours the other tumbler half full.*)

TYRONE (*Surprised*): Hello! I thought you never touched it.

JOSIE (*Glibly*): I have on occasion. And this is one. I don't want to be left out altogether from celebrating our victory over Harder. (*She gives him a sharp bitter glance. Meeting his eyes, which are regarding her with puzzled wonder, she forces a laugh*) Don't look at me as if I was up to some game. A drink or two will make me better company, and help me enjoy the moon and the night with you. Here's luck. (*She touches his glass with hers.*)

TYRONE (*Shrugs his shoulders*): All right. Here's luck. (*They drink. She gags and sputters. He pours water in her glass. She drinks it. He puts his glass and the pitcher back on the boulder. He keeps staring at her with a puzzled frown.*)

JOSIE: Some of it went down the wrong way.

TYRONE: So I see. That'll teach you to pour out baths instead of drinks.

JOSIE: It's the first time I ever heard you complain a drink was too big.

TYRONE: Yours was too big.

JOSIE: I'm my father's daughter. I've a strong head. So don't worry I'll pass out and you'll have to put me to bed. (*She gives a little bold laugh*) Sure, that's a beautiful notion. I'll have to pretend I'm—

TYRONE (*Irritably*): Nix on the raw stuff, Josie. Remember you said—

JOSIE (*Resentment in her kidding*): I'd be different? That's right. I'm forgetting it's your pleasure to have me pretend I'm an innocent virgin tonight.

TYRONE (*In a strange tone that is almost threatening*): If you don't look out, I'll call you on that bluff, Josie. (*He stares at her with a deliberate sensualist's look that undresses her*) I'd like to. You know that, don't you?

JOSIE (*Boldly*): I don't at all. You're the one who's bluffing.

TYRONE (*Grabs her in his arms—with genuine passion*): Josie! (*Then as suddenly he lets her go*) Nix. Let's cut it out. (*He turns away. Her face betrays the confused conflict within her of fright, passion, happiness, and bitter resentment. He goes on with an abrupt change of tone*) How about another drink? That's honest-to-God old bonded Bourbon. How the devil did Phil get hold of it?

JOSIE: Tom Lombardo, the bootlegger, gave him a case for letting him hide a truckload in our barn when the agents were after him. He stole it from a warehouse on faked permits. (*She pours out drinks as she speaks, a half tumblerful for him, a small one for herself*) Here you are. (*She gives him his drink—smiles at him co-*

quettishly, beginning to show the effect of her big drink by her increasingly bold manner) Let's sit down where the moon will be in our eyes and we'll see romance. *(She takes his arm and leads him to her bedroom steps. She sits on the top step, pulling him down beside her but on the one below. She raises her glass)* Here's hoping before the night's out you'll have more courage and kiss me at least.

TYRONE *(Frowns—then kiddingly)*: That's a promise. Here's how. *(He drains his tumbler. She drinks half of hers. He puts his glass on the ground beside him. A pause. She tries to read his face without his noticing. He seems to be lapsing again into vague preoccupation.)*

JOSIE: Now don't sink back half-dead-and-alive in dreams the way you were before.

TYRONE *(Quickly)*: I'm not. I had a good final dose of heebie-jeebies when you were in the house. That's all for tonight. *(He adds a bit maudlinly, his two big drinks beginning to affect him)* Let the dead past bury its dead.

JOSIE: That's the talk. There's only tonight, and the moon, and us—and the bonded Bourbon. Have another drink, and don't wait for me.

TYRONE: Not now, thanks. They're coming too fast. *(He gives her a curious, cynically amused look)* Trying to get me soused, Josie?

JOSIE *(Starts—quickly)*: I'm not. Only to get you feeling happy, so you'll forget all sadness.

TYRONE *(Kiddingly)*: I might forget all my honorable intentions, too. So look out.

JOSIE: I'll look forward to it—and I hope that's another promise, like the kiss you owe me. If you're suspicious I'm trying to get you soused—well, here goes. *(She drinks what is left in her glass)* There, now. I must be scheming to get myself soused, too.

TYRONE: Maybe you are.

JOSIE (*Resentfully*): If I was, it'd be to make you feel at home. Don't all the pretty little Broadway tarts get soused with you?

TYRONE (*Irritably*): There you go again with that old line!

JOSIE: All right, I won't! (*Forcing a laugh*) I must be eaten up with jealousy for them, that's it.

TYRONE: You needn't be. They don't belong.

JOSIE: And I do?

TYRONE: Yes. You do.

JOSIE: For tonight only, you mean?

TYRONE: We've agreed there is only tonight—and it's to be different from any past night—for both of us.

JOSIE (*In a forced, kidding tone*): I hope it will be. I'll try to control my envy for your Broadway flames. I suppose it's because I have a picture of them in my mind as small and dainty and pretty—

TYRONE: They're just gold-digging tramps.

JOSIE (*As if he hadn't spoken*): While I'm only a big, rough, ugly cow of a woman.

TYRONE: Shut up! You're beautiful.

JOSIE (*Jeeringly, but her voice trembles*): God pity the blind!

TYRONE: You're beautiful to me.

JOSIE: It must be the Bourbon—

TYRONE: You're real and healthy and clean and fine and warm and strong and kind—

JOSIE: I have a beautiful soul, you mean?

TYRONE: Well, I don't know much about ladies' souls— (*He takes her hand*) But I do know you're beautiful. (*He kisses her hand*) And I love you a lot—in my fashion.

JOSIE (*Stammers*): Jim— (*Hastily forcing her playful tone*) Sure, you're full of fine compliments all of a sudden, and I ought to show you how pleased I am. (*She pulls his head back and kisses him on the lips—a quick, shy kiss*) That's for my beautiful soul.

TYRONE (*The kiss arouses his physical desire. He pulls her head down and stares into her eyes*): You have a beautiful strong body, too, Josie—and beautiful eyes and hair, and a beautiful smile and beautiful warm breasts. (*He kisses her on the lips. She pulls back frightenedly for a second—then returns his kiss. Suddenly he breaks away —in a tone of guilty irritation*) Nix! Nix! Don't be a fool, Josie. Don't let me pull that stuff.

JOSIE (*Triumphant for a second*): You meant it! I know you meant it! (*Then with resentful bitterness—roughly*) Be God, you're right I'm a damned fool to let you make me forget you're the greatest liar in the world! (*Quickly*) I mean, the greatest kidder. And now, how about another drink?

TYRONE (*Staring at nothing—vaguely*): You don't get me, Josie. You don't know—and I hope you never will know—

JOSIE (*Blurts out bitterly*): Maybe I know more than you think.

TYRONE (*As if she hadn't spoken*): There's always the aftermath that poisons you. I don't want you to be poisoned—

JOSIE: Maybe you know what you're talking about—

TYRONE: And I don't want to be poisoned myself—not again —not with you. (*He pauses—slowly*) There have been too many nights—and dawns. This must be different. I want— (*His voice trails off into silence.*)

JOSIE (*Trying to read his face—uneasily*): Don't get in one of your queer spells, now. (*She gives his shoulder a shake—forcing a light tone*) Sure, I don't think you know what you want. Except another drink. I'm sure you want that. And I want one, too.

TYRONE (*Recovering himself*): Fine! Grand idea. (*He gets*

up and brings the bottle from the boulder. He picks up his tumbler and pours a big drink. She is holding out her tumbler but he ignores it.)

JOSIE: You're not polite, pouring your own first.

TYRONE: I said a drink was a grand idea—for me. Not for you. You skip this one.

JOSIE (*Resentfully*): Oh, I do, do I? Are you giving me orders?

TYRONE: Yes. Take a big drink of moonlight instead.

JOSIE (*Angrily*): You'll pour me a drink, if you please, Jim Tyrone, or—

TYRONE (*Stares at her—then shrugs his shoulders*): All right, if you want to take it that way, Josie. It's your funeral. (*He pours a drink into her tumbler.*)

JOSIE (*Ashamed but defiant—stiffly*): Thank you kindly. (*She raises her glass—mockingly*) Here's to tonight. (TYRONE *is staring at her, a strange bitter disgust in his eyes. Suddenly he slaps at her hand, knocking the glass to the ground.*)

TYRONE (*His voice hard with repulsion*): I've slept with drunken tramps on too many nights!

JOSIE (*Stares at him, too startled and bewildered to be angry. Her voice trembles with surprising meekness*): All right, Jim, if you don't want me to—

TYRONE (*Now looks as bewildered by his action as she does*): I'm sorry, Josie. Don't know what the drink got into me. (*He picks up her glass*) Here. I'll pour you another.

JOSIE (*Still meek*): No, thank you. I'll skip this one. (*She puts the glass on the ground*) But you drink up.

TYRONE: Thanks. (*He gulps down his drink. Mechanically, as if he didn't know what he was doing, he pours another. Suddenly he blurts out with guilty loathing*) That fat blonde pig on the train—I got her drunk! That's why— (*He stops guiltily.*)

JOSIE (*Uneasily*): What are you talking about? What train?

TYRONE: No train. Don't mind me. (*He gulps down the drink and pours another with the same strange air of acting unconsciously*) Maybe I'll tell you—later, when I'm— That'll cure you—for all time! (*Abruptly he realizes what he is saying. He gives the characteristic shrug of shoulders—cynically*) Nuts! The Brooklyn boys are talking again. I guess I'm more stewed than I thought—in the center of the old bean, at least. (*Dully*) I better beat it back to the Inn and go to bed and stop bothering you, Josie.

JOSIE (*Bullyingly—and pityingly*): Well, you won't, not if I have to hold you. Come on now, bring your drink and sit down like you were before. (*He does so. She pats his cheek—forcing a playful air*) That's a good boy. And I won't take any more whiskey. I've all the effect from it I want already. Everything is far away and doesn't matter—except the moon and its dreams, and I'm part of the dreams—and you are, too. (*She adds with a rueful little laugh*) I keep forgetting the thing I've got to remember. I keep hoping it's a lie, even though I know I'm a damned fool.

TYRONE (*Hazily*): Damned fool about what?

JOSIE: Never mind. (*Forcing a laugh*) I've just had a thought. If my poor old father had seen you knocking his prize whiskey on the ground—Holy Joseph, he'd have had three paralytic strokes!

TYRONE (*Grins*): Yes, I can picture him. (*He pauses—with amused affection*) But that's all a fake. He loves to play tightwad, but the people he likes know better. He'd give them his shirt. He's a grand old scout, Josie. (*A bit maudlin*) The only real friend I've got left—except you. I love his guts.

JOSIE (*Tensely—sickened by his hypocrisy*): Och, for the love of God—!

TYRONE (*Shrugs his shoulders*): Yes, I suppose that does sound like moaning-at-the-bar stuff. But I mean it.

JOSIE: Do you? Well, I know my father's virtues without you telling me.

TYRONE: You ought to appreciate him because he worships the ground you walk on—and he knows you a lot better than you think. (*He turns to smile at her teasingly*) As well as I do—almost.

JOSIE (*Defensively*): That's not saying much. Maybe I can guess what you think you know— (*Forcing a contemptuous laugh*) If it's that, God pity you, you're a terrible fool.

TYRONE (*Teasingly*): If it's what? I haven't said anything.

JOSIE: You'd better not, or I'll die laughing at you. (*She changes the subject abruptly*) Why don't you drink up? It makes me nervous watching you hold it as if you didn't know it was there.

TYRONE: I didn't, at that. (*He drinks.*)

JOSIE: And have another.

TYRONE (*A bit drunkenly*): Will a whore go to a picnic? Real bonded Bourbon. That's my dish. (*He goes to the boulder for the bottle. He is as steady on his feet as if he were completely sober.*)

JOSIE (*In a light tone*): Bring the bottle back so it'll be handy and you won't have to leave me. I miss you.

TYRONE (*Comes back with the bottle. He smiles at her cynically*): Still trying to get me soused, Josie?

JOSIE: I'm not such a fool—with your capacity.

TYRONE: You better watch your step. It might work—and then think of how disgusted you'd feel, with me lying beside you, probably snoring, as you watched the dawn come. You don't know—

JOSIE (*Defiantly*): The hell I don't! Isn't that the way I've felt with every one of them, after?

TYRONE (*As if he hadn't heard—bitterly*): But take it from me, I know. I've seen too God-damned many dawns creeping grayly over too many dirty windows.

JOSIE (*Ignores this—boldly*): But it might be different with you. Love could make it different. And I've been head over heels in love ever since you said you loved my beautiful soul. (*Again he doesn't seem to have heard—resentfully*) Don't stand there like a loon, mourning over the past. Why don't you pour yourself a drink and sit down?

TYRONE (*Looks at the bottle and tumbler in his hands, as if he'd forgotten them—mechanically*): Sure thing. Real bonded Bourbon. I ought to know. If I had a dollar for every drink of it I had before Prohibition, I'd hire our dear bully, Harder, for a valet. (JOSIE *stiffens and her face hardens.* TYRONE *pours a drink and sets the bottle on the ground. He looks up suddenly into her eyes—warningly*) You'd better remember I said you had beautiful eyes and hair—and breasts.

JOSIE: I remember you did. (*She tries to be calculatingly enticing*) So sit down and I'll let you lay your head—

TYRONE: No. If you won't watch your step, I've got to. (*He sits down but doesn't lean back*) And don't let me get away with pretending I'm so soused I don't know what I'm doing. I always know. Or part of me does. That's the trouble. (*He pauses—then bursts out in a strange threatening tone*) You better look out, Josie. She was tickled to death to get me pie-eyed. Had an idea she could roll me, I guess. She wasn't so tickled about it— later on.

JOSIE: What she? (*He doesn't reply. She forces a light tone*) I hope you don't think I'm scheming to roll you.

TYRONE (*Vaguely*): What? (*Coming to—indignantly*) Of
course not. What are you talking about? For God's sake,
you're not a tart.

JOSIE (*Roughly*): No, I'm a fool. I'm always giving it away.

TYRONE (*Angrily*): That lousy bluff again, eh? You're a
liar! For Christ sake, quit the smut stuff, can't you!

JOSIE (*Stung*): Listen to me, Jim! Drunk or not, don't you
talk that way to me or—

TYRONE: How about your not talking the old smut stuff to
me? You promised you'd be yourself. (*Pauses—vaguely*)
You don't get it, Josie. You see, she was one of the smut-
tiest talking pigs I've ever listened to.

JOSIE: What she? Do you mean the blonde on the train?

TYRONE (*Starts—sharply*): Train? Who told you—?
(*Quickly*) Oh—that's right—I did say—. (*Vaguely*)
What blonde? What's the difference? Coming back from
the Coast. It was long ago. But it seems like tonight.
There is no present or future—only the past happening
over and over again—now. You can't get away from it.
(*Abruptly*) Nuts! To hell with that crap.

JOSIE: You came back from the Coast about a year ago after— (*She checks herself*)

TYRONE (*Dully*): Yes. After Mama's death. (*Quickly*) But
I've been to the Coast a lot of times during my career
as a third-rate ham. I don't remember which time—or
anything much—except I was pie-eyed in a drawing
room the whole four days. (*Abruptly*) What were we
talking about before? What a grand guy Phil is. You
ought to be glad you've got him for a father. Mine was
an old bastard.

JOSIE: He wasn't! He was one of the finest, kindest gentlemen ever lived.

TYRONE (*Sneeringly*): Outside the family, sure. Inside, he
was a lousy tightwad bastard.

JOSIE (*Repelled*): You ought to be ashamed!

TYRONE: To speak ill of the dead? Nuts! He can't hear, and he knows I hated him, anyway—as much as he hated me. I'm glad he's dead. So is he. Or he ought to be. Everyone ought to be, if they have any sense. Out of a bum racket. At peace. (*He shrugs his shoulders*) Nuts! What of it?

JOSIE (*Tensely*): Don't Jim. I hate you when you talk like that. (*Forcing a light tone*) Do you want to spoil our beautiful moonlight night? And don't be telling me of your old flames, on trains or not. I'm too jealous.

TYRONE (*With a shudder of disgust*): Of that pig? (*He drinks his whiskey as if to wash a bad taste from his mouth—then takes one of her hands in both of his—simply*) You're a fool to be jealous of anyone. You're the only woman I care a damn about.

JOSIE (*Deeply stirred, in spite of herself—her voice trembling*): Jim, don't— (*Forcing a tense little laugh*) All right, I'll try and believe that—for tonight.

TYRONE (*Simply*): Thanks, Josie. (*A pause. He speaks in a tone of random curiosity*) Why did you say a while ago I'd be leaving for New York soon?

JOSIE (*Stiffens—her face hardening*): Well, I was right, wasn't I? (*Unconsciously she tries to pull her hand away*.)

TYRONE: Why are you pulling your hand away?

JOSIE (*Stops*): Was I? (*Forcing a smile*) I suppose because it seems crazy for you to hold my big ugly paw so tenderly. But you're welcome to it, if you like.

TYRONE: I do like. It's strong and kind and warm—like you. (*He kisses it.*)

JOSIE (*Tensely*): Och, for the love of God—! (*She jerks her hand away—then hastily forces a joking tone*) Wasting kisses on my hand! Sure, even the moon is laughing at us.

TYRONE: Nuts for the moon! I'd rather have one light on

Broadway than all the moons since Rameses was a pup.
(*He takes cigarettes from his pocket and lights one.*)

JOSIE (*Her eyes searching his face, lighted up by the match*): You'll be taking a train back to your dear old Broadway tomorrow night, won't you?

TYRONE (*Still holding the burning match, stares at her in surprise*): Tomorrow night? Where did you get that?

JOSIE: A little bird told me.

TYRONE (*Blows out the match in a cloud of smoke*): You'd better give that bird the bird. By the end of the week, is the right dope. Phil got his dates mixed.

JOSIE (*Quickly*): He didn't tell me. He was too drunk to remember anything.

TYRONE: He was sober when I told him. I called up the executors when we reached the Inn after leaving here. They said the estate would be out of probate within a few days. I told Phil the glad tidings and bought drinks for all and sundry. There was quite a celebration. Funny, Phil wouldn't remember that.

JOSIE (*Bewildered—not knowing what to believe*): It is —funny.

TYRONE (*Shrugs his shoulders*): Well, he's stewed to the ears. That always explains anything. (*Then strangely*) Only sometimes it doesn't.

JOSIE: No—sometimes it doesn't.

TYRONE (*Goes on without real interest, talking to keep from thinking*): Phil certainly has a prize bun on to-night. He never took a punch at me before. And that drivel he talked about owing me one— What got into his head, I wonder.

JOSIE (*Tensely*): How would I know, if you don't?

TYRONE: Well, I don't. Not unless— I remember I did try to get his goat. Simpson sat down with us. Harder sent him to see me. You remember after Harder left here I said the joke was on you, that you'd made this place a

gold mine. I was kidding, but I had the right dope. What
do you think he told Simpson to offer? Ten grand! On
the level, Josie.

JOSIE (*Tense*): So you accepted?

TYRONE: I told Simpson to tell Harder I did. I decided the
best way to fix him was to let him think he'd got away
with it, and then when he comes tomorrow morning to
drive me to the executor's office, I'll tell him what he
can do with himself, his bankroll, and tin oil tanks.

JOSIE (*Knows he is telling the truth—so relieved she can
only stammer stupidly*): So that's—the truth of it.

TYRONE (*Smiles*): Of course, I did it to kid Phil, too. He
was right there, listening. But I know I didn't fool him.

JOSIE (*Weakly*): Maybe you did fool him, for once. But
I don't know.

TYRONE: And that's why he took a swing at me? (*He
laughs, but there is a forced note to it*) Well, if so, it's
one hell of a joke on him. (*His tone becomes hurt and
bitter*) All the same, I'll be good and sore, Josie. I
promised this place wouldn't be sold except to him.
What the hell does he think I am? He ought to know
I wouldn't double-cross you and him for ten million!

JOSIE (*Giving away at last to her relief and joy*): Don't I
know! Oh, Jim, darling! (*She hugs him passionately
and kisses him on the lips*) I knew you'd never— I told
him— (*She kisses him again*) Oh, Jim, I love you.

TYRONE (*Again with a strange, simple gratitude*): Thanks,
Josie. I mean, for not believing I'm a rotten louse. Everyone else believes it—including myself—for a damned good
reason. (*Abruptly changing the subject*) I'm a fool to let
this stuff about Phil get under my skin, but— Why, I
remember telling him tonight I'd even written my
brother and got his okay on selling the farm to him. And
Phil thanked me. He seemed touched and grateful. You
wouldn't think he'd forget that.

JOSIE (*Her face hard and bitter*): I wouldn't, indeed. There's a lot of things he'll have to explain when he comes at sun— (*Hastily*) When he comes back. (*She pauses—then bursts out*) The damned old schemer, I'll teach him to— (*Again checking herself*) to act like a fool.

TYRONE (*Smiles*): You'll get out the old club, eh? What a bluff you are, Josie. (*Teasingly*) You and your lovers, Messalina—when you've never—

JOSIE (*With a faint spark of her old defiance*): You're a liar.

TYRONE: "Pride is the sin by which the angels fell." Are you going to keep that up—with me?

JOSIE (*Feebly*): You think I've never because no one would —because I'm a great ugly cow—

TYRONE (*Gently*): Nuts! You could have had any one of them. You kidded them till you were sure they wanted you. That was all you wanted. And then you slapped them groggy when they tried for more. But you had to keep convincing yourself—

JOSIE (*Tormentedly*): Don't, Jim.

TYRONE: You can take the truth, Josie—from me. Because you and I belong to the same club. We can kid the world but we can't fool ourselves, like most people, no matter what we do—nor escape ourselves no matter where we run away. Whether it's the bottom of a bottle, or a South Sea Island, we'd find our own ghosts there waiting to greet us—"sleepless with pale commemorative eyes," as Rossetti wrote. (*He sneers to himself*) The old poetic bull, eh? Crap! (*Reverting to a teasing tone*) You don't ask how I saw through your bluff, Josie. You pretend too much. And so do the guys. I've listened to them at the Inn. They all lie to each other. No one wants to admit all he got was a slap in the puss, when he thinks a lot

of other guys made it. You can't blame them. And they
know you don't give a damn how they lie. So—

JOSIE: For the love of God, Jim! Don't!

TYRONE: Phil is wise to you, of course, but although he
knew I knew, he would never admit it until tonight.

JOSIE (*Startled—vindictively*): So he admitted it, did he?
Wait till I get hold of him!

TYRONE: He'll never admit it to you. He's afraid of hurting
you.

JOSIE: He is, is he? Well— (*Almost hysterically*) For the
love of God, can't you shut up about him!

TYRONE (*Glances up at her, surprised—then shrugs his
shoulders*): Oh, all right. I wanted to clear things up,
that's all—for Phil's sake as well as yours. You have a
hell of a license to be sore. He's the one who ought to
be. Don't you realize what a lousy position you've put
him in with your brazen-trollop act?

JOSIE (*Tensely*): No. He doesn't care, except to use me in
his scheming. He—

TYRONE: Don't be a damned fool. Of course he cares. And
so do I. (*He turns and pulls her head down and kisses
her on the lips*) I care, Josie. I love you.

JOSIE (*With pitiful longing*): Do you, Jim? Do you? (*She
forces a trembling smile—faintly*) Then I'll confess the
truth to you. I've been a crazy fool. I am a virgin. (*She
begins to sob with a strange forlorn shame and humiliation*) And now you'll never—and I want you to—now
more than ever—because I love you more than ever,
after what's happened— (*Suddenly she kisses him with
fierce passion*) But you will! I'll make you! To hell with
your honorable scruples! I know you want me! I couldn't
believe that until tonight—but now I know. It's in your
kisses! (*She kisses him again—with passionate tenderness*) Oh, you great fool! As if I gave a damn what

happened after! I'll have had tonight and your love to remember for the rest of my days! (*She kisses him again*) Oh, Jim darling, haven't you said yourself there's only tonight? (*She whispers tenderly*) Come. Come with me. (*She gets to her feet, pulling at his arm—with a little self-mocking laugh*) But I'll have to make you leave before sunrise. I mustn't forget that.

TYRONE (*A strange change has come over his face. He looks her over now with a sneering cynical lust. He speaks thickly as if he was suddenly very drunk*): Sure thing, Kiddo. What the hell else do you suppose I came for? I've been kidding myself. (*He steps up beside her and puts his arm around her and presses his body to hers*) You're the goods, Kid. I've wanted you all along. Love, nuts! I'll show you what love is. I know what you want, Bright Eyes. (*She is staring at him now with a look of frightened horror. He kisses her roughly*) Come on, Baby Doll, let's hit the hay. (*He pushes her back in the doorway.*)

JOSIE (*Strickenly*): Jim! Don't! (*She pulls his arms away so violently that he staggers back and would fall down the steps if she didn't grab his arm in time. As it is he goes down on one knee. She is on the verge of collapse herself—brokenly*) Jim! I'm not a whore.

TYRONE (*Remains on one knee—confusedly, as if he didn't know what had happened*): What the hell? Was I trying to rape you, Josie? Forget it. I'm drunk—not responsible. (*He gets to his feet, staggering a bit, and steps down to the ground.*)

JOSIE (*Covering her face with her hands*): Oh, Jim! (*She sobs.*)

TYRONE (*With vague pity*): Don't cry. No harm done. You stopped me, didn't you? (*She continues to sob. He mutters vaguely, as if talking to himself*) Must have drawn a blank for a while. Nuts! Cut out the faking. I knew what I was doing. (*Slowly, staring before him*) But it's funny. I *was* seeing things. That's the truth, Josie. For a moment I thought you were that blonde pig — (*Hastily*) The old heebie-jeebies. Hair of the dog. (*He gropes around for the bottle and his glass*) I'll have another shot—

JOSIE (*Takes her hands from her face—fiercely*): Pour the whole bottle down your throat, if you like! Only stop talking! (*She covers her face with her hands and sobs again.*)

TYRONE (*Stares at her with a hurt and sad expression— dully*): Can't forgive me, eh? You ought to. You ought to thank me for letting you see— (*He pauses, as if waiting for her to say something but she remains silent. He shrugs his shoulders, pours out a big drink mechanically*) Well, here's how. (*He drinks and puts the bottle and glass on the ground—dully*) That was a nightcap. Our moonlight romance seems to be a flop, Josie. I guess I'd better go.

JOSIE (*Dully*): Yes. You'd better go. Good night.

TYRONE: Not good night. Good-bye.

JOSIE (*Lifts her head*): Good-bye?

TYRONE: Yes. I won't see you again before I leave for New York. I was a damned fool to come tonight. I hoped— But you don't get it. How could you? So what's the good— (*He shrugs his shoulders hopelessly and turns toward the road.*)

JOSIE: Jim!

TYRONE (*Turning back—bitter accusation in his tone now*): Whore? Who said you were a whore? But I warned you, didn't I, if you kept on— Why did you have to act like one, asking me to come to bed? That wasn't what I came here for. And you promised tonight would be different. Why the hell did you promise that, if all you wanted was what all the others want, if that's all love

means to you? (*Then guiltily*) Oh, Christ, I don't mean
that, Josie. I know how you feel, and if I could give you
happiness— But it wouldn't work. You don't know me.
I'd poison it for myself and for you. I've poisoned it
already, haven't I, but it would be a million times worse
after— No matter how I tried not to, I'd make it like all
the other nights—for you, too. You'd lie awake and
watch the dawn come with disgust, with nausea retching
your memory, and the wine of passion poets blab about,
a sour aftertaste in your mouth of Dago red ink! (*He
gives a sneering laugh.*)

JOSIE (*Distractedly*): Oh, Jim, don't! Please don't!

TYRONE: You'd hate me and yourself—not for a day or two
but for the rest of your life. (*With a perverse, jeering
note of vindictive boastfulness in his tone*) Believe me,
Kid, when I poison them, they stay poisoned!

JOSIE (*With dull bitterness*): Good-bye, Jim.

TYRONE (*Miserably hurt and sad for a second—appealingly*):
Josie— (*Gives the characteristic shrug of his shoulders—
simply*) Good-bye. (*He turns toward the road—bitterly*)
I'll find it hard to forgive, too. I came here asking for
love—just for this one night, because I thought you loved
me. (*Dully*) Nuts. To hell with it. (*He starts away.*)

JOSIE (*Watches him for a second, fighting the love that, in
spite of her, responds to his appeal—then she springs up
and runs to him—with fierce, possessive, maternal tenderness*): Come here to me, you great fool, and stop your
silly blather. There's nothing to hate you for. There's
nothing to forgive. Sure, I was only trying to give you
happiness, because I love you. I'm sorry I was so stupid
and didn't see— But I see now, and you'll find I have
all the love you need. (*She gives him a hug and kisses
him. There is passion in her kiss but it is a tender, protective maternal passion, which he responds to with
an instant grateful yielding.*)

TYRONE (*Simply*): Thanks, Josie. You're beautiful. I love you. I knew you'd understand.

JOSIE: Of course I do. Come, now. (*She leads him back, her arm around his waist.*)

TYRONE: I didn't want to leave you. You know that.

JOSIE: Indeed I know it. Come now. We'll sit down. (*She sits on the top step and pulls him down on the step below her*) That's it—with my arm around you. Now lay your head on my breast—the way you said you wanted to do— (*He lets his head fall back on her breast. She hugs him—gently*) There, now. Forget all about my being a fool and forgive— (*Her voice trembles—but she goes on determinedly*) Forgive my selfishness, thinking only of myself. Sure, if there's one thing I owe you tonight, after all my lying and scheming, it's to give you the love you need, and it'll be my pride and my joy— (*Forcing a trembling echo of her playful tone*) It's easy enough, too, for I have all kinds of love for you—and maybe this is the greatest of all—because it costs so much. (*She pauses, looking down at his face. He has closed his eyes and his haggard, dissipated face looks like a pale mask in the moonlight—at peace as a death mask is at peace. She becomes frightened*) Jim! Don't look like that!

TYRONE (*Opens his eyes—vaguely*): Like what?

JOSIE (*Quickly*): It's the moonlight. It makes you look so pale, and with your eyes closed—

TYRONE (*Simply*): You mean I looked dead?

JOSIE: No! As if you'd fallen asleep.

TYRONE (*Speaks in a tired, empty tone, as if he felt he ought to explain something to her—something which no longer interests him*): Listen, and I'll tell you a little story, Josie. All my life I had just one dream. From the time I was a kid, I loved racehorses. I thought they were the most beautiful things in the world. I liked to gamble, too. So the big dream was that some day I'd have enough dough to play a cagey system of betting on favorites, and follow the horses south in the winter, and come back north with them in the spring, and be at the track every day. It seemed that would be the ideal life—for me. (*He pauses.*)

JOSIE: Well, you'll be able to do it.

TYRONE: No. I won't be able to do it, Josie. That's the joke. I gave it a try-out before I came up here. I borrowed some money on my share of the estate, and started going to tracks. But it didn't work. I played my system, but I found I didn't care if I won or lost. The horses were beautiful, but I found myself saying to myself, what of it? Their beauty didn't mean anything. I found that every day I was glad when the last race was over, and I could go back to the hotel—and the bottle in my room. (*He pauses, staring into the moonlight with vacant eyes.*)

JOSIE (*Uneasily*): Why did you tell me this?

TYRONE (*In the same listless monotone*): You said I looked dead. Well, I am.

JOSIE: You're not! (*She hugs him protectively*) Don't talk like that!

TYRONE: Ever since Mama died.

JOSIE (*Deeply moved—pityingly*): I know. I've felt all along it was that sorrow was making you— (*She pauses —gently*) Maybe if you talked about your grief for her, it would help you. I think it must be all choked up inside you, killing you.

TYRONE (*In a strange warning tone*): You'd better look out, Josie.

JOSIE: Why?

TYRONE (*Quickly, forcing his cynical smile*): I might develop a crying jag, and sob on your beautiful breast.

JOSIE (*Gently*): You can sob all you like.

TYRONE: Don't encourage me. You'd be sorry. (*A deep conflict shows in his expression and tone. He is driven to*

go on in spite of himself) But if you're such a glutton
for punishment— After all, I said I'd tell you later,
didn't I?

JOSIE (*Puzzled*): You said you'd tell me about the blonde
on the train.

TYRONE: She's part of it. I lied about that. (*He pauses—
then blurts out sneeringly*) You won't believe it could
have happened. Or if you did believe, you couldn't understand or forgive— (*Quickly*) But you might. You're
the one person who might. Because you really love me.
And because you're the only woman I've ever met who
understands the lousy rotten things a man can do when
he's crazy drunk, and draws a blank—especially when
he's nutty with grief to start with.

JOSIE (*Hugging him tenderly*): Of course I'll understand,
Jim, darling.

TYRONE (*Stares into the moonlight—hauntedly*): But I
didn't draw a blank. I tried to. I drank enough to knock
out ten men. But it didn't work. I knew what I was
doing. (*He pauses—dully*) No, I can't tell you, Josie.
You'd loathe my guts, and I couldn't blame you.

JOSIE: No! I'll love you no matter what—

TYRONE (*With strange triumphant harshness*): All right!
Remember that's a promise! (*He pauses—starts to speak
—pauses again.*)

JOSIE (*Pityingly*): Maybe you'd better not—if it will make
you suffer.

TYRONE: Trying to welch now, eh? It's too late. You've got
me started. Suffer? Christ, I ought to suffer! (*He pauses.
Then he closes his eyes. It is as if he had to hide from
sight before he can begin. He makes his face expressionless. His voice becomes impersonal and objective, as
though what he told concerned some man he had known,
but had nothing to do with him. This is the only way
he can start telling the story*) When Mama died, I'd

been on the wagon for nearly two years. Not even a glass
of beer. Honestly. And I know I would have stayed on.
For her sake. She had no one but me. The Old Man was
dead. My brother had married—had a kid—had his own
life to live. She'd lost him. She had only me to attend to
things for her and take care of her. She'd always hated
my drinking. So I quit. It made me happy to do it. For
her. Because she was all I had, all I cared about. Because
I loved her. (*He pauses*) No one would believe that now,
who knew— But I did.

JOSIE (*Gently*) : I know how much you loved her.

TYRONE: We went out to the Coast to see about selling a
piece of property the Old Man had bought three years
ago. And one day she suddenly became ill. Got rapidly
worse. Went into a coma. Brain tumor. The docs said,
no hope. Might never come out of coma. I went crazy.
Couldn't face losing her. The old booze yen got me. I
got drunk and stayed drunk. And I began hoping she'd
never come out of the coma, and see I was drinking
again. That was my excuse, too—that she'd never know.
And she never did. (*He pauses—then sneeringly*) Nix!
Kidding myself again. I know damned well just before
she died she recognized me. She saw I was drunk. Then
she closed her eyes so she couldn't see, and was glad to
die! (*He opens his eyes and stares into the moonlight
as if he saw this deathbed scene before him.*)

JOSIE (*Soothingly*) : Ssshh. You only imagine that because
you feel guilty about drinking.

TYRONE (*As if he hadn't heard, closes his eyes again*): After
that, I kept so drunk I did draw a blank most of the
time, but I went through the necessary motions and no
one guessed how drunk— (*He pauses*) But there are
things I can never forget—the undertakers, and her body
in a coffin with her face made up. I couldn't hardly
recognize her. She looked young and pretty like some-

one I remembered meeting long ago. Practically a stranger. To whom I was a stranger. Cold and indifferent. Not worried about me any more. Free at last. Free from worry. From pain. From me. I stood looking down at her, and something happened to me. I found I couldn't feel anything. I knew I ought to be heartbroken but I couldn't feel anything. I seemed dead, too. I knew I ought to cry. Even a crying jag would look better than just standing there. But I couldn't cry. I cursed to myself, "You dirty bastard, it's Mama. You loved her, and now she's dead. She's gone away from you forever. Never, never again—" But it had no effect. All I did was try to explain to myself, "She's dead. What does she care now if I cry or not, or what I do? It doesn't matter a damn to her. She's happy to be where I can't hurt her ever again. She's rid of me at last. For God's sake, can't you leave her alone even now? For God's sake, can't you let her rest in peace?" (*He pauses—then sneeringly*) But there were several people around and I knew they expected me to show something. Once a ham, always a ham! So I put on an act. I flopped on my knees and hid my face in my hands and faked some sobs and cried, "Mama! Mama! My dear mother!" But all the time I kept saying to myself, "You lousy ham! You God-damned lousy ham! Christ, in a minute you'll start singing 'Mother Macree'!" (*He opens his eyes and gives a tortured, sneering laugh, staring into the moonlight.*)

JOSIE (*Horrified, but still deeply pitying*): Jim! Don't! It's past. You've punished yourself. And you were drunk. You didn't mean—

TYRONE (*Again closes his eyes*): I had to bring her body East to be buried beside the Old Man. I took a drawing room and hid in it with a case of booze. She was in her coffin in the baggage car. No matter how drunk I got, I couldn't forget that for a minute. I found I couldn't

stay alone in the drawing room. It became haunted. I was
going crazy. I had to go out and wander up and down the
train looking for company. I made such a public nuisance
of myself that the conductor threatened if I didn't quit,
he'd keep me locked in the drawing room. But I'd
spotted one passenger who was used to drunks and
could pretend to like them, if there was enough dough
in it. She had parlor house written all over her—a blonde
pig who looked more like a whore than twenty-five
whores, with a face like an overgrown doll's and a
come-on smile as cold as a polar bear's feet. I bribed
the porter to take a message to her and that night she
sneaked into my drawing room. She was bound for
New York, too. So every night—for fifty bucks a night—
(*He opens his eyes and now he stares torturedly through
the moonlight into the drawing room.*)

JOSIE (*Her face full of revulsion—stammers*): Oh, how
could you! (*Instinctively she draws away, taking her
arms from around him.*)

TYRONE: How could I? I don't know. But I did. I suppose
I had some mad idea she could make me forget—what
was in the baggage car ahead.

JOSIE: Don't. (*She draws back again so he has to raise his
head from her breast. He doesn't seem to notice this.*)

TYRONE: No, it couldn't have been that. Because I didn't
seem to want to forget. It was like some plot I had to
carry out. The blonde—she didn't matter. She was only
something that belonged in the plot. It was as if I wanted
revenge—because I'd been left alone—because I knew I
was lost, without any hope left—that all I could do
would be drink myself to death, because no one was
left who could help me. (*His face hardens and a look of
cruel vindictiveness comes into it—with a strange horrible
satisfaction in his tone*) No, I didn't forget even in that

pig's arms! I remembered the last two lines of a lousy
tear-jerker song I'd heard when I was a kid kept singing
over and over in my brain.

> *"And baby's cries can't waken her*
> *In the baggage coach ahead."*

JOSIE (*Distractedly*): Jim!

TYRONE: I couldn't stop it singing. I didn't want to stop it!

JOSIE: Jim! For the love of God. I don't want to hear!

TYRONE (*After a pause—dully*): Well, that's all—except I
was too drunk to go to her funeral.

JOSIE: Oh! (*She has drawn away from him as far as she
can without getting up. He becomes aware of this for the
first time and turns slowly to stare at her.*)

TYRONE (*Dully*): Don't want to touch me now, eh? (*He
shrugs his shoulders mechanically*) Sorry. I'm a damned
fool. I shouldn't have told you.

JOSIE (*Her horror ebbing as her love and protective com-
passion return—moves nearer him—haltingly*): Don't
Jim. Don't say—I don't want to touch you. It's—a lie.
(*She puts a hand on his shoulder.*)

TYRONE (*As if she hadn't spoken—with hopeless longing*):
Wish I could believe in the spiritualists' bunk. If I
could tell her it was because I missed her so much and
couldn't forgive her for leaving me—

JOSIE: Jim! For the love of God—!

TYRONE (*Unheeding*): She'd understand and forgive me,
don't you think? She always did. She was simple and
kind and pure of heart. She was beautiful. You're like
her deep in your heart. That's why I told you. I thought
— (*Abruptly his expression becomes sneering and cynical
—harshly*) My mistake. Nuts! Forget it. Time I got a
move on. I don't like your damned moon, Josie. It's an
ad for the past. (*He recites mockingly*)

"It is the very error of the moon:
She comes more nearer earth than she was wont,
And makes men mad."

(*He moves*) I'll grab the last trolley for town. There'll be a speak open, and some drunk laughing. I need a laugh. (*He starts to get up.*)

JOSIE (*Throws her arms around him and pulls him back— tensely*): No! You won't go! I won't let you! (*She hugs him close—gently*) I understand now, Jim, darling, and I'm proud you came to me as the one in the world you know loves you enough to understand and forgive— and I do forgive!

TYRONE (*Lets his head fall back on her breast—simply*): Thanks, Josie. I know you—

JOSIE: As *she* forgives, do you hear me! As *she* loves and understands and forgives!

TYRONE (*Simply*): Yes, I know she— (*His voice breaks.*)

JOSIE (*Bends over him with a brooding maternal tenderness*): That's right. Do what you came for, my darling. It isn't drunken laughter in a speakeasy you want to hear at all, but the sound of yourself crying your heart's repentance against her breast. (*His face is convulsed. He hides it on her breast and sobs rackingly. She hugs him more tightly and speaks softly, staring into the moonlight*) She hears. I feel her in the moonlight, her soul wrapped in it like a silver mantle, and I know she understands and forgives me, too, and her blessing lies on me. (*A pause. His sobs begin to stop exhaustedly. She looks down at him again and speaks soothingly as she would to a child*) There. There, now. (*He stops. She goes on in a gentle, bullying tone*) You're a fine one, wanting to leave me when the night I promised I'd give you has just begun, our night that'll be different from all the others, with a dawn that won't creep over dirty windowpanes but will wake in the sky like a promise of God's peace in the soul's dark sadness. (*She smiles a little amused smile*) Will you listen to me, Jim! I must be a poet. Who would have guessed it? Sure, love is a wonderful mad inspiration! (*A pause. She looks down. His eyes are closed. His face against her breast looks pale and haggard in the moonlight. Calm with the drained, exhausted peace of death. For a second she is frightened. Then she realizes and whispers softly*) Asleep. (*In a tender crooning tone like a lullaby*) That's right. Sleep in peace, my darling. (*Then with sudden anguished longing*) Oh, Jim, Jim, maybe my love could still save you, if you could want it enough! (*She shakes her head*) No. that can never be. (*Her eyes leave his face to stare up at the sky. She looks weary and stricken and sad. She forces a defensive, self-derisive smile*) God forgive me, it's a fine end to all my scheming, to sit here with the dead hugged to my breast, and the silly mug of the moon grinning down, enjoying the joke!

Curtain

Act Four

SCENE—*Same as Act Three. It is dawn. The first faint streaks of color, heralding the sunrise, appear in the eastern sky at left.*

JOSIE *sits in the same position on the steps, as if she had not moved, her arms around* TYRONE. *He is still asleep, his head on her breast. His face has the same exhausted, death-like repose.* JOSIE'S *face is set in an expression of numbed, resigned sadness. Her body sags tiredly. In spite of her strength, holding herself like this for hours, for fear of waking him, is becoming too much for her.*

The two make a strangely tragic picture in the wan dawn light—this big sorrowful woman hugging a haggard-faced, middle-aged drunkard against her breast, as if he were a sick child.

HOGAN *appears at left-rear, coming from the barn. He approaches the corner of the house stealthily on tiptoe. Wisps of hay stick to his clothes and his face is swollen and sleepy, but his little pig's eyes are sharply wide awake and sober. He peeks around the corner, and takes in the two on the steps. His eyes fix on* JOSIE'S *face in a long, probing stare.*

JOSIE (*Speaks in a low grim tone*): Stop hiding, Father. I heard you sneak up. (*He comes guiltily around the corner. She keeps her voice low, but her tone is commanding*) Come here, and be quiet about it. (*He obeys meekly, coming as far as the boulder silently, his eyes searching her face, his expression becoming guilty and miserable at what he sees. She goes on in the same tone, without looking at him)* Talk low, now. I don't want him wakened— *(She adds strangely)* Not until the dawn has beauty in it.

HOGAN *(Worriedly)*: What? *(He decides it's better for the present to ask no questions. His eyes fall on* TYRONE's *face. In spite of himself, he is startled—in an awed, almost frightened whisper)* Be God, he looks dead!

JOSIE *(Strangely)*: Why wouldn't he? He is.

HOGAN: Is?

JOSIE: Don't be a fool. Can't you see him breathing? Dead asleep, I mean. Don't stand there gawking. Sit down. *(He sits meekly on the boulder. His face betrays a guilty dread of what is coming. There is a pause in which she doesn't look at him but, he keeps glancing at her, growing visibly more uneasy. She speaks bitterly)* Where's your witnesses?

HOGAN *(Guiltily)*: Witnesses? *(Then forcing an amused grin)* Oh, be God, if that ain't a joke on me! Sure, I got so blind drunk at the Inn I forgot all about our scheme and came home and went to sleep in the hayloft.

JOSIE *(Her expression harder and more bitter)*: You're a liar.

HOGAN: I'm not. I just woke up. Look at the hay sticking to me. That's proof.

JOSIE: I'm not thinking of that, and well you know it. *(With bitter voice)* So you just woke up—did you?—and then came sneaking here to see if the scheme behind your scheme had worked!

HOGAN *(Guiltily)*: I don't know what you mean.

JOSIE: Don't lie any more, Father. This time, you've told one too many. *(He starts to defend himself but the look on her face makes him think better of it and he remains uneasily silent. A pause.)*

HOGAN (*Finally has to blurt out*): Sure, if I'd brought the witnesses, there's nothing for them to witness that—

JOSIE: No. You're right, there. There's nothing. Nothing at all. (*She smiles strangely*) Except a great miracle they'd never believe, or you either.

HOGAN: What miracle?

JOSIE: A virgin who bears a dead child in the night, and the dawn finds her still a virgin. If that isn't a miracle, what is?

HOGAN (*Uneasily*): Stop talking so queer. You give me the shivers. (*He attempts a joking tone*) Is it you who's the virgin? Faith, that *would* be a miracle, no less! (*He forces a chuckle.*)

JOSIE: I told you to stop lying, Father.

HOGAN: What lie? (*He stops and watches her face worriedly. She is silent, as if she were not aware of him now. Her eyes are fixed on the wanton sky.*)

JOSIE (*As if to herself*): It'll be beautiful soon, and I can wake him.

HOGAN (*Can't retain his anxiety any longer*): Josie, darlin'! For the love of God, can't you tell me what happened to you?

JOSIE (*Her face hard and bitter again*): I've told you once. Nothing.

HOGAN: Nothing? If you could see the sadness in your face—

JOSIE: What woman doesn't sorrow for the man she loved who has died? But there's pride in my heart, too.

HOGAN (*Tormentedly*): Will you stop talking as if you'd gone mad in the night! (*Raising his voice—with revengeful anger*) Listen to me! If Jim Tyrone has done anything to bring you sorrow— (TYRONE *stirs in his sleep and moans, pressing his face against her breast as if for protection. She looks down at him and hugs him close.*)

JOSIE (*Croons softly*): There, there, my darling. Rest in

peace a while longer. (*Turns on her father angrily and whispers*) Didn't I tell you to speak low and not wake him! (*She pauses—then quietly*) He did nothing to bring me sorrow. It was my mistake. I thought there was still hope. I didn't know he'd died already—that it was a damned soul coming to me in the moonlight, to confess and be forgiven and find peace for a night—

HOGAN: Josie! Will you stop!

JOSIE (*After a pause—dully*): He'd never do anything to hurt me. You know it. (*Self-mockingly*) Sure, hasn't he told me I'm beautiful to him and he loves me—in his fashion. (*Then matter-of-factly*) All that happened was that he got drunk and he had one of his crazy notions he wanted to sleep the way he is, and I let him sleep. (*With forced roughness*) And, be God, the night's over. I'm half dead with tiredness and sleepiness. It's that you see in my face, not sorrow.

HOGAN: Don't try to fool me, Josie. I—

JOSIE (*Her face hard and bitter—grimly*): Fool you, is it? It's you who made a fool of me with your lies, thinking you'd use me to get your dirty greasy paws on the money he'll have!

HOGAN: No! I swear by all the saints—

JOSIE: You'd swear on a Bible while you were stealing it! (*Grimly*) Listen to me, Father. I didn't call you here to answer questions about what's none of your business. I called you here to tell you I've seen through all the lies you told last night to get me to— (*As he starts to speak*) Shut up! I'll do the talking now. You weren't drunk. You were only putting it on as part of your scheme—

HOGAN (*Quietly*): I wasn't drunk, no. I admit that, Josie. But I'd had slews of drinks and they were in my head or I'd never have the crazy dreams—

JOSIE (*With biting scorn*): Dreams, is it? The only dream

you've ever had, or will have, is of yourself counting a fistful of dirty money, and divil a care how you got it, or who you robbed or made suffer!

HOGAN (*Winces—pleadingly*): Josie!

JOSIE: Shut up. (*Scathingly*) I'm sure you've made up a whole new set of lies and excuses. You're that cunning and clever, but you can save your breath. They wouldn't fool me now. I've been fooled once too often. (*He gives her a frightened look, as if something he had dreaded has happened. She goes on, grimly accusing*) You lied about Jim selling the farm. You knew he was kidding. You knew the estate would be out of probate in a few days, and he'd go back to Broadway, and you had to do something quick or you'd lose the last chance of getting your greedy hooks on his money.

HOGAN (*Miserably*): No. It wasn't that, Josie.

JOSIE: You saw how hurt and angry I was because he'd kept me waiting here, and you used that. You knew I loved him and wanted him and you used that. You used all you knew about me— Oh, you did it clever! You ought to be proud! You worked it so it was me who did all the dirty scheming— You knew I'd find out from Jim you'd lied about the farm, but not before your lie had done its work—made me go after him, get him drunk, get drunk myself so I could be shameless—and when the truth did come out, wouldn't it make me love him all the more and be more shameless and willing? Don't tell me you didn't count on that, and you such a clever schemer! And if he once had me, knowing I was a virgin, didn't you count on his honor and remorse, and his loving me in his fashion, to make him offer to marry me? Sure, why wouldn't he, you thought. It wouldn't hold him. He'd go back to Broadway just the same and never see me again. But there'd be money in it, and when he'd finished killing himself, I'd be his legal widow and get what's left.

HOGAN (*Miserably*): No! It wasn't that.

JOSIE: But what's the good of talking? It's all over. I've only one more word for you, Father, and it's this: I'm leaving you today, like my brothers left. You can live alone and work alone your cunning schemes on yourself.

HOGAN (*After a pause—slowly*): I knew you'd be bitter against me, Josie, but I took the chance you'd be so happy you wouldn't care how—

JOSIE (*As if she hadn't heard, looking at the eastern sky which is now glowing with color*): Thank God, it's beautiful. It's time. (*To* HOGAN) Go in the house and stay there till he's gone. I don't want you around to start some new scheme. (*He looks miserable, starts to speak, thinks better of it, and meekly tiptoes past her up the steps and goes in, closing the door quietly after him. She looks down at* TYRONE. *Her face softens with a maternal tenderness—sadly*) I hate to bring you back to life, Jim, darling. If you could have died in your sleep, that's what you would have liked, isn't it? (*She gives him a gentle shake*) Wake up, Jim. (*He moans in his sleep and presses more closely against her. She stares at his face*) Dear God, let him remember that one thing and forget the rest. That will be enough for me. (*She gives him a more vigorous shake*) Jim! Wake up, do you hear? It's time.

TYRONE (*Half wakens without opening his eyes—mutters*): What the hell? (*Dimly conscious of a woman's body— cynically*) Again, eh? Same old stuff. Who the hell are you, sweetheart? (*Irritably*) What's the big idea, waking me up? What time is it?

JOSIE: It's dawn.

TYRONE (*Still without opening his eyes*): Dawn? (*He quotes drowsily*)

"But I was desolate and sick of an old passion,
  When I awoke and found the dawn was gray."

(*Then with a sneer*) They're all gray. Go to sleep, Kid—
and let me sleep. (*He falls asleep again.*)

JOSIE (*Tensely*): This one isn't gray, Jim. It's different
from all the others— (*She sees he is asleep—bitterly*)
He'll have forgotten. He'll never notice. And I'm the
whore on the train to him now, not— (*Suddenly she
pushes him away from her and shakes him roughly*)
Will you wake up, for God's sake! I've had all I can
bear—

TYRONE (*Still half asleep*): Hey! Cut out the rough stuff,
Kid. What? (*Awake now, blinking his eyes—with dazed
surprise*) Josie.

JOSIE (*Still bitter*): That's who, and none of your damned
tarts! (*She pushes him*) Get up now, so you won't fall
asleep again. (*He does so with difficulty, still in a sleepy
daze, his body stiff and cramped. She conquers her
bitter resentment and puts on her old free-and-easy
kidding tone with him, but all the time waiting to see
how much he will remember*) You're stiff and cramped,
and no wonder. I'm worse from holding you, if that's
any comfort. (*She stretches and rubs her numbed arms,
groaning comically*) Holy Joseph, I'm a wreck entirely.
I'll never be the same. (*Giving him a quick glance*)
You look as if you'd drawn a blank and were wondering how you got here. I'll bet you don't remember a
thing.

TYRONE (*Moving his arms and legs gingerly—sleepily*): I
don't know. Wait till I'm sure I'm still alive.

JOSIE: You need an eye-opener. (*She picks up the bottle
and glass and pours him a drink*) Here you are.

TYRONE (*Takes the glass mechanically*): Thanks, Josie. (*He goes and sits on the boulder, holding the drink as if he had no interest in it.*)

JOSIE (*Watching him*): Drink up or you'll be asleep again.

TYRONE: No, I'm awake now, Josie. Funny. Don't seem to want a drink. Oh, I've got a head all right. But no heebie-jeebies—yet.

JOSIE: That's fine. It must be a pleasant change—

TYRONE: It is. I've got a nice, dreamy peaceful hangover for once—as if I'd had a sound sleep without nightmares.

JOSIE: So you did. Divil a nightmare. I ought to know. Wasn't I holding you and keeping them away?

TYRONE: You mean you— (*Suddenly*) Wait a minute. I remember now I was sitting alone at a table in the Inn, and I suddenly had a crazy notion I'd come up here and sleep with my head on your— So that's why I woke up in your arms. (*Shamefacedly*) And you let me get away with it. You're a nut, Josie.

JOSIE: Oh, I didn't mind.

TYRONE: You must have seen how blotto I was, didn't you?

JOSIE: I did. You were as full as a tick.

TYRONE: Then why didn't you give me the bum's rush?

JOSIE: Why would I? I was glad to humor you.

TYRONE: For God's sake, how long was I cramped on you like that?

JOSIE: Oh, a few hours, only.

TYRONE: God, I'm sorry Josie, but it's your own fault for letting me—

JOSIE: Och, don't be apologizing. I was glad of the excuse to stay awake and enjoy the beauty of the moon.

TYRONE: Yes, I can remember what a beautiful night it was.

JOSIE: Can you? I'm glad of that, Jim. You seemed to enjoy it the while we were sitting here together before you fell asleep.

TYRONE: How long a while was that?

JOSIE: Not long. Less than an hour, anyway.

TYRONE: I suppose I bored the hell out of you with a lot of drunken drivel.

JOSIE: Not a lot, no. But some. You were full of blarney, saying how beautiful I was to you.

TYRONE (*Earnestly*): That wasn't drivel, Josie. You were. You are. You always will be.

JOSIE: You're a wonder, Jim. Nothing can stop you, can it? Even me in the light of dawn, looking like something you'd put in the field to scare the crows from the corn. You'll kid at the Day of Judgment.

TYRONE (*Impatiently*): You know damned well it isn't kidding. You're not a fool. You can tell.

JOSIE (*Kiddingly*): All right, then, I'm beautiful and you love me—in your fashion.

TYRONE: "In my fashion," eh? Was I reciting poetry to you? That must have been hard to take.

JOSIE: It wasn't. I liked it. It was all about beautiful nights and the romance of the moon.

TYRONE: Well, there was some excuse for that, anyway. It sure was a beautiful night. I'll never forget it.

JOSIE: I'm glad, Jim.

TYRONE: What other bunk did I pull on you—or I mean, did old John Barleycorn pull?

JOSIE: Not much. You were mostly quiet and sad—in a kind of daze, as if the moon was in your wits as well as whiskey.

TYRONE: I remember I was having a grand time at the Inn, celebrating with Phil, and then suddenly, for no reason, all the fun went out of it, and I was more melancholy than ten Hamlets. (*He pauses*) Hope I didn't tell you the sad story of my life and weep on your bosom, Josie.

JOSIE: You didn't. The one thing you talked a lot about was that you wanted the night with me to be different from all the other nights you'd spent with women.

TYRONE (*With revulsion*): God, don't make me think of those tramps now! (*Then with deep, grateful feeling*) It sure was different, Josie. I may not remember much, but I know how different it was from the way I feel now. None of my usual morning-after stuff—the damned sick remorse that makes you wish you'd died in your sleep so you wouldn't have to face the rotten things you're afraid you said and did the night before, when you were so drunk you didn't know what you were doing.

JOSIE: There's nothing you said or did last night for you to regret. You can take my word for it.

TYRONE (*As if he hadn't heard—slowly*): It's hard to describe how I feel. It's a new one on me. Sort of at peace with myself and this lousy life—as if all my sins had been forgiven— (*He becomes self-conscious—cynically*) Nuts with that sin bunk, but you know what I mean.

JOSIE (*Tensely*): I do, and I'm happy you feel that way, Jim. (*A pause. She goes on*) You talked about how you'd watched too many dawns come creeping grayly over dirty windowpanes, with some tart snoring beside you—

TYRONE (*Winces*): Have a heart. Don't remind me of that now, Josie. Don't spoil this dawn! (*A pause. She watches him tensely. He turns slowly to face the east, where the sky is now glowing with all the colors of an exceptionally beautiful sunrise. He stares, drawing a deep breath. He is profoundly moved but immediately becomes self-conscious and tries to sneer it off—cynically*) God seems to be putting on quite a display. I like Belasco better. Rise of curtain, Act-Four stuff. (*Her face has fallen into lines of bitter hurt, but he adds quickly and angrily*) God damn it! Why do I have to pull that lousy stuff? (*With genuine deep feeling*) God, it's beautiful, Josie! I—I'll never forget it—here with you.

JOSIE (*Her face clearing—simply*): I'm glad, Jim. I was hoping you'd feel beauty in it—by way of a token.

TYRONE (*Watching the sunrise—mechanically*): Token of what?

JOSIE: Oh, I don't know. Token to me that—never mind. I forget what I meant. (*Abruptly changing the subject*) Don't think I woke you just to admire the sunrise. You're on a farm, not Broadway, and it's time for me to start work, not go to bed. (*She gets to her feet and stretches. There is a growing strain behind her free-and-easy manner*) And that's a hint, Jim. I can't stay entertaining you. So go back to the Inn, that's a good boy. I know you'll understand the reason, and not think I'm tired of your company. (*She forces a smile.*)

TYRONE (*Gets up*): Of course, I understand. (*He pauses—then blurts out guiltily*) One more question. You're sure I didn't get out of order last night—and try to make you, or anything like that.

JOSIE: You didn't. You kidded back when I kidded you, the way we always do. That's all.

TYRONE: Thank God for that. I'd never forgive myself if —I wouldn't have asked you except I've pulled some pretty rotten stuff when I was drawing a blank. (*He becomes conscious of the forgotten drink he has in his hand*) Well, I might as well drink this. The bar at the Inn won't be open for hours. (*He drinks—then looks pleasantly surprised*) I'll be damned! That isn't Phil's rotgut. That's real, honest-to-God bonded Bourbon. Where— (*This clicks in his mind and suddenly he remembers everything and* JOSIE *sees that he does. The look of guilt and shame and anguish settles over his face. Instinctively he throws the glass away, his first reaction one of loathing for the drink which brought back memory. He feels* JOSIE *staring at him and fights desperately to control his voice and expression*) Real Bourbon. I remember now you said a bootlegger gave it to Phil. Well,

I'll run along and let you do your work. See you later,
Josie. (*He turns toward the road.*)

JOSIE (*Strickenly*): No! Don't Jim! Don't go like that! You
won't see me later. You'll never see me again now, and
I know that's best for us both, but I can't bear to have
you ashamed you wanted my love to comfort your sorrow
—when I'm so proud I could give it. (*Pleadingly*) I
hoped, for your sake, you wouldn't remember, but now
you do, I want you to remember my love for you gave you
peace for a while.

TYRONE (*Stares at her, fighting with himself. He stammers
defensively*): I don't know what you're talking about.
I don't remember—

JOSIE (*Sadly*): All right, Jim. Neither do I then. Good-bye,
and God bless you. (*She turns as if to go up the steps
into the house.*)

TYRONE (*Stammers*): Wait, Josie! (*Coming to her*) I'm a
liar! I'm a louse! Forgive me, Josie. I do remember! I'm
glad I remember! I'll never forget your love! (*He kisses
her on the lips*) Never! (*Kissing her again*) Never, do
you hear! I'll always love you, Josie. (*He kisses her
again*) Good-bye—and God bless you! (*He turns away
and walks quickly down the road off left without looking
back. She stands, watching him go, for a moment, then
she puts her hands over her face, her head bent, and sobs.
HOGAN comes out of her room and stands on top of the
steps. He looks after TYRONE and his face is hard with
bitter anger.*)

JOSIE (*Sensing his presence, stops crying and lifts her head
—dully*): I'll get your breakfast in a minute, Father.

HOGAN: To hell with my breakfast! I'm not a pig that has
no other thought but eating! (*Then pleadingly*) Listen,
darlin'. All you said about my lying and scheming, and
what I hoped would happen, is true. But it wasn't his

money, Josie. I did see it was the last chance—the only
one left to bring the two of you to stop your damned pretending, and face the truth that you loved each other.
I wanted you to find happiness—by hook or crook, one
way or another, what did I care how? I wanted to save
him, and I hoped he'd see that only your love could— It
was his talk of the beauty he saw in you that made me
hope— And I knew he'd never go to bed with you even
if you'd let him unless he married you. And if I gave a
thought to his money at all, that was the least of it, and
why shouldn't I want to have you live in ease and comfort for a change, like you deserve, instead of in this
shanty on a lousy farm, slaving for me? (*He pauses—
miserably*) Can't you believe that's the truth, Josie, and
not feel so bitter against me?

JOSIE (*Her eyes still following* TYRONE—*gently*): I know
it's the truth, Father. I'm not bitter now. Don't be afraid
I'm going to leave you. I only said it to punish you for a
while.

HOGAN (*With humble gratitude*): Thank God for that,
darlin'.

JOSIE (*Forces a teasing smile and a little of her old manner*): A ginger-haired, crooked old goat like you to be
playing Cupid!

HOGAN (*His face lights up joyfully. He is almost himself
again—ruefully*): You had me punished, that's sure. I
was thinking after you'd gone I'd drown myself in
Harder's ice pond. There was this consolation in it, I
know that the bastard would never look at a piece of
ice again without remembering me. (*She doesn't hear
this. Her thoughts are on the receding figure of* TYRONE
again. HOGAN *looks at her sad face worriedly—gently*)
Don't, darlin'. Don't be hurting yourself. (*Then as she
still doesn't hear, he puts on his old, fuming irascible
tone*) Are you going to moon at the sunrise forever, and

me with the sides of my stomach knocking together?

JOSIE (*Gently*): Don't worry about me, Father. It's over now. I'm not hurt. I'm only sad for him.

HOGAN: For him? (*He bursts out in a fit of smoldering rage*) May the blackest curse from the pit of hell—

JOSIE (*With an anguished cry*): Don't, Father! I love him!

HOGAN (*Subsides, but his face looks sorrowful and old—dully*): I didn't mean it. I know whatever happened he meant no harm to you. It was life I was cursing— (*With a trace of his natural manner*) And, be God, that's a waste of breath, if it does deserve it. (*Then as she remains silent—miserably*) Or maybe I was cursing myself for a damned old scheming fool, like I ought to.

JOSIE (*Turns to him, forcing a teasing smile*): Look out. I might say Amen to that. (*Gently*) Don't be sad, Father. I'm all right—and I'm well content here with you. (*Forcing her teasing manner again*) Sure, living with you has spoilt me for any other man, anyway. There'd never be the same fun or excitement.

HOGAN (*Plays up to this—in his fuming manner*): There'll be excitement if I don't get my breakfast soon, but it won't be fun, I'm warning you!

JOSIE (*Forcing her usual reaction to his threats*): Och, don't be threatening me, you bad-tempered old tick. Let's go in the house and I'll get your damned breakfast.

HOGAN: Now you're talking. (*He goes in the house through her room. She follows him as far as the door—then turns for a last look down the road.*)

JOSIE (*Her face sad, tender and pitying—gently*): May you have your wish and die in your sleep soon, Jim, darling. May you rest forever in forgiveness and peace. (*She turns slowly and goes back into the house.*)

Curtain

MODERN LIBRARY COLLEGE EDITIONS

MODERN LIBRARY GIANTS

A series of sturdily bound and handsomely printed, full-sized library editions of books formerly available only in expensive sets. These volumes contain from 600 to 1,400 pages each.

THE MODERN LIBRARY GIANTS REPRESENT A SELECTION OF THE WORLD'S GREATEST BOOKS

MODERN LIBRARY GIANTS